Shadows of Trauma

Shadows of Trauma

Memory and the Politics of Postwar Identity

Aleida Assmann

Translated by Sarah Clift

FORDHAM UNIVERSITY PRESS
NEW YORK 2016

Copyright © 2016 Fordham University Press

All rights reserved. No part of this publication may be reproduced, stored in a retrieval system, or transmitted in any form or by any means—electronic, mechanical, photocopy, recording, or any other—except for brief quotations in printed reviews, without the prior permission of the publisher.

This book was originally published in German as Aleida Assmann, *Der lange Schatten der Vergangenheit: Erinnerungskultur und Geschichtspolitik*, © Verlag C. H. Beck oHG, Munich, 2006.

Fordham University Press has no responsibility for the persistence or accuracy of URLs for external or third-party Internet websites referred to in this publication and does not guarantee that any content on such websites is, or will remain, accurate or appropriate.

Fordham University Press also publishes its books in a variety of electronic formats. Some content that appears in print may not be available in electronic books.

Visit us online at www.fordhampress.com.

Library of Congress Cataloging-in-Publication Data

Assmann, Aleida.
 [Lange Schatten der Vergangenheit. English]
 Shadows of trauma : memory and the politics of postwar identity / Aleida Assmann ; translated by Sarah Clift.
   pages cm
 Summary: "The book traces the process of creating of a new German memory of the Holocaust after the fall of the Wall. Combining theoretical analysis with historical case studies, the book revisits crucial debates and controversial issues out of which Germany's new 'memory culture' emerged as a collective project and work in progress" — Provided by publisher.
 Includes bibliographical references and index.
 ISBN 978-0-8232-6727-9 (hardback) — ISBN 978-0-8232-6728-6 (paper)
 1. National socialism—Historiography. 2. Historiography—Germany. 3. Memory—Political aspects—Germany.
 4. Collective memory—Germany. I. Title.
  DD256.48.A8713 2015
  940.53'18072043—dc23
                                              2015017367

Printed in the United States of America
18 17 16   5 4 3 2 1
First edition

Reinhart Koselleck died in 2005, at the age of 82. No one influenced the postwar generation in Germany across disciplinary boundaries as he did, as a historian, a witness to contemporary history, an intellectual, and an artist. The following pages owe a great deal to the full breadth of his work. Above all, though, the doubts he raised concerning memory, the challenges he posed, and the contrary positions he developed over the years were what ultimately made him into my implicit addressee as I was writing. This book is dedicated to his memory.

CONTENTS

Preface to the English-Language Edition   ix

Introduction: Triumph and Trauma   1

Part I: Theoretical Foundations

1. From Individual to Collective Constructions of the Past   9
2. Basic Concepts and Themes of Individual and Collective Memory   45

Part II: Analyses and Case Studies

3. How True Are Memories?   97
4. False Memories: Pathologies of Identity at the End of the Twentieth Century   114
5. Incorrect Memories: On the Normative Power of Social Frameworks of Memory   127
6. Five Strategies of Repression   141
7. German Narratives of Victimhood   154
8. Points of Intersection between Lived Memory and Cultural Memory   174
9. Commemorative Sites in Space and Time   185
10. The Future of Holocaust Memory   202
11. Europe as a Community of Memory   216

Conclusion: Shadows of Trauma — 235

Notes — 243
Bibliography — 279
Index — 299

PREFACE TO THE ENGLISH-LANGUAGE EDITION

Jorge Semprun once said that the dream of every writer is to work on one book for his or her entire life, writing it and then continuously rewriting it. This dream can easily come true for those of us who work on memory, a topic that is vast, important, and fascinating enough—and that is continuously undergoing shifts, changes, and new developments—to warrant returning to it again and again. But it is not only new theoretical aspects of the topic that confront us with new ideas and challenges in the rapidly growing field of memory studies. In studying memory, we can never completely divest ourselves of our subjective perspective, but we also have to come to terms with our own position vis-à-vis the impact of historical events. So doing memory studies is not only about studying theories and acquiring knowledge; it is also about deepening our historical understanding of ourselves and others.

After the 2011 publication of *Cultural Memory and Western Civilization* (the somewhat grandiose title was the creation of the publisher), which takes a long historical view in examining the media and arts of memory mainly from the perspective of literary texts, English-speaking readers are now introduced to another version of my "never-ending" book, one focusing on acts of remembering within a contemporary political framework. The title indicates this shift in emphasis, from literature and art to autobiography, society, and politics. It analyzes German memory practices from the late 1980s up to the first years of the new millennium, bringing together conceptual work on the dynamics of individual and collective remembering with concrete case studies that examine the shadows of trauma in post-unification Germany.

Based on research conducted from 2000 to 2006, this book profited greatly from inspiring academic contexts, including a two-month residency at the Warburg-Haus in Hamburg in 2005 and a Sir Peter Ustinov Guest Professorship at the University of Vienna in the same summer. These opportunities allowed me to present a first draft of the book and to discuss it with students, whose interest, attention, and critical interventions were a constant source of inspiration. During the book's gestation period, I also had the invaluable opportunity to hold various guest professorships and to work with colleagues and students at Yale, Princeton, and Rice University. I am also endlessly grateful to my colleagues and friends Bernhard Giesen, Jay Winter, Geoffrey Hartman, and Jan Assmann, with all of whom I have co-taught seminars that have deepened my awareness and opened up new perspectives for me on the multifaceted topic of memory.

I am greatly indebted to a number of people and institutions that made this publication of my book in English possible. Marianne Hirsch was the first to suggest a translation on the occasion of a lecture that I gave at Columbia University in 2007, a plan enthusiastically picked up by the unforgettable Helen Tartar, who was also present at the event. I had long admired her creative energy in conceiving new projects in the humanities and so was deeply grateful for her personal investment in and keen support of the project, both of which were sustained by Thomas Lay following Helen's tragic death. The plan materialized in 2011 when Sarah Clift, a friend and esteemed colleague, offered to do the translation, funded by a Max Planck Research Award. I am both grateful to her and delighted to read my text in English, mediated as it is by her knowledge, experience, and insights.

Aleida Assmann
Konstanz, January 2015

INTRODUCTION

Triumph and Trauma

In January 1997, artist Horst Hoheisel finally received the official permission he needed to carry out a controversial public installation in the heart of Berlin. So, during the night of the 26th to the 27th of January, a year after German Federal president Roman Herzog inaugurated Auschwitz Memorial Day, Hoheisel mounted a light installation that projected an image of the gate leading into Auschwitz onto the Brandenburg Gate for the duration of only one night. "The two gates merged into a single image," commented the artist.[1] "At first, I imagined that the installation would be a grandiose gesture, but in the course of that cold January night it became much more modest. Since then, the Brandenburg Gate has not been nearly as significant to me." Although the artist's original intention for the piece was to stage a personal intervention aimed at breaking a taboo, its significance goes well beyond that event. For, by means of photography, it becomes possible to capture and preserve a one-time performance that was seen by only relatively few people and for only a very short time during a cold January night and to make it available to others who are distant in time and space. Materialized in photographic images, this fleeting moment could then enter the archive of cultural memory, which is of course how it could be used as the cover image for this book. So, while the artist felt that the provocative power of the work had been immediately exhausted by the installation itself, it retains that power in an altered form.

Hoheisel's light projection can be interpreted as a kind of thought image that gives us a way of looking at the complex history of Germany's memory culture. *First*, it highlights the significance of the Brandenburg Gate as a national historical symbol. As a general rule, the role of monuments is to formulate clear and unequivocal messages for future generations. But these are seldom taken to heart, which is why, contrary to their appointed task, monuments themselves soon become historical. If they continue to make any impression at all, it is solely as a material relic of a bygone era. The Brandenburg Gate is different in this respect, since its national symbolic value derives less from the dedication of its founders than from events relating to its structure, which has been seized upon many times in history. First erected in the 1790s, it was a highly self-conscious symbol of peace that had been secured through victory.[2] Already by 1806, though, this message had not just been invalidated: the Prussian loss against Napoleon was also symbolically carried out on the monument itself, the quadriga of which was humiliatingly transported to Paris as a spoil of war. However, after Napoleon's defeat in the battle at Leipzig in 1813, the tables were turned once again and the group of statues were brought back in a triumphal procession and reconstituted, with the additional feature by Karl Friedrich Schinkel of an iron cross placed in the hand of von Schadow's Athena-Victoria figure, as a visible sign of her superiority.

This monument not only traces Germany's history and exemplifies it: it has also repeatedly been the stage on which history itself has taken place, whether in moments of triumph or of trauma. Hitler's ascent to power on January 30, 1933, was celebrated there, with parades and huge military displays, and on November 9, 1989, it was also where the fall of the Berlin Wall was experienced most directly by Berliners as well as by those who followed the event over the media.

As Hoheisel was preparing the work, he came to realize that the Brandenburg Gate "appeared more and more like a mere projection screen" to him. So, the *second* point about this site is that it fulfills this function as projection screen not least in relation to the commercial demands for attention that are made in a free-market society: all kinds of companies and organizations jockeyed for position to have their oversized messages projected from this site. During an extensive renovation project that took place on the gate from 2000 to 2002, the German telecommunications company Deutsche Telekom agreed to pay a percentage of the costs in exchange for the right to place large-format advertisements on nineteen plastic sheaths. Then, in 2002, the Association for the Establishment of a Memorial for the Murdered Jews of Europe joined in on the commercialization of the site and used it to display a controversial billboard. Against the background of an idyllic Alpine landscape, complete with a shimmering blue lake and white-topped peaks, were the lines, "The Holocaust didn't happen." This fundraising drive was unsuccessful, but it is nonetheless a striking example of the tight interweaving of the historical monument, the high-end attention-grabbing strategies of advertising, and German memory culture.

Third, Hoheisel's work used the Brandenburg Gate as a stage to draw connections between this important national site of memory [or *lieu de mémoire*] and the Holocaust. Placing his light projection in the center of Berlin, he superimposed the triumphal with the traumatic *lieux de mémoire*: distant from one another geographically and even more remote from one another in terms of public awareness, the triumphant and the traumatic are here forced together by Hoheisel into what we might call a "reversible figure." According to sociologist Bernhard Giesen's meticulous work on the political dynamics of triumph and trauma in the wake of conflict, the triumphant and the traumatic are the two modalities according to which mythic narratives construct a sense of national identity. Where national identity is concerned, Giesen argues that historical experiences are always processed in one of two ways: either as the euphoric high point of a collective self-overcoming or as a profound disgrace and humiliation. In a certain way, Hoheisel's work is the figurative equivalent of Giesen's argument. But it also shows the central problem of German national memory. Triumph and trauma are mutually exclusive: the one suppresses the other, makes it disappear, ensures that it is forgotten—and yet the two moments are inseparably connected in Germany's national memory. The triumphant symbol of German reunification in the middle of Berlin exists alongside the traumatic low point of Auschwitz.

In contrast to Bernhard Giesen, who considers "triumph" and "trauma" to be transhistorical anthropological categories for the interpretation of collective experience, historian Reinhart Koselleck argues that Auschwitz represents a historic turning point in the problem of national memory. To support this claim, he differentiates between two forms of negative memories. There are those involving violence and defeats—examples of which abound in world history but that were in no way categorized as "meaningless"—that can still be "measured against a standard of justice or judged on the basis of demanded or idealized justice."³ According to Koselleck, this standard becomes wholly inadequate in the context of the extreme and abyssal violence with which the Holocaust was carried out. "There is no body of meaning," he concludes, "that can retrospectively redeem or bear witness to the totality of the crimes of the German people under National Socialism. The absence of such a body defines our remembrance."⁴

If the Holocaust represents a historic turning point in the extremity of violence involved in mass killing, this change also poses entirely new challenges to individual remembering and collective memory. It is therefore unsurprising that the resonances of this experience have caused the foundations and norms of remembering to shift; at the same time, these so-called "anomalies" have brought a great deal of academic attention to the process of remembering more generally.

What follows here is not a historical study; it makes no contribution to Holocaust research or to research concerning the events of World War II. It focuses exclusively on the belated reception of those events, inquiring into the ways those events are remembered individually, how they are passed on or silenced as collective experience, how they are publically recognized, and in what forms of media and ritualized commemorations they are being continually reconstructed. Psychological attitudes, political constellations, and cultural conditions of processes of remembering are particularly important in this regard, as are questions concerning normative frames of reference and the possibility or impossibility of making comparisons. In the post-traumatic era in which we currently find ourselves, practices of memory are closely linked to theories of memory. We are looking at ourselves, as it were, in our remembering. Individual and collective remembering are less and less frequently understood as spontaneous, natural, or sacred acts and more and more frequently recognized as social and cultural constructions that change over time and so have their own history.

The increased importance of the concept of trauma in our own day reflects a growing sensibility regarding the phenomenon of violence, both in terms of the suffering it causes and in terms of issues related to culpability. The Holocaust, which cannot be measured using conventional standards and cannot be treated or worked through using traditional psychological, political, and cultural methods, has opened the door onto an experience that has irrevocably changed the world. In its long shadow, the belated engagement with the Holocaust has produced an arsenal of concepts and norms that are now being applied both to contemporary forms of violence such as the sexual abuse of children as well as to other historical forms of violence such as slavery, genocide of indigenous peoples, colonial violence, and the First World War. This conceptual and discursive expansion of research into trauma in no way implies that the Holocaust be relativized or that its singularity be called into question, as the Historians' Debate twenty years ago feared might be the case. Rather, it signals a profound moral and cognitive transformation *in light of this event*, one that allows us to understand earlier incidences involving the excessive use of violence in new ways, and above all to describe and judge such events for which there had previously been no language or public interest.

This general context brings us to the heart of our thematic concerns. We shall inquire into the anomalies and specific features of this negative remembrance, such as Koselleck has defined it, both at the national and at the transnational level. We will also have to look at the ways in which the different sides of this negative remembrance—the one being characterized by guilt and the other by suffering—can either mutually exclude one other or can be connected in some way to one another. Further, we must clarify more precisely whether, when, and how individual recollection might be translated into a collective remembrance and what problems might arise in the process of such a translation.

The dominant focus in memory research today is on understanding the past as a construction that responds to the needs and possibilities of the present. The word *shadow* in the book's title here is meant to complicate that focus slightly by emphasizing the aspects of involuntariness and inaccessibility in the experience of those who engage with the traumatic past, both those who are directly affected by it as well as those who come after. So we shall also need to consider how to situate the constructivist notion of willful manipulation in relation to ideas of psychological pressure, inaccessibility, and ongoing affective power.

Memories are always situated somewhere between these poles of activity and passivity, ones that we can mark out by means of two contrasting positions. Both of these positions can be illustrated by means of examples from early twentieth-century literature: the first comes from Kari, the protagonist of Hugo Hofmannsthal's play *The Difficult Man* (1921), in which, among other things, the author deals with his traumatic experience of being buried alive during the First World War. That position can be stated as follows: "You can't call the past to witness like the police summoning evidence." The contrary position comes from the novel *Zeno Cosini* (1923) in which Italian writer Italo Svevo grapples with psychoanalysis. This position holds that "the present directs the past like members of an orchestra. It requires these shades and not others. Thus at times the past seems long, short at others. At times, it resonates; at times, it is silent. The part of the past that can work its way into the present is only the one that is meant to shed light on the present or to obscure it."[5]

The theme of this book is not the Holocaust or the Second World War but rather the dynamics of individual and collective memory in the shadow of a traumatic past. Memories do not exist as a closed system; they are always already affected, strengthened, inflected, modified, and polarized by other memories and by impulses to forget within the context of a given social reality. Therefore, in what follows, we will continually return to questions about how different memories are configured, how they intersect, and how they clash with one another. These topics have been the subject of intensive research for a decade now; in the interim, the studies that have come out of this research fill entire libraries. New case studies about individual and collective memory are always appearing on the market, but few have attempted to bring together the various disciplinary approaches to a memory discourse that has at times developed quite unevenly. The primary goal of this book is to do just that: to situate that discourse on a new level of interdisciplinary integration. A second goal consists of outlining and defining as clearly as possible some of the concepts used in the discourse of memory. Without this work of making distinctions and differentiations, which I hope will not seem too pedantic, the discourse quickly comes to a standstill. A third goal will be to bring this theoretical or conceptual work together with historical case studies, and, to this end, both parts of the book are constructed in such a way that each of them reflects, comments on, and fills out the other.

Finally, I should quite frankly add that the dynamics of individual and collective memory confront us with more problems than we can hope to answer. But according to Dirk Baecker, unsolved problems also have their uses. Those uses consist in "carrying them around as a lasting reminder of what has not yet been grasped. This means that one is constantly mobilizing mental and also practical resources to ask oneself whether it might in fact be possible to solve this hitherto unsolved problem."[6]

PART I

Theoretical Foundations

ONE

From Individual to Collective Constructions of the Past

As individuals, people may well be "indivisible," but they are never self-sufficient or unified entities. They always form part of a network of larger connections in which they are embedded and without which they could not exist. Every "I" is connected to a "we" that provides important foundations for the establishment of a personal identity. On the other hand, this "we" is not uniform either: it is also multi-layered, marking reference points that are partly meshed together and partly distinct and separate. The various groups with which an individual is connected reflect a spectrum of heterogeneous memberships that exhibit varying degrees of exclusivity. Sometimes membership in these groups takes place involuntarily (literally, "not consciously chosen"), as is the case with a family, a generation, an ethnicity, or a nation into which we are born. Alongside memberships that are determined by birth, there are groups we freely enter into by virtue of shared interests and abilities (such as a political party or a choir), performance and nomination (as in the case of academies and orders), or obligation (as in the case of compulsory military service for males of a particular age).

The different groups in which we find ourselves as individuals, into which we grow or develop, and that we choose and build ourselves vary in terms of their importance for our lives and in terms of how long they exert influence. The high school association, for instance, is a group to which we belong for a relatively short but highly impressionable time of our lives, and its influence on individuals will vary a great deal; it all depends on whether some of these connections continue to be maintained and cared for past their temporal horizon. The same goes for the local conditions in which we grow up: the neighborhood, the circles of friends, and the organizations. The reliability and the binding strength of the different groups to which the individual belongs vary a great deal. Informal groups and chosen communities like neighborhoods and circles of friends dissolve through mobility and changes in life phases; new ones take their place. But more formal groups are also not invariable or static components of our identities: religious identity can be given up or changed through conversion; nation and culture can be replaced through migration or reorientation. On the other hand, birth families, ethnicity, gender, and the generation into which we are born (usually) do not allow for change and therefore constitute an existential background that may take on very different shapes, but that we are not free to change in any fundamental way.

There are considerable differences in the temporal character of such groups. Informal memberships are usually short-term and lapse again after a few years or decades. Other more formal memberships end, at the very latest, in death. However, that does not apply to families, membership in which does not end with death. The life of the individual not only begins in the family, it is also prolonged after death in that same context; that is, the family is where the dead are remembered, memorialized. Even when other groups like academies, firms, or circles of friends take on this role, they model themselves after a family. So the family is the paradigmatic community that incorporates its dead, even though it must undergo continual ruptures in doing so. Seen from the perspective of the individual, the family is a long succession of generations in which the period of one's own life is fixed; it began before one's birth and, presuming there are children and grandchildren, it will continue after one's death. But more than that, the family is also an important framework of communication in which the different generations living at the same time overlap each other, and their different experiences, stories, and destinies also overlap. The individual takes part in a family memory, then, and in cases where there is a genealogical or historical interest, that family memory may be strengthened and even extended by means of records or documents. As a general rule, family memory tends to span three generations of people who are in contact with one another—that is, who know about each other and participate in cross-generational exchange. On the other hand, cultures, religious communities, and nations exist over a much longer period of time. By participating in such groups, the individual exists within various temporal horizons. While an individual's lifespan is, existentially speaking, quite limited, he or she nevertheless moves in ever-wider temporal dimensions beyond the scope of his or her own experience, ones that both recede into the past and project into the future. Therefore, the memory of the individual includes a great deal more than the events of his or her own experience; individual and collective memories are always interwoven in his or her memory.

In what follows, we will examine these different temporal horizons more closely, referring to them as "horizons of memory." To do this, we will assume that these groups each develop a specific form of memory: we will speak of the memory of the family, of the neighborhood, of the generation, of society, of the nation, and of the culture. It is not always easy to determine where one memory formation stops and another one begins, since the various levels pass through the individual person; they are intermingled and superimposed in those individuals. Nevertheless, it is useful to distinguish among the various levels and dimensions of memory because in part they have very different functions and dynamics. So, the opposition between individual and collective memory indicated in the heading for this chapter—an opposition that has gained currency in everyday language—should be made more complex by introducing four memory formations, each of which can be differentiated according to the criteria of spatial and temporal radius, of group size, and according to their brevity and their stability: these memory formations are the memory of the individual, the social group, and the political collectives of the nation and the culture.

Individual Memory

I begin this section on individual memory with a pessimistic assessment made by an English physician from the mid-seventeenth century on the human capacity for memory: "Darknesse and light divide the course of time, and oblivion shares with memory a great part even of our living beings; we slightly remember our felicities, and the smartest stroaks of affliction leave but short smart upon us. Sense endureth no extremities, and sorrows destroy us or themselves."[1] To be sure, the physician Sir Thomas Browne is writing under the influence of a pessimistic Christian worldview that places little hope in the human condition or its earthly aspirations. However, the view that is sketched out by today's neurologists and cognitive psychologists regarding the human capacity for memory is not much more positive. Focusing on the deceptive character of our memories, their research shows that memories are among the most fleeting and unreliable things there are.[2]

As questionable as our memories may be, the ability to remember nonetheless constitutes what it is to be a human being. We could not construct a self without memory, nor could we communicate with others as individual people. Biographical memories are indispensable since they are the material out of which experiences, relationships, and above all the sense of one's own identity are constituted.[3] However, only a tiny fraction of our memories is processed in language and implicitly forms the backbone of our life story. The majority of our memories, to put it in Proustian terms, "slumber" in us and wait to be "awakened" by an external inducement—at which point we become conscious of these memories; they achieve a sensual presence once again and can, under the right conditions, be articulated in words and recalled as part of an available repertoire. In addition to these available and unavailable "preconscious" memories, there are the inaccessible "unconscious" memories, those that are kept under lock and key and whose gatekeeper is known as "repression" or "trauma." These memories are often too painful or too shameful to come to the surface of consciousness without external aids like therapy or forms of outside pressure.

Our episodic memories have certain features in common. First, they are fundamentally *perspectival* and so are not interchangeable or transferable. Every individual with his or her life story occupies a unique space with a specific perceptual position, which is why memories, even if they intersect, are differentiated from each other. Second, memories do not exist in isolation but are *interlinked* with the memories of others. Through their structure, which consists of crossovers, overlapping, and connections, memories reciprocally confirm and strengthen one another. This is how they achieve not only coherence and credibility but also how they are able to generate a binding and community-building effect. Third, memories taken as they are in themselves are *fragmentary*; that is, they are limited in scope and quite formless. What flashes forth as a memory is, as a rule, a disconnected and isolated moment without a before or an after. Only through their belated recounting do memories take on a form and a structure that both completes them and at the same time stabilizes them. Fourth, memories are *fleeting* and unstable. Some change over the course of time with changes in the person and in their life situations while others fade or get entirely lost. Structures of relevance and frames of reference can change dramatically over the course of a lifetime, so that what was important at one time can gradually become unimportant and what was once unimportant can retrospectively become important. Memories that are linked together and often repeated in stories are best preserved; however, even they are given stable temporal boundaries: with the death of those who bear these memories, they necessarily disintegrate once again.

We can combine all of these features under the heading of "individual memory" [*Gedächtnis*], the dynamic medium through which individuals process their experiences. Of course, we should not conceive of it as an independent and purely private memory. As French sociologist Maurice Halbwachs's pioneering research into social memory showed in the 1920s, individual memory is always supported by the social milieu. According to Halbwachs, an absolutely solitary person could form no memories whatsoever, because these are first developed and stabilized through communication—that is, in verbal exchange with others. Similar to language in this respect, memory [*Gedächtnis*] is the cohesion of our memories that grows inward into the individual from the outside, and it is unquestionably language that constitutes its most important support. Accordingly, what we may term *communicative memory* arises within a milieu characterized by spatial proximity, regular interaction, collective forms of life, and shared experience.[4]

Not only do personal memories exist within a specific social milieu, but they also exist within a specific temporal horizon. This temporal horizon is largely determined by shifts in generation. After about eighty to one hundred years, there is a clear line drawn. This is the period in which different generations—three as a general rule, but on rare occasions, there can be as many as five—exist at the same time and develop a community through the personal exchange of experiences, memories, and stories. By telling stories, listening, asking questions, and further recounting, the scope of their own individual memories is expanded. Children and grandchildren adopt a share of the memories of the older family members in their own repository of memories, in which what has been personally experienced intersects with what they have heard about. As an existential horizon for personal memories, this "three-generational memory" is decisive for the orientation of the individual in the world. After eighty to a hundred years, it dissolves quite naturally once again, making room for subsequent generations in the fluid exchange of memories.

That is why we could also call such a memory supported by communication the *short-term memory* of a society.

Social Memory

In addition to the generations that exist within a family, social and historical generations also lend a certain rhythm to the temporal experience of a society.[5] Karl Mannheim was already paying special attention to generational memory in the 1930s, and sociologists have subsequently declared him to be one of the fathers of research into social memory, along with Halbwachs.[6] He proceeds on the assumption that the ages between twelve and twenty-five years are particularly formative ones and that what individuals experience during this time is decisive for the entire development of their personalities. As observers, actors, or victims, individuals are always caught up in the overarching dynamics of the historical process. Every person of a particular age group is informed by certain key historical experiences, and whether one likes it or not, one shares with one's peers certain convictions, attitudes, world perspectives, social values, and interpretative models. This means that individual memory, not only in terms of its temporal scope but also in terms of the ways it processes experience, is informed by the wider horizon of generational memory. An American psychologist formulated this in a somewhat extreme way: "Generational identity, once formed, is unchangeable."[7]

Generations thus share "a common understanding or grasp of the world."[8] According to sociologist Heinz Bude, they are "tentative communities of people close in age created on the basis of shared events and experiences" and are understood to be different from those of previous and subsequent generations. Therefore, Bude emphasizes, "communication between generations is about a limit of understanding that has to do with the temporality of experience. Age creates a truly existential divide, since no one can escape the confines of his time."[9] If one takes this sociological approach to generations seriously, the abstract unity of a historical epoch and its social memory can then be differentiated into different memories that are immersed in experience. The coexistence of and conflicts between various age groups are responsible both for a plurality of perspectives and for various tensions, clashes, and frictions. Every generation develops its own way of accessing the past; it is not simply given from the previous generation. The frictions that are so clearly felt in social memory are grounded in the different generational values and needs that are passed on from the previous frameworks for memory, ones that are, of course, only valid for a limited duration of time.

The dynamics of a society's memory are thus largely determined by generational shifts. With every such shift taking place about every thirty years, there is also a marked alteration in the cultural cross-section of memories. Attitudes that were once representative gradually move from the center to the periphery. What becomes clear in hindsight is that a shift in dominant generations dispels a particular atmosphere of experiences and values, of hopes and obsessions, and new impressions take their place. Generational shifts are always crucial for the renewal of a society's memory, but they have a particularly important role to play in addressing traumatic or humiliating memories. In post–World War II Germany, for instance, the repressive and complicit silence regarding historical guilt lasted into the sixties in West German society and was only broken by representatives of the younger generation, the so-called '68ers. This generation not only initiated the process of critically examining German guilt but acted as a leading participant in constructing monuments, developing ideas for museum exhibits, producing films, and engaging in other forms of public memory culture.

As a general rule, public memory culture of the kind that follows humiliating or traumatic events is first initiated after a period of fifteen to thirty years. In a comparative study of different American states, sociologists Pennebacker and Banasik examined one such instance of this belated impact of adverse historical experiences. They showed that in the city of Dallas, where John F. Kennedy was assassinated in 1963, no schools or streets had yet been named after the American president. The same situation applied to the city of Memphis, where civil rights activist Martin Luther King had been murdered: his name was not to be found on any streets or schools. Only after a period of thirty years were the citizens of both cities prepared to overcome their memory paralysis and build museums commemorating and documenting the assassinations that took place in those cities.[10]

A limited temporal horizon is characteristic of social memory, which is why we can speak of a social short-term memory in this context. Although this memory certainly relies on different media such as books, photo albums, and diaries, these supports nonetheless do not extend the duration of living remembrance. A remembrance is only alive insofar as a past is made present within a familiar context by means of conversation or verbal exchange. Psychologists have come up with a specific speech act to describe this form of remembrance: the term they use is *memory talk* or *conversational remem-*

bering.[11] By means of informal two-way communication, the past is not only made present but is also understood as teamwork. Once the network of this living communication is disrupted, the collective memory fades. The material supports for this living memory such as photography and letters then become relics or traces of a lost past, one that can no longer be spontaneously enlivened through such communicative acts of memory. The temporal horizon of social memory cannot be extended beyond the living interaction that spans a maximum of three to five generations. That is why it has the quality of a shadow running alongside the present, or of a horizon that is continually being closed as it advances.

Harald Welzer has a somewhat different interpretation of the concept of social memory. He has extended its application from voluntary and conscious acts of transmission and communication to include the ways in which history is conveyed unintentionally, incidentally, and in undetected ways.[12] Thus he pays particular attention to phenomena where the past is not really "constructed" but rather remains below the surface or is still present in more subtle ways.

Collective Memory—A Fiction?

Whereas the transition from individual to social memory is quite straightforward, the transition from social to collective memory tends to be more complex and indeed more controversial. Despite the fact that the idiom of collective memory has gained acceptance in everyday language and more and more frequently appears in the titles of books, a widespread skepticism regarding the term still exists. The historian Reinhart Koselleck has repeatedly stated that "there is no collective remembering," and for the Viennese philosopher Rudolf Burger, it is clear that "in spite of what is claimed by mystifiers today, there is no such thing as 'collective memory.'"[13]

The idea of collective memory was first introduced by French sociologist Maurice Halbwachs in the 1920s. People expressed misgivings about it from the very start, and it continues to raise doubts and misunderstandings.[14] In the context of his own direct engagement with the criticisms, Halbwachs explicitly rejects the notion that social memory represents a kind of mystical communion and describes it solely in terms of narrative, recall, and communicative exchange.

To clarify the issue, let's hear what another critic of collective memory has to say. In her book *Regarding the Pain of Others*, Susan Sontag writes:

> Photographs that everyone recognizes are now a constituent part of what a society chooses to think about, or declares that it has chosen to think about. It calls these ideas "memories," and that is, over the long run, a fiction. Strictly speaking, there is no such thing as collective memory. . . . All memory is individual, unreproducible—it dies with each person. What is called collective memory is not a remembering but a stipulating: that *this* is important, and this is the story about how it happened, with the pictures that lock the story in our minds. Ideologies create substantiating archives of images, representative images, which encapsulate common ideas of significance and trigger predictable thoughts, feelings.[15]

According to Sontag, a society can apparently decide without a will, think without a mind, and speak without a tongue. But it cannot remember without a faculty of memory. For her, the liberties of metaphorical language reach their limit with the idea of memory. Like Koselleck and Burger, she cannot think about memory independent of an organic basis or of an individual's own experience. The word she chooses to replace *collective memory* is *ideologies*, going on to define these ideologies in terms of repositories of provocative images that influence and steer people's beliefs, feelings, and opinions. The word *ideology* implies that such powerful images are accompanied by dangerous values and ways of thinking, and that these must be criticized and dismantled.

What in the politicized 1960s and '70s were treated as myths and ideologies came to be thought of as collective memory in the 1990s. This substitution is clearly associated with a generational shift, but it also contains a new insight about the unavoidability of images, including the necessity of political symbols. Instead of a critical rationality that categorizes images as a means of manipulation, the conviction has arisen that people are utterly dependent on images and collective symbols. Mental, material, and media images have important roles to play within a community that seeks to create for itself an image of itself. Of course, it is not just images that do this: stories, sites, memorials, and ritual practices do, too. Since the 1980s, a new branch of research has been developing that explores the question of how images (in the broadest sense) function for the constitution of communities. Concepts that are central to this development include the social imaginary (Jacques Lacan, Cornelius Castoriadis), the imagined community (Benedict Anderson) and, ever more consistently since the 1990s, collective memory. The fundamental premise of this paradigm shift from ideology critique to collective memory is by no means a postmodern relativism that rejects the principles of rationality and ethical commitment. Rather, it is guided by two insights: the first has to do with the enduring power of images and symbols and the second with their constructed character. This latter insight undermines the notion of false consciousness—from which the one carrying out the analysis always seems to be immune—because it is just as valid for one's own thinking as it is for the thinking of others. The insight that images and symbols were and are "made" is no longer automatically taken to indicate their fictional, untrue, or manipulative character, since the status of constructed (whether a long time ago or only recently) applies to all cultural artefacts. The task of the premise of ideology critique by no means led to the generalized development of a critical consciousness: to the contrary, one's own cultural horizon can no longer be exempted from those premises of critique, and so it too has become subject to the same modality of analysis. The task of memory research in the field of cultural studies is not just to describe and explain how images and symbols work, but also to evaluate them critically and to explore their destructive potential. The field of memory research in cultural studies, and specifically this particular research agenda, arose during the time when memory research was taking the innovative step from individual to collective memory. As we have seen, this step remains a difficult one, but there are also good reasons for it, ones that will be examined in greater detail in what follows.

Three Dimensions of Memory: Neural, Social, Cultural

The dispute over concepts can be settled if we stop relying on one of the three different levels and structures of human memory in isolation from all the others. In fact, none of these levels can function without the others. First, an analysis of how they interact can capture the complexity and potential of human memory. Then, distinguishing them from one another will allow us to make a clear theoretical description of the passage from individual to collective memory and to identify the different dimensions of memory.

The *first* level for the constitution of human memory is the *biological*. The fundamental requirement for memory is an organism with a brain and a central nervous system. This neural basis, currently the object of intensive research by brain researchers and cognitive psychologists, is not, however, an autonomous system: it requires fields of interaction within which it can be preserved and developed. There are two such fields of interaction that sustain and stabilize biological memory (and the brain more generally): the first is social interaction and communication and the second is cultural interaction supported by signs and media. The *neural* network is constantly interacting with both of these dimensions: with the *social* network and the *cultural* field. To the latter belong *material representations* in the form of texts, images, and memorials as well as *symbolic practices* such as festivals and rituals. Just as biological memory is formed and extended through interaction with other people, so too is it formed and extended through interaction with cultural artefacts and activities. Whereas what is reconstructed as social memory does not have a permanent or stable form, but rather unfolds in time as a dynamic process of negotiation and engagement, the media of cultural memory possess the stability and duration that are secured through institutions.

While as a general rule these three dimensions—neural structures, social interaction, and symbolic media—are all involved in memory processes, the various levels can be distinguished from one another on the basis of the emphasis each places on a particular aspect. On the first organic level, memory is a neural network in which brain waves pulsate and synapses are combined; certain forms of social communication as well as material carriers of memory—words or images—act as stimuli for this memory. At the second level, the social, memory is mainly a communicative network and thus can be understood as a social construction through which interpersonal relations and conversation are built up and sustained. Of course, this social memory could not exist without individual psychic organisms, and it also makes use of material supports in the form of recordings and images. Finally, at the third level, that of cultural memory, the focus is on symbolic media as carriers of memory, and this likewise involves a collective symbolic construction that is kept in motion through social communication and is strengthened and appropriated through the individual memories.

Memory is formed through the interaction of three components that have to work in concert with one another: there must be a carrier, an environment, and a support. In the case of neural memory, the carrier is the organism and its brain; the environment is the social setting and its frameworks of memory; and the support consists of strategies of memorization like repetition, "anecdotalizing," and media recordings or chronicles. In the case of social memory, the carrier is the social group that achieves stability through the regular and collective re-actualization of its collection of memories; the environment is constituted by individuals who exchange their individual versions of a collective experience with one another, and the supports are the symbolic media that they have at their disposal. In the case of cultural memory, the relation among the three components is even more radically inverted; for its carrier, this memory relies on transferable cultural objects that have been handed down, such as symbols, artefacts, media, and practices; as well, it relies on institutions that, by means of transmission, are able to extend the lifespan of those objects beyond that of finite human individuals, thus securing their long-term validity. Its environment is the group that creates its identity by means of these symbols, in that the group is always engaged in changing, renewing, and revitalizing this cultural pool; its supports are the individuals who appropriate these symbols and engage with them. Of special interest here are the transitions and boundaries among the various dimensions of memory. The transitions are quite fluid between neural and social memory. At the level of social memory, individual memory is interconnected with the memories of others, as Halbwachs had already emphasized. As a consequence, individual memory goes beyond itself and incorporates the memories of others. The boundaries between what one has personally experienced and what one has only heard about but then incorporated into oneself are therefore not always easy to identify. We will come back to the important question concerning the truth of individual memories later on. The enrichment of one's own experience that occurs through the experiences of others is of greater importance in the transition from individual to social memory, though, as is the way in which one's own perspectival memories are confirmed by means of others' memories.

Dimension:	Neural memory	Social memory	Cultural memory
Carrier:	Individual brain	Social communication	Symbolic media
Environment:	Social communication	Individual brain	Social communication
Support:	Symbolic media	Symbolic media	Individual memory

By contrast, the transition from social to cultural memory is not at all fluid, but rather traverses a breach and an abyss. The reason for this is that a decoupling and a recoupling of memory and experience take place at this level. This incredible broadening of horizon that takes place at the level of cultural memory is only possible with the aid of symbolic media, which give memory a lasting support. First, symbols that represent the carriers of cultural memories are externalized and objectivized. They represent a disembodied experience that can be taken in and appropriated by those who did not have the experience themselves. Second, this means that their temporal scope is not limited to a human lifespan but can potentially be extended indefinitely. The temporal duration of cultural memory is determined not by a finite human being, but by signs that are materially fixed and institutionally stabilized. Third, the disembodied and temporally indefinite content of cultural memory must always be brought together with living memories and appropriated by these memories. Appropriating this content by freely identifying with it allows the individual to achieve his or her cultural identity alongside his or her personal and social identity.

So at the level of cultural memory, the circle of people who act as carriers for this memory is substantially widened, and the temporal scope and durability of the memory are radically extended. While social memory is *a coordination of individual memories* brought about through collective life, conversation, and other forms of discourse, collective and cultural memory relies on a pool of experience and knowledge that has been released from its living carriers and *passes over into material media*. It is in this way that memories can be stabilized over generational thresholds. While social memory repeatedly vanishes with the people that keep it going, cultural symbols and signs are more durable. The range of social memory is tied to life rhythms and is therefore biologically limited, while memory that is generated at the level of culture—and that relies on external media like texts, images, monuments, and rituals—is temporally limitless: it has a long-term temporal horizon that can potentially stretch over centuries. Collective memory can be differentiated from family and generational memory by means of such symbolic supports, assuring that the memory has a future through succeeding generations. Monuments, memorials, yearly anniversaries, and rituals secure transgenerational memory by means of material signs or regular repetition. They offer occasions for later generations to grow into a collective memory without their having any personal connection to it.

Many misunderstandings regarding the legitimacy or illegitimacy of the concept of collective memory can be cleared up with this distinction between the organic, the social, and the cultural levels of memory. Of course, we cannot conceive of collective memory in terms of a simple analogy with individual memory. When such analogies are set up, critics who subscribe to the notion that memory is exclusively the domain of individual experience are right to do so. Institutions and associations, nations, states, the church, or a company do not "have" a memory; rather, they "make" one with the assistance of memorial signs and symbols. At the same time, institutions and associations are also "made" with the assistance of this memory.[16] So we can still speak of memory in a nonmetaphorical way under these very different conditions insofar as the construction of identity always makes some reference to the past.

With the help of the different components (carriers, environments, and supports) and the different dimensions of memory (organic, social, cultural), it becomes easier to distinguish the various formations of memory in which the individual participates through his or her multiple memberships in many groups. We will now examine these more closely. At this point, it becomes clear that the concept of "collective memory" is too vague to use for making adequate distinctions between one particular memory formation and any other. For collective stakes are included both in the social memory—such as that of families and close-knit groups—that necessarily exceeds the individual, as well as in the cultural memory that allows for communalization, one that not only exceeds the individual but that also extends beyond generations and epochs. In a narrower sense, "collective" can alone be called a memory formation when, together with strong ties of loyalty, it generates powerfully unified collective identities. This is particularly true for "national" memory, which is a form of "official" or "political" memory.

Memory Formations

Foundation:	**Biologically mediated**		**Symbolically mediated**	
Processing:	Neural	Communicative	Collective	Individual
Memory formation:	Individual memory	Social memory	Political memory	Cultural memory

In what follows, we shall turn our attention to the formation of political memory and explore a few aspects related to its emergence and its function.

Political Memory

Both individual and collective forms of memory are organized according to perspective. In contrast to the technical storage of knowledge and to archives, memory is not geared toward the greatest possible comprehensiveness; it assimilates nothing arbitrary but rather operates according to a more or less fixed principle of selection. Forgetting is therefore a constitutive part of individual and collective memory. Nietzsche describes this fundamentally selective and perspectival character of memory using a concept borrowed from optics.[17] He speaks of "horizon," by which he means a parameter of the field of vision that is bound to a particular standpoint. Nietzsche also talks about the "plastic power" of memory. He is referring to the ability to draw as clear a boundary as possible between remembering and forgetting, one that is able to distinguish between what is important and what is unimportant, what is relevant and what is irrelevant, what is in the service of life and what is not. Without this filter, he argues, individuals and groups would have no way of forming an identity (he himself spoke of "character" in this context), nor would they have any clear orientation as a basis for their activity. According to Nietzsche, when storehouses of knowledge become oversaturated, memory is actually weakened, thereby leading to a loss of identity.

In what follows, we will discuss the specifics and the problems of political memory using the example of national memory. The nineteenth century was both the century of nation building and the century of historical research, but the two projects were not necessarily as incompatible as Nietzsche had feared they were. He was writing during the age of historicism in which the archive of historical knowledge was undergoing a massive expansion, an expansion that, in his opinion, would lead to a terrible crisis of orientation. The task of his "untimely meditations" was to show what role the history writing could play for nation building and what forms a national memory could adopt.

RENAN AS THEORETICIAN OF NATIONAL MEMORY

We can speak of a political or a national memory when history is put to the service of identity formation, when it is appropriated by citizens and attested to by politicians. Contrary to the plural voices of social memory, which is memory "from below" and which repeatedly dissolves with generational shifts, national memory is a much more unifying construction that acts on society "from above": it is grounded in political institutions and invested in a longer temporal duration of survival.

A decade after Nietzsche, French writer and scholar of religion Ernst Renan highlighted the significance of collective memory for the nation in his famous Sorbonne lecture entitled "What Is a Nation?" (1882).[18] His analysis of the nation continues to be of great interest because of the ways in which it anticipates important perspectives in contemporary theories of the nation. In the lecture, Renan rejects the romantic discourse of nationhood that was so predominant in Germany at the time. Renan finds occasion to go through the traditional features of a possible definition of a nation in order to rule them all out and to replace them with something new. Race (collective roots, ethnicity), language, religion, and geography are, for him, excluded from the outset; nothing about them explains the kind of solidarity that is specific to the nation. According to him, it is precisely *not* the inalienable properties of the same blood, the same language, the same rituals, or the same morals that, from Herodotus to Herder, have constituted the benchmarks of national identity. For him, the nation is anything but a family writ large. In place of these traditional conceptions, he develops a modern conception of a willed or deliberate democratic nation born out of the spirit of the French Revolution, solidarity with which does not hearken back to a primordial collective origin but must be renewed through a daily plebiscite.

Renan was no supporter of a purely constitutional patriotism, however. Mere thirst for power or financial interests also fall short in terms of their unifying power, for the nation, he emphasizes, also has its sentimental side. To describe more carefully this affective side of the nation, he himself draws on the organicist metaphor that was so beloved in the nineteenth century: the nation not only has a body, he suggests, but it also has a soul.

> A nation is a soul, a spiritual principle. Two things that, in reality, are but one, constitute this soul or spiritual principle. . . . Human beings, I tell you, are not made overnight. The nation, like the individual, is the culmination of a long history of effort, sacrifice, and of devotion. . . . A heroic past, great figures, glory . . . this is the social capital upon which we base a national idea.
>
> (47)

It is surprising to hear Renan using the expression "*le capital social*" here, an idea we have come to associate with the work of Pierre Bourdieu. Of course, every epoch has a certain body of concepts at its disposal, and it must articulate itself in accordance with that conceptual framework. Notions like identity, imagined community, and collective memory were not available to Renan in the 1880s; nonetheless, my claim is that phenomena like these are already at stake in his work. With this notion of soul, he is not reverting back to the romantic discourse on the nation that was so deeply rooted in Germany, but is articulating a new perspective similar to Henri Bergson's vitalist theory of memory. Bergson's theory of memory is also expressed in organicist language; its lasting significance lies in the way it shifted memory research from a mechanical science of memorization à la Hermann Ebbinghaus to a dynamic constructivist paradigm, which has since become one of the foundations of modern memory research. With his emphasis on a collective soul, Renan places the nation as a community based on collective experience on equal footing with the nation as a willed community. And he had a very specific reference point for this: France had just had to cope with the 1871 defeat against the Prussians.

For Renan, soul means nothing more than a communal memory. Through firsthand experience, he was becoming aware that dramatic historical experiences constitute national identity. "For a people to appropriate history means, in fact, that they see it through the lens of their own identity."[19] What historian Christian Meier here calls identity is what Ernst Renan called soul. To see history through the lens of identity is clearly something different from what the project of historiography does; it is at precisely this point that historical research parts ways with national memory. Ian Buruma, who cites this line from Christian Meier, finds nothing in it but an echo of an outmoded nineteenth-century German way of thinking from which he emphatically seeks to distances himself: "All this rests on the assumption that there is such a thing as a national psyche. And to assume that is to believe in national community as an organic mass with history coursing through its veins. I think it is a romantic assumption, based less on history than on myth; a religious notion, expressed less through scholarship than through monuments, memorials, and historical sites turned into sacred grounds."[20] Buruma's argument follows the well-known logic of ideology critique, which pits scholarly facts against religious myths and believes that the latter can be cleared up for good. However, in the process he overlooks the sense that what he criticizes as so many obsolete and dangerous ways of thinking in fact have a great deal of force in our own time and thus urgently demand adequate methods of analysis. This analysis is in no way based on the romantic premise that the nation has a soul; its premise is much more that nations transform certain historical experiences into myths by dictating the ways in which they are processed, interpreted, and appropriated and that an "self-hypnotic" effect is generated when these myths are kept present with the help of monuments, memorials, and sites.

MYTH

The medium of collective memory (what we are calling political or national memory) is shaped in a much more durable way than social memory is. Peter

Novick sees its simplicity as its most important feature: "Collective memory simplifies; sees events from a single committed perspective; is impatient with ambiguities of any kind; reduces events to mythic archetypes."[21] To which we can add, in collective memory, mental images turn icons and stories into myths whose most important characteristics are their persuasiveness and their affective force. Such myths generally take historical events out of the context of the concrete conditions of their occurrence and reshape them into histories that are suspended in time and passed on from generation to generation. How long they are passed on depends upon whether or not they are needed—that is, whether or not they correspond to the desired self-image of the group and its goals. Their duration is not limited by the carriers' dying off, but rather through their replacement by other myths when they are no longer functional.

The word *myth* has a double meaning: in the one Buruma uses, it means a *falsification* of historical facts that can be refuted through historical research. Myth in this sense is the manifestation of a lie and a false consciousness that can be deconstructed and laid to rest by means of historical truth. There are, however, other ways of thinking about myth. It can also mean the form in which history is seen through the lens of identity; according to this meaning, myth denotes the *affective appropriation* of one's own history. Myth in this sense is a foundational history that possesses a lasting significance whose force is not neutralized by historicization: it keeps the past alive in contemporary society and gives that society an orientation for the future. History raised to the level of myth in the context of social reality is "contemporary in the way that past and present blend into one another in particular places and through particular activities."[22] Appropriating history in this way can often involve a falsification of that history, but that is not necessarily the case. To examine and differentiate these cases with greater precision, the research paradigm of ideology critique must be replaced by one focused on national memory. The interpretation and idealization of history in the form of memorials, monuments, and sacred spaces cannot be reduced to a simple falsification of historical fact, since these modes of relating to history are themselves historical facts. Not simply a myth in an ideological-critical sense, it can be understood as a cultural construction that has substantial effects on the present and the future. What is decisive about the construction of collective self-images is not their ontological status, but rather the potential impact of those historical experiences that end up getting interpreted and appropriated. Alongside the question "What happened and how?" is the following one: "How was the event experienced, and how is it remembered?" Today there are "mnemo-historical" questions alongside strictly historical ones, questions regarding the aftereffects, the imaginative interpretation, and the appropriation of history through the medium of stories that promote a kind of identification with them.[23]

Generally we could say that there are basically two paths to nation building. While they are by no means mutually exclusive, the one focuses on *modernization* and the other on *mythologization*. Benedict Anderson has clearly described the path of modernization in terms of the role played by institutions like the printing press and alphabetization; he also explores the literary genre of the novel and the role played by the newspaper in the process of democratic nation building. Regarding the dimension of the nation as a construct of identity or as a project involving identity, though, these evolutionary achievements say little. So to complement this kind of investigation, what is needed is an analysis of the national *Mythomotorik* without which nations would not be able to manage: nations as imagined communities are indeed more than just functional systems.[24] Albrecht Koschorke has shown in his studies on the relation between the images of corporations and the political imaginary that there is a clear dialectic between the empty abstraction of a modern functionalistic entity and the drive to mythologize this entity. Ernst Renan was concerned about this mythic dimension a hundred years before Benedict Anderson, which is the reason his prescient analysis places such emphasis on collective memory for the nation:

> More valuable than common customs and frontiers that conform to strategic ideas is to have a shared heritage of glory and regret, a common plan of action for the future, and to have suffered, rejoiced and hoped together. These we can all understand despite the diversities of race and language. I have just said, "to have suffered together." Yes, shared suffering unites more than does joy. As far as national memories go, acts of mourning are more potent than those of triumph since they impose duties and require a common effort.
>
> (47)

According to Renan, the nation has a collective will that is oriented toward the future. In order to be effective, however, this will must be strengthened by the construction of a collective past. It is this collective memory that makes the present meaningful as one stage in the course of a necessary and long-term development. The potential for the national memory of a historical event to act as a *Mythomotorik* lies precisely in this temporal orientation: it endows the present with orientation and meaning insofar as it is revealed to be an intermediate stage of a motivating narrative that includes the past and the future. The nineteenth century is not only the age of historicization, in which a modern historiography emerges that seeks to objectify the past in a professional and independent academic discourse. During the same time period, national myths also emerge that appropriate the past to the present by focusing on particular moments that will support an identity-constructing narrative. In that way, academic historical research was often put to the service of national constructions of memory, but problems often arose in terms of the tensions and dissonances between national narratives and historical truth. Again, it is Renan who brings out this contradiction when he writes, "Forgetting, I would even say historical error, is essential to the creation of a nation, which is why the advance of historical studies often poses a threat to nationality" (19).

Although Renan uses conventional nineteenth-century descriptions of the nation as a growing and organic being with a body and a soul, at the same time he is emphatic on the point that nations owe their existence to a political decision and a constitution that must be supported and strengthened by the construction of an imagined self-image. With this claim, he is anticipating the current "anti-essentialist" theory of the nation as an "imagined community" that is based upon an imaginative construction rather than on an undefinable "being."[25] In fact, there are at least four reasons to acknowledge Renan's work as an important precursor to theories of national memory: first, he emphasizes the importance of a relation to the past as a central affective tie for the solidarity of the nation; second, he privileges the binding force of suffering and grief over that of triumph and success; third, he draws attention to the constitutive importance of forgetting for the construction of national memory; and finally, he discusses in farsighted ways the conflicts that tend to arise between historical research and the construction of collective memory. Constructions of national memory are susceptible to the criticisms of academic historical research; according to Renan, conflicts and irreconcilable differences are liable to arise between the mythologization of the past and its academic treatment. This is an important point, one that I will take as an opportunity to add a brief excursus on the relationship between memory and history.

Excursus: Memory and History

In a series of groundbreaking studies on the semantics of history, historian Reinhart Koselleck has shown that the concept of history first took on its modern character in the second half of the eighteenth century. In these studies, Koselleck discovers in the word *history* an abstract collective singular that took the place of many histories as a *plural tantum*. Plural histories are always only partial views; each of them is decentralized and bound to a particular standpoint, and together they flow into the modern concept of history in the same way that rivers flow into a sea. Just like metaphorical rivers, these plural histories are taken up into the sea of abstract history. This image of the sea comes from Maurice Halbwachs, who used it to distinguish the concept of collective memory from history, understood in the sense of academic history. The historical world, he writes, "is like an ocean fed by the many partial histories. . . . The totality of past events can be put together in a single record only by separating them from the memory of the groups who preserved them."[26] Sixty years later, Pierre Nora would intensify this opposition in the introduction to his monumental work *Les lieux de mémoire* on the basis that memory and history,

> far from being synonymous, appear now to be in fundamental opposition. . . . Memory is a perpetually actual phenomenon, a bond tying us to the eternal present; history is a representation of the past. . . . Memory installs remembrance within the sacred; history, always prosaic, releases it again. Memory is blind to all but the group it binds. . . . History, on the other hand, belongs to everyone and to no one, whence its claim to universal authority.[27]

This antagonism between history and memory is by no means universal; rather, it has its own history. History and memory first diverged from one another with the emergence of academic history as a professionalized discourse in the nineteenth century; at that time, both memory and history discovered its adversary in the other. All earlier forms of history writing were understood to be forms of memory or a way of preserving a memory. So in ancient times the concepts of history and memory overlapped one another. From antiquity up to modernity, we see it repeatedly emphasized that the central function of historiography was to support memory. The task of historiography was to legitimate the origin and the memory of a dynasty, an institution or a state, and to attest to its continuity through evidence of its noble past. The primary function of history writing was what is now known as "the politics of history" or "the politics of the past":[28] it was a question of producing a memory that, as a "servant of authority,"[29] would lay the foundation for a political commonwealth. In so doing, it would support the interests of the ruling power of the day.

Cicero saw the writing of history as a weapon against forgetting. This formulation became something of a stock phrase and remained central for the ways in which history writing was understood, right up to the modern period. With this understanding, written forms of history took on and perpetuated important functions of the oral transmission of history: facts (*res gestae*) regarding past heroes and kings that were previously sung by bards began to be recorded by chroniclers to protect them from being forgotten and to ensure the dead a dignified remembrance. This blending of history and memory in myth is characteristic of oral cultures of history and of the history writing of early states.

As an instance of the loosening of these strong connections between history and memory, I would invoke the ancient Greek historian Herodotus. In the opening sentence of his *Histories*, he calls his own work of history *historiai*, which means something like "critical inquiry." Despite this basic stance, again in his proem he invokes the traditional connection between history and memory. In his work, history also remains an exercise of memory where memory is understood to be tightly bound to the concept of glory (*kleos*, *fama*). He records his histories so that "neither the deeds of men may be forgotten by lapse of time, nor the works great and marvellous, which have been produced some by Hellenes and some by Barbarians, may lose their renown."[30] There is of course a volatile displacement contained in this formulation, which emphasizes the memorial orientation of history writing in order to annul it in substance. The reference to the Greeks *and* the barbarians makes it clear that Herodotus's historiographical project exceeds a strictly ethnocentric standpoint. The audience for whom Herodotus carried out his inquiry is no longer clearly delimited, thereby loosening the reference to identity that is a basic requirement for every construction of memory.[31] For the individual as well as for the collective, memories are connected to a particular acting subject, and they work to strengthen its self-understanding. The memorial function of historiography was therefore always connected to an exclusive standpoint, a particular perspective, and an identity. At odds with this perspectivalism is Herodotus's "memory belonging to posterity," an entity that is already on the verge of losing the contours of this specific identity. In his work, history writing has a much broader memorial function, coming to possess a nonspecific cognitive function. It has more to do with knowledge than with memory; it is more about *curiositas* than *memoria*. That also confirms the clarification that follows the passages just cited: "In particular, one should know the causes as to why they waged war against each other."[32] This explicit combination of *what* happened with *why* it happened points to a new function of historiography, which is to enlighten. For Herodotus, it is a matter of getting underneath the events to uncover causes and regularities, from which the historian can distill general knowledge regarding human forms of activity and motivation.

Herodotus developed an interest in the past that goes beyond the horizons of "one's own" and so relaxes, even to the point of undoing, the strong connection between history and identity. To the extent that history writing approaches a meta-perspective and an idea of general knowledge, it also distances itself from memory. Under the influence of this decoupling, the ethnographic gaze is free to roam beyond its own concerns and can cultivate a new interest in foreign peoples and cultures. This historiography is initiated through historical curiosity and, no longer being tied to a sharply differentiated collective identity, can expand a body of historical knowledge whose reach is potentially limitless. It is not only released from specific viewpoints, but it is also taken up in a written discourse that no longer forms a part of the rulers' archive. In the final analysis, as Pierre Nora claims, this knowledge belongs to "everyone and to no one" and has a "claim to universal authority." History that relinquishes its ties to memory and identity—and nothing less is implied by this than the methodological imperative of objectivity—becomes the universal memory of humanity whose site is the archive of scholarship.[33]

History, writes Halbwachs, "can be represented as the universal memory of the human species. But there is no universal memory. Every collective memory requires the support of a group delimited in space and time. The totality of past events can be put together in a single record only by separating them from the memory of the groups who preserved them and by severing the bonds that held them close to the psychological life of the social milieus where they occurred, while retaining only the group's chronological and spatial outline of them."[34] Halbwachs is referring here to the tradition of critical historiography that followed in the wake of Herodotus. In the course of the nineteenth century, it came to be established as an academic discipline that developed independently of any political objections that might arise regarding standards of discursive truth and authority. Of course, despite this ideal of objectivity, professional historians were never entirely free of relations, loyalties, and prejudices. This new standard regarding the critical procedure of historical analysis by no means excluded the possibility that historical reflection might come to the service of nation building and understand its task "as giving to the state, the people . . . an image of themselves."[35] In the nineteenth century, history largely became—despite Nietzsche's fears to the contrary—

the foundation upon which collective identities were shaped. It imparted and strengthened feelings of belonging. All of this does not invalidate the historian's ideal of objectivity; as Bernard Lewis has emphasized, at the very least the historian must be conscious of how difficult this ideal is to achieve and "instead of indulging his prejudices, seek to identify and correct them."[36]

RAPPROCHEMENTS BETWEEN HISTORY AND MEMORY IN THE SHADOW OF THE HOLOCAUST

For a long time, historians did not consider personal memory to be a legitimate resource for history writing; rather, in attempting to reconstruct an objective picture of events, the historian would routinely bypass subjective memories, which were considered to be notoriously unreliable and biased.[37] Remembering and memory were understood to be the opponents of the academic historian, but this has undergone decisive changes in the aftermath of the Holocaust. Since the 1980s we have seen history and memory converge again in powerful ways. No longer considered to be polar opposites of each other, they are striking up new modes of relation. This convergence is associated with a fundamental revaluation of memory and oral traditions. Positivist historiography confronts its limit when its sources fall silent. At this limit, oral testimonies and modes of transmission can help where archival documents do not convey any perspective from within the experience, as is the case with postcolonial situations in which indigenous cultures have been destroyed or with a post-traumatic situation following genocide. It was in this context that a revaluation of lived experience and memory, as well as the genre of subjective testimony, took place. Of particular importance in this regard was the revaluation of the stature of the moral witnesses who had, at least to some degree, experienced firsthand what happened to the murdered victims.[38]

As an example of the new rapprochement between history and memory in the shadow of the Holocaust, we could name the historian Saul Friedländer, who is both a Holocaust survivor and the author of a powerful book on memory.[39] Moreover, he is also the cofounder of the journal *History and Memory*, which has been in publication since 1989 and which, among other things, takes up issues regarding official commemoration and state-sanctioned memory politics. The name Saul Friedländer is also associated with the Historians' Debate in 1986, which played out in German newspapers and journals regarding appropriate ways of representing this decisive historical event.

At the heart of the controversy surrounding that debate were the contrasting poles of historicization on the one hand and sacralization on the other. Should the Holocaust be given back to the historians and thereby promoted to the universal archive of scholarship, or should it be anchored in a collective memory? The passage from Nora cited previously makes itself felt once again: "Memory installs remembrance within the sacred; history, always prosaic, releases it again." Together with the so-called *Vergleichsverbot* (a ban on comparison, which itself became controversial), the strong claim about the Holocaust's radical singularity came to be associated with a commitment to its being remembered as a transnational and transgenerational "memory of humanity." There is a certain paradox here, since up until this point, this universalistic perspective had always been understood as the way to dissolve identity and thereby also to dissolve memory.

In the context of the Holocaust, memory plays a role at two completely different levels: at one level, there is the lived memory of survivors, and at another level, there is the imperative for humanity to remember. Saul Friedländer has pointed out that the growing social significance of the memories of Holocaust survivors first caused professional historical research to gradually move away from an exclusive engagement with problems "of the discipline" that the Nazi regime presented, and finally and decisively to begin directing its attention to the horrific findings regarding this state's homicidal machinery. He even claims that pop culture and the media had a hand in "forcing the academic discipline of history to pay more attention to the history of the Holocaust since the late 1970s."[40] Not least, he shows that the new rapprochement of history and memory has consequences for historiographical forms of representation. In his history of the Holocaust, he places a strong emphasis on the perspectives of people who became entangled in the events as victims or as executioners. By allowing for individual experiences and memories, he undermines the illusion of a coherent reconstruction of history, drawing attention to the irreducible plurality and diversity of these experiences. This strategy yields a multi-perspectival representation of the historical event and brings together the scholarly explanation of connections with subjective perceptions and experiences.[41] To some extent, this had already been the project of oral history since the '60s. Of course, in the context of the Holocaust, far greater value was given to the concept of "survivor testimony" than in oral history research, largely because of the specific memorial function this testimony had. The importance of these testimonials had less to do with individual fates and social developments that had not yet been registered by the discipline of history than it had to do with giving a voice to the murdered or silenced victims of Nazism.

In the course of this development, bridges were built over the once unbridgeable chasm between historical scholarship and a memory-oriented interpretation of the past. Subjective experience and objective concepts were no longer considered incompatible but were now seen as complementary. The importance of personal testimonials has since become generally recognized in historical scholarship, not only because they offer an additional resource for understanding past occurrences but also because they are monuments to the perspectives of the victims themselves. Ricoeur and Friedländer have both emphasized the importance of memory to the work of historians, for whom testimony and personal memory act as triggers for history writing in general and for Holocaust history writing in particular. The historian cannot and must not simply ignore personal memories, for, in the case of the Holocaust, its representation would be reduced to an abstraction, as remote from the experience of the time as it would be from the opportunity for a personal re-experiencing in the present.

Therefore, from the perspective of memory, there are three things in particular that enhance history writing: the emphasis placed by memory on the aspects of emotion and individual experience; its emphasis on the memorial function of history as a form of remembrance; and the emphasis it places on an ethical orientation.

Friedländer has underscored that the "implicit or explicit use of moral categories is unavoidable in interpretation." This development shows that alongside the roles history writing plays for self-aggrandizement or critique, there is a third function that we could call moral. It has to do with witnessing, conscience, and accountability. This corresponds to a definition given of history writing by Johann Huizinga. He describes it as "a spiritual form in which a society makes itself account for something."[42] With this definition, Huizinga is once again emphasizing the close connections that exist between the past, memory, and identity. Society is accountable for its *own* past, not for just any past whatsoever. The history that Huizinga has in mind takes the form of a collective self-questioning, and its fundamental relation to identity makes it into a form of remembering. In the post-traumatic situation, this function of history writing has taken on new significance. In the aftereffects of catastrophes, the historian is not only a storyteller, a "teller of tales" in Hayden White's sense, but is also a lawyer and judge in Carlo Ginzburg's terms, or a "remembrancer" in Peter Burke's sense. In the late Middle Ages in

England, *remembrancer* was the title given to debt collectors whose job it was to remind the citizens of a city what they would rather forget. While Burke clearly places himself in this tradition, he also combines the critical function of historiography with the moral function: "I prefer to see historians as the guardians of awkward facts, the skeletons in the closet in the cupboard of the social memory."[43]

Our current situation is not so much characterized by the dominance of history *or* memory as it is by the complexity of their coexistence. They are two competing ways of referring to the past, each of which corrects and supplements the other. In our involvement with the past, and especially in our involvement with the traumatic past, we need all these functions: both the memorial and the moral functions that tie history to memory as well as the critical function that separates them from each other. Nora writes that history and memory are opposites in every respect. That might very well be true, but he overlooks the fact that they also depend upon each other. Only by being exposed to each other can both history and memory fulfill their roles. In the words of Christian Maier, "memory motivates historical activity; historical research utilizes memory."[44] Historical research depends upon memory for orientation in terms of meaning and value, while memory depends upon historical research for verification and correction.

Cultural Memory

I would like to begin this final section on cultural memory with another pessimistic statement by Sir Thomas Browne, who, in the middle of the seventeenth century, realized that "our Fathers finde their graves in our short memories, and sadly tell us how we may be buried in our Survivors. Gravestones tell the truth scarce fourty years: Generations passe while some trees stand and old families last not three Oaks."[45] The basic law of life, Browne reminds us, is forgetting. The continual process of forgetting is not only a normal aspect of social life, but it is also a precondition for survival, and that is as true for groups as it is for individuals. Just as for the individual, a great deal must also be forgotten in society for it to be able to distance itself from horrific events, to overcome conflicts, to make room for the new, and to set tasks for the present. Particularly for a culture involved in the dynamics of the modern with its relentless rhythm of renewal and decay, forgetting becomes a central (and not just accidental) aspect of culture. Similar to the ways in which we're constantly phasing out older products to replace them with newer ones—clothing, furniture, cars, washing machines, computers, software—so too do memories, experiences, artworks, and systems of knowledge wane and then disappear as a consequence of social and cultural change.[46]

That is not the whole story, however. Forgetting is not just the unavoidable and quasi-natural consequence of a life of growth and renewal, but it is also a deliberate cultural aim. For instance, the heretical writings that ended up on the index of the Catholic Church, as well as those members of the church who were identified as heretics and excommunicated, were intentionally forgotten.[47] But so too were the writings and names of those who, following a political transformation or scholarly change in paradigm, dropped out of the framework of those recognized as having made lasting and significant contributions. Finally, those whose achievements were obscured by a narrow and exclusive method of selection were also forgotten: that is how the work of Graupner is overshadowed by that of Bach and how Mozart's work obscures Ignaz Holzbauer's.

The sociologist Zygmunt Bauman defines the task of culture as the "translation of the transient into the intransient."[48] Remembrance is always improbable and so requires a great deal of effort and support on the part of certain institutions and the media. Generally speaking, every culture invents ways of ensuring memory in order to combat Browne's idea of a relentless and universal forgetting. In both oral and literate cultures, different kinds of media are invented to ensure the preservation and transmission of knowledge considered indispensable for the expression and continued existence of a society's cultural identity. Notions like tradition, heritage, and cultural legacy (in French, *patrimoine*) indicate how central this striving for perpetuity and transmission is. When we replace this terminology with the idea of cultural memory, the dynamics of memory and forgetting—ones that were already inherent in the project—come to the forefront. How we ensure inclusion and survival always involves their opposites, such as exclusion, invalidation, and destruction, as well as the weaker forms of forgetting such as neglect, dissolution, and loss.

How did cultural memory ever come about? How is it that, out of memories, efforts, and achievements formerly belonging to the individual, a complex whole emerges that does not have to be newly constituted from generation to generation or from epoch to epoch but extends over centuries? To answer this question, we must revisit the issue of individual memories and their changing social horizon. As long as memories are not articulated and stabilized in external media, they are delicate and fragile. They often vanish within a lifetime: with the death of their carrier, they too are irrecoverably lost. Following a death, the material traces of that life also become fragmented. Residences are cleared out, their contents dispersed at flea markets and auctions. No one can identify the people in the photos of photo albums anymore. The family memory frequently and quite naturally dissolves after about eighty to one hundred years, making room for the memories of subsequent generations in a fluid process of changeover. Of course, not everything associated with this life is immediately lost: objects like furniture, letters, or photos remain and are retained as supports for the family memory even beyond the threshold of three generations.

There is clearly a difference between material remains and living memories, memories that, according to Siegfried Kracauer, can only be maintained through oral communication. Using the example of a photo of his grandmother, he closely analyzes this difference and finds that photography, with its down-to-the-last-detail accuracy of every ruffle of clothing and every wrinkle of a face, is the opposite of memory. It registers an outer shell that possesses the character of a mummy. For Kracauer, the quality of living memory is entirely different from that of exact photography. It is only established through scraps of verbal memory, through sayings and anecdotes. The grandchildren might not know very much about their grandmother, but they still know something, writes Kracauer in an autobiographical glance at his own past. They know "that in her later years she lived in a narrow little room with a view onto the old part of town and that, to amuse the children, she would make toy soldiers dance on a glass plate; they also know a nasty story about her life, and two confirmed utterances which change a bit from generation to generation."[49]

As a general rule, the material context of a lived life outlasts its owner. The heroine of an American novel from the nineteenth century makes precisely this observation on the occasion of inheriting a bureau: "'This piece of furniture,' her new husband shares with her, 'belonged to my father's mother and grandmother and great-grandmother, and now it has come to your hands.'" Her reaction is not one of pride over her new property, but rather insight into the paradox of duration: "'how long such an insignificant thing,' said Ellen thoughtfully—'outlasts its more dignified possessors.'"[50] Remnants that outlast their owners or everyday objects that possess functional, material, or sentimental value always enter into new configurations and new contexts. The last of these contexts that protects these remnants from destruction or forgetting is the museum or the archive. Museums and archives as well as research libraries are cultural sites in which a society preserves the remains and traces of its past, long after these have lost their living references and contexts. Alongside objects, we can add books, letters, and written testimonials, as well as pictures, photographs, and other carriers of information. As soon as these cease to be useful, they become silent witnesses to the past that must be newly interpreted by specialists.

Social Memory	Cultural Memory
Biological carrier	Material carrier
Limited (80–100 years)	Unlimited
Intergenerational	Transgenerational
Communication	Symbols and signs
"Conversational remembering"	Monuments, anniversaries, rituals, texts, images

STORAGE MEMORY AND FUNCTIONAL MEMORY

While living memory is irretrievably lost along with its carriers, the material remains of a culture have a chance at a second life through institutions that take them beyond their original context.[51] When they are placed in museums, libraries, and archives and are collected, conserved, and catalogued in such institutions, they stand the chance of surviving for a much longer period of time. That said, we are still very far from a complete description of the prerequisites and the conditions for the emergence of cultural memory, for not only does a cultural memory emerge in hindsight by means of collection and conservation, but there is also a forward-thinking principle of selection at work that aims to collect and communicate an inheritance for an indeterminant posterity.

For a better understanding of these two aspects of cultural memory, we must differentiate the dynamics of cultural memory between a society's storage memory and what I would call its functional memory. This difference is analogous to the structure of memory in which remembering and forgetting are intimately connected and engage with one another, for much of what we have forgotten is not irretrievably lost but is only unavailable for a certain amount of time.[52] What in personal memory sinks back onto the undifferentiated ground of forgetting will also resurface only under certain conditions, just as it does in the completely forgotten feeling that Proust's madeleine suddenly reawakens. As a general rule, what we usually call forgetting is in truth a latent memory, the key to which we have lost; if we accidentally stumble upon it, a segment of the sensuously lived past returns in a completely unexpected way. We can also speak of such a return when certain elements of an inheritance that have become sedimented in storage memory are illuminated in new ways by present modes of awareness, whereas conversely the thoughts of the present are shaped with the help of certain preserved elements of an inheritance. Thus, to use the language of Walter Benjamin, traces of the past come to light along with the thoughts of the present in a constellation of legibility. In this way, new affinities or, more precisely, elective affinities between past epochs and the ever-advancing present are always being developed. Perhaps we could say that what Proust's *mémoire involontaire* is for the individual, the archive or storage memory is for cultural memory: it is the basis and background for latent memories whose time lies either in the past or in the future. At the cultural level, the material remnants of earlier periods correspond to Proust's unconscious memory. These remnants are no longer needed or integrated into the present, but perhaps they are still available somewhere, for what has faded or been rejected, invalidated, or discarded by a society at a particular moment in time is not necessarily completely lost or forgotten: it can be collected in material traces, preserved, and brought out again during a later period in which it is newly discovered and reinterpreted.

This distinction between a culture's storage memory and its functional memory is most obviously at work in the institution of the art museum: its permanent exhibits fix a selection of its works in the awareness and the memory of its visitors, though it has a far larger collection of works of every genre and every period available in storage. A museum of this sort always fulfills two clearly defined functions: one is to establish a *canon* that is highly valued and determined according to a specific taste (as well as being a determinant of taste), while the other is to act as a historical *archive*. The conservation or upkeep of the collection is thus only one side of cultural memory. The other side involves rigid criteria of selection, active appraisal, and personal appropriation. There is never enough space for functional memory, so what ends up making the cut—from the canon of biblical texts to the canon of classics—has gone through a rigorous procedure of selection. This procedure of canonization, which both selects texts and images and endows them with a kind of sacred aura, secures a place for them not just in the passive cultural memory of a society but also in its active cultural memory, for canonization also signifies a transhistorical commitment to readings and interpretation. So, despite increasingly accelerated paces of cultural innovation, the collections of functional memory remain on the curricula of educational institutions, on the playbill of theatres, in the halls of museums, in performances at concert halls, and in publishers' programs. What has a place in the functional memory of a society is always subject to new performances, exhibitions, readings, interpretations, and engagements. This continual engagement prevents a particular cultural artefact from becoming foreign or mute; it is continually being revitalized across generations through the intervention of an ever-changing present awareness.

Storage memory is also a memory since, when considered from the perspective of a totality, it also only recovers a very small segment of the cultural legacy. It too is always the product of a forgetting: mechanisms like selection, invalidation, destruction, and loss are also at work here. But it has much more space, and therefore its content is not subject to such rigid processes of selection processes as functional memory, which is why the storage memory of libraries and archives is full to bursting. This overabundance of storage memory is, as Montaigne and later Nietzsche already noted, only the flipside of an empty memory. Conservation and care of the collection are therefore the preconditions for a cultural memory, but it is only through individual perception, appraisal, and appropriation and the ways they are conveyed through media, through cultural establishments, and through educational institutions that they become part of a cultural memory. Storage memory is the cultural archive in which a certain portion of the material remains of earlier periods are stored after these have lost their points of reference and contexts within a living culture. Visual or verbal documents become the silent testimonials to the past when the actual stories and memories to which they refer have been lost. Cultural artefacts that are preserved in storage memory distinguish themselves in decisive ways from artefacts preserved in functional memory, the latter being particularly well-protected against the processes of forgetting and defamiliarization. The institutionally established and long-term stability of artefacts does not, of course, foreclose the possibility of change or renewal within cultural memory. This possibility arises because of the porousness of the border between functional memory and storage memory; it can be transgressed in both directions. Elements from the willed and conscious active functional memory will continuously fall back into the archive when they are no longer of interest; new discoveries can be retrieved out of passive storage memory for the renewal of a culture's functional memory.

The structure of cultural memory arises within this field of tension between functional memory and storage memory, between what is remembered and what is forgotten, what is conscious and what is unconscious, what is manifest and what is latent. These dynamics serve to make cultural memory considerably more complex and open to change but also more heterogeneous, more precarious, and more controversial than national memory, which strives for an unambiguous unity. Like national memory, the task of cultural memory is to transmit experiences and knowledge over generations, thereby developing a long-term social memory. However, these different memory formations are distinguished from one another on the basis of how they are reproduced. While political memory achieves its stability through its radically restricted content, its powerful symbolism, its collective rituals, and its normative obligations, cultural memory is dependent upon the formal diversity of texts, images, and three-dimensional artefacts. Both depend upon various forms of media—be they forms of assuring duration through storage techniques such as writing and imagery or forms assuring repetition through performances such as rituals, which are a means of renewal, participation, and acquisition. For political memory, these means of acquisition are best celebrated collectively, while individual engagement is crucial for the acquisition of cultural memory.

The heritage of cultural memory involves inventories that include libraries, collections, sculptures, and architecture alongside activities occurring at regular temporal intervals, like festivals, customs, and rituals. In the midst of historical change, these inventories have to be constantly interpreted, discussed, and renewed, since they must be appropriated by succeeding generations and newly transmitted in keeping with the current needs and demands of the present. Whereas political memory tends toward unity and instrumentalization, cultural memory resists such reductionism due to its media-oriented and material character. Its inventory is never rigorously unified. Storage memory can withstand this unifying instrumentalization, since it stores precisely that which has lost its current reference point and thereby opens up its historical dimension. But functional memory can also withstand this unifying trend, since its contents are fundamentally open to a variety of interpretations and must be newly transmitted in light of that multiplicity of individual standpoints and experiences.

Cultural Memory

Functional Memory	**Storage Memory**
Ways of assuring repetition (symbolic practices)	Ways of assuring duration (material representations)
Traditions	Books, images, films
Rituals	Libraries
Canonization of artefacts	Museums
	Archives

Summary

To sum up the most important findings of our overview of the different forms of memory: the transition from individual to collective memory cannot be made in a single step; rather, it leads us over different levels that need to be more carefully examined. These levels take on the contours of various groups to which we as individuals belong and that influence our memories and our identities. We have become familiar with four such carriers of each specific memory formation: individuals, social groups, political collectives, and cultures. On these four levels, identities arise that each have their respective meaning, reliability, and range. While they are not necessarily incompatible, under certain conditions these identities can come into serious conflict with one another.

Through the individual's membership and participation in these various identities, a great deal more is adopted by our memories than is given by our own experience. Lived memory itself is always interwoven with the experience of others because it is built up through communicative exchange and therefore depends upon points of overlap and confirmation. With the appropriation of history as seen "through the lens of identity," our episodic lived memory is extended or broadened by means of knowledge-based memory. Although these formations—that gained through experience and that broader memory gained through learning—initially might have nothing to do with one another, nevertheless they do not remain completely distinct from each other. Intellectual stores of knowledge become a political and cultural memory insofar as connections are made to one's own identity and to one's world of experience and insofar as one participates in memorial rituals. Whoever participates in the many ritual marches through Belfast during holiday celebrations, as is the norm in Protestant Ireland, or whoever goes to

Auschwitz on a school trip to take history in at the level of bodily experience, thereby endeavors to overcome the strict boundaries between lived memory and memory based on knowledge. In that way, an absent primary experience can be replaced by a secondary experience.[53]

In response to critical or skeptical positions that reject the concept of collective memory as an unreliable metaphor, we have argued that the presence of two basic criteria justifies our speaking of a memory: the first is a *connection to identities* (along with all of the associated emotion and affectivity), and the second involves a *dialectic of remembering and forgetting* that, at all levels, leads to a dynamic that is unstable, shifting, and volatile. The criticism of the concept of collective memory that I myself have expressed has nothing to do with its supposedly mystical or metaphorical premises, but solely with its vagueness, which is why I have recommended here that it be replaced with the terms *social* and *political* or *national memory*.

We have differentiated among three supports of memory: the biological or neural system of the human brain that pertains exclusively to individuals; the social system of embodied interaction and verbal communication; and the system of symbolic articulations and technical media that is the basis not only for communication over long distances but also for a long-term cultural tradition. All three supports are involved whenever experiences are registered and then taken up again to reach out to more and more people. The communication radius of cultural memory is potentially unlimited in a temporal sense so long as storage techniques hold up and the institutions are reliable. Yet, the stability of storage media does not amount to a cultural memory: it must be continually translated into communication and experience.

Just as the Internet makes it possible to communicate in real time over vast geographical distances, cultural memory makes it possible to engage across temporal distances in exchanges that help to shape identity. So at the same time, cultural memory creates the conditions for communicating beyond one's own lifetime without interaction, which means that we are never exclusively contemporaries in our own period and that we use the experiential riches of earlier times. That is, we can critically reflect upon the knowledge and the abilities of earlier stages of humanity. Within this cultural dimension, the borders between present and past are systematically held open through the interplay of setting something aside and then later returning to it. Cultural memory is the precondition for communicating beyond the span of one's own lifetime and constitutes the possibility for continued encounters between self and other, between people from different historical ages.

We began with the image of a person who participates in many different groups and in whose own memory different group memories intersect, overlap, and occasionally experience friction. This conception also has a philosophical dimension, one that is most often emphasized by those who seek to problematize the idea of an autonomous subject. Hans-Georg Gadamer is one such thinker, and he writes, "long before we understand ourselves through the process of self-examination, we understand ourselves in a self-evident way in the family, society, and state in which we live."[54] In a very similar way, Alasdair MacIntyre has commented on the irreducible connection between individual and collective identity: "The story of my life is always embedded in the story of those communities from which I derive my identity. . . . What I am, therefore, is in key part what I inherit, a specific past that is present to some degree in my present."[55] In other words, to a very significant degree, we are what we remember and also what we forget. To complicate matters, our memory participates not only in the memories of other people, but in the symbolic universe of our shared culture.

TWO

Basic Concepts and Themes
of Individual and Collective Memory

In this chapter, we shall further develop the foundations of memory theory, taking into consideration the historical conditions, the psychic mechanisms, and the political strategies that are involved in constructions of memory. An attempt will be made to identify some basic concepts and mechanisms that determine the grammar of individual and collective memory, the notion of grammar being privileged over a typology that concentrates on a closed and static method of classification. When we use the term *grammar* in this context, we are referring above all to the ways in which grammar generates meaning—that is, the mechanism by which meaningful statements emerge. Linguists understand grammar to be the set of rules underlying verbal expressions as collective constructions involving psychic, social, and cultural elements. This set of rules conveys information about the conditions of those verbal expressions and allows us to measure their formal quality and their success or failure as acts of communication. Of course, this degree of normative rigor is out of the question when it comes to individual and collective constructions of memory, but my argument is that a set of rules underlies these as well and that this set of rules is closely related to narrative conventions and to certain types of dissemination.[1] In a kind of pragmatics or rhetoric of memory, what are the most important emotionally charged formulae that are deployed in response to corresponding challenges in particular historical situations? Do connections open up between the psychic mechanisms of memory on the one hand and social and political strategies of memory on the other? Can we identify certain basic patterns whose iterability makes it possible to generate comparisons and general statements? Of course, thinking about the logic implicit to the dynamics of individual and collective memory in terms of structural iterability does not imply that that logic is universal or timeless. On the contrary, alongside the task of identifying certain basic patterns and assumptions about constructions and configurations of memory, it will also be a matter of detailing the histories of their development and of pointing out significant historical turning points within that development.

The outline for these basic theoretical concepts and conventions is based on concrete examples that at this point will only be cursorily treated and for which I am able to rely on a substantial body of research that has been generated in particular over the last decade. This great body of research can only become a discourse of memory that is relevant to the field of cultural studies once it has been freed from its different disciplinary contexts and brought together beyond those disciplinary boundaries.[2] A focus of this kind on themes and formulae related to memory necessarily involves certain kinds of reduction. What I have had to leave out of this section will be addressed in the next section, where we shall deepen the issues by means of select case studies in their historical and social contexts.

Who Remembers?

In the essay mentioned earlier, "Forms and Traditions of Negative Memory," Reinhart Koselleck poses three basic questions:[3]

1. *Who* is being remembered?
2. *What* is being remembered?
3. *How* are they being remembered?

In what follows, we will begin with a fourth question, slightly different from the first: *who remembers [wer erinnert sich]?* We will need to examine how different perspectives influence different constructions of memory. Is it possible to speak of something like a psycho-logic as regards the formation of memory under the influence of pride and shame or guilt and suffering? Which political arguments and strategies foster constructions of memory?

THE VICTORS AND THE DEFEATED

To explain the constellation involving the victors and the defeated, we can again take up Renan's subtle analysis of nation building in the late nineteenth century:

> The nation, like the individual, is the culmination of a long history of effort, of sacrifice and of devotion.... A heroic past, great figures, glory (true glory, that is), this is the social capital on which we base a national idea.[4]

This assessment makes it quite clear what the selection criteria are for memory under the dictates of the nineteenth-century nation-state. What matters in this context are those points of connection to history that serve to strengthen a positive self-image and that can be harmonized with a particular course of action. Whatever turns out to be inconsistent with this heroic picture will be subject to forgetting. Victories are obviously more easily remembered than defeats. This is clearly the case in the Metro stations of Paris, where Napoleon's victories are commemorated, but not his defeats. Conversely, in London (so, the land of Wellington), there is a metro station bearing the name of Waterloo, which is clear evidence for the selective and perspectival character of national memory. One's own victory is committed to memory alongside the unstated defeat of one's neighbor, thus extending these historical confrontations far beyond their own time. Under changed political conditions, these constructions of memory can also create disturbances. So, for instance, on the occasion of the hundredth anniversary of the *Entente cordiale* between England and France that was celebrated in 2004, the name of the Waterloo Room in Buckingham palace was temporarily changed to the "Music Room."

However, this does not mean that only glorious victories have a place in national memory. Given certain conditions, defeats can also become central historical points of reference. Renan expresses himself clearly on this point:

> More valuable than common customs and frontiers that conform to strategic interest is to have a shared heritage of glory and of regret, a common plan of action for the future, and to have suffered, rejoiced and hoped together. These we can all understand despite the diversities of race and language. I have just said, "to have suffered together." Yes, shared suffering unites more than does joy. As far as

national memories go, acts of mourning are more potent than those of triumph, since they impose duties and require common effort.

(47)

A decade after the defeat of the French by Prussian troops at Sedan, Renan knew firsthand that the memory of those who suffer defeat has stronger affective potential than the memory of the victor. While a triumph celebrated by the victors inevitably becomes an aspect of its past, the memory of the defeated points to the future. The imperative to remember the defeat is substantially stronger, as are the means by which the defeated work through it. In a sense then, one can "lose" by winning and also "win" by losing. Renan directs this insight to the Prussians in the form of a paradox: "*Vae victoribus!*" [Woe to the victorious!].⁵ Defeats don't necessarily destroy a collective self-image; more often than not, they strengthen feelings of national solidarity. In fact, defeats are remembered and reactivated with the greatest degree of pathos and ceremonial expense in cases where a nation bases its identity on a sense of itself as a victim. In such cases, memories of injustice and harm suffered are kept alive to create a strong sense of communal solidarity in the face of external pressures, to legitimate claims, and to mobilize resistance. A particularly striking example of this dynamic involves the Serbian people, who remember the defeat in Kosovo against the Ottoman Empire in 1389 by recording the fallen heroes of that time in their national calendar of saints and acknowledging them in annual commemorations. Further examples include the Czech people, for whom the defeat of Bohemian groups in the battle of White Mountain (November 8, 1620) against the Habsburg Empire remains a national sore point to this day. Similar to the Czechs, alongside the Irish, the Poles also foster a memory that focuses on defeats. The latter have even earned the title trophy for suffering, thinking of itself as the "Christ of nations." In such a form, defeats can be ennobling; they can also strengthen the will to national independence over and against an imperial hegemonic power and perpetuate that sensibility over centuries. The mobilizing power of defeat also plays an important role for the citizens of Quebec, a francophone minority in English-speaking Canada. They remember the defeat of General Montcalm in the year 1759 against the colonial rule of the British and publically display this defeat up to the present day: their automobile license plate caption is "*Je me souviens.*" No further defeats can be sustained when it comes to cultural survival in an exclusively English-speaking place. In the 1960s, the state of Israel excavated the Jewish fortress Masada that had fallen under the Romans and built it up as its central political site of memory. Here too, a mobilizing force arises out of the memory of a defeat. It is not at all weakened by the memory of defeat; rather, its resolve is hardened by association with the warning, "Never Again Shall We Be Victims!"[6]

In each of these cases, the historical memory of the nation takes on the form of a narrative whose powerful affective charge is sustained over centuries through ritualized performances that ensure its regular repetition and reactivation. As well, a historical date from the past is chosen that can take on the quality of a mythical primal event. This allows for an enduring charisma of sorts to develop around the national memory, on the basis of which all further historical experiences can then be interpreted and evaluated.

Evidently, the national memory is just as receptive to historical moments of aggrandizement as it is to moments of humiliation, provided that they can be processed through the semantics of a heroic historical image. Giesen's formula, "triumph and trauma," seems to fit exactly with these findings. Renan spoke of "triumph and mourning." I propose that we talk about "triumph and disgrace" or "victory and defeat" in this context and reserve the word *trauma* for special cases, which we have yet to discuss. What makes a defeat different from a traumatic experience shall be briefly illustrated here, by comparing the ends of the two world wars.

After the First World War and the Versailles peace treaty, the national memory of the Germans was a typical memory of the defeated, for which the notions of humiliation and disgrace proved central. A loss of honor and the destruction of positive individual and collective self-images were at the heart of this experience. There was only one way to rebuild honor, according to this psychology: disgrace had to be transformed into heroic grandeur, and shameful humiliation and powerlessness had to become a manifestation of strength and determination. In accordance with the national code, the feudalist myth of honor constituted the common heroic tie between the victors and the defeated; the defeated had to win back at all costs the honor that they had lost through the defeat and all of its humiliating consequences. Two examples serve to verify the extent to which the Nazi dictatorship was influenced by a heroic memory of the defeated. During the Nazi period, the memorial site of the Neue Wache in Berlin was rededicated to commemorate the fallen "heroes of the movement." The date of Hitler's attempted putsch in Munich, November 9, 1923 (one hardly remembered today), became an important memorial day for the Third Reich. The other example was in the headlines not long ago, in the spring of 2006. Under the bell tower that was raised on the grounds of the Berlin Olympic Stadium in Berlin between 1934 and 1936, Langemarckhalle was erected as a national shrine to commemorate German casualties in November 1914 in the Battle of Langemarck. Just in time for the 2006 Soccer World Championships, the German Historical Museum took over the site and mounted an exhibition that engaged the theme of sports, history, and politics to act as (in their words) "an antidote, as it were, to the 'Langemarck myth.'"[7]

There was no peace treaty at the end of the Second World War; rather, there was an unconditional surrender that demolished Germany as a subject of international law. Under these conditions, the honor of the German nation was destroyed in an even more fundamental way than it had been before. The national memory in 1945 was no longer simply the memory of a defeated nation; in the context of the unleashing of extreme violence that had begun with the aggressive war of offense and ended with the Holocaust, the national memory became a perpetrator memory for which entirely new and historically unprecedented measures were needed. What was new was that for the Germans, every self-interpretation that had previously been based on the heroic semantics of honor—in which victors and defeated are bound to one another in ways that go well beyond their opposition—had to be forfeited. Wolfgang Schivelbusch has pointedly summarized this difference: "there are thus degrees of defeat and capitulation. As long as losing nations have an intact national identity at their command, they will stubbornly refuse to comply with the victor's demands for moral and spiritual surrender through demonstrations of regret, conversion, and willingness to be reeducated. The situation is different when, together with the physical properties of a nation, its spiritual and moral backbone has been broken. The losers in 1865, 1871, and even 1918 had not yet reached this nadir."[8] This historical turning point in the grammar of national memory takes the heroic semantics of honor and turns it into a discourse of perpetrator and trauma. Trauma is the very opposite of a heroic narrative; it does not signify the mobilization and strengthening of identity but rather points to a disturbance of identity or, indeed, to its destruction.

The important distinction between those who are defeated and those who are traumatized often gets blurred. Take, for example, the following: in an essay on "Large Group Identity and Selective Traumas," psychoanalyst Vamik Volkan transferred the psychological workings and consequences of traumatization from an individual level to a collective one and discussed them in terms of historical examples.[9] My objection here is not directed at the psychoanalytic interpretation of historical events and collectives, but solely at the blurring of the distinction between defeats and traumas. To make the distinction clearer, we might ask, "Was the defeat traumatic?" That could just as well have been asked of the First World War as of any other defeat. So the question must have something to do with how the defeat was processed. That is, was it repressed, silenced, or effaced from the collective narrative as being dishonorable, or was it presented by means of the semantics of heroism? Even such a presentation stabilizes the event in collective memory, which Volkan discusses in terms of selective trauma. In doing so, he confuses the heroic national semantics of defeat with the demand on the part of traumatized victims for recognition. Recognition of the kind that traumatized victims need can only come from the outside. But this is exactly what the Serbs didn't need: they produced a stable and self-contained national myth in which to preserve their heroic sentiments until such time as they could be reignited six hundred years later through Milosevic's political machinations in order to assert an ad hoc, collective right to exercise revenge and violence against their Bosnian and Albanian neighbors. In what follows, we will examine more closely the question of which historical events in a more narrow sense can be spoken of as traumatizing. One criterion will be that such experiences either fundamentally obstruct national narratives and heroic stereotypes or demand entirely new cultural forms and models of presentation.

WHO WRITES HISTORY: THE VICTORS OR THE DEFEATED?

One often hears it said that history is written by the victors, but the saying is seldom given much thought. There is no doubt that it has its relevance: the victors who are setting a course for the future do not simply allow the historical narrative to lead teleologically to the moment of their triumph, but they also tightly control those archives in which other perspectives might be discovered. Walter Benjamin's critique of history written from the perspective of the victor has had a great influence on the thinking of intellectuals from the so-called '68 generation. He taught them to empathize with the defeated as opposed to with the victors: "All rulers are the heirs of those who conquered before them. Hence, empathy with the victor invariably benefits the rulers. . . . Whoever has emerged victorious participates to this day in the triumphal procession in which the present rulers step over those who are lying prostrate."[10]

The historian Reinhart Koselleck has modified the saying somewhat; according to him, the defeated in history prove to be better historians than the victors. Whereas history written by the victors has a "short-term perspective" and is focused on "those series of events that, through their own efforts, brought them victory," the historiography of the defeated is more complex and instructive. From the "unique gains in experience imposed upon them spring insights of lasting duration and, consequently, of greater explanatory power. If history is made in the short run by the victors, historical gains in knowledge stem in the long run from the vanquished."[11]

Koselleck supports his argument using obvious examples, but freely admits that there are also counter-examples: "After 1918, the Germans were fixated on paragraph 231 of the Versailles Treaty, incensed over its fixing of guilt for the war onto them. They unleashed a moralistic debate about innocence, one which obstructed every insight into the deeper and longer-lasting reasons for the defeat."[12] Today we tend to differentiate more precisely between "the writing of history" or historiography and "the memory of history." The analysis of history from the point of view of the defeated such as was done by the Scottish social historians or by Alexis de Tocqueville has nothing to do with the resentment precipitated by Versailles because in the context of Versailles, it was less about the writing of history than it was a memory strategy. In a seminal essay, Peter Burke draws attention to the difference between *writing* history and *remembering* history: "It is often said that history is written by the victors," he writes; "it might also be said that history is forgotten by the victors. They can afford to forget, while the vanquished are unable to accept what happened and are condemned to brood over it, relive it, and reflect how different it might have been."[13]

In his book *The Culture of Defeat*, Wolfgang Schivelbusch examines the strategies of collective memory, along with their psycho-historical and mythologizing mechanisms, that emerge in the aftermath of defeats. By comparing three prominent defeats (of the American South after the Civil War, of France following the Prussian War, and of Germany after the First World War), he discovers certain patterns in the way such experiences were processed.[14] In line with Koselleck's argument, Schivelbusch argues that while the historiography on the side of the defeated can set into motion a reflective process of penetrating self-critique, their memory strategy is often geared toward self-aggrandizement and mythologization. The tangible experience of national humiliation is answered through an arsenal of fantastical interpretations: through the alternative of a spiritual or moral elevation, through cathartic purification or a new myth of honor, through a scapegoat myth or legends of being stabbed in the back and betrayal. Such strategies spare the defeated from disappointment; they allow the defeated to save face and to reinterpret their experience of humiliation as self-aggrandizement. In this way, a loss of honor can lead to an increase in honor; those defeated in combat can turn into spiritual victors.

COMING TO TERMS WITH THE PAST

In our own day, the difference between the victors and the defeated on the one hand and between perpetrators and victims on the other has become indispensable for comparing nations and the difficulties they have in engaging with their pasts. The example of the Spanish Civil War is highly relevant in this respect with its reciprocal warfare between the supporters of the fascist Franco regime and the Republicans who were Communist sympathizers. But just because the battle had two sides does not imply that there was symmetry between them. The Republican side not only was defeated, but it also had to contend with the pressure of a victor's memory—and continue to be stigmatized as enemies of the people, as so-called "red traitors"—for a further thirty years until Franco's death in 1975. In this case, it was the victors who wrote history: because of the dynamics of political power, the underdogs didn't stand a chance of telling their story. Given their political powerlessness, nothing remained for them except precisely their memory, which kept them alive as an oppressed political group of victims. This memory of the defeated remains an unofficial and subversive one, which in Benjamin's sense waits for the day of its redemption or recognition. Only once a social and political framework has been produced in which the suffering of this defeated group can be narrated and recognized, only once it has been taken up into the national self-image, can it be overcome and forgotten.

In the aftermath of civil war, the political goal of a politics of memory must therefore be directed toward achieving a compromise. As long as the painful asymmetry of remembering remains, so too does the war continue; through the triumphalism of the victor, the oppression is prolonged into peacetime. Civil war is only overcome when the symmetry of memories is reestablished and both sides can relinquish their opposing perspectives in the context of a common unifying framework. By means of this integration and by establishing common goals for the future, the conflict of opposing memories can be overcome, divisive resentments can be smoothed over, and the ardor of hatred and revanchism can settle. The politics of memory in the aftermath of civil wars must be directed toward dispelling the destructively divisive energy of memory, and this can never be accomplished by repressing a memory but only through mutual understanding. The goal in such a political situation is to "come to terms with the past," a notion that is inappropriate for the conditions of the German postwar period but is wholly relevant in the case of Spain. The goal of coming to terms with the past is to overcome a painful memory for the sake of a common and liberated future. As was the case in Spain, wherever the victor's memory triumphs over the memory of the defeated for a generation following civil war, a reestablishment of symmetry must first be produced in memory before one can finally turn away from divided pasts and face a common future.

Victim and Perpetrator

The notions of victim and perpetrator belonging to the domain of criminology are relatively new to historiography; until recently, one only spoke of the victors and the defeated. Throughout the course of the total war that Germans ruthlessly unleashed and with which they set the entirety of Europe ablaze, ever greater segments of the civilian population were pulled into the homicidal maelstrom. In this sense, the war was not restricted to military action. The insane project of the destruction of the European Jews was largely implemented under cover of this war's darkness. Following the war, therefore, it could not simply be a question of the victor and the defeated standing opposed to one another, but also of perpetrator and victim. The international tribunal of the Allied forces in Nuremburg, where German war criminals were made to account for themselves, was an utterly new historical phenomenon.

ON THE AMBIVALENCE OF THE NOTION OF VICTIM

To clarify the difference between the memory of the defeated and the memory of the victim, the ambivalence of the term *victim* [*Opfer*, both "victim" and "sacrifice"—Trans.] must first be taken into account. The notion emerges out of the religious paradigms of ancient and Judeo-Christian worship where it is most commonly associated with aggressive and deadly violence.[15] In the act of killing the victim, a taboo is broken that is considered sacred within the context of the worship. So the act of killing in connection with the worship itself turns into an eminently meaningful sacred activity: it becomes a sacrifice. The semantics of victimhood [*Opfersemantik*] was then reinterpreted in important ways: first, the sacrifice of animals or food replaced the human sacrifice, and second, these were replaced with spiritual sacrifices like singing, praying, and ascetic daily living. Another important change then occurred with the reintroduction of the human sacrifice. In the Hebrew Bible, God first commands Abraham to sacrifice his son Isaac before stopping his hand at the last minute and substituting a sheep. According to Christian commentators, this episode is redeemed in the New Testament through God's plan to have his own son die on the cross at Golgotha. So, the highest form of religious piety becomes the act of voluntary suffering, which takes the place of Abraham's unconditional obedience. What is significant about this reintroduction of the human sacrifice is the fact that it is freely accepted, that in it, the pure passivity (of Isaac) becomes bound to the activity of a willing acceptance (of Abraham). That is the form in which every *religious* martyr surpasses the Abraham story or reenacts the self-victimization of Christ. In that the religious martyr understands him- or herself to be a "sacrifice" or victim [*Opfer*] in this sense, he or she is reinterpreting a passive event—political oppression—so that it becomes an active undertaking. By reframing death as a religious message, the martyr undermines the political power of persecutory state violence. These semantics of victimhood were able to survive these explicitly religious contexts such that its meaning could be newly evaluated within the secular realm of national discourse. Thus God, as the recipient of the sacrifice and its greatest advocate, came to be replaced by other absolute values, such as the fatherland.

Differentiations within the terminology of *Opfer* have gone furthest in Latin: there we find the distinction between "victim" on the one hand ("sacrificium," "immolatio") and, on the other, the material sacrifice or offering ("hostia," "victima," both of which are nouns of the feminine gender, tellingly enough), whereby in each case this double aspect is concealed by the use of two separate words. While the range of meaning of the word *hostie* is limited to the ritual of communion, the words *sacrificium* and *victima* have been carried over as borrowed words into the vernacular and continue to govern the semantics of victim terminology in their most recent forms. What is new in the current situation is the polarization of the notions of *sacrificium* and *victima*, which today mark out two opposing poles of what actually coincide in the German word *Opfer*: the free commitment of one's own life within a religious or heroic semantics is derived from the Latin *sacrificium* (in English, *sacrifice*); from the Latin *victima* (*victim* in English) comes the passive and defenseless object of violence.

This new division of the concept of victim into an active and a purely passive variant has become absolutely essential to the contemporary discussion. Another form of memory corresponds to both categories. The victim memory of soldiers is encoded within the semantics of heroic nationalism, which has absorbed the religious meaning of martyrdom. The sacrificial deaths of the victors and the defeated are understood as "dying for": they are seen as a gift to the community and to the fatherland that will be repaid by the survivors and future generations with honor and glorification.

None of this is relevant to powerless victims in a situation of radically asymmetrical violence. It does not apply to slaves displaced from Africa, to the aboriginal populations of various continents that were eradicated through the introduction of weaponry and bacteria, to the Armenian genocide in the shadow of the First World War, to the genocide of the European Jews and the Sinti and Roma people, nor does it apply to the murder of other disenfranchised social minorities in the shadow of the Second World War or to persecuted and murdered civilians the world over.

HEROIC AND TRAUMATIC MEMORY OF VICTIMS

The crucial difference between the relationship of the victor to the defeated on the one hand and of the perpetrator to the victim on the other is that in the latter case, no form of reciprocity exists. When no battles are even being fought, but rather acts of persecution and extermination are being carried out in a terrifying asymmetry between a blindsiding power and those who are being delivered into powerlessness, the persecuted have no political goal, motive, or value to deploy against the powers of destruction. The majority of the persecuted were not even active as resistance fighters; rather, they were passive victims and were in no way prepared for what was happening to them, let alone in a position to mount resistance. Such experiences could no longer be grasped using heroic representations of experience and remembering. A problem thus arose regarding the shape of this new memory, one that first emerged only decades later and crystallized around the new concept of trauma.

The traumatic memory of the victim differs from the heroic memory of the victim in many ways. As easy as it might be to remember violence and loss in the mode of heroic victimhood, it is impossible to do this in the mode of a trauma victim. The heroic victim is identified as a martyr: "Martyrdom implies faith, in an ideal, in nationhood, in God. A martyr's death is terrible but it is instilled with deep meaning. The idea of millions of people murdered for nothing is unbearable. The temptation is to invent meaning, by calling them martyrs, by erecting crosses, by engaging in religious ritual."[16] This activity of meaning-making can be formulated just as well in accordance with a nationalist rhetoric as it can be within a religious one. In a GDR travel guide, for instance, the entry for the memorial site of Ravensbrück describes it as a monument to "our dead sisters, the immortal heroines of the antifascist struggle, who gave their lives for the freedom and independence of their countries and a happy future of all peoples."[17]

It is extremely difficult to remember traumatic experiences of suffering and shame because they cannot be integrated into a positive individual or collective self-image. For the trauma victim, there are no culturally tried-and-tested models of reception or traditions of memory. "Why," asks Louis Begley, "do we find it so difficult to admire those who are tormented and make no defiant gesture? Supposing they are neither meek nor proud but only frightened?"[18] Therefore it often happens that a traumatic experience will only be represented and socially recognized belatedly, often decades or even centuries after the historical event. Only then can it become a part of a collective or cultural memory. It is a long road, however, to get to that point of having an experience of traumatic victimization recognized and taken up as historical knowledge and collective memory. Whether or not the group experience of victimization takes on the form of a collective and cultural memory also depends upon whether the group affected succeeds in organizing itself as a collective and whether it develops commemorative forms that can span generations. In the absence of such symbolic memorial forms, it can also happen that the psychic wounds of trauma are unconsciously passed on to subsequent generations. In light of these difficulties, it is understandable that historical trauma is initially approached through the forms of heroic victim memory. That is why the Warsaw Ghetto uprising was at the center of the Jewish memory of the Holocaust for so long, and that is also why the heroic memory of the firefighters played such an important role in the commemorative ceremonies in New York after September 11, 2001.

The two meanings of the German word *Opfer* can be illustrated using two political initiatives undertaken by former German Federal Chancellor Helmut Kohl. In terms of the first meaning, victim in the sense of sacrifice, we could invoke the joint visit paid by Helmut Kohl and American president Ronald Reagan to the Bitburg military cemetery in May 1985. As part of a process of normalizing political relations between the two closely allied states, after forty years, their respective images of the past also had to be harmonized. The joint honoring of Allied and German fallen soldiers offered itself up as an inclusive ritual of mourning and reconciliation that could dismantle any remaining differences. But the opposite took place. Since the Bitburg military cemetery housed not only the graves of American soldiers and soldiers from the Wehrmacht but also those of members of the Waffen-SS, these latter were automatically included in the reconciliatory German-American pact of memory. All of them had made sacrifices for the fatherland. The tacit standardization of memory brought out the discrepancy in a scandal that marked the beginning of a new phase in Germany's history of memory.[19] Whereas the heroic meaning of *Opfer* (sacrifice) was celebrated at the Bitburg cemetery commemoration, the same federal chancellor staged the passive meaning of *Opfer* (victim) seven years later in an act that was meant to be no less unifying. In 1992, after the reunification of Germany, he turned the East German memorial site of the Neue Wache on Unter den Linden into a central memorial site for the reunified nation. He dedicated this site to "the victims of war and dictatorship." This category of victim brought German soldiers, resistance fighters, displaced persons, victims of bombing, and rape victims together with the murdered prisoners of concentration camps. This boundless memory of a universalized victimization not only served to abolish the gap between victim and perpetrator, but it also served to efface memory itself. What remained was the sense of a generalized and catastrophic fate shared by all people, along with a vague pathos in which every visitor to the monument could participate according to his or her own needs.

THE TURN IN VICTIM MEMORY

We are currently experiencing an ethical turn from sacrificial forms of memory to more victim-centered forms that clearly has nothing to do with these generalizing blanket gestures. The ethical significance of this turn does not consist in the inclusive assertion that we are all victims, but rather in the act of recognizing victims, calling them by name, and telling their stories. Whereas the sacrificial victim is confirmed within the context of his or her own community, by contrast, the passive victim whose memory is not borne by any comparable group is initially dependent upon the recognition of other groups to have this status conferred upon him or her. The memory of the passive victim cannot remain within the group of those affected but calls for the broadening of its reception in terms of public resonance and recognition. The testimony of the victim who is marked by trauma depends on this resonance and the reassurance found in an ethical memory—that is, in a memory that transcends group interests.

In the turn from heroes or martyrs who die for a cause and so sacrifice themselves for the community to victims who make claims for restitution and recognition, Henry Rousso sees "the significant passage from a political to a moral model of understanding the past. For has one ever seen 'heroes,' demigods in the Greek sense of the word, demand restitution before the courts? Although," he adds, "the identification with the victims who would actually have been forgotten in the traditional observation of history of states, victors, academics, etc. leads to an overvaluation of this perspective today."[20]

Many see this moralizing turn as an ambivalent one these days because there are two sides to it. On the one hand, it has led to a moral sensibility and to new legal and ethical standards that are no longer open to negotiation. On the other hand, the ethical turn has laid the ground for an emotionalization of history and a one-sided emphasis on suffering as the basis upon which collective demands are being made. At this point, we shall briefly consider both of these sides of the universalization of a new understanding of right and wrong (*Rechtsbewusstsein*) and of a victim-centered politics of identity.

We shall begin with the universalization of a new understanding of right and wrong. The ethical turn we're talking about here not only has to do with feelings and mindset but it also involves institutions. In a concrete way, it has to do with the lessons and principles that were to be drawn from the experience of World War II and the Holocaust. The principle of universal human rights is written into the preamble of the constitution of the Federal Republic of Germany as Article 1: "(1) Human dignity shall be inviolable. To respect and protect it shall be the duty of all state authority." Constitutional rights are based on this norm, rights that extend from the physical integrity of the person to the right to practice different religions and engage in different cultures and ways of life. The genocide of the European Jews and the persecution of other disenfranchised minorities went beyond the notion of war crimes; henceforth, they would be considered "crimes against humanity" not only in the sense that they exceeded the measure of what had previously been heard in the courts, but also in the sense that this law of a crime against humanity transcends national constitutions.

The counter-argument of those sentenced in Nuremburg was frequently articulated in terms of *nulla poena sine lege* (no penalty without law). This principle, which is also referred to as "ex post facto," contains the proviso that one cannot be judged for something that was not punishable under the corresponding regime at the time of the act. This argument was invalidated after the establishment of the fundamental ethical norm of human dignity that overrides all state constitutions and regulations. A new international institution was created in The Hague following Nuremburg that brings cases against those accused of crimes against humanity and prosecutes them. While juridical prosecution and punishment are an indispensable requirement for confronting these crimes, it is also true that in these cases where the murdering reaches vast and immeasurable proportions, this judicial process is never sufficient and so additional forms of engagement are demanded. The moral answer to such crimes against humanity is the establishment of a general and obligatory memory, to be borne by humanity as a whole. Crimes against humanity are destined to enter into the memory of humanity.

Those who deny the existence of this ethical turn in memory culture continue to speak of the healing powers of forgetting. When it comes to symmetrical relations, there is no question that collective forgetting is very important both historically and in the present: in the context of modern peace settlements, for instance, forgetting has been mobilized to play an important humanizing role in the aftermath of civil wars. There are, however, fairly narrow limits to the effectiveness of forgetting in cases of historical traumas, which, in contrast to acts of war, are not based on reciprocity but have a purely asymmetrical character. Honor, whether triumphant or aggrieved, has determined the code of national memory for centuries and given to that code the principle means of selecting what is worthy of remembrance. This cannot be the sole measure of assessing memory in the future. The new awareness of the long-term effects of traumatic historical experiences for the victim and the perpetrator has created new determinants for the organization of national memory. With regard to historical traumas that arise not out of acts of war but out of the exploitation, dehumanization, and extermination of innocent people, forgetting has no healing power. These kinds of crimes against humanity are not disposed of by means of forgetting but are preserved in a memory shared by the victim and the perpetrator.

This ethical turn, one that has brought the repressed and forgotten experiences of history's victims back into the center of culture awareness, has not been universally viewed as a positive development. So here we've come to the other side of the coin, a politics of identity that is focused on victims. The negative consequences associated with this ethical turn did not become evident in 1945 but rather first manifested themselves in the 1990s. There have always been passive victims in history, those who were exploited, tortured, and annihilated. What is new in this development is the attention that these victims draw to themselves, or wish to draw to themselves. So, does the ethical turn consist of developing a new historical narrative from the perspective of the victim? The project at stake here is actually much more specific: it is a matter of validating a victim's history from and for his or her own group. In other words, it is not a matter of *history* in general but of the *memory* of groups who can then build a new identity on this basis and for which they claim media attention and social recognition just as much as they do material restitution and symbolic reputation.

The ethical turn we're talking about here responds to two historical experiences that are of paradigmatic importance: the Holocaust and colonialism. Although the events are fundamentally different from one another in terms of their respective aims and methods of execution (and so cannot be leveled in any way), the retrospective treatment of both was the origin of a historically new phenomenon of victim discourse. As such, it was the first time that historical traumas were articulated from the perspective of those whose stories had been reduced to silence in the official history. For want of archives and other state institutions for preserving the past, these forgotten stories broke through as memories in the present and were the basis for the formation of new collective identities. Added to that was a further aspect that added a great deal of force to victim discourse: in 1980, trauma was recognized as an official medical diagnosis in the *American Handbook of Psychiatry*. As a consequence, trauma discourse gained currency, coming to include both historical traumas and biographical traumas such as childhood sexual abuse. At the same time, this development made it increasingly possible for other historical traumas to be publically recognized. After the Holocaust, slavery, and colonialism, further cases of collective powerlessness and suffering were brought to the fore, from older and more recent genocides both within and outside of Europe to the suffering of civilian populations during the world wars. The figure of the passive victim has belatedly moved to the very center of media attention and cultural valuation, marking the present as a post-traumatic era. What is the basis of the new and overwhelming importance of this figure? What constitutes its value, indeed, its irresistible aura?

The importance of the figure of the passive victim, which must be clearly distinguished from the sacrifice of the martyr, lies in its utter passivity and in its connotations of innocence and purity. In this passivity, it represents a reversal of the figure of the hero and his or her unparalleled activity. In a postreligious epoch in which the vulnerable body represents the highest value, the traumatized victim embodies this value through the stigmata of his or her physical and psychic wounds. The aura of the victim consists in the sense that he or she was innocently caught in the zone of death and has returned as an envoy from this other world. The emphasis on suffering and scars appears as part of a post-Christian passion story that lends an absolute moral authority to the victim. Through this inversion of the heroic and the traumatic, the theme of suffering that was devalued and suppressed through heroic values and was only an object of religious attention in the symbolic form of Christ's suffering has become a positive cultural value and social status that individuals and groups are increasingly reclaiming for themselves. What had remained up until recently a cause for shame has become a source of prestige and honor.

The traumatized group cannot, however, create this positive value for itself; it can only acquire it by means of recognition or compensation. Therefore, in the post-traumatic era, along with the discourse of victimhood, the problem of a praxis and politics of recognition has become central.[21] This recognition not only takes place through a "critical secondary witnessing" but in part also adopts the forms of reverence and piety.[22] While the ethical turn seeks to give back to the victim his or her *dignity* from within the framework of a universalistic perspective, in connection with an identity constructed on the basis of the victim, it has also involved the transformation of trauma into *honor*, in the sense of an aspiration and a positive self-worth.[23] The problematic effects of this development are, first, that a group whose self-image is secured by means of an exaggerated or mythic sense of its victimhood blocks its own possibilities of development through rendering itself passive, and second, that the group can become hardened to the traumatic experiences of other victims. A politics of identity that is based on the semantics of victimhood proves to be part of the problem and not its solution or, more precisely, part of a post-traumatic syndrome that is in no way an attempt to overcome that syndrome.

Yehuda Elkana has forcefully emphasized this self-destructive influence of an Israeli identity based exclusively on the Holocaust as a collective experience of victimhood, alleging that because of it, important cultural values have been suppressed or displaced. He is not arguing that the Holocaust should be forgotten; he is simply making a case against establishing the Holocaust as the central basis for the construction of a national identity.[24]

PERPETRATOR MEMORY

In the wake of the Holocaust and colonialism, whereas innocence and suffering have turned into clear positive values upon which to establish collective identities of victimhood, the contours of the identity of those responsible for such suffering have remained rather blurry. There is no clear sense of a memory of the perpetrators that would correspond to that of the victims because perpetrators do not seek public recognition; on the contrary, they prefer to remain invisible. Suffering strengthens a self-image, but guilt threatens to destroy it. It is from out of this difference that a fundamental asymmetry between the memory of the victim and that of the perpetrator arises. The exposure of a defenseless victim to extreme forms of violence turns up as a long-term trauma. The individual's consciousness will disassociate itself from what threatens to overpower it in an effort to protect itself from collapse during its most extreme exposure to violence.

Something else entirely takes place on the side of the perpetrator. Here it is not a matter of an inner dissociation from a traumatic experience as an unconscious strategy of survival, but of a defense against guilt as a strategy for saving face. Everything that is incompatible with one's own identity or profile is warded off. Whereas the suffering of harm and injustice is deeply registered in the body and soul of the victim, the perpetrators ward off their guilt under the pressure of the social effects of shame. Nietzsche registered this logic in a short aphorism, to which he gave the form of a psychological drama *en miniature*:

> Memory says, "I did that."
> Pride replies, "I could not have done that."
> Eventually, memory yields.[25]

Pride and honor shut down memory and prevent the recognition of guilt from occurring. Pride and honor determine the norms of a positive self-image, defined in accordance with social values. While a kind of "pride about suffering" has now emerged, there has been no corresponding "pride about guilt."[26] What is considered as incriminating or hateful within the context of a dominant value system is generally dealt with by means of silence. As we have seen, silence is ambivalent and has opposing meanings for the victim and the perpetrator. While silence for the victim represents a transitional phase of self-protection and a release from the pressures of pain, for the perpetrator it is the final refuge. Silence allows the victim to achieve a measure of distance from the dangers of the trauma for a certain amount of time, whereas it affords the perpetrator security and protection from prosecution. Making the deed into a taboo is therefore the goal of the perpetrator, whereas a memory that takes the past into account is the therapeutic and moral goal of the victim.

In the case of Nazi perpetrators, the defense mechanism described by Nietzsche began long before the imagined or real court proceedings did. What was warded off was, namely, the awareness of what should have been belatedly identified as culpability. Günther Anders has emphasized that "the act of repression [in the sense of concealing or hiding—A.A.] becomes just as terrible as the object of repression; and that repression occurs, in fact, not after the deed, but rather in and during the deed itself, no: before the deed, as the very condition of its taking place."[27] What had been blocked out by means of ideological delusion and a systematic anaesthetizing of moral feeling could never become a burden of conscience. Compassion in Nazism was programmed to stop abruptly at the boundaries of the group. Secondary virtues like the performance of one's duties and self-abandonment, fanatical collective egotism, and a high degree of social validation and recognition contributed to the gradual dissolution of every sense of injustice.

COLLECTIVE GUILT

The most extreme configuration of perpetrator-victim imaginable today was realized in the confrontation between German SS henchmen and Jewish prisoners in the extermination camps, or between the paramilitary death squads [*Einsatzgruppen*] and the defenseless populations of Eastern European cities during the Second World War. In the Holocaust the opposition between raw aggression and bare life, between unlimited discretionary power and defenseless subjection, was taken to its most shocking and unsurpassable limit.[28]

Aside from this paradigmatic perpetrator-victim configuration, there were also more complex kinds of perpetrators in the reality of National-Socialist Germany: there were followers, opportunists, and those who were unmoved, but there were also those who, to a greater or lesser extent, made bold gestures of assistance and resistance. Whether or not one pays attention to these differentiations depends upon one's perspective. While historians strive for differentiation, at the level of the collective, the paradigmatic configuration of perpetrators and victims has remained at a standstill. The Germans have been regarded as a "symbolic people" ever since, as have the Jews. C. K. Williams, who coined that term, understands it to mean the symbolic identity of a collective from an outside viewpoint.[29] In light of this outside viewpoint, Germans born later cannot freely construct their own national identity, but rather must realize "that their history shares in the historical suffering of the Jews. And that such a recognition must also be willingly accomplished."[30]

Identifying the Germans as a symbolic people is not to be confused with the notion of collective guilt. While the notion of a symbolic people does refer to a stigma that the Federal Republic, as the successor state to the Third Reich, has registered in its national memory and has made into an aspect of its political identity, the notion of collective guilt suggests an undifferentiated connection to liability. Accusations of guilt against the Nazi perpetrators before the courts did not yield bad consciences; rather, they elicited denials of guilt and justifications. A similar mechanism also captured postwar German society when it fell subject to the criticism of collective guilt. The notion of collective guilt was used for a few months following the war before being pulled out of circulation by the American occupiers as an unserviceable category. This brevity of the term's use has to do with the reorientation of the occupation policy from the punishment of the Germans to their rehabilitation.[31]

The claim of collective guilt has repeatedly surfaced, but in different forms. In 1988, Günther Anders declared that the terminology of collective guilt was "completely meaningless." And he adds, "at that time [in the 1940s], it may be true that this absurd phrase was being used, particularly in the U.S. But already by 1950 no serious person would dare use it: no one who seriously mourned the dead, nor any serious author, historian, or politician would use the phrase."[32] Anders argues that the phrase was being kept in circulation solely by Germans who needed the terminology in order to distance themselves from it or, to be more precise, to "put themselves in the right through this distancing," the right here consisting of being the "victim" of an indefensible accusation of collective guilt. He writes, "if there had been no such phrase, they would have had to invent it just so that they could define themselves in opposition to it."[33] In terms of its content, Hannah Arendt shifted the notion of collective guilt from the level of the crimes to the level of knowledge about them. Through confidants and accomplices, what she calls a "Volksgemeinschaft of crimes" was established, around which the wider German people were forced "at least to bear the onus of complicity and awareness of what was going on."[34] Primo Levi would later see in the "unsuccessful dissemination of truth about the concentration camps" and in the "willful ignorance" what he called "a weighty collective guilt in the German people."[35]

The Figure of the Witness

Whereas victors and the defeated identify themselves in relation to each other on the basis of their reciprocal action, identifying perpetrators and victims requires outside agents. Generally speaking, this means that a third party must accompany the dyad of victim and perpetrator, the third party being the one who assesses the acts of violence and undertakes to assign the roles.[36] The witness is a key figure in this outside assessment and in this assigning of roles.

Over the course of the past two or three decades, new attention has been paid to the victim, and, during that same time period, the role of the witness has also become more significant, which is why we cannot understand the one without the other. In what follows, therefore, we will examine the figure of the witness more closely, beginning with an exploration of the different institutions of witnessing.

FOUR BASIC TYPES OF WITNESSING

The Legal Witness

The importance of witnessing varies somewhat, depending on the institutional context. The courts are a public stage on which the dyads of victim/plaintiff and perpetrator/accused are redoubled in the prosecutor/defense and are presided over by the judge in the form of a triad. In this context, the witness (Lat. *testis*) is he or she who was present at the scene of the crime either by seeing or hearing something. His or her sensory perception of the events is brought in as evidence in the court proceedings and supports the judge in determining what happened and issuing a judgment. This makes it clear that a legal witness has a subordinate function in that he or she is acting in support of the proceedings. Construed in this way, an act of witnessing before the courts contains four important conditions:

- the impartiality of the witness toward both the victim and the accused
- sensory perception of the crime scene
- an accurate memory of what was perceived
- a commitment to the truth, ritualized and sworn under oath

But the witness also has a role to play outside of the courts, as for instance at the finalizing of a contract, the legality of which he or she guarantees as an independent third agent. As the linguist Émile Benveniste has pointed out, in such situations, the witness joins in as a third party. Benveniste elucidates the concept of the witness in the following way: "Etymologically, *testis* is someone who is present as a "third" (*terstis*) at a transaction where two persons are concerned."[37] In this case the witness is not interrogated; the act to which he or she bears witness is much more likely to become the object of his or her testimony in the context of a later situation.

The Historical Witness

In Greek tragedies, the historical witness is often personified as the messenger who is called upon to deliver news of a terrible event. He is the one who bridges the distance between the scene of violence or war and what is happening on stage. He is the point of connection between the site of a catastrophe and the site of distant unknowing. To strengthen the reliability of his statement, truth claims to that effect are allowed into the messenger's testimony. The typical formula for the truthfulness of the report goes as follows: I have added nothing, taken nothing away, and changed nothing.[38] In this case, the witness's testimony is not a simple notification, but a speech act in the form of an authenticated or authorized statement. While in the legal context, the witness is simply integrated into a broader process of determining the truth, in the context of a (theatrical) report by a messenger, it is more fundamentally a matter of communicating and transmitting decisive occurrences in a world without newspapers, reports, images, and news channels. The witness as messenger is quite often a survivor (Lat. *superstes*) who, as the only one to have escaped, is able to pass on the report of a catastrophe to the outside world. In this way, the fact of survival and the imperative to report the event become closely connected with one other.[39]

More generally, the historical witness is one who, by virtue of his or her proximity to an important event, conveys to the outside world his or her perception of it. Just as the testimony of a legal witness introduces evidence into the court record, the testimony of the historical witness plays a role in historical reconstruction. Despite the centrality of historical witnessing for history writing, or perhaps *because* of it, the status of the historical witness remains highly controversial, especially within the domain of professional history writing.[40]

Eyewitnesses gained new significance as witnesses to a particular time period [*Zeitzeuge*] in the context of oral history, a branch of historical research that emerged in the 1960s and has been officially recognized ever since. The goal of this new international direction in historical research has been to enrich our knowledge of historical events by introducing an experiential dimension and the dimension of a "history from below" into historiography.[41] However, what has been experienced and remembered cannot simply be recognized as a historical resource without further questioning. Therefore historians have developed criteria of reliability for oral sources or differentiated testimonies that are closer to the time of the event from those that are more distant in time from it: for instance, testimonies about the Holocaust that were recorded up until 1946 are classified differently than testimonies that were first recorded fifty years after the events.

The Religious Witness

While the Latin word for witness (*testis*) refers to a legal context, the Greek word, *martys*, points to a religious context. With the notion of martyr, it is no longer a matter of an impartial or escaped observer, but rather of someone who is included in the dyad of violence; here, the roles of victim and witness become interwoven with one another. In contrast to the purely passive victim, the religious witness is active. The martyr is the victim of a political violence that kills him or her, but at the same time he or she is able to triumph over it. The martyr escapes the persecuting violence in that the violence of "dying from" is translated into a "dying for." The message that is brought out before death and in death is the acknowledgment of a superior and more powerful God. The word *martyrion* originally means "the testimonial account of the sacrifice of a person."[42] In this sense, martyrdom is not yet exclusively constituted in terms of a violent death, but is first constituted as a *report* on the death. The report first divests the persecuting authority of the power of definition over the event in that it reinterprets a moment of the utmost lowliness and obliteration in physical death into an act of testimony that goes well beyond this death. This radical inversion of political inferiority into religious superiority, of trauma into triumph, also requires a doubled witness: the one through the dying martyr and the other through a secondary witness to the martyr. Since the martyr dies with the avowing testimony on his lips (*kiddush ha-shem*, "sanctification of His name," is the Hebrew precept for a martyr's death), there is no guarantee that this act can acquire an enduring meaning and have continuing effects on earth. Therefore, the witness-as-martyr requires a second witness who will bear witness to his or her death, recognize him or her as a victim ("sacrificium"), and pass on his or her experience as a meaningful testimony. This testimony, which translates political inferiority into religious superiority, is anything but impartial: it is the act of religious piety par excellence. The Gospel accounts of Christ's martyrdom belong to this category of secondary witnessing, as do the persecuted and murdered martyrs that the Catholic Church canonizes as saints. These secondary testimonies are in no way simply an epiphenomenon of martyrdom; first and foremost, they interpret the religious message, commit it to writing, and formulate it into a foundational story on which religious communities can be based.

The Moral Witness

In the aftermath of the Holocaust, another type of witness has emerged: the moral witness.[43] This type of witness has adopted characteristics from all the other kinds of witnesses but at the same time distinguishes itself from them in essential ways. So, in order to bring out these differences, we first needed to sketch out this rudimentary typology of the witness. In common with the religious witness, the moral witness brings together the role of victim and the role of witness. What differentiates him or her from the martyr, however, is that he or she does not become a witness by *dying*, but by *surviving*. As a survivor (*superstes*), the moral witness not only resembles the historical witness but also bears resemblance to the partisan religious witness who becomes the witness for those who have not survived—the voice for those who have been decisively silenced and for their obliterated names. Through this proximity to death and to the dead, his or her testimony not only takes place as an accusation but is also a lament for the dead, which is why this testimony also involves the silence of not being able to speak.[44]

The second, no less important, difference from the religious witness is that the moral witness has no positive message to impart, such as the power of a superior God for whom it is worth dying. In strict opposition to these semantics of sacrifice, the moral witness reveals an enormous crime and tells exclusively of an evil experienced firsthand. In this way, his or her message corresponds to a negative revelation that is neither the stuff of meaning-making nor the stuff of a foundational history upon which communities are based.

Like the religious witness, the moral witness is also dependent upon further witnesses to take up his or her message. Without the message of the moral witness being taken up by others, his or her survival—which has imposed the urgent responsibility to bear witness—would become meaningless. In his poem "Ashglory," Paul Celan expresses it this way: "Nobody/witnesses for the/witness [*Niemand/zeugt für den/Zeugen*]."[45] In 1967, when Celan's collection of poetry first appeared, the tide had already begun to turn. A secondary community of witnesses prepared to take up the testimony of survivors had gradually begun to take shape. In his study on triumph and trauma, Bernhard Giesen has convincingly worked out this connection between primary and secondary witnesses, between traumatized victims and a moral community as a third party between victims and perpetrators. During the actual period of persecution, humiliation, and murder, traumatized victims have no faces, no voices, no place, and no histories. A broader community beyond the perpetrator-victim dyad, consisting of uninvolved third parties, must first be developed, which listens to the testimony and gives the status of victim to the witness.[46] Understood in this way, "victim" is not a natural category; rather, it arises in the first instance as a social construction through a moral community in a public space. The moral community, which distances itself from victimizing power on the basis of civil societal values, tends to include the whole of humanity because it touches on the universal values of human dignity and respect for the physical integrity of all humans. As an inclusive universalistic community, it is grounded in the potentially unlimited public arena of discourse, which pits it against the development of exclusive groups marked by clear borders of identity. With its function of founding a moral order and the emphasis on guilt and responsibility, this discourse takes up certain premises from judicial systems and universalizes them. Without competing with the legal system, this universalistic discourse does manage to account for the force and extent of a crime that is dealt with only in a very fragmentary and incomplete way through processes of criminal prosecution.[47] What begins in the courtroom is continued in a social practice and in a politics of recognition outside of the courtroom. The secondary witnessing of a society follows after judgment and conviction in the form of a memory culture that takes historical responsibility and is borne on an empathy for and solidarity with the victims.

An important chapter of Avishai Margalit's book *The Ethics of Memory* is devoted to this new type of moral witness. In his analysis, Margalit pays particular attention to three aspects of moral witnessing: the embodiment of the testimony; the construction of a moral agent; and the mandate of truth.[48] First, regarding *embodiment*, Margalit carefully distinguishes the role of the moral witness from the neutral and impartial observation that characterizes the legal and messenger witnesses. For Margalit, it is utterly crucial that the victim and the witness be the same person: the victim and the witness have both experienced firsthand the crime to which they bear witness. Since they were exposed to the violence in an unmediated and defenseless way, they have registered that violence in their bodies and in their souls. The body of the persecuted and traumatized is the continued scene of criminal violence, but at the same time, it is also the witness's memory, one that is not so easily disposed of as a message might be for a messenger to communicate. The moral witness does not simply bear a message; in this case, the bearer of the message *is* the message.

The old question regarding the truth of testimony returns here in the form of a question about authenticity. It is strengthened neither by an oath, as with messengers, nor by some other kind of validating formula. The truth and authority of this testimony lie solely in the unmediated connection to the Holocaust, in the inexpressible bodily experience of violence. In a certain way, his or her body carries "the invisible watermark in an imaginary passport that is stamped by history itself."[49] Therefore the embodied truth of the witness is ultimately more important than the exactitude of his or her report. What moral witnesses offer, writes Jay Winter, "is not unvarnished truth, but rather a very subjective construction of the extreme conditions under which they lived."[50] As the embodiment of a traumatic experience and at the same time as victims, they are also living proof of the crime about which they speak.

According to Margalit (and his reflections are very close to those of Bernhard Giesen here), a further distinction to be made between the legal witness and the moral witness is that the testimony of the moral witness to crimes that have been committed is not inscribed within the institution of the courts but rather, in the much more general public arena of a *moral community*. Morals are certainly no substitute for law, but they do supplement law and respond to the excessive nature of crimes that outstrip legal frameworks. Insofar as the witness is able to find an audience for his or her testimony outside of the courts, he or she performatively creates a moral community, one with no concrete form or institution. It only arises by virtue of its being appealed to. It is first through this third party, the detached addressee, that an agent emerges who is being appealed to, one who listens to the victim's story and bears witness to his or her testimony.

Aside from embodiment and the creation of a moral agent, Margalit also emphasizes the *mandate of truth* as a third characteristic of the moral witness. The mandate of truth assumes a world in which the testimony of the traumatized victims is not heard, is denied, forgotten, falsified, or whitewashed in some way or another. The mandate of truth held by the moral witness is directly opposed to the need for concealment on the part of the criminal perpetrator. The one belongs to the other as the convex belongs to the concave; the one brings the other onto the scene. The desire characteristic of perpetrators is to efface historical traces and to defend themselves against guilt through denial and other evasive strategies. The perfect crime is one in which the criminal leaves no traces, in which even the fact of the crime itself is successfully concealed. "Who still remembers the Armenians today?" asked Hitler in the 1930s. His wish was that the "final solution to the Jewish question" would also leave behind no traces.[51] Forgetting protects the perpetrator and weakens the victim, which is why remembering in the form of testimony has become an ethical duty and a form of belated resistance. This is also at the core of truth and reconciliation commissions following regime changes and civil wars, the task of which is to reconstruct the historical truth of traumatic, violent events in as uncorrupted a way as possible, bracketing processes of legal prosecution.

In the case of the National Socialist crimes of genocide against the Jewish people, forgetting and the erasure of historical traces were not belated cover-up strategies; they were actually aspects of the crime itself. This strategy of concealment and secrecy shows—at least indirectly—that the perpetrators were subjectively aware of their criminal guilt. Here we should recall Günther Anders's suggestion that "repression often happens not after the act but in the performance of the act itself, during the act, no: before the act, precisely as its presupposition, is even actual."[52] The victim's desire for moral testimony is inversely related to the perpetrator's desire for forgetting. Whereas the one is directed toward forgetting and cover-up, the other is committed to saving traces, to remembering and to narrating. The mandate for truth of the moral witness is directed against the impulses and strategies of forgetting and denial: "Moral witnesses," writes Jay Winter, "are people who retain a sense of anger, of outrage, of frustration to the lies, distortions, re-workings, or sanitizations of their painful past."[53] Winter uses striking examples to show that, in order to be heard, the memories of traumatized survivors must not only overcome the resistances of society but must also overcome its heroic stereotypes. Although they cannot relinquish certain narrative conventions, they do reject quite a number of those that lead to a romanticized and meaningful narrative: according to Winter, the moral witness consists not least of a critical engagement with and a resistance to the human need for heroism, consolation, and hope—themes that are so often used in society as a means of self-protection against the corrosive power of evil and as a way of making unbearable experiences more bearable.

How Does Remembering Happen?

We have considered the question of "who remembers?" from a number of different perspectives: from the perspectives of the victors and the defeated, from the perspectives of perpetrators and victims as well as of witnesses, and we have placed these within the context of their historical conditions, their psychological dispositions, political strategies, and moral projects. We shall now extend this examination of the basic concepts and themes of individual and collective remembering to a consideration of the specific ways in which remembering and forgetting take place. Trauma, silence, forgetting, and mourning are all key terms under which to consider different forms of memory or, indeed, of its blockage.

TRAUMA

The paradox has by now become commonplace: the more the horrors of the Holocaust objectively recede in time, the closer they seem to us at a subjective level. This paradox describes what psychiatrists call the dynamics of a "post-traumatic" situation. The long-term nature of the effects is evidently an important symptom of what is designated under the clinical term of *trauma*.

But what exactly is meant by it? The word *trauma* stems from the Greek and literally means "wound." In medicine, this terminology has long been associated with the very general meaning of "injury." By contrast, the new and more specific use of the concept refers to a psychic wound that brings about perplexing symptoms and poses entirely new problems for medical practitioners. Psychic trauma can be traced back to life-threatening and deeply injurious experiences of extreme violence, the force of which can shatter the stimulus shield of perception and cannot be processed psychically because of the strange and identity-threatening quality of those experiences. In order to survive such an experience, a psychic defense mechanism arises that psychiatrists call "dissociation."[54] In cases of dissociation, an unconscious strategy of splitting occurs by means of which the threatening experience is held at a distance or cut off from the victim's conscious mind. The event is certainly registered, but at the same time the links to consciousness are broken off. What can neither be remembered nor forgotten in such cases remains isolated from consciousness, meaning that these experiences move into a latent state where they remain subliminal and inconspicuous for a long period of time until they make themselves known through a language of symptoms. Memory that is not conscious is, as they say, registered in the body. Exemplary in this regard are the facial tics and motor disturbances that could be observed in devastated soldiers returning from the First World War. Another example is the syndrome of "multiple personality disorder," a pathological division of identity observed in victims of childhood sexual abuse.

The notion of trauma has a relatively short history. Although already in circulation in psychiatric circles by the end of the nineteenth century, it was not recognized as an official diagnosis in the *American Handbook of Psychiatry* until 1980, in the context of the political and social aftermath of the Vietnam War.[55] This recognition not only had therapeutic consequences but legal ones as well, especially in the United States. It now became possible to demonstrate that psychic injuries from a long time ago were directly related to current disorders, the result of which was that the statute of limitations for certain crimes like sexual child abuse was lifted. This in turn caused a flood of lawsuits (along with an organized defense against them). Of course, the traumas of war, sexual abuse, and the persecutions of the Holocaust are all very different phenomena, but nonetheless, in all of these cases, victims experience long-term disturbances in the development of their personalities because of the presence of a past that is threatening, imprisoning, and unmanageable. The symptoms of trauma can often appear for the first time years after the traumatizing experience. The potential for psychic disturbance expressed in the development of different symptoms can also be unconsciously passed on from one generation to another. This intergenerational nexus of trauma can only be interrupted when the segments of the trauma that are unconscious or cut off from the conscious mind are successfully converted into a conscious form.[56] Therapy therefore aims at liberating the trauma from its encapsulation through language and turning it into an aspect of the victim's conscious identity. This is not possible through individual therapeutic situations alone, however; for this to happen, a social and political environment is needed. To be more precise: a "framework of memory" is required in which these detached and repressed memories can be empathically heard and can find a place in the social memory.

Ever since it became established within a medical context, the notion of trauma has been exclusively associated with the perspective of the victim, which means that *suffering* [*Erleiden*] physical violence and psychic intimidation have become essential components of the idea. In the victim, suffering turns into injury [*Leiden*], and passivity is converted into passion.[57] The most important examples in the hundred or so years of trauma research are train accidents, "shell shock" (the syndrome of soldiers who were immobilized by the grenade explosions that blew up their comrades and that appeared en masse for the first time during the First World War), sexual child abuse, political persecution, torture, and the historical experience of genocide. Freud did not really take part in the psychiatric discussion regarding shell shock; his focus was on the family problem of sexual child abuse, but he treated this diagnosis through his "seduction theory"—that is, by relocating the event exclusively in the imagination of the person concerned—in such a way that there is no direct route leading from his work to contemporary trauma research. Freud is therefore not the father of this new branch of research; rather, the fathers of trauma research were investigators like Pierre Janet in France or W. H. Rivers in England, who laid the notional and experimental foundations for today's conceptualization of trauma as well as for methods of its treatment.[58]

THE TRAUMA OF PERPETRATORS AND THE TRAUMA OF VICTIMS

Another reason Freud cannot be called the father of modern trauma research is because he brought the concept of trauma primarily to bear on the perpetrators: in his psycho-historical studies *Totem and Taboo* and *Moses and Mono-*

theism, he used the term *trauma* exclusively in relation to the perpetrators. According to his interpretation, the trauma incurred by the horde of brothers as a consequence of murdering their primal father was repeated on Moses as the religious founder. So for Freud, there is a bad conscience at the origin of culture and religion, and it takes the form of a perpetrator trauma. According to his analysis, this event led to a collective repression that forms the latent subtext for the biblical tradition and its particularly compulsive character up to the present day. The literary scholar Cathy Caruth has reworked the concept of trauma for its reception in cultural studies and has likewise taken Freud's work as her starting point, but her work is based primarily on the literary analysis of an episode from Tasso's *Gerusalemme Liberata*. In this case, of course, one can hardly speak of perpetrators, since the death occurs unintentionally in a tragic moment of misreading the true relations.[59]

Although the practice of referring to perpetrator trauma as well as to victim trauma is still widespread, I would like to make the case that the concept of trauma should only be used in the context of specific forms of victim experience. In contrast to victims, perpetrators are not traumatized because the event that they are called to take responsibility for is one that they willed, planned, consciously carried out, and, moreover—in the case of the crimes of National Socialism—is one that they justified to themselves at the level of ideology. As perpetrators of extreme criminal violence, they were not suddenly or unwittingly confronted by an overpowering and incomprehensible occurrence that threatened their physical integrity and their personal identity: they were not defenselessly handed over to the events. These are all conditions of trauma that are to be found only on the side of the victim. Whereas the Holocaust victim was defenselessly pulled into the continually increasing violence of a murderous machine, the perpetrators were in no way unprepared as they entered into these developments. To be sure, they gave up their individual egos when they became members of a collective whose ideological mission they adopted as their own, one that committed them to violence and programmed them for insensitivity. We cannot speak of traumatization in this context, however, but of indoctrination. The absence of traumatization and the absence of feelings of guilt and regret show just how deeply processes of ideological programming, conditioning, and hardening can go and just how little can be spoken here of the shattering of identity that accompanies traumatization. Traumatic shocks were certainly also possible in a perpetrator biography. The moment when Hitler left his followers in the lurch through his suicide is one such example: those who had given up their egos for the Führer suddenly realized that they were unhinged marionettes that had had their strings cut. For those in this situation who did not themselves choose suicide, a completely unknown life awaited them, one that Adolf Eichmann described in the following way: "I myself felt it immediately on the 8th of May, 1945, that I had my own difficult life to live without a Führer: I couldn't expect to get any orientation from anywhere, no orders or directives, no clear standards. In brief: a life emerged that was completely unknown."[60] If National Socialist perpetrators experienced trauma at all, it was a trauma that involved the sudden and shocking confrontation with their individual responsibility and conscience.

Bernhard Giesen, who holds to the idea of perpetrator trauma, focuses on this shift in awareness. For him, perpetrator trauma arises when a triumphant fantasy of all-powerfulness suddenly comes up against its own limits:

> The perpetrator understands himself as being above the world's legal order, and as being in the position to decide on the state of exception, in Agamben's sense. This self-procured absolute subjectivity only turns into a trauma when it is confronted with reality, so in the German case, when the war was lost and the fantasy of all-powerfulness of the community is revealed to be a deception. A prior legal order is made valid once again or a new one is created, the act is evaluated in relation to it and the experience of all-powerfulness is exposed as a crime. In the case of Anna O., had the sense of reality not kicked in, there would have been no hysteria; had Nazi Germany won the war, there would have been no perpetrator consciousness.[61]

According to Giesen, then, this sudden suspension of frameworks of thinking, evaluating, and acting led to a National Socialist perpetrator trauma. But what precisely does this involve? Certainly not a sudden awakening of conscience, but perhaps they became conscious of their dramatic humiliation through a complete loss of face. One might say that the shocking confrontation with an opposing horizon of values as their crimes became public led to a "trauma of shame" that goes along with the destruction of a self-image.[62] The long-term destruction of a self-image that is so decisive for trauma is not readily conceivable in the case of the perpetrators, however. On the contrary, those interrogated in the Nuremburg or Frankfurt courts reacted with persistent arrogance and stereotypical declarations of innocence rather than with appeals and collapses. Their general posture involved a defense against guilt through dissociation and repression, as well as a tabooing through silence, all of which would be better understood through the notion of taboo than through the idea of trauma.[63]

As problematic as the concept of perpetrator trauma may be, the issue of a trauma of guilt besetting subsequent generations and potentially leading to reactions ranging from acceptance to denial is unavoidable. The guilt from which the perpetrators had arrogantly distanced themselves is one that the Germans as a nation still have to confront; the crimes of the fathers and the grandfathers have been taken on by their children and grandchildren. Giesen has also drawn attention to this shift:

> The cross-generational collective identity in Germany therefore consists of the perpetrator trauma of by-standers and not that of willing executioners. The willing executioners . . . were dying out whereas the guilt of by-standers is the decisive cross-generational element, one that is hidden and in that way, constitutive of identity.[64]

SILENCING

How did the comparison between victim and perpetrator trauma ever come about, given the striking and unmistakable differences between them? One reason could have to do with certain parallels in the reactions of each to the historical trauma of the Holocaust. For the first decade and a half following the war, there was no general sense of a need to thematize the recent events of the war and the mass extermination, either in Israel or in West Germany. Both were busy with the task of constructing a state, for which all available energy was being directed toward the future. There are many reasons to think that the traumatic past was being held under lock and key for both sides so as not to endanger the development of a new life and a new identity.

Of course, beneath these surface similarities very different psychological dynamics were playing themselves out in families: on the one side, there was a tabooing of the past under the weight of enormous guilt, and on the other side, a silence had developed around suffering for the sake of a life-affirming perspective and for the sake of one's own survival and that of one's children.

Let us begin by turning to the situation of victims of the Holocaust in the postwar period. Traumatic experiences, we have determined, are tied to long-term aftereffects; they need time and are often approachable only years later. At the same time, as concerns the historical trauma of the Holocaust, in many cases a disparity also arose after the war between the personal willingness of the victims to remember and recount on the one hand and, on the other hand, a social environment that did not want to hear their memories. So delay and belatedness are based on psychological as well as on social conditions, on traumatization as well as on tabooing, conditions that made not only perpetrators but, in part, also victims reluctant to remember after the war and Holocaust. Dan Bar-On has described this situation using the image of a "double wall of silence"; when the survivors made a hole in the wall that enclosed them and were finally prepared to talk, they came up against a second wall of silence that their society had put up as a protective wall against trauma.[65] Primo Levi movingly portrays the nightmare of the witness in which he is finally able to share his experience but finds no receptive group for his words: "It is an intense pleasure, physically inexpressible, to be at home, among friendly people, and to have so many things to recount: but I cannot help noticing that my listeners do not follow me. In fact, they are completely indifferent: they speak confusedly of other things among themselves, as if I was not there."[66] Primo Levi's account was printed in 1947, but he was unable to find an Italian publisher willing to print a new edition. The book was rejected by Natalia Ginzburg, an Italian Jew, who like Levi belonged to the Communist resistance and whose husband was murdered by the Gestapo in 1945. Levi's book would have to wait a decade before being republished in 1958.[67] Like Primo Levi, Elie Wiesel, in the quasi-biblical role of moral witness to history, committed his memories to writing immediately after the liberation of the concentration camps. He has François Mauriac to thank for the circulation of his survivor testimony *La Nuit* (1958). The original version, written in Yiddish, was characterized by a fervent tone of hate and revenge, one that Mauriac had Wiesel change for the French version, in order to change the reception of the text and give it a new foundation.

Other Holocaust survivors who wrote down their memories for the first time much later have reported similar stories. For example, in the autobiography Ruth Klüger wrote almost a half century after her experiences in German concentration camps, she describes the stifling effect of the pressure to forget that survivors in American society had to endure in the 1950s. In Israeli society as well, there was virtually no receptive audience at first: at the time, Israel was entirely occupied with building a new world for itself, and the memories of the horrors that survivors had recently suffered were seen as detrimental to this project. This lasted until the 1960s, at which time the traumatic past finally became approachable in a public way. In particular, the Eichmann trial

(1961) shaped the traumatic memories into an objective form for the new state, in that its court setting necessarily involved an institutional and media public. The end of the '70s brought the TV series *Holocaust*, which was produced in the United States. This series also had a huge presence in German media and prompted a sudden rush to identify with the victims.

Silence in the sense of "keeping quiet" (*Verschweigen*) has a long tradition on the side of the perpetrators, one that leads directly back to the beginning of the crimes. In his book *Extermination and Memory*, Dirk Rupnow points out a paradox among the Nazi elite who planned and carried out the crimes of the Holocaust. They experienced a kind of double exigency, on the one hand to efface all traces of their crimes and on the other hand to preserve a heroic portrayal of their acts for posterity. In the infamous Posen speech in which Heinrich Himmler prepared those who would be responsible for carrying out the mass extermination of the Jews for what was being demanded of them, there is talk of "a page of glory in our history which has never been written and which is never to be written." An unwritten page of glorious history is a paradoxical phenomenon, established somewhere midway between remembering and forgetting. In another speech given two days later, he emphasizes even more strongly the importance of strict secrecy regarding the mass murder:

> At some much later date, one may consider the possibility of telling the German people a little more. I believe it is better that we all bear this together for our people, as we have done, and take the responsibility on ourselves (the responsibility for a deed, not just for an idea) and take this secret with us to our graves.[68]

Himmler not only describes the project of mass murder here using the exalted language of nationalistic heroics, but he also uses a veiled Christian symbolics of self-sacrifice with which to stylize the mass murder into a mission that is at once national and religiously based. At the same time, he also insists that disclosure be forbidden for the purposes of this mission, which was categorized as a crime and therefore had to be kept hidden. Keeping silent, secrecy, forgetting, and the desire for honor, glory, and recognition intersect here in an extreme perversion of values.

After the war, this silence accommodated the wish of the perpetrators not to get further involved in the atrocities of the recent past. Perpetrators were extremely resistant to engage in acts of remembering before the courts. In postwar Germany, this silence dovetailed with the demand for a bottom line, a leitmotif that pervaded the speeches of the Bundestag at the time.[69] Moreover, in the first decades following the war there was general consensus that neither guilt nor experiences of suffering should be made a topic for public debate.[70] This thematic taboo would later be described by the philosopher Hermann Lübbe using the notion of a communicative silencing. Divesting it of any negative moral connotation, Lübbe characterizes the notion of silencing as a necessary and productive social environment in which the transformation of postwar Germany into a democratic society could take place.[71]

Of course, Hannah Arendt saw things differently: after total mobilization and the Final Solution, for her the silence exercised by the perpetrators and by those of their wider society after the war resulted in "the onus of complicity."[72] The task of the following generation was to liberate itself from this complicity and to break the silence, which was in any case about to be transformed into a forgetting in the transition from the generation of perpetrators and witnesses to the generation of their children. Since the 1980s, in light of outright Holocaust denial on the one hand and the threat of forgetting through the disappearance of witnesses on the other, maintaining silence has met with increasingly negative assessments. To remain silent was starting to look like a retrospective fulfillment of Hitler's wish to have the genocide followed by a mnemocide, his formulation for which being "Who today remembers the Armenians?" Whoever privileged silence made themselves guilty of complicity: communicative silencing turned into a complicit silence. As a result, after claims had been made regarding the impossibility of expressing the trauma of the Holocaust, on the side of the victims there was an increasing demand for expression, and bearing witness and the genre of testimony took on a sacrosanct status. Breaking the silence became a kind of religious duty; one's own history must be told and the memory of the dead must be kept alive to prevent their second death through forgetting.

In West Germany in the 1970s and '80s there was a wave of so-called father literature in which the second generation grappled with the biographies of their parents in Nazi Germany. These texts are written against the silence of that first generation; they are often triggered by the death of the parents, carrying out a surrogate dialogue that never took place in life. Something similar happened on the side of the victims. A literature of the second generation arises here as well, in which themes become approachable that the parents had kept hidden from themselves and from their children. David Grossman's *See under: Love* is an impressive example of the interest a child takes in the memories of the generation of grandparents who are pushed to the margins of society and whose terrifying stories circulate amongst themselves at a remove from any mainstream social interest.

After a latency period of about fifty years, the social and political climate has fundamentally changed. As they age, many surviving victims have begun to put their memories on record and write their histories. The political framework has also changed: Yad Vashem has become a memorial site of central importance, one that, in addition to being an archive for research, is also a site of liturgical remembrance and political commemoration. Since no corresponding impulse to remember has occurred on the side of the perpetrator generation, a massive asymmetry in the memory situation has arisen: on the one side, there is the void of silence and on the other side, there is an overflowing archive of witnesses in various media such as books, films, and videos. This asymmetry in memory still exists but is starting to be gradually dismantled through a new German literature of memory that adopts the form of the intergenerational family novel.

Although we cannot speak of a real parallel between perpetrator and victim trauma in the first generation, we can make out certain indisputable similarities in the second generation and recognize comparable psychological wounds. The silence regarding key experiences in the generation of the parents has triggered mechanisms of unconscious transmission to the children on both sides. The Israeli psychotherapist Dan Bar-On worked with injured parties of the second generation on both the sides of the victims and the perpetrators and even successfully managed to bring these groups together. Parallel damages appeared in the process, the mutual recognition of which was somewhat liberating for both of the groups involved.

The decisive return of memory in the 1980s first created an impulse to reconcile the divided memories of victims and perpetrators. In the United States, the new concept "Holocaust" (the title of a popular television series) became central for a new social and academic discourse.[73] In the Germany of the '80s, a series of memorial days (1985 marked forty years since the end of the war; 1988 was the sixtieth anniversary of the November pogroms; 1989 marked the fiftieth anniversary since the beginning of the war; and 1986 was the Historians' Debate) brought the past into public consciousness, and new forms began to be developed to grapple with events that were still very much present in lived memory.

FORGETTING

Much has been written about the uses and the disadvantages of forgetting. Forgetting is a central aspect of remembering; we can only remember because we can also forget and in fact are always unconsciously doing it. The waning and loss of memories and experience are part of a normal and everyday process. The memory is not an exact storage system but rather a dynamic entity that adapts to a changing present and so can always accommodate the new.

In connection with the themes of individual and collective memory, forgetting is of interest above all as an intentional strategy and a resource. I commence, then, with three nineteenth-century theoreticians of forgetting, all of whom emphasized its importance. The first is again Ernest Renan, who, in his speech on nationhood, touches on the theme of forgetting twice. For him, the "essence" of the nation is constituted by a group of people who have "a great deal in common and also [who] have forgotten a great deal."[74] The other reference is as follows: "Forgetting—I would even say historical error, is essential to the creation of a nation, which is why the advance of historical study often poses a threat to nationality" (21). A decade before Renan, the philosopher Friedrich Nietzsche addressed this thesis in his influential essay "On the Uses and Disadvantages of History for Life." For Nietzsche, in the face of the unlimited growth of historical knowledge, knowledge had to be limited so that it could be put to the service of a capacity to orient and act, to preserve and strengthen collective self-images. Without forgetting there is, for Nietzsche, neither life, happiness, future, nor even conscience: "Cheerfulness, the good conscience, the joyful deed, confidence in the future—all of them depend, in the case of the individual as of a nation, on the existence of a line dividing the bright and discernible from the un-illuminable and dark."[75] Forgetting is a capacity that characterizes the strong: "That which such a nature cannot subdue it knows how to forget; it no longer exists, the horizon is rounded and closed, and there is nothing left to suggest there are people, passions, teachings, goals lying beyond it."

This last sentence sounds very much like the formulations one finds in an essay by American philosopher Ralph Waldo Emerson, whose works we know that Nietzsche read with great interest. Emerson describes a great conqueror as one who immediately forgets what he has overcome. On the other hand, whoever says of himself "see how completely I have triumphed over these black events" shows that he has not yet completely forgotten, since that which has been overcome is still preserved in language. In contrast to the victors, the defeated are chained to their memory: "Not if they still remind me of the black event—they have not yet conquered." Victory, overcoming, and forgetting are a single thing for Emerson, who, speaking in the first person plural, voices an emphatically "male" experience: "The one thing which we seek with insatiable desire, is to forget ourselves, to be surprised out of our propriety, to lose our sempiternal memory, and to do something without knowing how and why."[76]

On the political stage, forgetting has a role to play not only on the basis of psychological mechanisms but also on the basis of intentional strategy and decrees. There are essentially two forms of "prescribed forgetting." In one case, forgetting is understood as a punishment, and in this context we can speak of "*damnatio memoriae.*" In the other, it is a blessing and a mercy, in which case we describe it as "amnesty." The *damnatio memoriae* is a form of persecution through the eradication of the name; here it is a question of effacing the traces of a person's existence, of erasing him or her from the annals of history writing and, by means of restrictions on communication, from the social memory. Excommunication also imposes a mantle of silence and forgetting on a person, thus erasing his or her membership within a community. But prohibiting communication can also have a healing and restorative social function when it does not involve forgetting glorious acts, names, and existence but rather when it is an issue of forgetting guilt and of relieving those who are guilty of that guilt: in cases of amnesty, forgetting is coupled with acquittal. This granting of a reprieve can, however, only be socially effective when the group is also committed to keeping the exonerated person clear of bad memories. This becomes a real problem especially in the aftermath of civil wars when parties who were previously divided and made into enemies must be reintegrated with each other after a political turning point has been reached.[77]

The Viennese philosopher Rudolf Burger takes up this tradition of forgetting in his book *Kleine Geschichte der Vergangenheit* [*A Short History of the Past*] and summarizes it in the following way: "Lethe is a remedy."[78] In the context of a reading by Adorno of Goethe's *Faust*, he explains that forgetting represents a vital resource without which life and survival are not possible: "It was the highest achievement of civilization," writes Burger, "when Greek philosophy managed to break through the mythical commandment of memory and to replace it with its negation, with the commandment *not* to remember."[79] According to Burger, we broke with this civilizing tradition after 1945 and are returned "to the Biblical pathos of an eleventh commandment 'Thou shalt never forget!'" (24).

What are his arguments against remembering? On the one hand, Burger invokes the fantastical story by Jorge Luis Borges about a "mnemopath" whose serious illness makes him incapable of living because he suffers from an inability to forget. The evidence provided by this literary fiction, as Burger slavishly recounts it, underhandedly suggests an argument against remembering in general and in particular against voluntarily committing oneself to the memory of the Holocaust and other traumatic histories, which he places in a perfidious series along with the crimes themselves:

> The mythogenic twentieth century, which at the height of technological modernity and bureaucratic rationality produced crimes of tellurian proportions in the name of a quasi-religious, eschatological doctrine of salvation, was also the first to break with the civilizing tradition of not-remembering and once again made the archaic "Never Forget!" valid as a moral responsibility.
>
> (24)

To be sure, the commandment to remember the Holocaust has a quasi-religious character. However, it does not follow that it be made equivalent to a Nazi doctrine of salvation. Burger's book is a plea for bringing the discussion to an end; while his book is not new in making such a demand, the philosophical dignity he lends to it certainly is.

One can object to Burger on the grounds that Lethe may be a remedy, but it is no cure-all. In his praise of forgetting, he overlooks the important distinction in memory research to which we have been repeatedly making reference: the distinction between symmetrical and asymmetrical relations of power. Symmetrical relations of power prevail between the victors and the defeated (despite the inequality that is made manifest through the victory and defeat), ones that are grounded in reciprocal acts of war. Particularly after a civil war when the reintegration of former adversaries becomes an urgent problem, Lethe can be a remedy for restoring the equality necessary for peace. On an everyday level, this is also true of the day following an election: as soon as the outcome of the vote is announced, the campaign slogans must be forgotten so that the irreconcilable opponents can again become partners in a collaborative effort. Asymmetrical relations of power persist between perpetrators and victims, however, and there is no corresponding form of reciprocity, nothing comparable to a decreed forgetting ("*perpetua oblivio et amnestia*" is the relevant formula in the Westphalia peace agreement). The asymmetry between unrestrained perpetrators and defenseless victims is carried on into a memory asymmetry, since after a political turning point has been reached, the perpetrators are able to save themselves by forgetting while the victims protect memory as a priceless good. As such, this asymmetry can never be dismantled through collective forgetting but only through collective remembering. Under these conditions, instead of forgetting as a form of *coping with the past*, collective memory and the *preservation of the past* that is accomplished by the following generation are the only ways to establish symmetry.

The institution of the "Truth and Reconciliation Commission" (TRC), founded in 1996 in South Africa and overseen by South African archbishop Desmond Tutu, lies midway between memory and forgetting. In the context of the transition from the apartheid regime to a democracy, the goal of this commission was to make public the crimes of the past without involving the courts. It was a matter of "remembering" the crimes against humanity and at the same time, and in the same act, of "forgetting" the consequences of judgment. Since the goal was to bring the white and black populations together within a democratic society and to open up a collective future for it, the rituals of the TRC were focused above all on forgiveness and reconciliation. The traumatic injuries of the victims had to be recognized; for them, a space of hearing had to be created. Even more than that: those injuries were re-experienced in a cathartic process of public mourning so that the community could overcome them collectively. The offering made to the victims was the truth and not the law; if the guilty had been sentenced, the foundation of the new state would have been destroyed.[80] Therefore, in South Africa one ultimately remembers in order to be able to forget. It is not a coincidence that a bishop presided over these events of the TRC: not only did they have a ritualized character but they were also informed by a Christian symbolics of purification and reconciliation.

MOURNING

The Inability to Mourn is the title of a well-known book by Alexander and Margarete Mitscherlich, and it has since become a kind of catch phrase. The inability that was the focus of the Mitscherlichs's research—that of the German people in general—had in fact been entrenched in German society well before the aftermath of the Second World War: it was entirely consistent with the long-term educational program associated with Prussian militarization, one that had become a standard of conduct for the German Empire. Young men especially were broken of the ability to mourn; "boys don't cry" became one of the most common and most deeply internalized tenets of this upbringing.[81] Beyond that, severity and self-discipline characterized the behavior expected of women, even playing a role in the socialization of babies and small children.[82] Where a decades-long disciplinary regime had exerted its influence, the sensibilities of Germans after the war could not be easily changed. Political structures may change overnight, but a transformation of mentalities and modes of perception takes a long time, even longer for a culture where affect is expressed through unconscious behaviors.

Ian Buruma recalls a scene in Günter Grass's novel *The Tin Drum* in which the guests in an old German postwar pub are given a small chopping board with a kitchen knife and onion. This onion, Grass writes, "did what the world and the sorrows of the world could not do: it brought forth a round, human tear. It made them cry. At last they were able to cry again. To cry properly, without restraint, to cry like mad."[83] What had struck Buruma in 1994 first became clear to German intellectuals only some years later: in self-critical liberal circles, "there has been—still is—much reflection and apology. But the mourning of the German dead—the soldiers, and the civilians killed by Allied bombs, or by vengeful Polish, Czech, or Slovak neighbors, who drove them from their homes—such mourning was an embarrassing affair, left largely to right-wing nationalists and nostalgic survivors, pining for their lost homelands."[84]

The subject of the inability to mourn was again taken up by writer W. G. Sebald in a lecture series he delivered in Zurich in 1997. In those lectures, Sebald develops the claim—one that subsequently became very controversial—that the aerial bomb war of the Allied forces holds no place in German historical consciousness or long-term memory because writers failed to give an adequate and transmissible form to these events.[85] Sebald speaks of a "scandalous deficiency" (70) in this context, by which he could mean both the absence of grief in response to German suffering and the lack of knowledge regarding German guilt. For Sebald, this absence of grief is reflected in a lack of authentic literary treatments of this historical experience: "Those who had escaped the catastrophe were unreliable and partly-blinded witnesses" (24). The psychoanalyst Werner Bohleber, who comments on this sentence, rightly draws attention to Sebald's untenable premise that at the time one could have immediately captured this experience in language and represented it "adequately." The absence of grief can be traced back to a traumatization, to the incursion of a nameless terror that "people shut away in order to go on living."[86] In other words, the absence of grief can itself be a symptom of trauma.

Grief is a spontaneous and profoundly intimate affect that is experienced following the loss of relatives and close friends; since it arises in the context of those close relations, it is not immediately self-evident that it can be transferred to an anonymous group. In the era of nation building and general military conscription, however, the affect of grief was transferred to the nation as a whole, which was imagined to be an oversized family with its corresponding bonds of piety and loyalty. To this end, grief had to be cast into ritual forms and symbolic acts that gave meaningful expression to these affective ties binding a political entity. Renan knew that for collective memories, "mourning is more important than triumph, because it imposes responsibilities, because it demands communal struggles." In brief, mourning brings about community and continuity. Buruma also emphasizes that grief is not just a personal experience but also has an important social function: "The ritual expression of grief and loss strengthens the sense of continuity and community."[87] In the aftermath of war, a nation has the task of taking up the soldiers killed in action into the community of survivors. At the same time, by "raising" the dead into collective memory, the nation strengthens the awareness of belonging to an identity. Grief or mourning in this sense is not simply about a feeling of inclusivity; to the contrary, in the remembrance of "our dead" over and against "your" and "their dead," it also always reinforces a powerful sense of differentiation.

Helmut Kohl took up the semantics of national mourning once again in 1993 with his reconception of the Neue Wache memorial site. Given the extent to which the Nazi state had exploited these semantics within the framework of a memory of defeat, it was no longer tenable to use them for the following generation. This abstract collective affectivity of mourning then gave way to a new form of emotional participation, that of generalized somberness. This mood linked the personal and, indeed, intimate feeling of grief to a vague and abstract social or political engagement. This individualistic attitude of dismay or affliction, which had its high point in the 1980s, replaces mourning through an indirect, generalized, and largely gratuitous form of empathy.[88]

Karl Heinz Bohrer argues that, in addition to ways in which National Socialism suppressed the ability to mourn, there are two other reasons for the German incapacity for historical mourning. In a thoroughly secularized society in which individualism has been established as the highest value, there are no longer tenable foundations for the expression of communal ritualistic forms. "Those who ritually mourn must be highly conscious of the public figure they project. For mourning is always doubly coded, subjectively and objectively. Objective mourning for those who were murdered, subjective mourning for one's own damaged history."[89] The other reason has to do with the absence of a long-term memory that might take the individual beyond his or her own lifetime. According to Bohrer, Germany has "only an historical short-term memory that more or less ends with the so-called Zero Hour of total collapse in 1945" (1140). The deficit of memory and that of mourning are thus mutually dependant. A counter-model to this would be Martin Walser and his notion of inner pathos.

What form of mourning can convincingly break from a fixation on the personal or collective "one's own" and attend to the other beyond that border, to the Jewish victims? In connection with Walter Benjamin's philosophy of history, Burkhard Liebsch describes a form of mourning that is "not genealogically, ethnically or politically 'patronizing.'" He describes it as an "ethical mourning" that is also a "form of protest": "The heart of ethical mourning is protest—under the banner of the difference, never to be wholly effaced, between what was and what could have been, or what should never have happened."[90] In contrast to historicism's nostalgic mourning triggered by the sense that a lived present has irrecoverably vanished, an ethical mourning is triggered by the sense that what happened should not have happened. In this context, Benjamin was thinking in particular about those who died a violent death and whose hopes for the future were left unfulfilled. Philosopher Paul Ricoeur develops this ethics with his notion of the promise: "History is a promise not to be indifferent in the face of the other's violent death."[91] Ethical mourning for this irretrievable loss is the "obligation" [Schuld] (in the sense of promising, commitment, conscience) that responds to a "guilt" [Schuld] (in the sense of crime) for which there are no reparations and raises it beyond the borders of the national collective.

Jörn Rüsen has also reflected on the limits of both individual and collective forms of mourning in light of the mass crimes of the Holocaust. He speaks of a new era requiring new modes of mourning.[92] By mourning, he understands more than a mere feeling; rather, he also sees it as an "intellectual category." Mourning for Rüsen takes shape at various levels: in the relation of generations to each other, in the self-image of the (perpetrator) nation, and at the level of universal values. Of particular interest here are his reflections on mourning as a response to the destruction of the national self-image as well as the destruction of the nation's memory. Where responsibility in the form of obligation must be taken for crimes against humanity, any form that adopts a semantics of heroism is certainly out of the question, but this does not rule out the possibility of national identity construction per se. Following the period of genocidal triumphalism in Germany, "historical mourning" implies work on an identity that is only possible through painful transformation: "The loss is substantial, and recovery is only possible by integrating negative elements into one's own history."[93] Rüsen also understands this work of mourning as a cultural praxis "that subjectively realizes an objective loss of this kind and, at the same time, wins a collective self, the nation, out of this loss, indeed, with this loss newly transformed."[94] Even the complicated syntax of this sentence makes it clear that it is not a question of a simple "cultural practice": Rüsen admits that what is at stake here is an entirely new historical phenomenon, one for which there are no compelling models.

CHANGES IN THE POLITICS OF HISTORY

As long as the central values of a social and political public realm remained those of honor, reputation, and image, grappling with one's own guilt did not stand a chance. This is why perpetrator memory tended toward what Dolf Sternberger calls a "vigorous forgetfulness." It is as difficult to be mindful of one's own guilt as it is easy to remember the guilt of others. For such an awareness to occur, powerful external pressure has to be applied. In the context of West German postwar society, the Mitscherlichs accurately described the paralyzing effects of a perpetrator memory that longed for a bottom line to be put in place through compulsive forgetting. Already in the mid-1960s, they were drawing attention to the opposition between perpetrator and victim memory and specifically to the striking discrepancy between "our own limited capacity for memory and that of our former wartime enemies and victims, which is in no way impaired." They point out that "it is not for us alone to determine at what point the implications have been sufficiently drawn out of a past that destroyed the lives and happiness of such a huge number of victims." Entirely in keeping with the argument that would later come from the global moral community, constituted in terms of an appeal to the moral witness, the Mitscherlichs were already pointing to "a world public that has in no way forgotten what occurred in the Third Reich and are not yet prepared to." And they add, "We had the opportunity to observe how it was only the pressure of opinion outside Germany that forced us to proceed with the legal procedures against the Nazi perpetrators, to extend the statute of limitations or to reconstitute the events of the mass crimes."[95]

The truth of these statements has been repeatedly confirmed over the last thirty years. As long as the memory of the perpetrators remains enclosed within a self-referential national memory, the distancing strategies that work to deflect guilt, along with the heroic values of honor and a positive self-image, will always prevent the acknowledgment of a negative memory. Austria is a striking example of this. By appealing to its neutral status, Austria afforded itself the doctrine of victimhood that allowed the country to see itself as Hitler's first victim. Now, this doctrine is appropriate in the context of politicians who survived the concentration camps, but it certainly falls short as the formula for a national self-description. The pressure of a global public first arose in Austria in the 1980s with the Waldheim affair, which was reinforced by a change in public consciousness over the course of a generational shift and which, in the end, was officially consolidated through claims of shared responsibility.[96]

Although the psychological mechanisms and strategies associated with the repression of guilt were not fundamentally different in Germany, the general framework for remembering certainly was. In contrast to Austria, Germany could not develop its own self-determining politics of memory but rather had to construct its memories within the frameworks of the West and East political blocs.[97] After the postwar period came to an end in 1989, the framework of memory underwent another decisive shift. As the Mitscherlichs had emphasized, what then became important was "a world public that has in no way forgotten what occurred in the Third Reich and are not yet prepared to." Under the influence of this transnational framework, the defenses against guilt were gradually weakened: admissions of guilt and personal confrontations with negative memory were taking on new forms, such as those being developed in connection with Daniel Goldhagen's book tour and the Wehrmacht exhibition in the 1990s.

Meanwhile, throughout the 1990s, the global public attested to by the Mitscherlichs acted as the trigger for other criticisms about how national memory should be constructed. Until recently, traumatic experiences of history could hardly be addressed from the side of the victims, let alone from the side of the perpetrators, because there were no cultural examples to draw on for how to process such memories. Gradually at first, forms of collective memory have been developed that no longer fall within the model of a retroactive and heroic meaningfulness; rather, they aim for the universal recognition of suffering and for therapeutic recovery from its paralyzing aftereffects. Connected to these new forms is a new engagement with the guilt of perpetrators in the memory of their descendants. No longer able to avoid the dark chapter of their history by forgetting it, these descendants are starting to take responsibility for that history by stabilizing it within collective memory and integrating it into a collective self-image.[98] As such, the reception of a victim's traumatic experience into collective memory is no longer bound up with resentment and revenge as it had been in cases of heroic military defeats, but is now being associated with claims of recognition and restitution.

The admissions and confessions that are increasingly being made worldwide by state and church leaders, apologizing for the crimes of the past committed by their state or their institution, are responding to these claims of traumatized victim groups. It is not just the Germans who are preoccupied with legacy issues relating to their history; in many places around the world, remembering historical crimes is providing a new basis for the coexistence of ethnic groups and nations and is helping to establish connections between their respective memories.

This is an utterly new phenomenon in history and, on a general level, it can be related to the growing significance of individual and collective memory.[99] Along with changes in social sensibility, a paradigm shift has also taken place in the politics of history. Previously, in the aftermath of wars, a collective forgetting was decreed so as to neutralize memories that could endanger the peaceful coexistence of the victors and the defeated. For historical traumas caused by crimes of exploitation and by the extermination of innocent and defenseless people, however, forgetting has no such healing power, not least because there is no authority that can forgive these crimes. Such "crimes against humanity" are not done away with by being forgotten, but rather are preserved in a memory shared by victims and perpetrators.

Over the past decade, we have witnessed this worldwide transformation in the way national memories are constructed. Honor, triumphant or injured, which for thousands of years dominated the grammar of national memory, is no longer the sole criterion. To name just a few events here, from 1998 alone: in January, the Canadian government apologized for the injustices carried out by its predecessors on the native people; in March, President Clinton apologized in Uganda for the active participation of the United States in the global crime of slavery; and in October, Japanese Prime Minister Obuchi apologized for the crimes committed under the Japanese government against female Koreans (the so-called comfort women).[100] At the very least, these official admissions of guilt are connected to a new awareness of the long-term and transgenerational effects of traumatic historical experience. This awareness has in turn generated new demands for how national memory is organized, both from the perspective of the victims and from that of the perpetrators. One of the most important developments here is the decoupling of remembering and revenge. Between perpetrators and victims today, collective remembering is seen as a substantially better foundation for peaceful coexistence than collective forgetting. In the case of a traumatic memory like that of the Holocaust victim, the maxim of the healing power of forgetting has given way to the ethical demand for collective memory.

How can we explain this dramatic change in the rhetoric of national memory? I trace it back primarily to two causes. In a world of globalized media and economies, nations can no longer afford to construct their memories in a way that is self-centered and isolated from the rest of the world. The second reason is closely connected to the first. We are currently experiencing an ethical turn in the cultural practice of remembering in which notions like recognition and responsibility play particularly important roles. The "global public" (as the Mitscherlichs called it) has entered as a third figure into the space between victims and perpetrators. This global public, based as it is on a globalized media, is also connected to a new global ethos that upholds universalistic normative and intercultural standards against the limited perspectives of what Peter Sloterdijk describes in terms of the collective egotism and self-hypnosis of the nation.[101] Those who are still under the influence of heroic self-images in their constructions of national memory must henceforth be prepared for critical interrogations from the outside world about the damaging consequences of its images of history for bilateral national and intercultural relations. In a world of globalized media and transnational association, nations today can no longer uncritically preserve their mythologizing self-images and memory constructions; above all, they can less and less afford to forget the victims of their own history.[102]

PART II

Analyses and Case Studies

THREE

How True Are Memories?

In the second part of this book, we return once again to the topic with which we began the first part: individual memory, its structure, its dynamics, its potential, and its problems. In particular, we shall seek to deepen our exploration of this topic by proposing conceptual differentiations and examples, the focus of which will primarily be the question concerning the truth of memories. This question will be answered in different ways depending on whether we are seeing things from an academic outside perspective or from the more intimate perspective of experience. Regardless of whether one takes the question regarding the truth or authenticity of memories seriously or whether one rejects it from a more skeptical point of view as misguided, the same realization applies that the problem is not going to go away and that it has left its trace in the discourse.

I-Memory and Me-Memory (Günter Grass)

"I remember. . . ." With these words, Günter Grass began a speech that he gave on October 2, 2000, in the city of Vilnius on the occasion of a

Lithuanian-German symposium on "The Future of Memory."[1] The Goethe Institute had invited four authors (another two of whom were also Nobel Prize winners) to return to the Baroque city that had once been a multicultural center in the middle of Europe and that became the capital city of an independent Lithuania in 1990. It being fifty-five years since the end of the war, Grass and the other authors returned, bringing with them their own burden of individual memories of persecution, extermination, and expulsion that are so typical of twentieth-century biographies.

Having begun his speech with the words "I remember . . . [*ich erinnere mich*]," Grass continues with the following: "or I am reminded [*ich werde erinnert*] by something that stands in my way, something that left its smell behind or hid in age-old letters marked with certain treacherous words, waiting to be remembered."[2] In this contorted sentence, Grass carries out an abrupt grammatical shift from the active to the passive voice, and in so doing, he empties out the subject position (the "I") and recovers himself in the position of object (the "me"). The word *something* then shifts into the subject position, which is at first nothing more than a vague placeholder. Grass then makes this blank space more concrete through words such as *smell* and *treacherous words*.

In registering a change in orientation with the tiny little word *or*, Grass is drawing attention to two fundamental modes of autobiographical memory that I would like to differentiate here as "I-memory" and "me-memory." While the one is verbal and declarative, the other is fleeting and diffused, though not without sharpness or definition; it appeals more to the senses than to the understanding. Psychology and psychotherapy have worked intensively with "I-memory" and have assigned the notion of "story" (among others) to it.[3] The therapeutic premise of this notion is that we are constituted by the stories that we tell about ourselves. According to this perspective, an identity is constructed with the help of a story that orders the unsorted reserves of our autobiographical memories and, by placing them within a memorable form, also gives them a meaning. So, an active I-memory undertakes to recall conscious memories and give them a narrative form that both makes them meaningful *and* opens up the possibility of a perspective on the future. Autobiographical memory is not automatically structured in this way; in order to give those reserves of unsorted memories a form, one must achieve distance from oneself, adopt a dialogical stance, and take on a position. These autobiographical memories also have a social component: we must be in the position to recount them either to ourselves or to others.

How True Are Memories? 99

While psychologists and philosophers have had a lot to say about I-memory, much less attention has been paid to the disorganized and preconscious memory. Here we have to follow writers like Proust or Grass. So let us return to the Grass speech that we just cited and take a look at a longer passage:

> And when we travel to the places of our past, which were destroyed or lost and now bear strange-sounding foreign names, memory suddenly catches up with us. Which is what happened to me in the spring of 1958 when, for the first time after the war I visited Gdansk, a city slowly emerging from the rubble still being cleared and where I hoped in the back of my mind to run into traces of Danzig. To be sure, the school buildings were still there, their corridors alive with the well-preserved fug of school. The paths that I used to take to school, on the other hand, seemed shorter than I remembered. But then, as I was looking for the former fishing village Brösen and discovered that the slapping tide of the Baltic had not changed, I suddenly found myself standing in front of the bathhouse, as derelict as the boarded-up kiosk next to its entrance. And all at once I saw that cheapest of my childhood pleasures bubbling up: raspberry- and lemon- and woodruff-flavored fizz powder in little bags which I would buy at that kiosk for a few pfennigs each. Hardly had the remembered refreshment begun to register in my mind that it began to hatch stories, true stories of lies waiting only for the right code word. The simple, harmless, and water-soluble fizz powder released a chain reaction in my head: The effervescence of first love, that tingling sensation experienced once and then never again.
>
> *(282–83)*

The brilliance of this passage lies in how the author is able to put several different things into play all at once: he manages to recount an episode from his childhood, to call up memories, and in addition, figuratively captures the process of memory itself. In the description of a soft drink that releases unexpected memories and gives them sensual presence, we sense the influence of Proust, the great literary father and explorer of the autobiographical memory, which he called *mémoire involuntaire*. What for Grass is the imaginary fizz powder is, for Proust, the taste of a madeleine cookie dunked in linden blossom tea that leads him to the epiphany of a deeply buried moment of the past, as sudden as it is overwhelming.

But in Grass's case, the autobiographical memory is also initiated by real sensual impulses. He returns to the places of his childhood such as his elementary school in Gdansk or the beach in Brösen; we could call these sites of memory *lieux de souvenir* to distance them in their subjective and private quality from Pierre Nora's collective and cultural sites of memory, the *lieux de mémoire*. Places and objects are the most important triggers for me-memory. As Grass writes, "silent objects trigger memory in us." They can be mute relics and photos, but they can also be simple everyday pleasures like fizz powder that suddenly awaken sensations that are laden with memories.

What kind of magic is it that inhabits these inconspicuous places and objects, such that they are able to move us so suddenly and so powerfully? Where does that power over us come from? The answer to these questions is clear: before they can have this effect on us, we ourselves must have invested something in them. From this perspective, the magical power of memory that dwells in objects and places is comparable to the power of ancient *symbola*. The word refers to objects possessing the value of a token. Such a token would be broken in two when a contract was made, and each of the parties would keep one half as a mark and a means of identification. Once the two halves were brought together again, the legality of the contract and the identity of the two parties were confirmed.

According to this analogy, we can think of many of our autobiographical memories—especially those stored in our me-memory—as being divided into two halves: one half remains in us and the other is externalized in places or objects. In a similar way, many invisible fibers and threads tether the body and the senses to the outside world. Me-memory is activated when the externally preserved half is brought together again with the bodily half. Places and objects are powerful triggers for this somatic memory, for which there is of course no key, no map, and no otherwise conscious and controlled entry. We can never survey or control it from the outside, since it has gained access to the very fibers and joints of our inaccessible sensations. That is why we blindly trip about here, as Grass writes, over every imaginable pitfall and hindrance. We do not have at our disposal a divining rod for these memories, since we ourselves are not the agent but rather the medium of these effects: we ourselves are the divining rod. This is also why it is not easy to gain access to this me-memory: we cannot simply call up the memories stored in it but rather must wait until they (through corresponding contingencies and passwords) come forward. The memories lie dormant in me-memory in the form of implicit and hidden dispositions; they constitute a dispersed and latent standby system that unexpectedly responds to certain external stimuli. Where stimulus meets disposition, somatic memories are activated and can be translated from the preconscious me-memory into the conscious I-memory.

The French philosopher Henri Bergson once wrote that "the characteristic of the man of action is the promptitude with which he summons to the help of a given situation all the memories that have reference of it; yet it is also the insurmountable barrier that encounters, when they present themselves on the threshold of his consciousness, memories that are useless or indifferent."[4] This perspective develops the core of an argument that Nietzsche had put forward twenty years earlier in his work "On the Uses and Disadvantages of History for Life." Men of action whom Nietzsche and Bergson so admired are virtuosos of I-memory; authors like Proust and Grass, on the other hand—and we could also include James Joyce and Virginia Woolf—are virtuosos of me-memory, those who have explored the labyrinthine and rhizomatic structure of our preconscious memories. At the same time, these memories constitute an invisible network by virtue of which our bodies are bound to the object world.

It is thus permissible to differentiate between two different systems within autobiographical memory: the I-memory that is based on the conscious work of reconstruction and the disorganized and unorganizable preconscious me-memory. Whereas the former is developed in interaction with other people, the latter is activated through interaction with places and objects. These places and things act as triggers to complete the "halved" dispositions of feeling that lie dormant within us, whereupon they—as with Grass—can be raised to the level of consciousness through introspection and reallocated to the I-memory. With that movement, however, the memory is qualitatively changed. The me-memory is nothing other than a system of resonances or strings that can potentially be made to sound. Which strings are hit—if and when a vibration in the labyrinthine network of our souls arises—is not really in our control; rather, it is based largely on happenstance and chance occurrences. However, one precondition seems to be that the experience be forgotten and in a state of latency over an extended period of time, and that during this time, its specific "freshness" has been preserved. To a certain extent, Oscar Wilde's saying "Touch it and the bloom is gone" also applies to psychosomatic me-memory, for every further reactivation of this me-memory serves to strengthen its encoding as a conscious and linguistic utterance and so also automatically weakens the underlying sensual and experiential substance. This transfer is an essential aspect of memory: the permanent recoding from the preconscious into the conscious, from the sensual and embodied into the linguistic and figurative, from images and speech into the written. Unlike the

102   *Analyses and Case Studies*

material conservation that takes place in libraries, storage areas, and archives, living memory always takes place in the process of such translations. Indeed, we can truly say that *to remember is to translate*, and for that reason, memories always remain malleable.

Problems of Authenticity

The act of translating memories also always implies change, displacement, and delay. What on the one hand can be seen as a means for keeping memory alive can, from another perspective, also be regarded as a danger or a threat. On this point, Christa Wolf expresses the most radical kind of skepticism when she writes, "The way something is recounted is the way that it *didn't* happen."[5] Her skepticism involves the insurmountable gap between experience and memory. Indeed, Wolf's critical sense of the insurmountable discrepancy between impression and expression provides the foundation for her artistic sensibility, informing her own memory work in terms of how she reflects on the possibilities of and limits to artistic representability. By means of this assertion, Wolf is raising the fundamental question regarding the truth or truthfulness of memories, one that I would like to pursue in what follows here. To do that, I have chosen two completely different memories of Auschwitz, which at the very least also illustrate the irreducible perspectivalism of lived memory.

TWO MEMORIES OF AUSCHWITZ (PRIMO LEVI AND REINHART KOSELLECK)

Primo Levi gives us a shocking account of what took place in the Buna-Monowitz camp, close to Auschwitz, on January 27, 1945.[6] He depicts the final days of the camp "outside of the world and time," before the arrival of the Russian army. The camp leadership had fled and taken 20,000 prisoners with them, almost all of whom died or were murdered on the evacuation march. Those who remained in the camp were the sick, the dying, and the deceased, including Primo Levi himself, who was suffering from scarlet fever. The infrastructure of the camp had completely broken down by the time it was evacuated. In –20° C weather, the few who remained in the camp busied themselves with the basic necessities: with finding sources of heat and lighting and with procuring meager provisions. Despite these small steps taken toward reestablishing a sense of self-determination and humanity, in light of the utter filth of the barracks, the suffering of those who were dying, and the sheer number of corpses, the dominant feeling remained one of powerlessness and self-loss:

> *January 26th.* We lay in a world of death and phantoms. The last trace of civilization had vanished around and inside us. The work of bestial degradation, begun by the victorious Germans, had been carried to its conclusion by the Germans in defeat.[7]

Primo Levi wrote this account immediately following his return from the camp. Entitled *If This Is a Man*, it has become something of a collective cultural memory for subsequent generations of both perpetrators and victims.

The autobiographical sketch that historian Reinhart Koselleck published in a daily newspaper fifty years after the end of the war points to a completely different lived memory.[8] For Koselleck the soldier, Liberation Day was the day of his arrest, as it was for countless other members of the Wehrmacht. He describes how his unit was handed over by the Americans to the Russians and how they headed off eastward in a huge prisoner convoy. These prisoners marched past Birkenau and finally reached Auschwitz, where they were moved into the barracks. At that time, the name *Auschwitz* meant nothing at all to Koselleck. The German prisoners of war first heard from the Russians that millions had been gassed in Birkenau, and many of them thought it was a deception on the part of Soviet propaganda. Such was not the case with Koselleck: he says that he immediately believed these reports to be true, and he also describes the circumstances under which, in Auschwitz, the truth about the place struck him with an almost physical violence. A former Polish concentration camp prisoner was appointed to monitor the German prisoners of war and forced them to do hard labor. At one point, he grabbed a footstool and menacingly held it in the air. But before he smashed it on top of Koselleck's head, he suddenly stopped himself and said, "What should I smash up your skull for—*you* gassed people . . . millions of them." The stool flew into the corner and broke to pieces. Koselleck continues: "it became strikingly [*schlagartig*]—to be taken literally—clear to me that he was telling the truth. Gassed? Millions? That could not have been invented" (21).

At this point in the text, Koselleck considers the truth of his own memories. He writes that "there are experiences which flow into our bodies like fervid lava to be congealed there forever. Unmoved and immovable, they can always be recalled without the least change. Not many of these experiences can be transformed into authentic memories; if that happens, however, such memories are founded on a powerful sensuous presence. The smell, the taste, the noise, the perception of the visual environment, in short: all the senses, in joy or pain, are immediately reactivated and require no conscious effort of remembering in order to be true and remain true. This was the nature of my experience, and I know it today as if it had happened only a moment ago" (21).

Koselleck had been taken to Auschwitz as a Russian prisoner of war, not as a victim of Nazism. He had no firsthand experience of the crimes carried out there; he knows this horrifying place only after liberation, and the only information he has about it comes to him secondhand. Nonetheless, he develops his ideas about the sensual presence of truth by the improbable means of a memory for which he himself has no direct experience whatsoever. His account bears witness to the shock effect that was triggered by sudden insight into the truth about the news of the Nazi crimes. The force of this news hit him harder than a possible blow to the head with a footstool ever could.

Some might be tempted to discredit Koselleck's insistence on the authenticity of his recollection as some sort of self-deception, especially in light of current neurological and psychological research into the general unreliability of human memories. But in fact, there is an exception to the rule in more recent memory theory that corresponds exactly to the type of memory Koselleck is describing. For memories such as these, which are subjectively experienced as authentic and unshakeable, psychologists have coined the term *flashbulb memories*.[9] Flashbulb memories are characterized by a high degree of vividness; they preserve unforeseeable, exceptional experiences with a high degree of exacting detail. Not only are flashbulb memories noted for their primary and vivid quality, but they are also described as being remarkably persistent: "flashbulb memories appear to endure for years and decades without noticeably degrading."[10] Flashbulb memories represent a special form of autobiographical or episodic memory that consists of remembering exactly where one was and what one was doing when one received news of an important historical event. The most common triggers for flashbulb memories are radical historical transformations that suddenly enter the consciousness of contemporary witnesses and have an immediate impact on their lives. This kind of impact occurs particularly in cases of historical events that usher in a new era and that also give new and unexpected direction to the lives of those who experience them. The most frequently cited triggers for flashbulb memories in the literature are the outbreak of the Second World War, the news of

Hitler's death, the assassination of John F. Kennedy on November 22, 1963, and, more recently (and worldwide), September 11, 2001.

Trace and Pathway: Two Models of Memory

Koselleck differentiates these unmediated memories, which he likens to fervid lava in the body, from those that are mediated by language. While the former preserve a kind of sensual immediacy or "presence of truth" for an indeterminate length of time, the latter are strengthened through repeated telling—though, in the process of retelling, they lose their sensual power over time:

> Of course there are countless memories that I have recounted time and again, but the concrete presence of truth has long since vanished from them. They remain for me purely literary stories; in hearing them myself, I can confer on them a kind of belief. I can no longer vouch for their sensual certainty.

Whereas knowledge can be shared in language, experiences stored in the body remain incommunicable and irreplaceable, both at the level of their immediate presence and in terms of the powerful impression they make. We experience them as particularly authentic insofar as they register a radically individual perception of a past reality and so at the same time vouchsafe the unique character of one's own existence.

Koselleck, we could say, distinguishes between two ways of storing memory: the body and language. In each case, memories are stabilized in entirely different ways. We can relate these two forms of storage to the neurological terms of *trace* and *pathway* (this is also roughly Freud's terminology). This distinction is already to be found in Samuel Butler (Maurice Halbwachs drew attention to this), who noted the following:

> We observe, therefore, that we remember best what we have done least often . . . and what we have done most often, with which, therefore, we are most familiar; our memory being mainly affected by the force of novelty and the force of routine. . . . But we remember impressions which have been made upon us by force of routine, in a very different way to that in which we remember a single deep impression.[11]

A trace develops by means of a one-time impression and a pathway or trail by repeated movement over the same stretch. Bodily memories are preserved by means of the intensity of the sensory impression; memories encoded in language are preserved through continual repetition. Sensory memories are influenced by the strength of the affect, the stress of the pain, or the force of the shock. They remain in memory regardless of whether or not they are consciously recalled.

By contrast, the basis of verbally encoded memories is not to be found in the body but in social forms of communication. Maurice Halbwachs has shown that memories are constituted through verbal exchange with other people and with their memories. We are able to recall many of our own memories in large part because we have occasion to talk about them. This narrating represents an act of elaborative encoding, translating what was experienced into a story. "Elaborative encoding is a critical and perhaps necessary ingredient of our ability to remember in rich and vivid detail what has happened to us in the past. . . . If we do not carry out elaborative encoding, we will be left with impoverished recollections."[12] The only problem is that the more frequently one talks about something the less one is remembering the experience itself and the more one is remembering the words used to narrate it. Memory is stabilized through elaboration and repetition, and that also means that what isn't repeated is lost. In a novel by Christa Wolf, we find the following sentence: "It was eleven years ago, another lifetime. His memory of it would have vanished if he hadn't preserved it in words, with the help of which he can recall the event as often as he wants to."[13] As for Koselleck, for Wolf too the anecdote she tells is the epitome of a verbalized memory that can be retrieved and reproduced at any time: "it becomes brightly polished by being often told," she explains, describing a form of memories that become fixed in verbal formulae and entirely lose the "sensory presence of truth."[14] However, this does not mean that verbally encoded memories are necessarily "false"; they just exist in another mode—namely, that of language and not that of the body.

Koselleck's contrast between sensory and language-based memories can be related to the difference between the passive remembering of "me-memory" and the more active "I-memory." He emphatically claims that under certain conditions, sensory memories are "reawakened and require no memory work at all to be true and to remain true." He considers what is stored in sensory impressions to be distinctly more immediate and truer than what is stored through the medium of verbal repetition. Beyond that, these two forms of memory, that of the trace and that of the pathway, can be associated with two different theories of memory, ones that we could designate by the terms *retention* and *(re)construction*. Retention points to the idea of a permanent bodily trace of the memory that, like Koselleck's glowing lava, will be preserved unchanged over long periods of time; by contrast, reconstruction refers to the idea that memories can only be stabilized by being newly produced and so are always being made present in new and somewhat different ways.

Since the 1970s and '80s, the neurosciences have radically challenged our understanding of memory as a kind of protective receptacle for remembrances and have come to see it instead as an activity that is highly malleable and so also fundamentally unreliable. However, this way of seeing things is not all that new. As early as the beginning of the twentieth century, writer Italo Svevo expressed the same idea in a formulation that should again be cited at greater length here:

> The past is always new. It is always changing as time moves on. Parts of it that seem to have been forgotten then resurface, while other parts fade when they are no longer important. The present directs the past like members of an orchestra. It requires these shades and not others. Thus at times the past seems long, short at others. At times, it resonates; at times, it is silent. The part of the past that can work its way into the present is only the one that is meant to shed light on the present or to obscure it.[15]

In this passage, Svevo is basically describing the mechanisms of Proust's *mémoire volontaire*. Proust contrasted these with his *mémoire involontaire* and with the central claim of his work, which reads as follows: "The book whose hieroglyphs are patterns not traced by us is the only book that really belongs to us." And he continues: "Only the impression, however trivial its material may seem to be, however faint its traces, is a criterion of truth."[16]

Amid all these propositions and theories, a basic existential question is opened up: are we the bearers of a memory writing that is buried in us once and for all, or do we ourselves write the past, continually doing this in ever new ways? How passive or how active is recollection? Are memory and consciousness mutually exclusive, as Freud assumed, or is consciousness involved in the act of memory? Perhaps questions in this form are already badly posed, since the two often overlap in the act of memory. In what follows, therefore, we will not examine retention and construction, or preservation and remaking, as opposites or as mutually exclusive but as complementary processes that are related to each other.

In testimonials like Koselleck's that are based in subjective memory, the reassurance of authenticity often plays a large role. One of the most important arguments used to underscore the authenticity of memories consists of the emphatic separation of figurative and verbal memories. Proust had already looked for his authentic recollections precisely in the place that language could not reach, in sensory impressions that resurface through involuntary stimuli. Of course, he himself has partially captured these memories in language, and so has made them communicable. However, that kind of "translation" does not necessarily always happen. Many of them remain isolated below the threshold of consciousness. "Our arms and legs are full of dormant memories," he writes. They persist without being grasped and are "awoken" by consciousness. That is why Proust also likens this cryptic presence of the embodied past to photographic negatives where nothing is fundamentally predictable, whether they are developed at some point or not.

The metaphor of photography has a particularly important role to play in arguments concerning the authenticity of recollections. When the doctor, experimental psychologist, and painter Carl Gustav Carus (1789–1869) was writing his memoirs, it occurred to him that "all I retained from the earliest years of my life were distinct images," from which he infers "that the earliest memories never contain a thought, but only unique sensual impressions which were imprinted into memory as on a daguerreotype plate."[17] The images that Carus has in mind permanently imprint themselves on the child's impressionable soul, compared here to a photographic plate. In Carus's model, the memory of a sensual impression bypasses the filters of language and consciousness, which otherwise process and organize perception. Early childhood images are inscribed in memory in just as an unmediated way as the world of appearances is in the silver salts of the photographic plates.

This metaphor of involuntary bodily inscription follows the trace model of memory, not that of the pathway, and is tied to a claim, if not of objective truth, then certainly of subjective truthfulness. The world is obviously not inscribed onto the human soul as automatically as it is with the shutter release of a camera. In the case of recollection, the shutter is activated by an affect that constitutes the core of emotional memory. Without the focusing adjustment of the attention through a certain affect no image will arise, but this affect will always shape the recollection.

Recent brain research has largely discredited the stark opposition of the paradigm of "inscription" (or "engram"[18]) on the one hand and that of the "canalized pathway" on the other. It has taken aspects of both and combined them in the following manner:

> Engrams are the transient or enduring change in our brains that result from encoding an experience. Neuroscientists believe that the brain records an event

by strengthening the connections between groups of neurons that participate in making the experience. A typical incident in our everyday lives consists of numerous sights, sounds, actions, and words. Different areas of the brain analyze these varied aspects of an event. As a result, neurons in the different regions become more strongly connected to one another. The new pattern of connections constitutes the brain's record of the event: the engram.[19]

Remembering and Imagining

There is another source of uncertainty that can obscure the sensory evidence of autobiographical memories, and it too can be illustrated with an example. Psychologist Alan Baddeley writes:

> Knowing something, but not being able to access it, is a very common experience. This occurred to me recently when my wife referred to a visit we had made to the town of Aldeburgh on the Suffolk coast before we were married. I simply could not recall the incident, although I was sure that I had been to Aldeburgh, and could conjure up a vivid visual image of a long-sweeping, rather grey pebbly beach with strong associations of Benjamin Britten and his gloomy and romantic opera *Peter Grimes*. To what extent I was actually remembering something I had experienced or something I had conjured up by reading or watching television, I found it hard to judge. And I confessed no, I could not remember the visit. "You remember, it was when you sat in the seagull dung!" my wife said. Immediately the memories came flooding back—not at all like the mournful romantic image of Aldeburgh I had previously been scanning![20]

With this example, Baddeley makes it clear how difficult it can be to differentiate between memories of one's own experience and those one has acquired from other sources. Forgetting happens in this case not through the failure of a memory to materialize but through the intervention of another memory. In such cases, this other memory is a mental image that has been generated by information communicated to us through various cultural media. The image can, in some cases, be so *vivid* [*lebhaft*] that it can be confused with one's own *bodily* [*leibhaften*] memory. How does one differentiate vivid imaginings from bodily memories? How is the authenticity of memories safeguarded in this difficult border zone? Baddeley has a simple answer to this question: through seagull droppings! In his case, seagull droppings provide the litmus test for the authenticity of his memory, since they function, clearly and with lightning speed, as the dividing line between what we might call metaphorical and metonymic memories. One stands before a metaphoric memory, as one would before a mental image, whereas with a metonymical memory, one is oneself stuck in it. While metaphorical memory is not specific to the individual and is transmissible without loss, with metonymic memory there is a bond connecting the recollection with the person doing the remembering. Even Baddeley, who was for a moment still purely an observer, suddenly rediscovers himself in the picture and the picture in him.

Baddeley's example highlights another aspect of the question regarding the authenticity of memories. Alongside sensuality, imagery, and fragmentation—qualities that could be attributed to all of our mental images—he adds embodiment as a form of direct physical contact with the recollected scene. Vivid imaginings and bodily memories are not always easily distinguishable in our memory—they overlap each other and often blend together. Subjective recollections intersect with the objective knowledge that we take in through images, reading, and music; recollections of what one has gone through oneself are always supported by, transformed, and occasionally also repressed (which is another source of unreliability for our memories) by what is already known. Baddeley's example vividly illustrates the fact that our memories do not survive in a vacuum. Our memories, in which recollections and mental images intersect, are always bound up with external collections of text and image provided by the media and by the broader cultural archive.

Summary

How true are our memories? There is no blanket answer to this question, but there is a new understanding of how important it is to make differentiations, a few of which I would like to introduce here. Psychologist Daniel Schacter speaks of a "murky twilight zone where memory and reality grope for each other, usually coupling nicely but sometimes yielding strange concoctions."[21] From the perspective of brain research, there is no basis for talk about authenticity. This was confirmed yet again by Wolf Singer, director of the Max Planck Institute for Brain Research in Frankfurt, in his address to the 43rd Congress of the Historical Sciences. In this talk, he describes memories as "fabrications supported by data."[22] Human memory is by nature geared toward adapting itself to a changing environment and does not aim for exact retention. Brain research has shown that every reactivation of a memory trace is at the same time a new inscription that necessarily transforms the original experience.

It would, however, be misguided for us to adopt a generalized attitude of skepticism regarding memory on the basis of these findings.[23] On the contrary, what is required is a critical awareness that can be expressed in the form of questions and differentiations. Recollections are strengthened by the clear perception, the emotional power, and the depth of an experience as well as by its expression in language. The "contents of memories are, to a large extent, subject to changes in their use."[24] The argument that memory images are preserved as clearly and in as fixed a way as photographs are might possess a certain rhetorical force, but it is not factually accurate. The memory is not an apparatus for precise registration and conservation, as a camera is. Rather, the continual rewritings and adaptations of our memories can be more readily compared to the practice of retouching, filtering out accidental and disruptive elements from the photograph, and embellishing, strengthening, enlarging, and inflating what comes into focus. In the same way that the official censorship mechanisms of a ministry of propaganda might function in relation to the self-image of a totalitarian state, so too does a form of inner censorship function in relation to one's own self-image and one's own history. The exception that proves the rule in this case would be the very specific instance of flashbulb memories, those situations and scenes of epoch-making or perceptual turning points that are preserved over long periods of time in unusually sharp detail. But there are also those cases of fraudulent and deceptive false memories, ones that can have devastating effects—especially within the social framework of the court, where decisions are made regarding guilt and innocence.[25]

Generally speaking, our recollections are both *imprecise* and *variable*. As a rule, we cannot depend upon the details. We frequently experience this unreliability when we are informed from an external source about something that we mean to remember. For most of our memories, there is no external evidence; however, when there are other memories competing with our own, or even evidence from historical documents, we are directly confronted with the weakness of our memory. Furthermore, memories are open to interpretation. Since our memory does not preserve a coherent sequence, but rather always makes available only tiny pieces and segments out of which we construct an image for ourselves, the retrospective narrative can change in the course of a lifetime without it being the case that we are falsifying the memories themselves.

To illustrate how imprecise memory can be, let us take an example. If we were to ask an auditorium of people how many airplanes were involved in the September 11 attacks, we would not get much agreement. Those who answered with "two" would have in mind the images of the burning Twin Towers that were repeatedly aired on television. Those who answered "three" would also be thinking about the images of the destroyed Pentagon building. Those who said "four" would also be remembering the plane that crashed in Pennsylvania, of which there were no images. Mass-mediated memories have turned members of a global society into participants in a traumatic event, in real time and on a global scale. Of course, these mass-mediated memories consist of isolated impressions that are remembered with varying intensities in words and images, but are not necessarily connected to a process of elaborative encoding. To move directly from findings about this kind of imprecision to claims about the falsity, artifice, and, finally, to the fiction of the underlying event—as memory skeptics are wont to do—is, however, to go decidedly too far.

Are we justified in continuing to pose questions regarding the authenticity of memories, in light of the critical examination and important deconstructions of the myths and fictions of memory, as well as the legitimate skepticism voiced regarding them? Generally speaking, such a question is never so starkly posed. Memories are not normally used for reality testing because we neither have nor do we require documentary evidence for subjective experiences. They are primarily apodeictic and so are self-legitimating. It is often of little consequence whether a memory is true or not; in the context of a social situation, for example, the point of a great story is often more important than its factuality; within the framework of an autobiographical retrospective, experiences are necessarily going to be reinterpreted and brought into a new context that supports the relevant self-image. To be sure, memories do not exist solely in the brain but are also moored to the social sphere and the object world: this mooring gives them additional supports and also allows for possibilities of correction, which places the question regarding truth on another level.

"We must keep in mind," Schacter writes, "that errors and distortions in remembering, though startling when they occur, are far from the norm in our mnemonic lives. Most of the time our memories reliably handle the staggering variety of demands that our day-to-day activities place on them."[26] The problem of truth is controversial only in certain institutional contexts, as in the case of testimonials during trials or in cases of statements made by a moral witness, where an emphatic claim to factual or biographical truth is being made. To dismiss outright the (subjective) claims we make to the truthfulness of our recollections would mean that we are turning into a society of Alzheimer's patients, in which no more promises can be made and no more debts repaid. So, taking the unreliability of our memories into account in no way implies that, either as individuals or as members of a society, we could simply stop engaging in questions of truth and taking on responsibilities and duties. Therefore, we shall need to continue submitting our own memories to scrutiny and augment them with a self-questioning discourse, examples of the kind I have introduced here. This discourse, oscillating between retention and construction or between authenticity and fabrication, is necessary in order that we can evaluate our own experiences and can anchor ourselves in the real world. In this sense, authenticity is less a fact than a criterion, an indispensable criterion for reality testing and for the assurance one has of one's own identity. In terms of its function as a requirement for one's own identity, authenticity is clearly indispensable, although, as we have seen, it is not uncontroversial.

FOUR

False Memories: Pathologies of Identity at the End of the Twentieth Century

In this chapter, we shall further examine the truthfulness of autobiographical memories by looking at two spectacular cases of false memory. The term *false* can be used to refer to memories that have been unconsciously changed, but it can also imply conscious falsification. Further, the issue of truth and falsehood here also involves the close connections between *memory* and *identity* under very specific autobiographical, social, and historical conditions.

Psychologist Erik Erikson took up the concept of individual identity and gave it new significance by situating it in relation to the often difficult, even crisis-ridden, process of creating continuity and coherence throughout different life stages.[1] Since then, the concept has enjoyed a huge boom and is now also being applied with increasing frequency to the collective.[2] Over 250 years before Erikson, though, philosopher John Locke was already writing about identity, introducing a new concept of personhood on the threshold of modernity that many commentators see as determining "the terms of the debate about the concept of person up to the present day."[3] So Locke's arguments shall serve us here as a kind of yardstick for the two case studies.

Locke's Concept of Identity

Writing about the relation between memory and identity, Spanish author Javier Marías states the following: "I don't believe that the faculty of memory alone is any guarantee that a person remains the same in different times and different places."[4] With this statement, Marías is questioning a claim first made by early modern British Enlightenment philosopher John Locke. In a chapter of his *Essay Concerning Human Understanding* entitled "Of Identity and Diversity,"[5] Locke grapples with different theories of identity in order to develop a more up-to-date or modern notion. Locke conceived the notion of identity in a substantially broader way than previous thinkers had done, in that he—to use Ricoeur's language—supplemented the "idem-identity" (identity understood as substantial equality, or sameness) with a notion of "ipse-identity" (identity understood as selfhood).[6] On the one hand, idem-identity involves the claim that two objects are identical, like two copies of a book or two cars from the assembly line of a factory. The notion of ipse-identity, on the other hand, can only be applied to people who have an awareness of time and change and who have the capacity for self-relation and self-consciousness. Locke realized that individuals undergo many changes over time; however, in spite of these manifest changes, they can recognize themselves as themselves, and, what is more, they first develop a sense of identity in light of these changes. His question, then, becomes: in what does a stable identity consist throughout these changes? And in what is this unity anchored?

In addition to a generic rationality, according to Locke, a person also has consciousness at its disposal that produces self-reflexive knowledge. It is first at this level that identity can be meaningfully defined. Locke therefore defines personal identity as a reflexive self-relation; it is not only rational but above all, it is relational. The person is born as a physical and rational being but must produce and answer for this identity him- or herself. Locke was writing at the beginning of the era of civil society, so at the very historical moment when modern bureaucracies of identity were beginning to develop their criteria that are now so familiar to us, such as date of birth, place of birth, name of parents, sex, eye color.[7] However, Locke disregarded such external factors of identification and anchored personal identity exclusively in an inner self-relation.[8] The most important prerequisite for this self-relation is, for him, consciousness, which we can also equate with memory, since, according to Locke, consciousness is an extended retrospective projection into the past. Personal identity arises when a person recognizes itself as a self over the course of time. According to Locke, the term *person* stands for

> a thinking intelligent Being, that has reason and reflection, and can consider it self as it self, the same thinking thing in different times and places; which it does only by that consciousness, which is inseparable from thinking, and as it seems to me essential to it.... And as far as this consciousness can be extended backwards to any past Action or thought, so far reaches the Identity of that *Person*; it is the same *self* now as it was then; and 'tis by the same *self* with this present one that now reflects on it, that that Action was done.
>
> (§9, 335)

Locke's notion of personal identity seeks to provide the groundwork for a new anthropology of human beings as citizens. In this context, we might recall that Locke's concept of identity had a long prehistory in the cultural practices of sixteenth- and seventeenth-century Puritan autobiography writing. Therefore, as concerns Locke, one can likewise speak of the "birth of the person out of the spirit of responsibility." Locke understands *person* to be a forensic term related to the goals and effects of action: he defines people as "intelligent Agents capable of Law, and Happiness and Misery" (§25:346). So, legal accountability becomes a precondition for the person as citizen. Striving for happiness and success is grounded in this accountability. For only he or she who is capable of debt can also register profits, and only he or she who is capable of suffering can strive for happiness. Locke emphasizes that for all this, above all one needs a reliable memory, thus replacing what used to be external norms and powers with consciousness and memory. Identity will henceforth be expected of the "I"—that is, the coherence of a person's life will depend upon a conscious self.

Locke based his concept of personal identity on the ability of the person to remember. Everything that we can attribute to our consciousness and that falls within the scope of our memory constitutes our identity:

> That with which the consciousness of this present thinking thing can join it self, makes the same Person, and is of one self with it, and with nothing else; and so attributes to it self, and owns all the Actions of that thing, as its own, as far as that consciousness reaches, and no farther; as every one who reflects will perceive.
>
> (§17:341)

So, the identity of a person arises for Locke when an individual identifies with his or her life story, in the sense of what actions they are prepared to appropriate to their own consciousness. I would now like to demonstrate the relevance and limitations of this Lockean model for understanding two sensational cases of identity from the 1990s.

The Schneider/Schwerte Case

Locke was a philosopher of consciousness; for him, there was still no complex psychology that could surreptitiously deform the pathways of memory. Therefore, for him, what I can no longer remember and so cannot attribute to myself does not constitute part of my personal identity. The first case we are looking at here demonstrates that, under the pressure of guilt and shame, the willingness to remember is drastically reduced and the unifying force of personal identity is destroyed. When one does not want to face up to one's conscience and take responsibility for earlier experiences, memories are suppressed and a new identity is forged. At any rate, that is how things went in the case of Schneider/Schwerte, where two different personal identities were experienced consecutively in one body and one biography. With Schneider/Schwerte, we are dealing with a new variation on the doppelgänger—not the well-documented nineteenth-century version that oscillates back and forth between two opposing manifestations but rather one that is divided into an earlier and a later person, into Hans Schneider and Hans Schwerte.

There is a certain affinity between the Schneider/Schwerte doppelgänger and the many so-called "conversion objects" [*Konversionsobjekte*] on display in German museums. The term *conversion objects* refers to everyday objects that were produced in 1945 out of military cast-offs. The most famous object, one that went through a conversion on a mass scale from being an instrument of the military to being a civilian object, was the Wehrmacht helmet, which was turned into a kitchen sieve by poking holes in it and attaching two handles.[9] *Hans Schwerte* experienced a similar transformation (though not exactly a conversion). Following a quick run through the qualifying phase at the University of Erlangen (he received his doctorate in 1948 and his habilitation in 1958), in 1965, he became professor of German literature at the University of Aachen. His habilitation work on *Faust und das Faustische: Ein Kapitel deutscher Ideologie* [Faust and the Faustian: A Chapter of German Ideology] (1962) was widely celebrated. Further, he championed a reformed German canon that placed Kafka and Celan at the center and, among other things, campaigned for the establishment and development of the new research area of Jewish studies in German departments. As left-liberal rector of the university, he battled on the side of the youth during the student revolts and steered a bold course of reform. After his retirement in 1978, he was deeply committed at a personal level to nurturing international relations. No wonder that this storybook scholar from the Federal Republic of Germany made a lot of friends and enjoyed a high standing, not least in Israel.

The news first came out in April 1995 that this highly respected and internationally renowned former rector at the Technical University of Aachen (who had also been awarded the Federal Cross of Merit) had a doppelgänger when, at age 85, he submitted a voluntary self-disclosure to the university.[10] In that document, he admits to having changed his name shortly after the war: he had not been born in 1910 in Hildesheim as Hans Schwerte, but rather in 1909 as Hans Ernst Schneider in Königsberg. It turns out that Hans Schneider had had a no less brilliant career than Schwerte, but in Nazi Germany as German professor and Hauptsturmführer in Himmler's Ahnenerbe, an institution that placed culture at the service of a racist and imperialist domestic and foreign politics. As one of the chief ideologues of the Indo-Germanic folk myth, Schneider had used the influence of his scholarly propagandistic work to underwrite the politics of National Socialism. When the war came to an end, he avoided arrest and prosecution by changing his identity. He let Hans Schneider die and came to life again as Hans Schwerte under the guise of a brother-in-law who had been killed. Such subterranean existences, as they were known at the time, were not uncommon in times of war and in the midst of the confusion caused by dysfunctional postwar bureaucracies.[11] Hans Schwerte married his wife, the "widow" of Hans Schneider, for the second time and took on the role of father to his own children. Of course, he could no longer make reference to the academic degrees he had earned previously. But he was able to put together a new set of works out of the now worthless resources of his scholarly writing fairly quickly by changing the main ideas and the terminology. His training and development made him vastly superior to most returning soldiers, so that he quickly got through his second course of study in German studies and could soon resume his career at the point when it had been interrupted by the end of the Third Reich.

The personal identities of Schneider and Schwerte mirror the value systems of their respective societies down to the smallest detail: each of them conformed perfectly to his society, so much so that many have understood the Schneider/Schwerte case to be exemplary of the institutional transition from Nazi Germany to the Federal Republic of Germany and the "zero hour" ideology that went along with it. "The radical discontinuity between the two identities," Ludwig Jäger writes, "suggests a new start, one that shirks the burden of coming to terms with the past."[12] Similarly the sociologist Claus Leggewie, after having sought out Schneider/Schwerte at his retirement home in Bavaria and conducted extensive interviews with him, sees the case as a parable for the history of memory in the Federal Republic. According to this view, after the war, he got rid of his memories in the course of the imposed reorientation, but then is forced to confront them again a half-century later in all kinds of different ways. Schwerte himself emphasized that he had not *worked through* his past, but had *worked it off*, in which case he understood his second life to be a kind of atonement and compensation for his first, which he thought to have been undone bit by bit over the course of that second life. Leggewie, who has reflected deeply on this case, describes the personality issue of Schneider/Schwerte as a case of "diachronic schizophrenia."[13]

I myself would prefer to speak of a "diachronic doppelgänger." Diachronic schizophrenia or a diachronic doppelgänger is a substantially different phenomenon from the practice of conversion. With conversion, there is also a change in identity: a Saul can become a Paul in accordance with a changed set of values. The difference between the two is that in cases of conversion, this change is not only a willed decision, but it is also accompanied by consciousness and memory. In fact, a successful conversion depends on a high degree of awareness concerning a clash of values between the before and the after and concerning the public possibilities for the new identity. Conversion is entirely consistent with Locke's schema, since in both cases, consciousness binds the different identities together in a continuity by means of memory; furthermore, it ensures accountability following the radical break: Paul remains aware of the fact that he was a Saul before. Such is not the case with a diachronic doppelgänger, for whom the second identity not only destroys the first—which also happens with conversion—but the act of destruction itself is forgotten, or rendered unconscious. While in cases of conversion, memory and consciousness shed strong light on the pivotal moment, with the diachronic doppelgänger, it is kept secret and hidden. The memory is disposed of, together with what Locke found so important: its function as a bridge. Schwerte described his difficulties with memory in the following way: "Everything that's now coming to the surface about Schneider strikes me as if it had to do with a complete stranger."[14] The second identity could only arise for Schwerte "at the cost of a largely effaced recollection of the Schneider identity." The second life is not, as Ludwig Jäger emphasizes, "a purported response to the first in light of the knowledge of the past; rather it is like a second attempt at a roulette table: new chances, new luck."[15] In Locke's terms, we are dealing with two personal identities in one body; put otherwise, we are dealing with a diachronic doppelgänger.

The Case of Bruno Dössecker / Binjamin Wilkomirski

Fragments: Memories of a Wartime Childhood [*Bruchstücke: Aus einer Kindheit 1939–1948*] is the title of a shocking Holocaust biography that was first published by the Jewish Branch of the Suhrkamp Press in 1995. Translation into twelve different languages immediately followed, along with ringing endorsements: "No portrayal of the Holocaust told from a child's point of view has touched so many readers since the publication of Anne Frank's diary."[16] The book's positive reception came to an abrupt halt three years later when an article appearing in a Swiss magazine proved that the author of *Fragments*, who went by the name of Binjamin Wilkomirski, had not in fact spent his childhood in Eastern European death camps but had spent its entirety in Switzerland. The Swiss writer Daniel Ganzfried conducted research into public records (birth certificates and school records) and revealed that "Binjamin Wilkomirski" was born as an illegitimate child; Bruno Grosjean had been his name, and, after spending some years in an orphanage, he was adopted by the Swiss couple Dössecker and grew up in a sheltered middle-class family.[17]

The writer Binjamin Wilkomirski functions just as Locke had described: he bases his identity on his memories. His book not only evokes memories as material for his life story—as is of course typical of autobiographical testimonies—but he also comments on the indisputable certainty of those memories. At the beginning of the book, he explains the quality of his memories in the following way:

> My earliest childhood memories are planted, first and foremost, in exact snapshots of my photographic memory and in the feelings imprinted in them, and the physical sensations. Then comes memory of being able to hear, and things I heard, then things I thought, and last of all, memory of things I said.[18]

Wilkomirski also draws on photography in his argument about the absolute reliability of memories that are shaped by images and by the senses. His claim to authenticity is further strengthened by the disconnected and fragmented quality of the memories. Here he speaks of fragments that resist the desire for order and the logic of "having become an adult." When he wants to write about the images of his childhood, for instance, he says that he must "dispense with an ordering logic and the perspective of a grown-up." The force and authenticity of his memory images are incompatible with a retrospective construction of identity. The logic of his argument goes as follows: the more *identity* there is at stake, the less *authenticity* there is. So the autobiographer denies the presence of any retrospective interference in his account: there is no bridge connecting the self of the past with the self of the present. He declares that his memories had remained untouched and encapsulated over the course of all the intervening years. Indeed, his claim about their immediacy and authenticity is based on this notion as well, a claim that is supported by the evidence of photography as a medium that has no linguistic or conceptual aspects. For photography does not produce an image of reality but retains an imprint of it.

Wilkomirski belongs to the tradition of the discourse of authenticity described above; he secures the truth of his early childhood memory *images* by distancing them from the domains of language, self-reflexive thought, and the logic of the adult world. This strategy proved very successful with his readers. The Rumanian writer Norman Manea, himself a Holocaust survivor, praised Wilkomirski's *Fragments* for this very reason: "There is not the coherence of literature to this book. You don't have the mind of the artist. So this incoherence felt like a kind of authenticity to me."[19] The incoherence and fragmentariness of sensory-motor memories—ones that we register as being so authentic—seem especially plausible in cases of traumatic experiences. Traumatic situations are not registered like other perceptions; they become deformed under the pressure of overwhelming emotion. Whatever can be recalled of one's memories is exploded into fragmented individual images. Henry Krystal, a psychiatrist at Michigan State University who has worked with Holocaust survivors for over four decades, describes these exploded and incoherent shards—which the memory will try to hide following the traumatic event—as "spotty."[20] Different from the flashbulb memory that briefly but coherently reveals a scene, the "spot" always only illuminates a selective and, for the subject, unbearable and incomprehensible segment of an event. For Krystal, though, these fragments are not immediate reflections of factual events. For him, the authentic dimension of traumatic memories consists far more in their distortion.

> What survivors remember many years later is the incomplete story that contains many defense mechanisms like deferral, falsification and above all, changes that shield against painful feelings associated with shame and guilt. . . . A part of the change to memory has to do with the construction of protective screen-memories, false memories that take the place of the unthinkable.[21]

Even the memory itself is not able to withstand the violence of trauma; no objective registering of the event takes place here, as with a camera. Rather, the registering apparatus is also deformed by the traumatic event.

The tone Wilkomirski uses to argue for the precise accuracy of his memories is not only apodeictic but also smacks of an apologetics. This is how someone speaks who wishes to efface his former self, who wishes to assert his memories against a hostile or an incredulous environment, someone who wants to facilitate the breakthrough of someone else's prior social identity with the assistance of memories. In an interview, he presents his family milieu as an environment characterized by a repressive silence, and in so doing, he is seizing on a common trope among survivors who, in their trauma, are often confronted with an indifferent environment. "'Children have no memories, children forget quickly, you must forget it all, it was just a bad dream.' These were the words, endlessly repeated, that were used on me from my schooldays to erase my past and make me keep quiet. So for decades I was silent, but my memory could not be wiped clean."[22] It is entirely possible that, by doing this, his adoptive parents had hoped to release their son from his earlier history and thus give him a new identity. These reassurances, if they occurred, had the opposite effect; they gave way to a restless search for a lost memory and another identity.

Of course Wilkomirski was by no means as independent and self-contained as he suggests. Rather, he was heavily dependent on written and visual documents as well as on the help of many friends. At home, he had compiled an extensive Holocaust library and a visual archive; beyond that, he participated in therapy sessions and established contact with two self-help groups that, under the guidance of experienced therapists and survivors, organized regular trips to the death camps of Majdanek and Auschwitz. With these supports, he was eventually able to articulate what he took to be, or at least doled out as, his long-repressed traumatic memories.

The memory images that Wilkomirski so emphatically sought to distance from the domains of language or thought do not exist in the kind of vacuum—in which they are conserved, protected from external influences—that he would like us to believe they do. Over 130 years ago, the English novelist Anthony Trollope wrote that "we have become a novel-reading people."[23] And he continues, "Our memories are laden with the stories which we read, with the plots which are unraveled for us, and with the characters which are drawn for us." The dominant medium has changed since Trollope; it is no longer print media that pervade our horizon with stories but rather the visual media of television, film, and video. In a thoroughly mediatized world, our conscious and unconscious minds tap into image banks such as books and television, film, and video. Free-floating images that circulate in these image banks are just as fragmentary and isolated as the memory fragments of Wilkomirski are.

Locke could not even have dreamed of such a scenario in which the authenticity of our memories is so radically threatened. Nonetheless, he was already thinking about the problem posed by Wilkomirski. In one section, he asks himself whether it would be possible for the awareness of a past action to be transferred from one person to another. Since memories, he emphasizes, are indeed only depictions of past actions, the problem could easily arise that the memory provokes something that never really happened. Memory, as Locke considers it, "being but a present representation of a past Action, why it may not be possible, that that may be represented to the Mind to have been, which really never was . . . [and] why one intellectual Substance may not have represented to it, as done by itself what it never did, and was perhaps done by some other Agent, why I say such a representation may not possibly be without reality of Matter of Fact, as well as several representations in Dreams are, which yet, whilst dreaming, we take for true, will be difficult to conclude from the Nature of things" (§3:337–38). If something of this kind were to happen, Locke suggests that it would be God's cruel trick, one that would destroy his notion of self-transparency and an identity based on self-evident infallibility.

Here we are confronted once again with the fluctuating boundary between memory images that refer to what happened to us and imaginary pictures that are appropriated through reading or films.[24] In an essay with the wonderful title "The Seven Sins of Memory,"[25] Daniel Schacter has put together a list of the different kinds of forgetting, some of which are relevant to the Wilkomirski case. For instance, *misattribution* is a term Schacter uses to describe a mistake of the memory that has nothing to do with problems of recall, but involves false attribution regarding the contents of the memory: here it is a matter of having memories of events as if one had experienced them oneself, or of having memories of events that did not take place at all. What Schacter terms *suggestibility* is even more relevant to the present case, which he understands to be "the creation of subjectively compelling false recollections of autobiographical episodes." He also calls these memories "illusory." They do not arise out of a conscious desire to deceive—for then there would be no question of a mistaken memory—but rather because of the different forms of influence exerted in the process of remembering. "Suggestibility in memory refers to the tendency to incorporate information provided by others."[26] As previously mentioned, Wilkomirski was surrounded by friends, therapists, and counselors, all of whom acted as confabulators, not to say as midwives, to his memories.

Social Frameworks of Memory

Locke created a modern concept of personal identity based entirely on the capacity for self-awareness and the ability to remember. However, he still had very little idea of how unreliable and deceptive this ability to remember can be and how problematic it is to define a person solely on the basis of a subjective orientation. Hans Schneider/Schwerte and Bruno Dösseker/ Binjamin Wilkomirski are examples of men with two heads who lived two consecutive lives within a single biography. They are good examples of the pathologies of identity that arose in the aftermath of the Second World War and the Holocaust. The one based his new identity on a forgetting of what he had done, while the other based it on the memory of what he himself did not experience. The one kept quiet and disposed of his memories as a perpetrator to avoid persecution, while the other wrote and implanted victim memories in himself in order to gain public attention and global recognition against the background of the ethical turn we talked about earlier: the turn from a sacrificial form of memory to a victim-based one. Both opportunistically adjusted their memories and their identities to suit the conditions of their respective presents, something about which Locke could have known nothing.

These two cases draw attention to a difference between memory and consciousness. Dieter Teichert has already argued that Locke's theory of personal identity is based less on memories per se than it is on a consciousness of past ego states. However, these earlier ego states are less important for our memory than the self-image that we project backward onto the past in a particular present moment. The idea that memory and identity should be characterized more as a reconstructive draft was first developed much later by French sociologist and theoretician of memory Maurice Halbwachs—

though Halbwachs anchored personal identity not in the individual as Locke had done, but in the social group. With this change in premise, the coordinates of the entire theory shift. According to Halbwachs's argument, identity is not the result of memories, but rather is their condition: it is much more so the case that memories arise and are formed in the first place because of social ties, identities, and group loyalties—they are always imbedded in communicative relationships. Precisely not isolated individuals, but rather these "social frameworks," as he calls them, are decisive factors in remembering and forgetting. With this concept of frameworks, Halbwachs provided memory research with an entirely new foundation.[27] He was able to show that the content of the memory does not provide a stable reference point, but rather is changed in accordance with the social and political conditions of the present moment in which we call up our memories. That is what is meant by the constructive power of memories: we tend to make them tacitly conform to the values and demands that our self-image of the time seeks to accommodate. Whatever does not fit into these frameworks has a difficult time coming to memory and language.

In order to adapt to the social framework of the Federal Republic and to become a member of the West German academic elite, Hans Schneider had to "forget" a great deal after the war ("forget" in the sense of conceal, repress, or dissociate). In the other case, in order to adapt to the framework of a society oriented around a post-traumatic association of affliction and suffering and, in the mid-1990s, to become a member of the group "Children of the Holocaust," Bruno Dössecker had to "remember" a lot ("remember" in the sense of appropriate, make an aspect of his person). In order to belong, we recollect and we forget—in this sense, the two diachronic doppelgängers confirm Halbwachs's constructivist theory of memory.[28] Locke's notion of individual consciousness and memory as the bridge for different ego states and his emphasis on a retrospective self must be supplemented with Halbwachs's theory of an identity that is reconstructed in the present within the context of social groups. Locke still assumed remembering to be a cumulative registering of individual states, neglecting not only the constructed character of identity but also its programmatic character. Sebastian Rödl emphasized the latter, speaking of a "normative framework" in relation to the construction of identity. His central claim is that normativity and subjectivity mutually constitute one another. To elaborate on this, he introduced the term *normative self-characterization*, which he describes in the following way: "We relate to our own thoughts and actions not descriptively, in the sense of deliberately stating and reporting them, but rather normatively. This relation to an 'ought' is that which makes a perspective particular and personal, and that which constitutes subjectivity and self-consciousness."[29]

At this point, we can lend more precision to the discussion about what Schwerte and Wilkomirski did to their own doppelgängers. They changed their identities, in that they completely switched one normative self-characterization for another. At the same time, in both cases these normative frameworks were "social frameworks" in Halbwachs's sense: they were social givens. Both of our protagonists expertly internalized these social and normative frameworks. The three-year and fifty-year success stories of these men show how well their performances worked: both of them constituted ideal types in the public eye at a particular historical juncture. That the truth about both of their tailor-made identities was eventually leaked has to do with the fact that identities are not only constructed within social frameworks but are also bureaucratically controlled and managed. So, beyond their being consistent with subjective processes and social norms, constructions of identity remain subject to external criteria of verification.

Set against the background of these two case studies, Locke's concept of personal identity falls short in two ways. On the one hand, Locke considered the activity of memory to be a purely mental and wholly reliable activity. In that sense, he underestimates the way that remembering is always driven by affects and so not only encloses and integrates but also rejects and dissociates. He assumes that humans are perfectly transparent to themselves but, as Nietzsche and Freud after him have shown, this self-transparency cannot be generally assumed. Equally untenable is his assumption of the solipsistic character of human beings. Remembering and consciousness always take place in a social context; identity is socially constructed and so is always dependent on the changing norms of the cultural and political environment. Therefore, we should perhaps read Locke's important chapter on identity and difference less as a description and more as a challenge: as a challenge to include those parts of one's biography from which one would most like to distance oneself. In any case, his premise involves precisely that which our two doppelgängers lack: namely, a reflexive self-relation that distinguishes even the best performers of certain social roles from personal identity. We only have one life and, despite all of our heterogeneous impulses, experiences, and stages of life, only one identity. Whoever lives out one sub-identity at the expense of the others and individualizes him- or herself twice, as happened in the two case studies, will become his or her own doppelgänger.

FIVE

Incorrect Recollections: On the Normative Power of Social Frameworks of Memory

In connection with the cases of false memory that we looked at in the last chapter, the question still remains regarding the enthusiastic reception enjoyed by Wilkomirski's book, especially among Holocaust survivors. After all, it was not only Wilkomirski himself who attested to the authenticity of his *Fragments*, but so too did his readers. Many of them found that Wilkomirski had articulated their own traumatic experiences, experiences that had reduced them to silence, with striking clarity. The subtitle of his book is *Memories of a Wartime Childhood*. But he didn't compose *a* childhood out of fragments; rather he dispersed exemplary "shards of a mirror," in which many individual stories of suffering found themselves refracted.[1] The book owes its success to a blank space that it came to fill in. He offered powerful images (in the sense of the *imagines agentes* of ancient rhetoric) to fill the space beyond language that the imagination turns away from, and then his traumatized readers could turn those fictional episodes back into an expression of their own authentic biographical experiences. So in a certain sense, Wilkomirski was the opposite of what *The New Yorker* called him. He wasn't so much a "memory thief" as he was a substitute, articulating the memory of the victims in their place; that is, he gave back to them memory that had been destroyed by the enormous degrees of suffering they had undergone.

The Holocaust as a Framework of Memory

Wilkomirski wrote his false memories in such a way as to have them fit perfectly into the then-current memory framework of Holocaust victims. His memories are not authentic, but they are "correct." They were correct not only in that they were serviceable from the perspective of the victims, but also in the sense that they were socially accepted. The privilege given to this victim perspective as the officially recognized memory not only explains the huge success of the book, which lasted three years, but it also produced the book in the first place. The sociocultural backdrop to the book is constituted by a change in sensibility related to the emergence of a victim culture. In the context of this change, as Novick has argued, the disaffected and contemptuous attitude toward victims changed into one of "enthusiastic approval." In that sense, "on the individual level, the cultural icon of the strong, silent hero is replaced by the vulnerable and verbose antihero. Stoicism is replaced as a prime value by sensitivity. Instead of enduring in silence, one lets it all hang out. The voicing of pain and outrage is alleged to be 'empowering' as well as therapeutic."[2] Wilkomirski did not experience the Holocaust as a historical event, but rather as a social construction.

When did the Holocaust become the Holocaust? This question, which has in the interim become the subject of various studies, already begins with the name. Neither the perpetrators nor the victims had any idea that they were involved in or gripped by the "Holocaust." At the beginning, there were very different names, such as, for instance, "the final solution" (starting in 1942), a term from a politically motivated code language on the side of the perpetrators or, on the side of a small group of victims, "stochastic process," a phrase going back to the work of physicist Bogdanov that means something like *chaotic resolution*.[3] Following the liberation of the concentration camps by the Allied troops and the full exposure of the Nazi crimes, the word *atrocities* took center stage, one that generalized the terror of this domination and made it just as undifferentiated as the term *Nazi barbarities* did. Over the next fifty years in Germany, the name *Auschwitz* came to stand for the genocide of the Jews and other victim groups. At the end of the 1960s, Elie Wiesel seized on the term *Holocaust*, which had been adopted into American everyday language (and which means an all-consuming sacrifice by fire) and had already been used as a translation for the Hebrew word *Shoah*. After the American television series chose to use this word as its title, nothing stood in the way of its general acceptance. The trauma, itself an empty signifier, had received its name. And to name an event is also part of a retrospective coping strategy. Along these lines, Ivan Illich once wrote that "one of the ways to bring an era to an end is to find a fitting name for it."[4] In this context, the opposite seems to be the case: with the naming, a new phase of the history of memory began.

The historian Peter Novick has closely examined the process by which the Holocaust gradually came to occupy the center of American culture following a period of relative indifference.[5] His book is not only an impressive example of mnemohistory (the history of memory) but also offers up a diagnosis of social developments and makes interventions into current debates about social values. He reconstructs the chronology beginning with the first two decades after the end of the Second World War in which there was no general interest in the topic and shows how, since the 1970s, the Holocaust gained its name and its particular focus, weakening its connection to World War II and, in the 1980s and above all in the '90s, making it into a global icon of guilt and trauma. Novick not only pursues this direction in the culture of the United States, but also looks at the impact this crescendo of memory has had on American culture and society, "thousands of kilometers away from the place and 50 years after the time of the event" (11). His criticism of the American engagement with the mass murder of the Jews is twofold. On the one hand, he argues that the general acceptance of the Holocaust as a key symbol in an American orientation toward the past "costs nothing and is painless." Of course Novick is not referring to material expense here; rather, because such an engagement involves no confrontation with one's own guilt, it is therefore, according to Novick, apolitical, uncontested, and inconsequential (350).

The other point of his critique has to do with the important role played by the Holocaust in the development of a new Jewish-American identity during a time when group identities were privileging victim status "on the basis of race, ethnicity, gender or sexual orientation" (8). In this respect, he alludes not only to problems that arise in the context of identities that are constructed on the basis of a victim culture but also to a change in attitude on the part of American Jews toward their surroundings. He is of the opinion that "the centering of the Holocaust in the minds of American Jews has contributed to the erosion of that larger social consciousness that was the hallmark of the American Jewry of my youth—post-Holocaust, but pre-Holocaust-fixation" (10).

Shortly after Novick's book came out, a work by Norman Finkelstein appeared that can, in certain respects, be seen as the work of someone "jumping on the bandwagon." Written in substantially shriller tones than Novick's work, Finkelstein's essay introduces the concept of the "Holocaust Industry." In his book, he differentiates between two versions of the Holocaust: written in capital letters, THE HOLOCAUST refers to an ideological construct that is marketed and deployed as a political weapon; by contrast, the historical event is designated with the words "mass extermination of the Jews by the Nazis." Finkelstein is writing as the American son of Jewish parents who survived the concentration camps and who have the event "in their bones" as a traumatic primary experience. Against this backdrop, he resists all forms of idealized religiosity, symbolic consolidation, and ritual stagings of memory, in all of which he sees only the expression of ideological delusions and collective self-interest. Despite all of the differences in temperament and presentation, Finkelstein's position is very close to Novick's cosmopolitan orientation. He too resists a particularistic appropriation of the Holocaust as the foundational myth of a new form of Jewish collective identity.

Although he does not cite him by name, the sociologist Jeffrey Alexander writes against Finkelstein's premises. The clear line that is drawn by Finkelstein between the actual historical Holocaust and its representation in the media seems to be methodologically out of the question for him. According to Alexander, since there is no direct access to the past and we are always engaged in ways of making the past present, historical events are always already mediated, represented, and culturally encoded. As soon as trauma is no longer an individual medical diagnosis and becomes a generalized concept, the issue starts to involve representations that have been culturally constructed within a more general framework. The notion of construction here is in no way equivalent to fiction; rather, it might be comparable to social fact or social reality. Alexander emphasizes that all facts regarding trauma are emotionally, intellectually, and morally mediated. "This screen has a trans-individual cultural status; it is symbolically structured and sociologically determined."[6] As he suggests, no trauma interprets itself; interpretation necessarily happens in the context of the discursive frameworks that he seeks to examine, beginning with the immediate postwar period and moving up to the present. He realizes too that the Holocaust was not always what it is today; rather, it only acquired the cognitive and moral status it has for the historical consciousness of a society as a consequence of a long and protracted process. What was experienced as a trauma by the victims who were directly affected was, for a very long time, not considered as such by the society to which these victims had returned. For it to become a trauma, the unrepresentable first had to be represented, and, beyond issues of representation, forms of identification and empathy had to be generated. This cultural work on trauma had to be accompanied by interpretations of the Holocaust, which had gone from being a narrative of progress in the 1950s to becoming a tragic narrative in the '80s and '90s. Thus Alexander traces the processes by which the Holocaust was universalized, first by being consolidated into a discourse of uniqueness and then becoming a free-floating signifier that allowed for the development of analogies. In contrast to Novick and Finkelstein, he describes the significance of Holocaust discourse not only for America, but also worldwide in terms of the development of a transnational universal ethics. It is obviously the case that in the process of this universalization, the specific conceptual content of the word would become somewhat thinner.

Halbwachs's Theory of a Framework of Memory

Here we return once again to the notion of a framework of memory, which we have just encountered in relation to false memory. Wherever there is a collective incentive to homogenize that puts a normative grid on top of heterogeneous individual memories, the influence of social or political frameworks of memory is at work. In *On Collective Memory*, Maurice Halbwachs introduces the idea that we always reconstruct our memories "under the pressure of society."[7] These social frameworks reflect, as he says, "the commands of our present society"[8] in which modes of perception, structures of bias, and collective self-images that are relevant at any given time have been taken up. We always remember, according to Halbwachs, *in the present and under the pressure of society*, which means that the past is always already made to conform to our current conditions and desires. Far from Proust's search for lost time and authentic memory, Halbwachs defines memory as "a reshaping operation as it applies to the past" (49). He argues that we can never really escape the dictates of the present (except maybe in dreams) and that our personal memories are generated and communicated exclusively in such social frameworks. So, just as we would never be able to perceive anything "without the help of the thinking of the group" in which we live, so too we could not develop or communicate any memories without this social support (363). So the group or society is not something exterior to the formation of memories; rather, that group both encompasses and forms precisely the private or inner person, who for Halbwachs is always already a social person.[9]

Other theoreticians have formulated arguments that are similar to Halbwachs's. For American philosopher George Herbert Mead, "the estimate and import of all histories lies in the interpretation and control in the present.... The implication of [Halbwachs's] position is that the past is such a construction that the reference found in it is not to events having a reality independent of the present which is the seat of reality."[10] The French philosopher Jean-Paul Sartre put the same point this way: "The meaning of the past is strictly dependent on my present project.... I alone can decide at each moment the *bearing* of the past: I do not decide it by debating it, by deliberating over it, and in each instance evaluating the importance of this or that prior event; but by projecting myself toward my ends, I preserve the past with me, and by action I decide its meaning."[11] These thinkers all agree on what we could call a nonessentialist understanding of the past. The word is misleading, though, in that it feigns an objective status that the past precisely does *not* have: its existence is always dependent upon acts of recollection—that is, on representations and frameworks of interpretation and on constructions belonging to a particular present, which are directed by contemporary needs and desires. By means of such social frameworks, personal memories become both meaningful and social. In turn they become communicable and a common possession that holds the group together. Since the world and societies change over time, social frameworks also change. Things that were unimportant yesterday can suddenly become highly topical once again. For example, the year 1945 was much more distant from us [in Germany—Trans.] in 1962 or 1975 than it was in 2003 or 2005. A social framework of memory first had to be established for the recognition to take place of the many histories that are meanwhile pressing to be heard. As long as the normative values were those of honor and fatherland or guilt and nation, there was no attention paid to stories involving German experiences of suffering.[12]

As a theorist of reconstructed memories in the present, Halbwachs could not conceive of a past that had some degree of independent power and influence over the present.[13] The questions that he posed in 1925 are crucially important today as we examine the memory of National Socialism even if the answers he gives to them are not always particularly satisfying for us. He was conducting his studies on memory after the First World War, and, oddly enough, he does not discuss its traumatic effects on families and on society at all.[14] What could still be ignored in the first decade after the First World

War can, however, no longer be denied many decades after the Second World War: we live in the shadow of a past that encroaches upon the present and haunts successive generations with emotional conflicts and moral dilemmas.

Martin Walser has often commented on this topic of memory frameworks and in doing so takes up a position that is diametrically opposed to that of Halbwachs (whom he does not name and whose work he perhaps does not even know). In his autobiographical novel from 1998, *Ein springender Brunnen* [A Leaping Fountain], he delves into the problem of irreconcilable frameworks and speaks out against the normative dictates of the present over the past. In this context, he does not speak of frameworks but, significantly, of roles:

> Some have learned to reject the past. They develop a more convenient past. They do this for the sake of the present. We experience all too acutely what kind of past we should have had if we separate ourselves from the currently dominant present. . . . The past as role. Not much in our arsenal of consciousnesses and comportments has the character of a role as much as the past does. It is wishful thinking to believe that men with different pasts could hope to live together as the different people that they, by virtue of their pasts, are. In reality, our relation to the past becomes more tightly regulated with every passing decade. As this relation becomes more and more regulated, the more our conception of the past is shown to be a product of the present.[15]

While Halbwachs suggests that the work of reconfiguring the past is a social fact and so is outside of our control, Walser sees it as a form of dissimulation and self-deception. In this sense, he takes the side of Proust, who wanted to free himself from the *mémoire volontaire* by means of which we adapt the past to our requirements and open himself up (if not in an uninterrupted way) to *mémoire involontaire*, which he hopes will be a muse for his autobiographical project. "To desire a present for the past over which we are not masters. . . . The goal of wishful thinking: a disinterested interest in the past. If only it could come to us of its own accord."[16]

Walser has been criticized for not having mentioned the word *Auschwitz* in a novel that explicitly engages with the past. This criticism is a typical example of how the interests of the present govern the way in which the past is taken up in public discourse. In fact, Walser had already anticipated this dilemma ten years earlier when he wrote:

> I have the feeling that I am not utterly free in my relationship with my memories. For example, it is impossible for me to adjust an established memory in light of a newly acquired fact. . . . The images [of my memories] remain unchanged. Noth-

ing that I have experienced since has altered these images.... My knowledge of the crimes of the Third Reich remains separate from my previously formed memory. In any case this is so as long as the memory remains private. As soon as I would like to allow someone else into this world, I realize that I cannot communicate the purity of my memory.... I'm obliged to speak of the Third Reich in the terms set out by today so that nothing is left but the one speaking in the present. One more person, who speaks of the past as if he had been then who he is today.... Most representations of the past are therefore reports on the present.[17]

Walser is making every attempt here to keep separate what coincides in Halbwachs's understanding of frameworks of memory. He does not want to engage in self-deception, which is of course commendable and, as part of a literary project, also convincing. Walser's concern has to do with the (literary) authenticity of the past, and this must, at all costs, be kept separate from a social construction in the present. His pure memories, he writes, are incommunicable, however. Walser agrees with Halbwachs on the point that, as soon as he enters into the social sphere, he is also bound to its social frameworks, in which case he should also be in a position to realize how untenable the innocence of memories regarding a brutal dictatorship is.

The differences between the two authors' positions become clearer if we take into account the different media that form their respective points of departure. While Halbwachs is thinking primarily about spoken communication, Walser's focus is on literary writing. While it is true that we are integrated into our environment by means of oral communication, we can also disengage ourselves from this communicative framework a little through writing and make it into an object of our reflection. Max Frisch had already drawn attention to this difference, writing in a note to his work *Wilhelm Tell: A School Text*: "If we, like the *Ur*-Swiss of those days had only oral tradition (the pub, grade school, etc.), there would, for instance, have been no pro-Hitler upper bourgeois and officers etc. in the Switzerland of 1933 to 1945 after a mere quarter century of oral tradition."[18]

According to Frisch, historical documents and sources act as necessary correctives for frameworks of memory; they are the rock on which the inaccuracies of memory get broken up. Sometimes families have written documents, too, though they can easily be gotten rid of when they don't conform to the prevailing self-image. It should perhaps be added that the plasticity of memory that Halbwachs so vividly describes only really holds true for oral traditions; he does not take into account how written sources are often in conflict with the dictates of the present and can make their own claim on the past. Without a feeling for the alterity of the past, we could never develop a historical consciousness but rather would live in an eternal present.[19]

Wilkomirski's memories—inauthentic, but correct—are comparable to other memories like Walser's, which are authentic but not correct. Like Wilkomirski, Walser also insists on the radical difference between the past of his experience and the present of his remembering. In that sense, for him too, what matters is the authenticity of his recollections, which he wants to save from the falsifications of retrospective influence. Walser is broaching a limit of communicability here, but one that has nothing to do with the idea that, for some memories, there are simply no words to be found. The issue here is not about how articulable his memories are, but rather how communicable and socially acceptable they are, in a society in which presuppositions and attitudes have altogether changed. And the greater the discrepancy between the experiences of the past and the system of validation in the present, the stronger the pressure will be to make this past conform to the norms of the present. The result would be, as Walser well knows, a past that is "completely closed, screened, cleansed, permitted and utterly appropriate."[20]

The comparison of Walser to Wilkomirski shows that the question about the truth of memories not only has a psychological aspect to it but also has a social dimension. Whether memories are taken to be true or not depends not least upon whether or not they are seen as being correct—that is, on whether or not they are communicable within a public sphere of communication and acceptable within a particular social framework.

The question regarding correct and incorrect memories also involves questions of genre and institutional contexts. First, the question of genre: Wilkomirski retroactively tried to mitigate the problem of the truth of his book by claiming that "it is at the discretion of the reader to take my book as literature or as a personal document"[21] The distinction he is making here has to do with various genres, also articulated through the categories established by publishers and bookshops: the genres of history, testimony, and documentary have to do with historically accurate portrayals and accounts; the fiction genre, as we know from Aristotle, concerns itself not with truth but probability (which is also the case with the genres of fictional autobiography and historiographical metafiction): with literature, greater license is taken with historical truth. Wilkomirski's book contains facts couched in a biographical fiction. So he cannot very well leave it to his readers to resolve the problem of truth; rather, this must happen precisely at the level of genre and in the pact entered into between author and reader. The genre of witnessing commits the author as moral witness not only to the truth of the factual (*What is it precisely* that I went through?) but also to the truth of the biographical (what is it that *I went through*?). Therefore, as Sigrid Weigel has noted, there can be no fictional testimony, only a simulated one.²² Second, institutional contexts always have corresponding norms and communicative parameters: Martin Walser generated a great deal of controversy and confusion on the occasion of his being awarded the 1998 Peace Prize in St. Paul's Cathedral in Frankfurt precisely because his speech failed to meet the criteria of this genre. Whoever delivers an official speech of this kind will invariably offend the sensibilities of his or her audience if, instead of offering sober reflections, he or she resorts to breaking taboos and issuing idiosyncratic complaints, however well-intentioned those may be.

The Jenninger Case

The most charged example of an incorrect memory is the official speech made by Philipp Jenninger, president of the German Bundestag, on November 10, 1988, in a special session devoted to commemorating the fiftieth anniversary of *Kristallnacht* (as it was called at the time). Just as Walser had been criticized for not having used the word *Auschwitz* in his autobiographical novel, so too was Jenninger criticized for not having used the words *grief* or *mourning* in his speech. What transpired during this public commemoration? What taboo was Jenninger guilty of breaking?

Jenninger had no intention of distancing himself from this speech. Heinz Galinksi, then-chair of the Central Council of Jews in Germany, could have intervened in the proceedings, although Jenninger had already rejected such an intervention in an argument that appears at the very beginning of his speech: "Today we find ourselves together in the German Bundestag, in Parliament to remember the pogrom of November 9 and 10, 1938, because, not the victims, but we ourselves, in whose midst the crimes took place, must remember and make a reckoning; because we Germans want to become clear in our understanding of our history and in the lessons it has for the political organization of our present and future."²³ He might well have taken the general direction for his speech from a text by historian Christian Meier, who demands that we "pose the question to ourselves as to how such a thing [that is, such an unimaginable crime as the Holocaust—A.A.] could happen." Such would be "a memory in which those doing the remembering would, at least intellectually, be exposed to attempts and difficulties, to endless entanglements—instead of the morally certain but inconsequential form of remembering to which we have grown so accustomed."[24] Jenninger had intended no less for the Bundestag commemoration, which he had chosen to develop into a peculiar kind of history lesson.

In his overview of the period between 1933 and 1938, he begins by highlighting how the constitutional state of Germany had been transformed into an illegitimate one, and how such a process met with the general willingness of Germans. With a view to "Hitler's political victory parade," he even speaks of a "fascination" and reconstructs—using mostly direct speech—the general public opinion of the then-contemporaries, those who were just as responsive to Hitler's achievements as they were unresponsive to the suffering of the Jewish population. People blamed the Jews themselves for their fate: "And if things got even worse, as they did in November 1938, one could always just say, in the words of one contemporary, 'Why should we care about it? If you're horrified, just look the other way. That's not going to be our destiny.'"[25]

Jenninger contrasts this understanding of the German mentality of the time with his reflections, warnings, and citations from great authors, along with an extensive eyewitness account of a 1942 mass murder of Jewish people. He delivered the entire speech in a flat tone of voice, so that one could not make out either the particular emphasis he wanted to give or his personal investment. What he said publically was one thing; what his public heard was another. While he was speaking, an atmosphere developed in the room that was a combination of outrage, embarrassment, and shame. Such an atmosphere makes it virtually impossible to listen in a focused way: one hears only what one does not want to hear, or what one is afraid of hearing. Regardless of how well-intentioned it was as a text, its effect as a performance was utterly scandalous.

The disastrous overall impression of the speech can be attributed not only to the miscellany of quotations combined with the flat voice in which he delivered it, but also to the optics of the event. The Jewish actress Ida Ehre was sitting right next to Jenninger's podium and had just finished reciting Celan's *Todesfuge* before Jenninger's speech. In pictures, she is seen covering her face with her hand while he was speaking. Most probably, this gesture contributed to the potentially scandalous effect of the speech: one could react with nothing short of outrage when it had so obviously pained and shocked the Jewish woman!

When Jenninger finished his speech and many audience members were indignantly leaving the hall, a few things looked a bit different. Ida Ehre, when asked about her impression of Jenninger's speech, stated that she had heard almost nothing of it. The recitation of Celan's poem had left her so shaken that the rest of the commemorative event had for the most part escaped her.[26] Jenninger later realized his mistake in having spoken right after Ida Ehre's recitation. He should not have followed Ida Ehre's reading of Paul Celan's poem. "'It was so moving,' he said, and then, 'but not the ideal preparation for a sober historical speech.'"[27] Here too the question can be raised regarding the appropriate genres and speech acts of commemorative ceremonies. A dry history lecture is clearly the wrong genre for such an occasion. Jenninger's speech made visible the normally invisible border that separates the social memory of Germans from their political memory. On the one side, there is a lot of room for the exchange of perspectives and for critical self-questioning. On the other side, this is not the case: the historical-political positioning of the state must be summed up in effective symbols and clear language. Arguments, voices of dissent, and instruction are obviously out of place in the speech act of a ceremonial commemoration; they destroy the somberness and the ceremoniousness of the occasion. At this level, where a ritualized statement must send a clear signal not only to the victims of National Socialism but also to neighboring European states, there is simply no place for Jenninger's inner struggle with culpability, as important as this might be in other contexts. Jenninger's speech fell far short of the need for clarity, and the day after his speech he resigned his Bundestag presidency.

Jenninger's speech could provide German politicians with schooling in the rituals of commemoration; they could learn from his mistakes.[28] So there is clearly something like a grammar of commemoration that structures the general conditions for the success of rituals. That Jenninger's speech was not false in the sense of contradicting the facts has been repeatedly demonstrated since then. This was best shown when Ignatz Bubis, Galinski's successor as chair of the Central Jewish Council of Germany, put it to the test. In the mid-1990s, he read the taboo speech aloud, to vigorous applause. Only afterward did he reveal its source. Jenninger's "incorrect" speech is often compared to the "correct" speech that Bundestag president Richard von Weizsäcker had given three years earlier. Effusive praise on the one hand and condemnation on the other not only demonstrates the difference between a successful and heart-wrenching speech and one that is both unsuccessful and confusing; it also reveals something of the deep-seated uncertainty Germans feel in dealing with the genre of commemoration.

As scandals, Jenninger's speech to the Bundestag and Walser's speech in the Church of St. Paul had greater impact on the German history of memory than any appropriate event or function could ever have. Walser reported that he received a thousand letters regarding his speech; in the case of Jenninger, three thousands letters were received.[29] It would be worthwhile to collect these letters and save them in an archive. Should there be historians in one hundred years' time who wish to write about the 1980s and '90s of the past millennium, they might find these letters of interest.

Useful and Useless Memories

The dependence of memories on overarching frameworks of memory can be demonstrated on all kinds of levels. We are not conscious of the normative force of such frameworks so long as we remain in unison with them; we don't feel them as a source of inner orientation, but only ever as forms of external pressure. They become particularly noticeable when they are replaced due to shifts in necessities, interests, and values. If we take Halbwachs's theory of the frameworks of memory seriously, we could say that memories on the collective level are not forgotten when they become dysfunctional or useless, but are displaced. Peter Novick has shown how memories that had been dysfunctional for a long time can become functional by means of a new framework of memory. His example is the memory of the suicide by Jews imprisoned in Masada prison, which has been entirely absent from Jewish memory for over 2,000 years, "though the text describing the event was readily available. This was not because Masada was a 'trauma' that was 'repressed' but because traditional Judaism focused on survival and holy study rather than on military resistance.... Zionists in the twentieth century found Masada more relevant to their self-understanding and self-representation, and a new collective memory emerged."[30] As a counter-example of a useful memory turned useless, Novick cites the scriptural book of Esther stories with their implicit revenge fantasy. These were ritually brought to life during the festival of Purim, but have subsequently disappeared from those rituals in the age of ecumenism.

Radical regime changes and changes in political systems are also always accompanied by changes in memory frameworks. The toppling of Lenin statues from their pedestals and the renaming of streets and public squares after 1989 are powerful examples of these dynamics. Generally less well-known are the kinds of distortions in memory that took place in 1945. Peter Novick explains the American silence around the theme of the Holocaust after the war and into the 1950s by emphasizing the political worthlessness of this memory. After the war, a far-reaching ideological reorientation took place in the United States, "after which talk of the Holocaust was not just unhelpful but actively obstructive."[31] In the context of the Allied forces, Americans and Russians fought against the Germans, their irreconcilable enemies. "All of this changed with breathtaking speed after 1945. The Russians were transformed from indispensable allies to implacable foes, the Germans from implacable foes to indispensable allies. . . . The apotheosis of evil—the epitome of limitless depravity—had been relocated, and public opinion had to be mobilized to accept the new worldview."[32] In the context of the Cold War, remembering the Holocaust was useless in the sense that it would have undermined this new military alliance. The creation of a victim culture and the changes that took place in 1989 were what first eased this framework of memory (or rather, of forgetting) and shifted the course of things in favor of memories.

SIX

Five Strategies of Repression

In the introduction, we touched on how inventive the human psyche can be, especially when it comes to developing strategies against guilt. The primary form of defense against guilt is justification. As early as the book of Genesis, with its story of the first fratricide, we find a guilt-ridden Cain responding to the question "Where is your brother?" with the knee-jerk justification of "I do not know. Am I my brother's keeper?" An admonition is always the best defense when the aim is to alleviate the weight of a bad conscience. The history of memory in Germany offers many powerful examples of such strategies for alleviating guilt and easing its burden, five of which shall be introduced and developed here by means of brief examples: these five strategies are offsetting, externalizing, erasure, remaining silent, and outright falsification. In general, these strategies all reflect a deep desire to dispose of the past: while this desire undoubtedly characterizes the mentality of a majority of Germans after the war, it can in fact surface in all kinds of situations, whenever the impetus is to save face before oneself or others, maintain a positive self-image, or dissociate or distance oneself from painful, shameful, or unsettling experiences.

Offsetting

First, the tactic of offsetting, which is frequently used both as a strategy against guilt and as a way of discharging it,[1] shall be illustrated by means of two paradigmatic statements from the proceedings of the Nuremburg trials. They both come from Hans Frank, ex-governor-general of the occupied Polish territories. The first took place during the proceedings from Maundy Thursday in 1946. Under the pressure of that day's cross-examination, he took responsibility for the extermination of the Jews—a spectacular exception among the many accused—and even added the following: "A thousand years will pass and still Germany's guilt will not have been erased."[2] What is striking about this statement is how it reflects the mythical style so characteristic of the mentality and language of the Nazi functional elite: instead of a thousand-year reign of glory, a thousand-year reign of guilt comes to take its place.

The second comes six months later and contains Frank's closing statement before the Nuremburg tribunal. The statement reads as follows: "The enormity of the heinous mass crimes that, as I have now discovered, have been and are still being perpetrated on Germans mostly in East Prussia, Silesia, Pomerania, and in Sudetenland by Russians, Poles, and Czechs, these crimes even now completely eradicate whatever possible guilt our people might have."[3] The perpetrator seeks refuge in the memory of a victim: what we have here is the enduring model of an age-old and extremely tenacious strategy of self-exculpation. In this rhetoric of offsetting, one guilt is weighed against the other so that they mathematically cancel each other out, so to speak. Suffering and guilt, which here collide as irreconcilable opposites in a discourse of self-justification, then come to oppose each other in an equally direct way in the following generation. Many members of that first generation persisted in denying or contesting their shared responsibility for the crimes of Nazism by systematically presenting themselves as victims, which in turn meant that their children had to bear the guilt that they had refused. Being the heirs of the guilt from which their parents had dissociated themselves and actively engaging with it was one side of the memory project of the '68 generation, the other side being a reorientation toward the Jewish victims, whose testimonies they listened to and with whose histories and culture they sought to identify themselves.

Externalizing

Externalizing is an idea introduced by sociologist Rainer M. Lepsius.[4] It refers to the tactic by means of which one dissociates oneself from guilt and assigns it to others. Using this idea of externalizing, which is complemented by the notion of internalizing, Lepsius describes the different positions that each of the German states took with respect to the politics of the past: the East German state externalized insofar as it handed off guilt and responsibility to the West German state, while West Germany internalized by entering into a treaty with Israel and paying reparations. The idea of externalizing should also be extended here to include psychological phenomena so that we can distinguish an offensive strategy of externalization from a more defensive form. The offensive form is akin to the strategy of scapegoating that René Girard has explored. "It was him!" or "It was them!" is the cry befitting the creation of the scapegoat. In Germany, the entire Jewish people was forced into this role and was "eliminated" as the symbolic bearer of the guilt that had been attributed to them. After the war, this offensive strategy of externalization was replaced by the defensive form. So the formula became "It wasn't me . . . it was the others." Though superficially similar, this statement actually plays an entirely different role on the psychic landscape. For instance, the wording in the title of Hannes Heer's book *Hitler war's: Die Befreiung der Deutschen von ihrer Vergangenheit* ["It Was Hitler": The Liberation of the Germans From Their Past] does not make Hitler into a scapegoat for the Germans, but rather has to be understood in the context of a strategy of belated apologetics.[5]

As an example of this kind of externalization, I am relying on a document that appeared in 1999 in German translation but was already available in 1946 in its original English.[6] It is a report from an American Jew by the name of Saul Padover who, born in Vienna in 1905, was a medieval historian by profession. As an unarmed intelligence officer, beginning in 1944, he accompanied advancing American troops from Belgium to Germany. Using the medium of the interview, his assignment had been to research the attitudes of Germans before the end of the war, taking as broad a sampling as possible. The dossier that he created for the Office for Strategic Services contains a summary as well as a record of hundreds of conversations with Germans from every profession and age group.[7] Padover's dossier is exceedingly interesting for our understanding of the German history of memory. With great clarity and vividness, it reveals another pattern of repression to which Germans often resorted when it became clear to them that the war was a lost cause. The attitude of the overwhelming majority of those with whom Padover came into contact was a unanimous condemnation of National Socialism, although it was a condemnation that categorically rejected a shared responsibility of any kind. Padover registers a "traumatic shock of Stalingrad" that led to a radical change of mood, without however promoting a change in disposition. He writes that the tendency of Germans "to pin all the blame and responsibility on Hitler should have been attentively registered. From a psychological point of view, Germans wanted to avoid punishment and moral responsibility, in that they offered to the world the guilty party, one they had worshipped as a demi-god just a little while before." There was no hint of self-reflection in this condemnation of Hitler. No one, he continues, "criticizes the aggression as such. What is criticized is the failed aggression. Hitler is criticized for having lost the way and not for having started it."[8]

This mode of interpreting one's own experience of the Nazi past was the best way to adapt to the newly formed Federal Republic. In his autobiographical novel, Uwe Timm shows how after the war, this posture was reflected in the communicative memory of small family groups and circles of friends:

> My father could not allow himself to grieve, only to feel anger, but because he saw courage, duty, and tradition as inviolable virtues he directed his anger not at the real causes but only at military bunglers, shirkers, traitors. That was the subject of his conversation with his old comrades. They came around in the evening, sat together, drank coffee and cognac and talked about the war. They tried to find explanations for why it had been lost. Battles were fought all over again, wrong orders put right, incompetent generals dismissed, Hitler deprived of his command of the army. It is hardly imaginable now to think of that generation discussing such subjects all evening.[9]

This stance, which had not yet resigned itself to the recent political turn of events, focused on figuring out whom to blame. By identifying the guilty party, one turns oneself into an innocent victim. The victims assert their own victimhood by means of complaints and accusation. One was lied to and deceived; one knew nothing of the atrocities; under the conditions of tyranny, there was no question of resistance; only the Nazis are guilty, while the Germans are innocent because they were only following orders.

Even before the end of the war, Saul Padover analyzed this prevalent way of reacting and draws the following compelling conclusion from his interviews:

> We have been out and about here for two months, we have spoken to a lot people, asked a lot of questions, and we haven't found a single Nazi. Everyone is an opponent of Nazism. Everyone is against Hitler. They were always against Hitler. What does this mean? It means that Hitler carried out whole thing entirely alone, without help or support from any Germans. He started the war, conquered the entirety of Europe, overran most of Russia, murdered five million Jews, killed seven to eight million Poles and Russians through starvation, established four hundred concentration camps, built up the largest army in Europe and on top of all that, ensured that the trains ran on time.
>
> *(46)*

After the war, strategies that were developed in relation to accusations of guilt were similar on both the individual and collective levels. Typical in this regard is the appeal made to the so-called superior orders, where the blame is to be placed on one's superiors, as well as in the notion of a criminal gang, from which one can readily distance oneself. The most radical variation of these exercises in self-exculpation consisted of drawing a line between the guilty Hitler and the innocent German people who had been "misled" and so became Hitler's victims.[10] This same strategy of externalization was repeatedly deployed in different situations and political configurations, and the line between innocence and guilt was constantly being shifted and redrawn. After the war, Christian Meier observes that we completely turned away "from what the Germans had been in the years between 1933 and 1945, wanting it not to have been *us*."[11] The GDR established the line between guilt and innocence as that separating the Federal Republic from themselves; the 1968ers drew it between themselves and the generation of their parents; Daniel Goldhagen can also be affiliated with this perspective, for he draws it between innocent and guilty generations. The exhibition that dealt with the crimes of the Wehrmacht then served to blur that line between "respectable Germans" and "guilty Germans."

This strategy of externalization was followed by a tentative attempt at internalizing—that is, those born afterward began to acknowledge German guilt and to engage with it willingly. This willingness is still reflected in today's engagement with the legacy of National Socialism, whether through the literary genre of the family saga or through research done by the second and third generations. To the extent that those who were directly responsible for the crimes are disappearing, the tension seems to be dissipating, and there is an increased general willingness to participate in an engagement with guilt.

Erasure

Perhaps much of what Padover heard from his interviewees wasn't the whole truth. But how is one to determine the truth in these circumstances? Was there a lie detector that could break through the masks of self-protection with which Padover was repeatedly confronted [the German translation of Padover's work is *Lügendetektor*, or Lie Detector—Trans.]? Of course, I very much doubt that the problem here is one that could be solved with the help of a lie detector. For the problem lies much deeper, since the Germans, who were being asked to give information about their own attitudes here, quite possibly lied not only to the American officer but also, and in the first instance, to themselves.[12] Their moral sense and their personal conscience had been anaesthetized when they adopted an inflexibly self-centered ideology of the collective and internalized a brutally functionalistic bureaucracy. The old anti-Semitic prejudices had been raised to the level of an ideology that focused on the irreconcilability of Germans and Jews and that had been stylized into an either/or survivalist alternative. The old and deeply internalized phantasm according to which the existence of Jews posed an immediate threat to Christians was being replayed using racist premises. Now, the deep insecurity was no longer to be found in the threat that Judaism posed to sanctified Christian symbols—and in particular, the consecrated host—but in a paranoid anxiety regarding the sacred purity of the body and blood of the German people.

Because this long tradition of engrained cultural prejudices had been passed on for generations, any possibility of empathy being exercised toward Jews by the vast majority of the population was undermined at the very point that Jews were being stripped of their rights, humiliated, tormented, persecuted, deported, and murdered. The foreignness of the Jewish people and the indifference toward them, learned over centuries and millennia, drastically narrowed perceptual horizons. What should have been an object of criticism, outrage, revulsion, grief, indeed, of trauma, was closed off from awareness and banished from consciousness. One couldn't very well draw upon such an amputated moral sensibility later on. In a psyche that had been distorted so fundamentally and for so long, the tasks of relearning, rethinking, and indeed of "refeeling" were well-nigh impossible. That also clarifies why, after the war, guilt and responsibility were externalized—that is, detached and transferred onto a small group of criminals. It was always the *others* who were guilty; there was always another perpetrator onto whom one could pin one's own guilt.

The problem of Germany's history of memory begins precisely at this point. It is impossible for something to become an object of memory that is not really registered at the time, owing to resistances and defense mechanisms. The logic of memory is extremely simple: in order to be able to remember something, a memory trace is required. To have a memory trace, something first had to have been perceived and stored that can be later called up as a memory. One cannot remember blind spots. Freud puts it in the following way: something that "could never have been 'forgotten,' because it was never at any time noticed—was never conscious" can also not be remembered in hindsight.[13] Since Freud, the branch of cognitive psychology that focuses on errors and gaps in memory has paid a great deal of attention to this problem. Psychologist Daniel L. Schacter's "seven sins of memory" differentiates between two types of errors: errors of retention and errors of recall. In accordance with Schacter's schema, the blind spots of the Germans would correspond to an error of retention that came about through a lapse of attention during the act of perception. Schacter writes, "A good deal of forgetting likely occurs because insufficient attention is devoted to a stimulus at the time of encoding or retrieval or because attended information is processed superficially. Such incidents of forgetting associated with lapses of attention during encoding or during attempted retrieval can be described as errors of absent-mindedness."[14]

Psychologists and neuroscientists who examine the dynamics of remembering and forgetting at the level of individual brain function confirm that the memory is not a static container in which experiences are conserved in an unchanged state. Personal remembering is a dynamic process in which one's involvement in the past varies depending on the conditions and requirements of the present. So, one admits precisely as much of the past as one needs or can tolerate. The same goes for memory and its social and political framework. Society determines frames of reference and modes of interpretation both for the perception of the present and, belatedly, for memory: these social structures are decisive for how and what (of the past) should claim attention and be brought forward. Changes to the framework of memory are dependent upon internal and external factors. The most important of these are the following:

Social: Generational shifts within a society
Domestic politics: A change in political system, as happened, for instance, with German reunification

Foreign affairs: The relation to other states like the United States, Israel, and European neighbors. Some of these neighbors, like England and France, belonged to the victorious Allied forces, and some of them, such as Austria or Italy, were in close collaboration with Germany. However, all of them, Poland and Russia especially, were victims of German aggression and its destructive violence.

Remaining Silent

As we saw earlier, remaining silent has two sides: the speechless silence [*das sprachlose Schweigen*] of the victim is the expression of a continued lack of power, and the silence of the perpetrator, insofar as it is about concealment [*das Verschweigen*], can be understood as the expression of a continued power.[15]

Silence is also an essential feature of the literature of high modernism, about which a great deal has been written. George Steiner has led the way in this research, repeatedly grappling with this theme in his various works.[16] According to him, modernism and the crisis of language are inseparable. He claims that, around the turn of the century, people were abandoned by language. Hofmannsthal's *The Letter of Lord Chandos* from 1903 stands as the paradigmatic example of the retreat of the essential into silence. But it was first with the historical experience of two world wars and in particular the Holocaust that the crisis of language took on the character of a collective trauma. Similarly, silence became a symptom of the excesses of an unlimited gratuitous violence that also shattered modes of mental processing and categories of language. "Before we know the event, the activity of the mind fails us," writes Lionel Trilling, and George Steiner emphasizes that the experience of the Holocaust lay "beyond the normative syntax of human communication."

In his 1958 Bremen speech, poet Paul Celan meditated on the condition of the German language, burdened as it is by complicity with the perpetrators and deformed as it has become under the pressure of trauma. The fragile esotericism of his poetic language, marked by trauma, retains an affinity with silence. Celan formulated in the following way the paradox of a speech that keeps silent and a silence that speaks:

> Reachable, near and not lost, there remained in the midst of the losses this one thing: language. It, the language, remained, not lost, yes in spite of everything. But it had to pass through its own answerlessness, pass through frightful muting,

pass through the thousand darknesses of deathbringing speech. It passed through and gave back no words for that which happened; yet it passed through this happening. Passed through and could come to light again, "enriched" by all this.[17]

The two forms of silence, that of the victim and that of the perpetrator, collided in dramatic ways on the occasion of a meeting between Paul Celan and Martin Heidegger. Between July 1967 and May 1970, the two of them met three times. Celan's poem "Todtnauberg" came out of the first meeting, a summer day trip from Freiburg to Heidegger's cabin in Todtnauberg. In that poem is a line, a slightly revised version of which Celan also wrote in the cottage guestbook: he wrote "about a hope, today, of a thinking man's coming word in the heart."[18]

Although there were two other meetings between the two, this hoped-for word from Heidegger never came. George Steiner sees this later silence of Heidegger's in the period from 1967 to 1970 as a greater scandal than his 1933–34 speeches as rector of Freiburg University. Much later a letter was discovered in the Literature Archive in Marbach that Heidegger had sent to Celan on January 30, 1968, six months after their encounter. In it, he thanks Celan for a first-edition copy of the poem "Todtnauberg," which Heidegger interpreted as a heroic monumentalization of himself and of the place where he worked. He is grateful that the language of the poet speaks "'Todtnauberg,' names the place and the landscape where thinking attempts to step back into the narrow." For him, the poem is "both encouragement and warning." Heidegger himself celebrated Celan as a second Hölderlin. With this comparison, not only did he assign Celan a central place in his system of values and in his thinking, but he also felt himself to be connected with Celan in a holy alliance of "poet and thinker [*Dichter und Denker*]." Prophetic gifts had been bestowed on both of them, and they were both destined to articulate existential experiences and interpret the inscrutable shape of the world. Such a destined connection was already clear to Heidegger from the very first meeting:

> But it already happened on the evening of your unforgettable reading when we first met at the hotel. [And then he abruptly continues.] Since then, we have remained silent with each other about many things.
>
> I think that one day, some of them will be brought out of the unspoken in conversation.

Insofar as he is able to, Heidegger is facing up to the demand of Celan's poem in these lines. Rather than recognizing the rupture between the Jew and the

German, Heidegger chooses the mythical figure of an alliance between the poet and the thinker. The silence is for him both the sign of this alliance and its medium. It does not separate the two masters of the word, but rather connects them, those two who are bound to each other in their silence about that which lies beyond words. Heidegger's lines are borne on the confidence that silence does not separate but rather binds the two all the more closely to each other in a wordless proximity.

Celan took this message in an entirely different way, however. For him, the meeting was not simply a rapprochement with a great philosopher but was also an extremely risky encounter between a traumatized Jew and a compromised German. Two further meetings took place, and still no German-Jewish dialogue ever came out of it. The last meeting between the two was very much characterized by the impossibility of communication. In the end, Celan's psychological strain led him to defend against any further attempts at rapprochement and appropriation. He took his own life four weeks later in Paris.

The episode between Heidegger and Celan played itself out between 1967 and 1970, during a time in which the protests of the '68 generation made it impossible for silence to continue as the self-evident response to the crimes of the Nazi regime. At that time, youth protests and revolts were gradually undermining the communicative silencing that had dominated the culture of the fifties. Heidegger, though, continued to embody the stance of this communicative silencing, which Hermann Lübbe later praised as a "mode of functioning geared toward the integration of the post-war population into the citizenry of the new republic."[19] However, when compared to Celan's, Heidegger's silence failed as "a mode of functioning geared toward integration," making palpable both exclusion and rupture. The silence that integrated the perpetrators was such that it prevented any bridge from being built to the victims.

However, this communicative silencing did make it possible to withdraw from the public realm in West German postwar society. The recent past disappeared from collective consciousness; engagement with it gave way to what Lutz Niethammer describes as the sinkhole of private coping.[20] The situation in the 1950s reflects not only the inability of postwar society to mourn but also its inability to engage in the democratic medium of public discourse and communication. The time-honored separation of private issues from politics in Germany continued to dominate and led to an atrophying of the public sphere. On top of that, silence was given a kind of heroic value, and the public sphere was accordingly devalued. Heidegger played a particularly important role in this devaluation by elevating silence as "another essential possibility of discourse," over "'idle talk'" and the "speaking that has forgotten being."[21] He dismissed public life as a "way of being of the 'They'" that is "insensitive to every difference of level and of genuineness." In the public sphere, Heidegger writes in *Being and Time*, "everything gets obscured, and what has thus been covered up gets passed off as something familiar and accessible to everyone."[22] That is to say, what is generally accessible to and known by everyone is, for that very reason, already worthless. Over and against a culture of public life and open dialogue, Heidegger values a culture of secrecy and silence. This same silence is also reflected in an entire generation of parents who said nothing to their own children and so have taken their secrets with them to the grave.

Falsification

In 2002, a collection appeared under the title *Verbrechen Erinnern* [Remembering Crimes]. It contains work by sociologist Harald Welzer, who carried out empirical studies on how German families transmitted the memory of National Socialism and the Holocaust. He writes, "While Germany has developed an enlightened practicable norm at the level of the politics of the past, of memory, and of commemorative culture, this still says nothing about how people remember the same past in non-public spheres, like the family for instance."[23] Immediately following, he anticipates the result of his study and claims that "contrary to popular opinion, neither Nazi crimes nor the Holocaust play an important role in German families—this in marked contrast to memories in which family members themselves appear as victims of the 'Third Reich,' as ordinary resistance fighters, but never as 'Nazis.'"[24]

According to Welzer's study, which goes into these results in detail, there are two different references made to the National Socialist past: one in terms of the retention of knowledge or *lexicon*, and one in terms of family memory or *album*. Once again, we see the category of cognitive knowledge of history (in the sense of a historical account that is as objective as possible) at odds with emotional memory (in the sense of a processing of experience from a particular viewpoint). Whereas in the first decades following the war, history had not yet been made a stable part of a socially binding framework of memory, grandchildren today grow up under the auspices of a historical curriculum that includes pedagogy on the Holocaust. The gap between public history and private memory can lead to experiences of cognitive dissonance and to moral dilemmas that can, however, be quietly rectified in the context of familial communication. The falsification of personal history takes place under the pressure to adapt to new moral standards. Under these conditions, problematic family members are transformed into moral beacons according to the new framework of memory. Welzer's findings are most striking when, as an exception, there had been talk in family circles about the guilt of certain family members for murders and shootings. These remarks were simply ignored or not heard, in stark contrast to how attentive family members were to references that proved useful for a positive account. "Some of the interviewees do talk about their experiences during the war in ways that show them as perpetrators. This does not, however, lead their listeners to dismay, to conflicts, or even to embarrassing situations. It leads to nothing at all. It is as if such tales were not heard by the family members present."[25]

As the powerful examples of Welzer and his research team have demonstrated, social memory is a highly malleable affair. It is not very good at reliably transmitting experiences, but it is good at conforming to the constantly changing frameworks of memory. In particular when it is passing through generations, family memory can be so flexible and versatile that on occasion it resembles the children's game of "telephone." Welzer rightly emphasizes that his "study of how the German past gets transmitted in inter-generational memory is not a study of the past but rather of the present."[26] This present is constantly shifting. And indeed, configurations, motives, and emphases have shifted in significant ways since the third postwar generation in Germany's history of memory has arisen. Not least, this includes a desire to see the old asymmetry dismantled that had so strongly determined German postwar memory.

Asymmetries in German Memory

The five strategies of repression are highly relevant to the social and individual memories of the Germans, but less so to statements made at the level of official politics. As much as Germans may have personally felt themselves to be Hitler's victims or his unwitting captives, it was obviously out of the question that this become the official doctrine concerning the politics of the past. In light of the strong tendency to develop ways of easing the burden of the past on the one hand and, on the other, the political responsibility that must be taken at the national level, a clear discrepancy of frameworks for remembering emerges that is characteristic of the German situation.

This asymmetry, which continues to give rise to tensions, scandals, and eruptions in Germany's history of memory, can be defined from both perspectives. On the one side, it must be noted that much of what is officially commemorated in Germany is not personally remembered. We see this even in the choice of the symbolically important official memorial days. In 1996, January 27 was made a new memorial day in the German national calendar. The liberation of Auschwitz by the Red Army took place on this day, and no Germans have any personal memory of it based on their own experiences. Those who had any personal experience of this place had already quickly left the scene of their crimes with the majority of surviving prisoners, before the Russians had even arrived. By contrast, November 9 has to do with historical dates like the pogrom of 1938 and the fall of the Berlin Wall in 1989, events that do resonate strongly in the biographies of individual Germans.[27] However, because of its ambivalence as both a national day of mourning and a day of celebration, November 9 has been eliminated as a national memorial day.

On the other side, much of what is personally remembered is not subsumed into the official political narrative. These elided memories bear particularly on German experiences of suffering, especially those undergone in the last phases of the war and in its immediate aftermath. Of concern in the next chapter shall be these individual memories and what might be at stake in their recovery. In that context, we will also need to ask if these memories really were subject to a decades-long communicative silencing and had no claim to being publicly recognized, represented, and communicated.

SEVEN

German Narratives of Victimhood

Commemorative years occurring in regular temporal intervals mark and produce the memory of historical events. In particular, national memory is made manifest on such occasions of ritualized memories. At the same time, since these occasions are also found in the engagement calendars of journalists, publishers, television editors, local politicians, and museum curators, public memory and official memory become intertwined with one another on such occasions. To understand the changes in Germany's history of memory, we need to ask to what dwindling extent the lived memory of those who were directly present still constitutes the basis for such occasions and how much of this is being transformed and replaced by media representations. The year 1985 is generally thought to be a threshold year for the memory of 1945: on May 8 of that year, Richard von Weizsäcker, then-president of the Bundestag, gave a commemorative speech that managed to shift the interpretation of the year of 1945 from defeat and catastrophe to liberation. In that regard, he also succeeded in shifting the general consensus of the Federal Republic over to the perspectives of surrounding nations and above all to the victims of National Socialism. To the extent that those who had lived through the experience of the war's end were decreasing in number, the willingness to reinterpret that experience intensified.

Klaus Naumann has likewise described the year 1995 as a "threshold year in memory culture."[1] After having closely examined the resonance in the press of that year, he realizes that contemporary witnesses to the period had played an important role for the last time. Most notably, he realizes that in comparison to 1985, a significant displacement had taken place in the themes of commemorative events, which were now focusing more on the issues of aerial bombing, escape, and expulsion. Not least, he sees this shift toward a victim perspective as a consequence of German unification, by virtue of which Dresden began to attract general interest as one of the more prominent memory sites, a status it had already had in the GDR. Naumann makes the further claim that there was a shift from ritual to dialogue—that is, from an imposing and solemn set of gestures to a critical questioning and problematization. Paradoxically enough, this questioning begins at the precise moment when the contemporary witnesses, those who could still have been questioned, were dying off.

Beginning in 1995, there has indeed been a gradual upsurge in accounts of German experiences of victimhood in the public discourse of memory. But we can now see in hindsight that the threshold was not 1995. The breaking wave, indeed the dam-bursting surge of these memories, would first happen seven or eight years later.

Aerial Warfare (W. G. Sebald and Jörg Friedrich)

The traumatic experiences of war suffered by the civilian population in Germany only gradually became a topic for public discussion. When this did eventually happen, the engagement focused largely on three sets of experience: the aerial bombardment of German cities, the rape of German women, and the expulsion of Germans from areas in Eastern Europe. All these experiences were in no way forgotten after the end of the war, but they could only be partially approached and in a very limited way. The wave of incidences of sexual violence was what social psychologists would call a "silent event." The social taboo against talking about it was so powerful that it didn't even have a place in the protected enclave of family memory.[2] By contrast, the memory of the expulsion not only played a large role in the memory of families but also resonated strongly in the public sphere (we shall return to this issue). Between the tabooed trauma of rape and the politicized trauma of expulsion, the third memory of victimhood among the German population involved the memory of the aerial bombardment of German cities by Allied forces. By no means did this memory disappear after the war. The memory of the nights spent in air-raid shelters, of the many dead and the blanket destruction of German cities was, to borrow a phrase from Avishai Margalit, a "common" but not "shared" (in the sense of socially communicated) memory.[3] Directly after the war, exchanges certainly took place about the terror of the nights of bombing that had just occurred; however, these exchanges never coalesced into an account to be borne, stabilized, and transmitted by society as a whole. Generally speaking, to play the role of Lot's wife and to look back into the debris and ashes was probably just too painful and humiliating, and it was generally thought to be more important to look to the future, to clear away the debris and begin the work of reconstruction.

W. G. Sebald's 1997 Zurich lecture series was devoted to searching for memory traces and for some trace of the pain left by the bombings in the memory of the Germans. In those lectures, he comes to the conclusion that this traumatic experience—buried in the foundation of the Federal Republic, along with its hundreds of thousands dead—never found any real literary expression.[4] He examines the postwar literature of authors like Böll, Andersch, and Peter de Mendelssohn looking for traces of this "shameful family secret" that "remained under a kind of taboo"[5] and comes to the conclusion that none of them had even come close to doing justice to the traumatic content of this experience. Given everything we have learned in the interim about trauma and the period of latency associated with it, Sebald's surprise at the absence of an appropriate working-through of this experience is itself surprising. His text is important because it itself possesses the character of a symptom in this whole psycho-historical process: it serves to indicate the completion of this latency period.

We now know that Sebald's search was not entirely exhaustive. Gert Ledig's 1956 novel *Vergeltung* escaped him,[6] as did the trilogy *Das Haus auf meinen Schultern* [The House on My Shoulders], by Dieter Forte (1992). The merit of Sebald's lecture series has less to do with the soundness of his argument than it does with his impetus even to recognize the problem and to raise it in such a way as to encourage serious debate. His foray enabled him to raise the veil of a taboo still hanging over German memories of victimhood. These memories had been stigmatized as a shameful abomination: it was feared that highlighting experiences that Germans had had as victims could serve to displace other experiences, namely those of the victims of the Holocaust that had finally been recognized and formalized in German society (the watchword here is "compensation"). And we shouldn't forget about the discourse regarding German experiences of victimhood that were associated with a strong right-leaning resentment. In 2002, at the same time as the publication of Grass's *Crabwalk* (which we'll come back to shortly), the book *Verbotene Trauer* [Forbidden Mourning] by Klaus Rainer Röhl appeared. The subtitle reads, "The End of a German Taboo."[7]

Like Grass, Röhl was born in 1928, grew up in Danzig, and was subject to the expulsion. His mother and his sister had tickets for the *Wilhelm Gustloff*, but they switched over to rail transport for fear of seasickness. Röhl's report would be an important and gripping testimony were it not so thoroughly poisoned by hatred and resentment. His portrayal is not a reworking of trauma, but rather an extension of it: it is a document attesting to anxiety, hatred, and bitterness. The representation of the past leads him to make one single argument against the terror of the Allied forces, against reeducation, against history, and against the foundations of the new German state. So the process of writing does not offer him the chance to loosen the grip of a traumatic cramping of memory, but rather serves to tighten it up into an ever-more threatening fist.

What is new about Sebald's and Grass's engagements with this taboo issue is that they are not being advanced by Holocaust deniers or relativists, and the usual rhetoric of resentment is entirely absent. Authors like Sebald and Grass are themselves renowned for attempting to integrate Jewish experiences of victimhood into German cultural memory. For them, the issue is not about making comparisons, and it is certainly not about weighing one experience of suffering against another, as it so clearly is for Röhl. There is no revisionist argument behind their desire to do justice to memory. They have no political agenda; theirs is a literary and therapeutic enterprise that seeks to consciously revive the traumatic experiences of history and to offer the chance of coming to terms with them after a certain period of latency.

After just sixty years, the psychic latency period of the trauma came to an end in Germany and an increasing need developed to approach a topic that strategies of defense had kept under wraps for so long. This work of recovering German memories of victimhood from their torpor and encapsulation did not meet with universal agreement and understanding, however. On the international scene, it unleashed disquiet and heavy resistance. How will the weights and balances of the international politics of memory shift? How can

Germans conform to the international image of the victim? Interesting in this context are some of the opinions voiced in *The New Yorker* in reaction to reviews of the American edition of Sebald's lectures. These letters to the editor reveal the contours of the new taboo. Someone who had experienced the German aerial attacks in Coventry wrote about how "shocked and insulted" they were by Sebald's book. Another accused Sebald of borrowing from Nazi rhetoric and of engaging in a moral relativism that he believes must be countered with the following admonition: "Hamburg, Dresden, and Berlin will be forever trumped by Auschwitz, Sobibor, and Buchenwald." This letter writer demands that Germans *publicly* remember the Holocaust but *privately* keep their own suffering to themselves.[8] Aside from how problematic such a demand may be, placing limitations on dialogue through editorial control is not easily enforced in the age of global information and communication technology. As soon as books like Sebald's or Grass's *Crabwalk* are translated, they reach an international literary audience.

In his lectures, Sebald points to a gap, a "self-imposed silence" or an "absence," that characterizes not only literature but is "also typical for other areas of discourse, from family conversations to historical writings." The only exception to this is one chapter in a work by military historian Jörg Friedrich.[9] Sebald died in 2001 and so didn't live to see Friedrich's 2002 study of the Allied bombings, *The Fire*, that would become an overnight bestseller and change the German memory landscape. The book provoked lively and controversial debate both in the public arena and among historians.[10] The book reconstructs the carpet-bombing of German cities from the perspective of Germans on the ground, bringing information into historical discourse that was known at the time but had been suppressed and distilling it into an argument. Friedrich portrays the Allied air offensive as a "war of destruction" against the German civilian population in general and against German culture in particular in terms of its architectural and cultural treasures.

The initial cause of the uproar in these debates was not the blurring of the boundaries between victims and perpetrators. It actually began with the language used. Over the previous two decades, engagement with the Holocaust had generated a standardized terminology that had been taken up meanwhile in the context of other traumatic experiences. When Nobel prizewinner Toni Morrison prefaced her novel *Beloved*, which is about the trauma of slavery, with a dedication to "Sixty Million and more," the reference to the six million Jewish victims of the Holocaust is unmistakable. When Günter Grass in his novella *Crabwalk* has the survivor of the *Wilhelm Gustloff*, the bombed and sinking cruise ship turned refugee carrier, say, "You've got to write it all down. . . . Someday I'll tell you the whole story, exactly what happened, and you'll write it all down," he is relating his literary work of memory to the genre of Holocaust testimony. When Jörg Friedrich in his book describes the bombing as a "collapse of civilization," the bomber fleets as "the Einsatzgruppen" ["task force" in English—Trans.], the burning bomb shelters as "gas chambers" or "crematoria," and the dead as "the exterminated,"[11] he is in effect using the language of the Holocaust to describe the suffering of Germans. Now the question becomes: is the Holocaust being used here as a paradigm of trauma to help in the articulation of other traumatic experiences, or should these writers be accused of using this kind of terminology in order to take part in a kind of competition between victims?

The fervent academic debate surrounding the book had less to do with the facts themselves than with the *representation* of the facts—that is, with their interpretation and evaluation within the existing framework of memory. Related questions then arose: do we need to maintain this framework of memory, or does it have to be replaced, rebuilt, or broadened? We also need to be clear that recognizing Germans as victims in no way minimizes or even neutralizes the basic situation of Germans as a perpetrator people. They find themselves on both sides, both on the perpetrator side and on the victim side. The more clearly we establish moral coordinates, the more stable the memory of the victims of the Nazi regime will be and the more readily will we be able to engage this experience of victimhood. But that can only happen if Germans are not passively stigmatized as a (symbolic) perpetrator people but rather themselves become active carriers of the memory of those victims. Once the Jewish experience of victimhood is rooted in German memory, other histories of suffering can be included in the picture without having to reorient or shift the entire framework. The traumas suffered by the German civilian population can only gain a position alongside the traumas suffered by the victims of the Holocaust after an awareness of historical connections has been established. It cannot be the case that Hamburg and Dresden are trumped or canceled out by Auschwitz and Treblinka. Rather, Hamburg and Dresden should be remembered together with Auschwitz and Treblinka. In an interview, Dieter Forte explains this historical nexus of perpetrator and victim experience in German memory:

> We committed a terrible injustice, and a war broke out because of it. The work by Gert Ledig is called *Payback*. That is the correct title, it says it all. Then came the "payback." When I describe this payback, the crux of the thing is indeed given.[12]

As unbefitting as the notion of trauma is in the context of the perpetrator, it is nonetheless clearly appropriate in the context of German experiences of victimhood. When writers and historians begin discussing these experiences a half-century after their occurrence, they are attesting to the end of a latency period, one that cannot be extended through acts of censorship.

By the turn of the new millennium, the time had come to face up to these experiences of suffering and give them a chance to be heard, if the latency period of trauma and its unconscious dynamics were not to be further drawn out. Having deeply frozen memories "thaw out" is always a risky business and can, as we know from the years following 1989, lead to certain disturbances in Europe's domestic bliss. Memories can upset the balance of powers, though, it has to be said, only when they are tied to resentment, hostility, and revenge. The memories themselves are not damaging, but the claims and arguments sometimes connected to them certainly can be. Clear boundaries must be established against those revisionist stances that seek to invert the positions of guilt and innocence. But no restrictions and taboos should be imposed on the memories themselves. On the contrary, when authors like Grass, Sebald, and Forte bring them back into cultural memory, those memories contribute to a gradual dissolving of taboo areas that can then be brought into a wider dialogue. For, the downward spiral of hate and violence can always come back into play through rationalizations, and it can only be interrupted in the long term once this traumatic history becomes narratable and has a chance of being heard with empathy.

When Memories Come Flooding Back

In 1997, Sebald points to a self-imposed silence or an absence in the context of the experience of the aerial war. In 2000, Grass marvels at "how lately and with such hesitation we remember the suffering inflicted on Germans during the war."[13] Grass wrote this when he was working on *Crabwalk*, the novella through which he sought to bring awareness to the theme of mourning those German victims. His book was only one of many media events in 2002 and 2003 that drew attention to German suffering, all of which were not so much aimed at changing attitudes as they were at introducing a change into the historical culture of suppressing emotion. In 2003, memories of the suffering that Germans had undergone fifty-eight years earlier broke out with unexpected force and particularly emotional intensity. The themes presented in the media by means of images and reports, books and films, interviews and documentaries and discussed with high degrees of emotional investment were focused on the expulsion and fleeing of Germans from the East, the carpet-bombing of German cities, and the mass rape of German women at the end of the war.

In an article for the *Süddeutschen Zeitung*, Ulrich Raulff asked why it was that these memories could not have waited until 2005, when they could have reentered public consciousness on the nice round number of sixty years.[14] This heavy burden of memory has returned, irritatingly enough, before an orderly memorial date. The return of memory—particularly those of a painful, unsettling, and shameful quality—follows other rhythms than those regulated by the calendar. Traumatization and social taboos inhibit memories over long periods of time, and this, in turn, causes them to emerge belatedly. Was it a question here of breaking a taboo? Had the duty finally come to an end to keep silent about an experience that, over long periods of time, had little chance of being brought up for discussion? To be sure, the topic of German histories of suffering is nothing new. In the context of families, they were told so often that they had assumed an almost formulaic shape. The writer Uwe Timm, born in 1940, was only a small child when he experienced the firebombing of Hamburg in July 1943. He retained only a few isolated images of this experience that he would include in an autobiographical text, written sixty years after the fact:

> Another clear picture, and my own memory begins here: huge torches to the right and left of the street. Burning trees.
> And this picture too: little flames floating in the air.[15]

Timm makes every effort to distinguish between the unsettling power of the images he himself retained from this experience and the family narrative that was formed retrospectively about these events on the other.

> It was not until later, when people talked about them, that the little flames floating in the air were explained: scraps of net curtains torn from the burning buildings by the firestorm.
> Years after the war the tales of these events, tales which accompanied me through my childhood, were told over and over again, gradually taking the edge off the original horror, making what happened intelligible and finally entertaining. . . . It was strange, the way in which shock, alarm, horror gradually became comprehensible through repeated telling, the way experiences slowly faded when put into words: *Hamburg in rubble and ashes. The city a sea of flames. The firestorm.*[16]

Timm's account is at odds with Sebald's claim about the family secret, insofar as he talks about narration as a form of therapy. From out of its prior state of inexpressibility, talking about the trauma made it possible to retrieve it, express it, and make it part of the social life of families and inner circles. In that sense, the stories became a means of reconnecting family members to each other. Nothing comparable to the important role played by these stories at the level of private identity happened at the public level. Here again we see the discrepancy that is so characteristic of German postwar history, between private remembering and official commemoration.[17] When Grass refers to a background theme, he captures the informal character of family memory that does not extend to the level of public representation or German national identity. Overstepping the boundary between private conversation and public/political dialogue was evidently taboo.

That is not to say that German memories of victimhood never came up in the political discourse of the postwar period. In fact, attempts had been made from the very beginning to politicize such experiences. The theme of expulsion that Grass discusses played a particularly important role in West Germany during the two decades immediately following the end of the war. Indeed, it was far more than a background theme: from 1953 to 1962, the most notable historians of the time (Werner Conze, Theodor Schieder, Hans Rothfels) carried out an extensive oral history project, published under the title *Dokumentation der Vertreibung der Deutschen aus Ost-Mitteleuropa* [Documentation of the Expulsion of Germans from East-Central Europe] by the Federal Ministry for Refugees, Displaced Persons and Victims of War.[18] While these historians sought to integrate this chapter of history into a more complete picture of the German war of destruction, the politicians of the time were more stalwart in their interest in the topic. For them, the displaced people constituted a sizable part of the electorate; materials were being collected with an eye to future negotiations with neighboring European states. Up until the late 1970s it had become customary to use the rhetoric of compensation and to compare the seven million displaced persons to six million murdered Jews, a style of argument that would be discredited a few years later by the Historians' Debate. Whoever reverts back to this kind of rhetoric on a political level today touches on a taboo and risks his or her position, as was shown by the scandal involving German Bundestag member Martin Hohmann and General Reinhard Günzel of the German army.[19]

For decades, the Federation of Expellees was the self-appointed representative of this experience, generating not a social memory but a political one.

It was a special-interest group that, with its reactionary voting and folksy reenactments, attracted less and less attention to itself over the years and so gradually became even less popular than it had been. Visitor numbers at the many museums that had been established by the Federal Ministry of Displaced Persons had been on the decline over the years, which is why Gustav Seibt describes them as "cold storage." How, then, can the resuscitation of this past in the mode of a kind of emotional reliving of it be explained? The answer is: by shifting the terms of the memory, reclaiming it from a special-interest politics, and providing it with a new basis. But how exactly did this happen?

A first explanation might be that the mass media have discovered the theme and fabricated a wide popular response. The assumption here would be that a large-scale media campaign, indeed a media offensive, exploited the malleable emotions of older and younger Germans in the short term, but which effect would just as quickly fizzle out as they invariably do with such fleeting media events. An argument against this explanation might involve recognizing that in modern democracies, social discourses are supported by the media, including such varied formats as books, films, reviews, newspaper articles, television documentaries, and talk shows. But the presence of the media does not generate the meaning of these memories, nor can the media call it into question. Memory can certainly be stimulated by the media and by a staging of attention, but the sustained public response to it is another issue: despite highly refined market strategies, that response is not arbitrarily subject to manipulation. Something else seems to be going on here. There is obviously a certain disposition on the part of the public as well as a question of timing involved. The media has, in the past, embraced the theme of German suffering before without producing a similar effect. Reports, films, documentaries, textbooks, and novels had been produced, without, however, igniting a broad public debate shared by the entire society.

A second explanation might be that, outside of close family circles or specialized research, these memories had not yet had a chance to be communicated as part of German history or come up for discussion in terms of their emotional dimension and shared with empathy in the public sphere. This memory was politically blocked from two sides: from the right by the revisionism of the special-interest group of expellees, and from the left by the attitude of the '68 generation, which was much more concerned with pinning the guilt on their parents than with listening to their stories of suffering. The question today has to do with the role this returned memory might play in the development of national identity. Perhaps the memory of German suffering is a welcome narrative because it includes experiences of both East and West Germans and so offers an important antidote of empathy between two communities more often marked by divisiveness. Drawing on these common experiences emphasizes an underlying link between the two German states that transcends political boundaries and differences. This shared experience of victimhood offers itself up as a new national myth connecting East and West.[20]

A possible third explanation would be to argue that the lived memory of these events is about to vanish as the last of those who lived through them are passing away. All social memory is subject to the biological rhythms according to which one generation supersedes another, and we find ourselves engaging the topics of expulsion, fleeing, and the bombing of German cities at the precise moment when this lived memory is dissolving and will vanish entirely in the foreseeable future. However, this does not mean that this experience will simply vanish into silence; to the contrary, it is now being emphatically reclaimed, and to great effect. At the present time, it is remarkable how many writers of the second and third generations are currently taking up on this theme, thoroughly researching it and devoting themselves in entirely new ways to their oral and written family memories.[21] In these bestselling semi-autobiographical novels, the authors inscribe themselves into a long-term family memory and place their own biography within the continuum that spans three or four generations.

Following a relatively long period of conflict and breakdown between generations, it would seem that harmony and continuity have become priorities once again. Unlike the '68 generation, the third generation no longer seeks a radically new beginning. Instead of a radical break, members of this generation focus on longer historical continuities. Most of this writing is still motivated by the desire to come to terms with guilt and with the haunting of a legacy. This theme, however, is no longer dramatized in father-son relationships but reaches further back and gains a somewhat epic breadth through a new and longer perspective. To a certain degree, the dominant tendency of the 1970s and '80s toward critique and accusation is giving way to a more apologetic attitude. The generation that experienced the events is being replaced by those of the so-called confessional generation, which is taking over the experiences and memories of its parents and striving to express that generation's attitudes, wishes, and values.

Expulsion (Günter Grass, Crabwalk)

As we've seen, one of the distinctive features of historical traumas is their belated reappearance long after the decisive events occurred. In the Vilnius speech that we have looked at a number of times, Günter Grass hesitantly moves from individual to collective memory, replacing the first person singular of the Baltic refugee and writer with the first person plural of Germans as a nation:

> At present, not a week goes by in which we are not warned against forgetting. Now that we have sufficiently often remembered the Jews who emigrated, who were persecuted, and who were murdered in inconceivable numbers, we're belatedly remembering the transport and murder of tens of thousands of Roma and Sinti.[22]

Grass registers here a chronological succession of waves of memory. The past is never accessible in its entirety but reveals, reluctantly and in stages, one facet at a time. When confronted by trauma, the process of remembering becomes more difficult in that it has to overcome resistances. It was only after resistances to remembering Jewish victims had been overcome that memories of the Sinti, the Roma, and the forced laborers came into their own. Grass also places the Germans on this list, though in a separate paragraph. Here too, he observes resistances and a lack of recognition, ones that he will go on to make the subject of his 2002 novella.

> Yet it is strange and troubling to think how lately and with what hesitation we remember the suffering inflicted on Germans during the war. The consequences for us of that unscrupulously initiated and criminally executed war, that is, the destruction of German cities, the death of hundreds of thousands of civilians through Allied carpet bombing, and the forced expulsion and privation of twelve million emigrant Germans from the East, have been relegated to the background.[23]

By "relegated to the background" Grass might be referring to that portion of memories that is restricted to the privacy of family circles, or to parts of an unofficial conversation that are cultivated in the pub and other informal venues. Bringing such memories into the foreground can then be a way of giving them social recognition, political relevance, or cultural meaning.

In any case, Grass's 2002 novella *Crabwalk* treats the 'background theme' of the expulsion. The novella is about a ship that, overcrowded with German refugees, sank in the Baltic Sea at the end of the Second World War. To portray the Germans from a victim's perspective is a risky undertaking, especially given that it was precisely this self-centered perspective of victimization that had blocked the recognition of other victims for decades, be they Jewish, Polish, or of whatever origin.[24] Grass's novella reconstitutes a repressed personal memory within the context of German collective memory; at the same time, however, the work is an object lesson in the fundamental mechanisms and dynamics of memory and in strategies of the politics of history.

The history that Grass reclaims from personal to cultural memory over half a century later is that of the sinking of the *Wilhelm Gustloff* by Russian torpedoes in the icy Baltic Sea on the evening of January 30, 1945. One part of the novella is devoted to the *prehistory* of the disaster and is written in the style of a dime-store novel. This part is constructed around the trio of historical figures that ended up in an unexpected historical configuration with the sinking of the ship: Gustloff, the ship's namesake, Frankfurter, his assassin, and Marinesko, the commandant of the Russian submarine who ordered the release of the torpedoes. The other part of the novel involves the *posthistory* of the accident—that is, how, in postwar Germany, the event gets remembered, suppressed, forgotten, then gets reexcavated, reconstructed, and even repeated in that reengagement. The trio of historical characters corresponds to the three fictional characters who act as bearers of memory: the mother, the son, and the grandchild.

The narrator of Grass's novella is a reluctant one. His mother, a survivor of the *Gustloff*, has been pestering him for years to tell her story and pass on her testimony to future generations. The mother's oral narrative runs throughout the book in fragments written in thick East Prussian dialect. Her neverending story has hardened into a litany of constantly repeated formulations. She is desperately searching for a witness, for someone to tell her story and turn it into an object of an enduring public memory. Her first choice is her son who, as member of the '68 generation, shares his generation's aversion to family stories of hunger, horror, and deprivation. He has also grown up in a world that sees this history as useless and counterproductive. From the 1960s to the 1990s, the event had not only been forgotten but repressed—that is, edged out by the Holocaust that, following a period of delay, had finally been politically recognized and had become a public memory. Despite his every effort, however, the son cannot entirely free himself from the history of his own origins. For he himself was born on January 30, 1945, the very night of the accident, after his seventeen-year-old mother was taken into a lifeboat.

Thus from the very outset, the claims he emphatically makes to a generational detachment and a radically new beginning are ironically undercut.

One message of the book is, to borrow a line from Grass's Vilnius speech, that there is no virgin territory in German history, not even in its future, in which its past has not already staked a claim.[25] The other message is that the blind spot in the moral consciousness of the '68 generation became the ground for an unwieldy return of the suppressed Nazi past. For, the story that the son does not want to tell is one that the grandchild is feverishly intent on telling. He becomes the hobby historian of the family legends and a willing crown witness for the grandmother. He even relocates to be with her in the former East Germany precisely at the time when, following the fall of the wall, it is actively reconfiguring its political memory. The Internet is the new medium of this generation, and Grass brilliantly puts it into play as the flipside of the official national memory and as a dynamic projection screen for tabooed language and suppressed memory. The ship that, at one time, had gone under in the Baltic Sea and was then banished from public memory resurfaces once again in the digital cyber world (127). Grass reconstructs the mechanism by which the emotive dynamics masked under a façade of political correctness become grist for the mill of the neo-Nazis. At the same time, he also makes it clear that the expellees' memories of suffering can in no way trump the memory of suffering of the victims of the Holocaust. This memory of German victimization can have a place in German collective memory only on the condition that no direct legal consequences or political standards for action follow from it—be they of revenge, changes to borders, or claims for compensation. The condition for recognizing this memory of victimhood is its depoliticization: for Grass, depoliticization is the only way that recognition can relax tensions and lead to the introduction of important differentiations in German collective memory.

By dividing up the memory of *Gustloff* into these three generations (1928, 1945, and 1984), Grass generates a long-term perspective on the discrepancies between personal memory and collective memory in Germany's history of memory. The convoluted dynamics of remembering and forgetting are not only influenced by generational shifts and changes to communications technology; changes in the political system also play a crucially important role. Cultural practices like funeral ceremonies, commemorative rituals, the construction of memorials, and the naming of streets, schools, and ships help to create a political memory that has a potentially unlimited claim on the future. But at the same time, a regime has to be in place to stabilize such claims.

The National Socialist state erected a pompous "Hall of Honor" as a perpetual memorial for Gustloff in his hometown of Schwerin. The East German state destroyed this commemorative site, letting it become overgrown and renaming the surrounding streets. With a subtle sense of irony, Grass draws attention to the paradoxical sense that, during times of political upheaval or regime change, the personal memory of the individual can often outlive the short-term politics of history.

Personal memory only comes up in Grass's novella in the case of the mother, a survivor of the *Gustloff*. The main activity of the narrator and his son is not to remember—indeed, they have no firsthand experience of the incident—but to do research, to reconstruct what happened, and to present their information. For them, the oral testimony of the (grand)mother is only one source among the many they have at their disposal. They carefully sift through—like the author himself does—all the sources available to them, be they fictional or historical, including various books, a film, archival material, letters, and photos. Indeed, one of the traces preserved in this cultural memory is even a feature film that was screened in West German cinemas in 1958 and was still geared toward the generation that lived through the experience. Grass presents this film in a surprising way: at the very moment in the novel when he could have described the actual sinking of the ship, he instead veers to a description of the film (119). By not presenting the disaster, but rather presenting a representation of it, Grass leaves the trauma as an empty site, one that he does not *fill in* with the screen memories of the film but rather *marks* as empty. To be sure, historical information had been stored in the cultural archive and so was available, but it would take a long time for the occurrence to make it into German collective memory or become part of Germany's historical consciousness. Grass's widely acclaimed novel raises this memory above the constrictions and predetermined expiration dates of social memory and places it in Germany's cultural memory. In the process, he has made the memory more widely accessible and more easily passed on across generational divides.

The Incompatibility of Suffering and Guilt

Ernst Renan once wrote that "collective suffering binds more than joy does." At the present time, the topics of guilt and suffering are bringing about a rapprochement between history and memory, and yet the two are also utterly incompatible with one other. In what follows, we will examine the question of their incompatibility more closely.

When Grass expresses surprise in his Vilnius speech at how slowly the memory of German suffering at the war's end was able to enter into general consciousness, he himself gives the answer to this question of incompatibility: "one injustice concealed the other. It was forbidden to compare them or even to estimate damages."[26] With these lines, Grass gets to the heart of the psycho-logic of the German memory problem. In point of fact, immediately after the war it was the Germans' own sense of themselves as victims that prevented them from taking into account the suffering of others, particularly that of the Jews. The subsequent establishment of a worldwide Holocaust memory meant that Jewish suffering pushed aside acknowledgment of the suffering of non-Jewish Germans. Today perhaps it is German suffering that is pushing aside memories of the Holocaust and blunting the consciousness of German guilt. Is it a question here, as Heidemarie Uhl has asked, of "an alternate- or counter-narrative to Holocaust memory?" Has the media market or a new nationalistic discourse gained the upper hand against the Germans' conscience and a practice of critical self-questioning? Is Germany possibly "leaving behind this phase of confrontation with its own past that, since the '80s, has appeared under the sign of a question about guilt"?[27]

The topic of the incompatibility of suffering and guilt is also reflected in competing historical accounts. This is illustrated with particular clarity in the confrontation between two historians, both of whom made it their task to convey the history of the Second World War to a nonprofessional audience. They both agreed (and in this respect they differed from their colleagues) that their research should be presented in such a way as to target the emotions of the public, and so used stirring rhetoric and shock effects to reach the hearts of their readers. For all their similarities of method, however, their basic tenets are diametrically opposed; one, Hannes Heer, exposes German guilt, while the other, Jörg Friedrich, chronicles experiences of German suffering.

Heer, born in 1941, conceived the exhibit "War of Annihilation: Crimes of the Wehrmacht, 1941–1944," which toured German cities from 1995 to 1999 under the auspices of Hamburg's Institute for Social Research. The popular traveling exhibit was seen by almost a million visitors throughout German cities and gave rise to heated debate. The exhibition was discontinued in 1999 on account of some photographs that had been given erroneous captions, but in 2001 it returned in revised form, and toured Germany under the slightly revised title "Crimes of the Wehrmacht: Dimensions of the War of Annihilation 1941–1944."

In its original form, the exhibition put forward three principal arguments. The first was that the idea of an unblemished Wehrmacht was untenable; the second was that there was no basis for distinguishing between Führer and Volk; and the third was that anti-Semitic racism and anti-Bolshevism were key motivations for, and instruments of, the war of annihilation. Heer wanted to show that responsibility for the mass-murder of the Jewish population did not simply lie with Hitler's inner circle and the special forces units, but that the Wehrmacht, and indeed the whole adult male population involved in it, took an active role in these crimes. Insofar as Heer personalized the guilt and dramatically extended its reach within the German population, he was also pitting himself against current discourses that sought to diminish this guilt by isolating it to a small clique of criminals or by placing it on modern industrial and administrative structures.

In the interim, the historical exhibit has acquired a history of its own, which Heer has written about.[28] He sees the exhibition as part of the memory climate of the 1990s, which was shaped by Victor Klemperer's diaries and Daniel Goldhagen's lecture tour. Since the beginning of the new millennium, following the appearance of new and controversial books on memory written from the perspective of the victim, the tone and themes have shifted in German memory discourse. In the context of an engagement with guilt and suffering, the last chapter of Heer's book is of particular interest in that he explicitly takes his opponent, Jörg Friedrich, to task.[29] Earlier we touched on Friedrich's book about the aerial war and pointed out its problematic use of terms like "collapse of civilization," "Einsatzgruppen," and "gas chambers." The proximity of this language to the Holocaust did not, of course, escape the reviewers, who criticized Friedrich for his "undisciplined use of language" and for the slippage of his semantics.[30] The person who complained of slippage had clearly not understood that the terminology used in the book was in fact an inseparable part of its argument: the book about the firestorm was itself playing with fire. Heer understood this extremely well and knew that this Historians' Debate had less to do with the facts themselves than with their representation. Friedrich's style contains explanations and arguments that are conveyed to the reader without explicit argumentation. In this context, the duel between Hannes Heer and Jörg Friedrich is being fought out over the rules of discourse and representation and, behind these rules, the taboo of comparison and offsetting: on the one side was the apologist for German suffering, on the other was the proponent of German guilt. Whereas it may be obvious "that today no serious contemporary denies Auschwitz or disputes German guilt," Heer still triggers the alarm, for he sees in Friedrich's book a "smokescreen . . . behind which major changes in historical writing are being developed in a relatively unnoticed way."[31] Heer reacts like a fireman to the "arsonist" Friedrich, as he puts it in his book. Between these two positions, there is no mediation possible; each is a mirror image of the other. In their work and their debate, they reactivate and perpetuate this old contest between suffering and guilt.

The duel between Friedrich and Heer dramatizes once again what Grass describes in terms of a forced alternative: one injustice conceals and suppresses the other. For Grass, comparing them or setting one against the other is out of the question, but that is precisely what Friedrich and Heer do in their historical-political dispute: on the one side, German suffering, which should make it possible to "absolve the perpetrators" of guilt; and on the other side, German guilt, which excludes any experience of suffering. Once again, this configuration promotes the sharpest possible contours in the categories of victims and perpetrators. Polemics and suppression thrive on this kind of rigid classification system, but it certainly doesn't allow for any nuances, contradictions, dilemmas, or ambivalences.

We should certainly not downplay the readiness of Germans to use the role of victim in order to avoid their own historical responsibility. At the same time, it would also be wrong to interpret any reference to suffering as a strategy of avoidance or as a means of denying guilt—besides which, saying that the stories of suffering in German family memories are politically incorrect is certainly not going to make them go away. But the either-or logic in which the problem of the incompatibility of guilt and suffering is currently being discussed always leads to a dead end. There is such a thing as a human right to one's own memories, however uncomfortable those memories may be, and this cannot be negated by censorship and taboos. How, then, can we get out of the tiresome situation produced by this forced alternative?

Hierarchization of Memory

One possibility suggests itself in looking more closely at the norms of memory praxis in democratic states. We know that memories are perspectival in nature and, therefore, basically heterogeneous. They become homogenized only when they are taken up in representations, for these tend toward harmonization and absorption. Symbolic representations, however, also mark out differences and erect boundaries between values, loyalties, solidarities, and commitments. In any society highly divergent memories and group experiences always exist side by side that do not create conflicts because they are not elevated to a public level; on the level of public discourse and national identity, however, the question arises as to how one can integrate divergent and even contradictory memories into a generally acceptable framework.

The solution to the problem of the heterogeneity of memories is, I believe, to be found in hierarchizing them. The idea of hierarchy involves questions of value, priority, and power. Memories subsist and are constructed on all kinds of levels, ones that involve varying levels of commitment, such as the individual, the family, society, and finally at the national level. On the lower levels, it is not necessary to impose norms or make decisions, while on the national level, by contrast, the level of politics, such norms are essential. I would like to illustrate this issue of norms by taking another look at the example of the memory of displaced persons.

Erika Steinbach, president of the Federation of Expellees, does not belong to the generation that lived through the expulsion but to the following generation, which identifies with those events and recaptures their impact and importance for their own identity. She is known for having taken on the task of establishing her family memory not just on an individual and social level but also on a national one. Though a member of the '68 generation, she does not seek confrontation with the guilt-ridden generation of her parents, but, on the contrary, claims the legacy of her parents and becomes the heir of their suffering. To elevate this very particularistic memory of the expellees to the level of a national memory, a symbolic space has to be created. Her project is to establish the Center against Expulsion in central Berlin, where it would enter into a symbolic relation with the Memorial to the Murdered Jews of Europe (the proposal immediately became a source of great tensions with European neighbors). In addition to this symbolic space, Steinbach's other goal was to establish a new commemoration date on the German calendar that was voted on and recommended by the Federal Council of Germany, after having been repeatedly rejected by the government. This day would be August 5, the day in 1950 when the Charter of the German Expellees had been signed.

This episode gives a detailed picture of how a particular memory can be reconstructed as a national memory. Certain frames of reference have so far prevented it from happening—and this brings us back to the normative side of memory. The norm of the German national framework of memory is the Holocaust, the recognition and working-through of German guilt, and the assumption of historical responsibility for the atrocities of the Nazi regime. This is the normative framework into which all other memories have to be integrated. Returning to the question of the different levels of memory, there is a national level that normatively marks out the parameters of the frameworks of memory, and there is a social level where heterogeneous memories of suffering, guilt, and resistance can exist side-by-side without disrupting the entire framework. Integrating these memories into that general framework will allow them to gain some much-needed context and be recognized as part of that "unscrupulously initiated and criminally executed war."[32]

Finally, given how dynamic and volatile social memory can be, certain normative parameters are indispensable. There is little point in trying to control the discourse by appealing to political correctness or to a strict either-or scenario. The clearer the normative standards are at the level of national memory, the more flexible social memory can be. The memory of suffering within families must never supersede the national memory of guilt, but the national memory of guilt must also not function to close off stories of suffering. Social memory is a complex and multifaceted arena that, to some extent, takes its normative cues from national memory. For an experience to be considered representative or generally relevant, it must be compatible with the national memory, or at least be capable of being integrated into it. On the one hand, this hierarchical structure ensures that the social memory of a national democratic state remains within certain limits; on the other hand, it can help national memory to become more complex, subtle, and flexible.

Where some critics see a troubling change of perspective in German memory, others see a broadening of perspective.[33] I myself belong to the second group, convinced as I am that imposing rules of discourse and taboos will not help us better understand the dynamics of memory. This is also true of historical research, which must always be open to new developments; it must be willing to shed light on previously ignored aspects of the field and be able to differentiate between these new insights. As long as the normative national frame remains in place, this dynamism can contribute to a greater diversification and complexity of German memory.

EIGHT

Points of Intersection between Lived Memory and Cultural Memory

A question that is often posed concerning the memory of the Second World War and the Holocaust has to do with the future of this memory once it is no longer grounded in the memories of those who lived through the experience. What will change when that lived memory vanishes along with survivors and contemporary witnesses? What exactly is happening at the current juncture? At the beginning of the 1990s, Reinhart Koselleck described the transition from the biographical memory of lived experience to an externally mediatized memory in the following way:

> The research criteria are becoming more austere, but they are—perhaps—also less vivid, less saturated with the empirical, even though they promise to recognize or appreciate more in their objectivity. The moral consternation, the disguised protective functions, the accusations and the designations of guilt by historiography—all these techniques of mastering the past [*Vergangenheitsbewältigungstechniken*] lose their quality as existential political matters; they fade in favor of individual academic research and analyses controlled by hypotheses.[1]

Koselleck, who is a historian, sees the transition beyond the memory of those who lived through the events as a virtually natural process of change that can be summed up in a phrase: what was once memory grounded in experience becomes the subject matter of objective history. However, there are very few signs of this linear process of change at the present time. These memories are still highly volatile in the political sphere, and there is no evidence to suggest that this hot topic is cooling down. What is becoming clear, though, is the sense that the historian no longer has a monopoly on the reconstruction, representation, and interpretation of this past. Alongside the discipline of history, these tasks are now shared by many other cultural institutions and media avenues. Historical writing and the process of historicization no longer dominate the field; rather, we are witnessing a proliferation of the modes and shapes in which memory takes place. At times, the field of academic history is compatible with these different forms, and at other times it enters into conflict with them.

So if we cannot assume that memory simply yields to history, the question then becomes how this memory gets extended beyond the reach of lived memory and what changes it undergoes in the process. At this point we would do well to recall some of the basic arguments that were introduced in Chapter 1. Particularly important in this context is the argument we developed concerning how the memory of the individual is already embedded within broader frames of reference with which it constantly interacts: the social group of the family or the generation, for instance, the ethnic and/or national group, and the set of cultural symbols adhering to them. So we have to take another, more concrete look at the various points of intersection where the memory of the individual participates in these larger structures of memory formation.

From Individual to Social Memory

One inevitably takes on a social memory simply by being born and raised in a human society. As we learn to speak, we also learn different forms of interaction, including the speech act known as memory talk or conversational remembering. As Maurice Halbwachs has shown, the frames of reference governing these practices are required to develop a memory in the first place. So our individual memories are always already socially grounded. The family memory plays a particularly important role in this social memory insofar as it both allows for different perspectives and arises out of a common body of stock anecdotes, formulations, and attitudes. This nexus between individual perspectives on the one hand and a shared body of family stories on the other explains why it is often difficult to distinguish between what one has experienced oneself and what one has been told by others.

Another form of social memory is generational memory, which is also related to autobiographical memory. Harald Welzer talks about how "narrative standardization lends coherence to experience" and that it is on that basis of narrative standardization that group- and generation-specific experiences get strengthened.[2] "Conversely, individual autobiographies draw on fitting stories from the standard inventory and integrate one or the other of them into their own life stories, without even really noticing."[3] This generation-specific standardized narrative is not produced by the individual, but rather emerges retrospectively in terms of how different experiences can be related to each other. Texts, images, and films also exert a powerful influence on this narrative. Welzer cites Bernhard Wicki's film *The Bridge* as an example in which the film's director relates his own memories of the Hitler youth and the so-called Flak-assistant generation in terms of experiences of other people that he heard about and went on to record. Although the film was broadly understood to be a generalized aesthetic presentation of a generational experience, that is not exactly the case, since the director, born in 1919, actually belongs to another war generation. Furthermore, the 1959 film was released at the height of the nuclear disarmament and peace movement and so also contains a more universal message. The international success of the film—enthusiastically acclaimed in Moscow, New York, Tokyo, and Rome—confirms the broad appeal this German postwar film had beyond the concerns of a specific generation or group. On the other hand, we could name Wolfgang Borchert's play about soldiers returning home, *The Man Outside* (1947), as a generation-specific work that depicts the experiences of an entire generation of uprooted and disaffected German youth. The content of the play—the most frequently staged in postwar Germany—is indeed "paradigmatic for the consciousness of a generation."[4]

Insofar as works of art are generalized aesthetic presentations, they always form part of the cultural memory and so are never the exclusive property of a particular generation. As a work of art, a novel or film opens up the experience of a generation and makes it accessible to a wider public. Of course, the reception of the generation that lived through the events will be different from the reception of those not directly affected: the one side will recognize the experience depicted as their own and might have their own memories triggered by it, and the other side will realize what happened and experience empathy for those who went through it. In both cases, there are intellectual and emotional operations involved that substantially broaden the horizons of our own experience.

From Individual to Collective Memory

How does the passage from an individual memory to a collective memory come about? To have a national identity one must possess a passport,[5] but how does one get a national memory? A general answer to this question might be through participating in rituals. Rituals take place at specific times and in specific places. Particular activities take place on national holidays: days of triumph and victory are joyously celebrated with fireworks, as in the Fourth of July in the United States and the First of August in Switzerland; in other cases, days commemorating historical trauma and grief are marked by a minute of silence, as is the case with the Fourth of May in Holland and the Yom HaShoah in Israel (the Twenty-seventh of Nisan).

On national memorial days, historical events become remembered ones. Past events are interpreted, communicated, and practiced in such a way that they become present, in such a way that "past and present blend into one another in particular places and through particular activities."[6] Israeli schoolchildren experience the presence of the past when they travel to Auschwitz or other death camps where their relatives were murdered. Here they take up Israel's national memory, the Holocaust, and make it a part of their own identity in a bodily way: they imaginatively relive their relatives' history of suffering, and as they do this, they are wrapped in the national flag as if it were a secularized prayer shawl. Adolescent American Jews who go on organized tours to Auschwitz and Treblinka to relive the collective historical trauma on a personal level often report afterward that they were "never so proud to be a Jew."[7] In his book *The Holocaust in American Life*, Peter Novick describes another example of this kind of initiation into a collective memory. During the Jewish coming-of-age rituals of bar and bat mitzvahs, the youth is taken up into the religious community. "In a growing number of communities," Novick writes, "the child is 'twinned' with a young victim of the Holocaust who never lived to have the ceremony."[8] The murdered adolescent is taken up into living memory at the same time as the living adolescent is taken up into the shared history of the Holocaust. The religious ceremony functions as a kind of double initiation, which binds the religious community to the Holocaust as a shared historical experience. Such rituals generally require the voluntary participation of individuals to bring past events into the present in powerful and affective ways. If such symbolic rituals are lacking, the ties to collective memory will be weaker. Such is the case in Germany, where most official rituals are carried out by politicians or other dignitaries and not by the population.

From Individual to Cultural Memory

Our individual memories contain much more than recollections of events that we ourselves lived through. The human brain is wired to have our memories enhanced through interaction with other people and with concrete symbols: our relation to the world is always a mediated one. Linguist Jürgen Trabant draws attention to the importance of this mediation when he stresses that "we in our cultures gain a lot more knowledge through the mediation of symbols than we do through direct emulation, direct experience, or even through our own activity and our own handling of things."[9] So, he argues, there is "*no* gap at all between my own knowledge and the social dimension"; for the majority of my knowledge is indeed not "drawn from my experience of the world, but through the mediation of symbols."[10] The sociologist Edward Shils has expressed a similar thought:

> The individual as he perceives himself includes things which are not bounded by his own experiences. . . . Memory is furnished not only from the recollections of events which the individual has himself experienced but from the memories of others. . . . From their accounts of their own experiences, which frequently antedate his own, and from works written at various removes, his image of his "larger self" is brought to include events which occurred both recently and earlier outside his own experiences.[11]

Cultural memory allows every individual to stand on the shoulders of giants: we are connected not only to a cultural body of knowledge but also to a cultural body of memory. The contents of cultural memory differ from generalized or specialized knowledge in that we do not take it up in order to master it or achieve particular goals, but to grapple with it and make it part of our identities.

Embodied Recollection—Disembodied Media Memory

For a lived experience to become a cultural memory, symbolic extension and psychological identification are required.[12] Memory and experience turn into communicable information through representations (and by that, specifically we mean symbolic encoding, inscription onto material storage devices, reproduction, and dissemination). In order to become knowledge, this information must be taken up by people who are interested in it and are willing to engage with it; otherwise, in the very best case, it will lose its relevance and be placed in storage memory. Finally, in order that this knowledge becomes a cultural memory, it must be appropriated by means of psychological identification and intellectual engagement and must also be grasped as a part of one's own identity.

Information	**Knowledge**	**Memory**
	Processing of information (cultural storage memory)	Appropriation of knowledge (cultural operative memory)

For a memory to become symbolically extended, it must be separated from the person who originally possessed the memory. Psychological identification occurs when that memory is then taken up by someone else or by some other carrier. What happens when an individual's memory of his or her own lived experience turns into an individual memory that draws its content purely from cultural memory? What is the difference between a memory of lived experience and a memory that relies on external forms of media representation? Martin Walser gives a general answer to this question when he writes, "One can move around in the past that is shared by everyone as if one were in a museum. One's own past is inaccessible."[13] We might say that it is inaccessible precisely because it has not been externalized and made into something objective. As both an accessible I-memory and an inaccessible me-memory, it is an inseparable and inexpressible part of the self. The memory of lived experience is *embodied*, ingrained. Memory that is taken up in representations is different in that it is *disembodied*, externalized. Insofar as it has become detached from living memory, it has also become available for other kinds of memory on a different, but equally legitimate, basis.

The writer and former Buchenwald prisoner Jorge Semprun describes the collision between a memory of lived experience and a cultural memory in a moving scene in his book *Literature or Life*. At the same time he powerfully analyzes the difference between the two modes of memory.[14] Three months after his liberation from Buchenwald, Semprun went to the cinema in Locarno. Before the feature film, as was usual at that time, a newsreel was being screened, and in this particular incident, Semprun was shown what he had just been through, which was still fresh in his own memory:

> Suddenly, after reports on a sports event and some international conference in New York, I had to close my eyes, blinded for a moment. When I opened them again, I hadn't been dreaming, the images were still there, on the screen, inescapable. . . .
>
> These scenes had been filmed in different camps liberated by the Allied advance a few months before. In Bergen-Belsen, in Mauthausen, in Dachau. There were also some images of Buchenwald, which I recognized.
>
> Or rather: which I knew for certain came from Buchenwald, without being certain of recognizing them. Or rather: without being certain of having seen them myself. And yet I had seen them. Or rather: I had experienced them. It was the difference between the seen and the experienced that was disturbing.

Up until that day, Semprun had managed to avoid such images. He alone possessed the embodied images that haunted him in intermittent flashbacks. But there were also other intimate images, memories that he could consciously recall and that "to me were as consubstantial, as natural (despite their unbearable element) as those of my childhood." When confronted with these images on screen, something unexpected happened to him:

> All of a sudden, though, in the quiet of that movie theater in Locarno, where whispers and murmurs died away into a rigid silence of horror and compassion (and disgust, probably), these intimate images became foreign to me, objectified up on the screen. They also broke free of my personal procedures of memory and censorship. They ceased being my property and my torment, the deadly riches of my life. They were, finally, nothing more than the externalized, radical reality of Evil: its chilling yet searing reflection.
>
> The gray, sometimes hazy images, filmed with the jerky motions of a handheld camera, acquired an inordinate and overwhelming dimension of reality that my memories themselves could not attain. . . . As if—although this might seem

strange at first—the dimension of unreality, the context of fiction inherent in any cinematic image, even the most strictly documentary one, gave the weight of incontestable reality to my inmost memories.

Few authors have been able to describe the relation between an embodied memory of experience and a disembodied objectivized memory in as vivid, subtle, and thoughtful a way as Semprun does here. What makes his account all the more remarkable is the fact that it involves a traumatic memory—that is, a memory that is even more inseparable from the person, since it cannot be fully transformed into a conscious recollection. What is most intimate and ungraspable is suddenly placed outside him in the space of the cinema. To be sure, he is just as distant from the pictures on the screen as the other people in the cinema are. In that sense, the images flickering on the screen are the object of an anonymous collective experience. But Semprun has personal recollections available to him in addition to the external ones on the screen; for him, the "seen" is combined with the "experienced," and he sinks into an anguished reverie as a consequence. What was his and his alone has ceased to belong to him; it has become foreign and objective; at the same time, this movement to the outside irrefutably confirms and substantiates his own memories. The images from the newsreel de-realize his experience, but at the same time, they validate it. One's own past is not accessible in itself; only when it is disembodied through material images and symbolic representations does it become accessible and communicable to others. From that moment onward, these images become available to unlimited numbers of people, who can then assimilate them into their own memory.

On the Asymmetry of Victim- and Perpetrator-Memory

Steven Spielberg's sevenfold Oscar-winning film *Schindler's List* (1993) launched a veritable explosion of films that approach the Holocaust in a more or less fictional way. As is widely known, this film appealed to a large audience and made sizable profits. One Internet site puts it this way: "Since 1997, in German cinemas alone there have been about 15 million 'Holocaust filmgoers.'"[15] The Holocaust film has not only been proven to be a successful business venture in the entertainment industry, but it has also come to be an important part of cultural memory: members primarily of younger generations are increasingly turning to such films for their knowledge of and perspective on the extermination of the Jews. Spielberg, who uses fictional scenes and dialogue in his films to intensify their impact and to illustrate the facts more vividly, took the bulk of the profits that he made from the film and established the "Shoah Visual History Foundation" to record testimonies of actual survivors. In an interview, he commented on this project: "The archive now holds more than 50,000 video interviews in 31 languages with survivors from 57 countries. This amounts to 14 years of back-to-back playing time, and enough videotape to wrap the entire earth."[16]

This huge project of recording video testimonies and producing such a massive collection of them meets the requirement that, alongside fictional treatments, survivors—with their real-life stories of suffering—be allowed to speak; projects such as these also ensure that these fragile voices will be heard in the future. According to Spielberg, it is by virtue of these videotapes that "the survivors will be able to speak to future generations for a long time after their death."[17] As long as they are preserved in archives, secured, and copied onto up-to-date storage systems, these video testimonies could transform a social memory of limited duration into a long-term cultural memory. Under such conditions, they take on the quality of a testament and—wherever these testimonies can be reaccessed and listened to—can go from being an *inter*generational memory to being a *trans*generational memory.[18]

Through a myriad of memorials, museums, and archives, and also through countless books, films, and videos, the memories of Holocaust victims and the memories we have of them have been firmly entrenched in cultural memory. However, the same cannot be said of perpetrators: we hardly have any memory of the perpetrators, much less any given from their perspective. On the one hand, many people may welcome such a thing, because the lack of a memory amounts to a *damnatio memoriae* and because high-profile treatments of episodes from perpetrator history—this was discussed on the occasion of Oscar Hirschbiegel's film *Downfall*—always run the risk of elevating or aggrandizing the Nazi past. On the other hand, the dramatic asymmetry between a vocal victim memory and the near-total absence of a perpetrator memory also represents a kind of burden or weight that is only now, a full sixty years after the traumatic events, becoming increasingly noticeable.

The fact that the Holocaust in Germany is a family history—as Raul Hilberg once put it—has had very little impact on the memory of families until now.[19] While, generally speaking, surviving victims of an advanced age want to record their memories, silence continues to dominate on the side of the perpetrators. There are, however, signs that this is changing with the second and third generations as actual perpetrators pass away. In most popular mass media formats, the Nazi past does tend to get treated as entertainment, following heroic or sensationalized generic formulae that keep National Socialism at a safe distance. However, we are seeing a new approach to the theme of guilt recently being developed in art, literature, and documentary film, one that does not seek to distance it as much. A generational shift and a shift in social memory were required for this new perspective: after Helmut Kohl's famous statement regarding "the mercy of a late birth" applied to everyone (since the actual perpetrators are no longer present in the family or in society) and so became irrelevant, the later generations are now developing their own position beyond the avoidance of guilt that characterized the confrontational and defensive stances of the 1970s and '80s. These strategies of avoidance are being replaced with engagements that place questions of guilt within family histories, since artists of the present generation now see themselves as a part of those families. As was discussed earlier, representatives of the second and third generation tend to see themselves in terms of familial continuity: they are interested in events that have influenced their own biographies and their own personalities beyond what they have consciously chosen for themselves. They are less interested in questions of historical *entanglement* than they are in articulating their own historical *enchainment*, a focus that is entirely consistent with the following statement by Nietzsche:

> For since we are the outcome of earlier generations, we are also the outcome of their aberrations, passions and errors, and indeed of their crimes; it is not possible wholly to free oneself from this chain. If we condemn these aberrations and regard ourselves as free of them, this does not alter the fact that we originate in them.[20]

The desire to draw out new dimensions in engaging with guilt is entirely in keeping with Nietzsche's insight regarding the heavy chain of generations: individuals are powerless to break free on their own resolve. Artistic work revolves around this chain, around the conditions and aftereffects of National Socialism in families; it seeks to translate the heavy burden of this unconscious heritage into a conscious relation and to transmit it in more affirming ways through historical reconstruction and imaginative re-experiencing. In *In My Brother's Shadow*, Uwe Timm describes the public "demoting" of the fathers under the occupying forces as a pivotal experience of the generation of 1968:

Overnight the big people, the grown-ups, had shrunk. An observation that I shared with many of my contemporaries. There is probably a connection between this impression and the anti-authoritarian student revolution against our parents' generation.[21]

He also writes about how National Socialism retreated into families once the fathers' humiliation had made it disappear out of the public sphere. "Our fathers had lost the power of command in public life and could exercise it only at home, within their own four walls."[22] While it was no doubt challenging to stand up to fathers who were still there to order them around, such a confrontation was made substantially more difficult in the case of family secrets or of deceased fathers, whose values had entered the family legacy in more elusive or subliminal ways.

Explorations of family secrets and fixations, such as those found in novels by Uwe Timm, Tanja Dückers, Stefan Wackwitz, and Dagmar Leupold or in films such as those by Malte Ludin, are transforming the heavy burden of an unconscious cross-generational legacy into a form of emotional and intellectual engagement and distancing.[23] Artistic representation of these private problems makes them more objective. As the artists and writers gain distance from their family histories, their readers are given the chance to become more aware of their own histories in light of these intensely thought-provoking treatments: what starts out as particular, private, and even idiosyncratic becomes more accessible through a generalized aesthetic formulation.

The biographical can indeed be refracted through the fictional. These artistic or autobiographical engagements with German guilt help bring what has remained unspoken to language and, similar to the memories of experiences of suffering, they often initiate dialogue and act as triggers for memory. Indeed, stories can often multiply: for instance, the discussions following the screening of Malte Ludin's eighty-minute film (*2 or 3 Things I Know about Him*) often last longer than the film. Art not only is a stand-in portrayal of memories but, as the example of Grass has already shown, it can also act as a social trigger for the release of blocked memories. Perhaps this indicates that the asymmetry between victim memories and perpetrator memories is already starting to be dismantled, and the gap between different memory formations is being bridged somewhat. With the help of art, private recollection is becoming part of social and cultural memory, and the memory of individuals and the memory of the collective are further coming into contact with one another and finding new points of intersection.

NINE

Commemorative Sites in Space and Time

The role of commemorative sites is to bring a particular moment of the past into the present, both spatially and temporally. This recollection of the past happens at topographical sites through "forms of safeguarding longevity," and it happens in time through "forms of safeguarding repetition."[1] These forms, which also complement each other, are fundamental for the ways in which collective and cultural memory turn into objects of individual experience and memory across generations. So in this chapter we will also be looking at some exemplary points of intersection between individual and collective memory that have become normative components of political self-representation and the politics of the past. We will first look at commemorative sites in terms of their spatial dimension before turning to the issue of anniversaries.

Memories are not only stored in symbols and objects but also in places, rooms, courtyards, cities, public squares, and landscapes. Whoever returns to such places after a long period of absence becomes a tourist of his or her own childhood and youth and reencounters him- or herself there decades later, just as Günter Grass did when he smelled the stale air in his school hallways or when he heard the lapping of the waves of the Baltic in the fishing village of Brösen. We have described such places—so meaningful for an individual life story—as *lieux de souvenir*, to distinguish them from *lieux de mémoire*, which we shall discuss here. To do that, we will be shifting from media that is used by individual memory to that used by collective memory.

Cultural memory is given a future not just by its being stored in libraries, museums, and archives but also by its being anchored in places. This site-specific aspect of cultural memory is not mobile but immobile: one must travel in order to experience—literally—the character of this memory. As a matter of fact, since antiquity people have had to travel to gain direct access to a person or to a historical event in their genuine locations. Crusaders who recaptured the Holy Land from the Muslims, pilgrims who searched out the reliquary shrines of their saints, tourists who want pictures taken of themselves in front of the pyramids of Cheops or the Taj Mahal, and not least the tour groups of Israeli youth who wrap themselves in their flag when visiting Auschwitz in order to consolidate their identity—all of these practices are grounded in the assumption that certain sites represent a kind of contact zone between present and past, that a secret door opens at these sites onto a past world. Pausanias mentions that the ancients were shown places that descend into the underworld. Odysseus gets directions from Circe to the exact place where he can enter the realm of the dead. At such places, time and space, past and present are linked together.

"Great is the power of memory that resides in places"—this claim of Cicero's neatly sums up the significance of sites for memory.[2] When we reflect on the localized dimension of memory, we can begin with the difference between the concepts of *space* and *site*. Space is the dimension that is measured, mapped, structured, and modeled in accordance with the human spirit of exploration and planning. Space is available: something can be made from it, and it too can be formed and re-formed. In contrast to this abstract sense of space as a dimension of human organizing, acting, and regulating, concrete sites are individualized through names and histories: they are where interaction has already taken place. Human destinies, experiences, and memories adhere to sites differently than they do to spaces; they are projected onto them partially with the aid of monuments.[3] The concept of space contains a potential for planning that points to the future; by contrast, the concept of site retains a knowledge that refers to the past.

Memorial Sites

Since we can only touch on a small area of this vast topic, we shall limit ourselves to an examination of Holocaust memorial sites that were part of a conception to join East and West Germany after 1990 and become an aspect of the newly unified Germany. Throughout this process the national memorial sites of the GDR were reconfigured and, in the year 2000, were established on the basis of a federal strategy for the promotion of memorial sites as institutions that, like theaters, community colleges, and museums, are part of the basic cultural configuration of the Federal Republic. Volkhard Knigge, director of the memorial sites at Buchenwald and Mittelbau-Dora, has reviewed some of the historical-political events of the recent German past—such as the establishment of a Holocaust memorial day in the year 1996 by the Federal president Roman Herzog and the decision of parliament on June 25, 1999, to go ahead with the construction of a central Holocaust memorial in Berlin to the murdered Jews of Europe, as well as the adoption of the Federal memorial site strategy in 2000—and has summarized these engagements under the heading of the "nationalization of negative remembrance."[4] However, he adds that this nationalization was not the result of a conscious political strategy but rather developed as a more or less contingent process or as a sequence of particular and partially antagonistic interests and initiatives. In a democracy, the creation of a national memory is preceded by special-interest-group memories, ones that are then taken up into it. The institutionalization and nationalization of negative remembrances, he emphasizes, is "historically novel, unprecedented, and in international comparison, until now one of a kind" (444). What is new about it is that it does not involve remembering crimes *suffered*—as it still was during the GDR—but rather remembering crimes *committed* and crimes that must be *answered* for. Negative remembrance is a perpetrator memory and not a victim memory.

In the case of traditional commemorative sites, founders and role models from a particular culture are commemorated in the service of an edification of the present. The fundamentally positive staging and meaningful functioning of commemorative sites are independent of whether or not the past events in question are comforting, sublime, or horrifying. Memories of the crucifixion at Golgotha, of the martyrdom of saints, and of the victims of battlefields are no less heroic and normative than memories of political role models and geniuses. Normative power arises wherever something exemplary has been achieved or endured. Memory can convert historical events involving persecution, executions, or defeat into a positive account with an affirmative message. Therefore traumatic sites that uphold a negative memory are distinguished from commemorative sites not on the basis of whether or not the events in question are pleasing or upsetting, but rather on the basis of whether or not they obstruct an affirmative construction of meaning. Just as with national memory, religious memory also abounds in bloodshed and victims; indeed these memories refer to acts of violence that have been *suffered* and not to those that have been *committed* and still need to be *answered* for. Endured suffering can still be cast in a positive light and used in the formation of a collective identity.

The transformation of the Buchwald concentration camp into a national memorial of the GDR is a good example of how a traumatic site can be turned into a heroic commemorative site. A decision was made—one that is incomprehensible to us today—to situate the memorial site on the Etter Mountain near Weimar, about five kilometers away from the real site. Its formative conception and symbolic message could be all the more effective the less it actually engaged with the site's historical vestiges. In 1958, artist Fritz Cremer summed up his idea for this commemorative site with the words "Opfer, Tat, Aufstieg" [Victim, Act, Ascent]. These words sum up a heroic narrative and capture the symbolic layout of Ehrenhain Buchenwald: the visitor is first led through a gate and proceeds downward along a path of stelae adorned with reliefs and plaques, before climbing up at the end to the so-called Tower of Freedom that looks out from the same height of the Etter Mountain over the surrounding area. This arrangement embodies "a secularized, political path toward purification," offering an interpretation of history that is consistent with the GDR regime and also cryptically drawing on the motif of the Christian passion (the path of stelae can be read as the stations of the cross) and the symbolism of resurrection (the tower as the architectural equivalent of ascension).[5]

In 1960, Jorge Semprun, former political prisoner in Buchenwald who had been caught off-guard in a Locarno cinema by newsreel images of the camp's liberation, responded to an invitation to visit this commemorative site with a decisive "No": "For fifteen years, I had tried not to be a survivor, I had succeeded in not becoming a member of some association or other of former deportees. I was always horrified by the pilgrimages, which is what these organized trips for former deportees and their families to the sites of former camps were called." Semprun shocked his interlocutor with his dream "that the camp be left to the slow work of nature, of the woods, roots, rain, erosion, and seasons. That one day, we would stumble upon the buildings of the former camp, inexorably overgrown by trees."[6]

An unusual memorial site can be found on the grounds of the former central detention center of the Ministry for State Security in Berlin-Hohenschönhausen. In the early 1990s, former prisoners began to get involved in the creation of a memorial site on the grounds of the detention center. In 1992, the prison area was put under heritage protection, and it opened for visitors in 1994. In addition, research into the history of the Hohenschönhausen detention center from 1945–89 is conducted there. Through exhibitions, events, and publications, visitors are given comprehensive and hands-on information about the forms and consequences of political persecution and repression during the period of the Communist dictatorship. Using the example of this very prison, the system of political justice is also represented.[7] This place is different from the memorial sites of the Holocaust in that former perpetrators involved in the GDR network of informants and justice system do not try to maintain a low profile but are in fact vocal opponents of the site. On this memorial site, then, an intense battle for the interpretation of history continues to this day.

Traumatic Sites

After two world wars and the Holocaust, the memorial landscape of Europe is dominated by historical sites of mass violence and murder. In contrast to monuments that are built on neutral ground and other kinds of constructed commemorative sites, these traumatic sites are multilayered, indeterminate, and inhabited by different memories and interpretations. The discursive strategies we ordinarily use—to historicize or relativize events, to make them meaningful—come up against their limits in such places. So they are often the context within which difficulties, conflicts, and confusion arise, not least because of how the cultural imperative to remember trauma and therefore to conserve these traumatic sites is inseparable from the impossibility of aesthetically representing the horrors of the Third Reich and of adequately communicating them. However, these difficulties have also led to some original ideas on the part of memory workers and artists in recent years. Of the many innovative directions that have been taken, we can only point to a few artistic works here.

The work of Hamburg artist Sigrid Sigurdsson is grounded in a refusal to substitute living memory with art, architecture, or other symbolic markers. She understands her role as an artist to be more about offering support, indeed even being a midwife of communicative memory, prompting citizens in their local contexts to engage in memory work and helping to frame these memories and to connect them to each other. Such a work came into being as Memorial Center Concentration Camp Out-Station Braunschweig Schillstraße, which was opened to the public in 2000. The memorial consists of a stepped pedestal connected to an open archive, inviting residents of Braunschweig as well as local organizations, associations, and institutions to leave their personal mementos, thoughts, and documents. Since 1997, more than seventy library cases have been compiled for the archive. To ensure that the work continues to have an impact on the public, texts are then selected on a rotational basis and exhibited on metal plaques affixed to the wall of the Memorial Center's periphery. Thus, the artist has made this commemorative site into a focal point for the interconnected memories of the city. Here the imperative to remember is not relegated to politicians or artists but has become a citizens' project.[8] The artist describes her open archive as a "man-made living entity much like gardens, which must be cultivated in order to maintain its interactivity. It can't just endlessly continue to grow, but since it consists mostly of handwritten documents and originals, it will always bear witness to a living part of a period of time."[9]

In the context of the debate about the still-to-be-realized memorial for the murdered Jews of Europe in central Berlin, Jewish historian Marianne Awerbuch expressed her own position by declaring that "the entire country is a memorial!" Sigrid Sigurdsson incorporated this claim into her project "Germany—a Memorial—a Research Task" (1996, ongoing). She realized that there was as yet no survey map of all of the sites at which Nazi crimes took place. So, working with a historian, she undertook to document all the sites of detention and mass murder from 1933 to 1945 on a map of Germany, which is still published and on sale today, showing the borders of December 31, 1937. The black markings on the map are a glaring illustration of the density and dispersal of these former sites of horror and show the extent of the terror system of National Socialism, which encroached well into residential areas. Since its inception, this project has grown to become an open digital archive that brings together academic research and the communicative work of memory into a large network.[10]

To illustrate the complexity of traumatic sites, we need to highlight four characteristics:

1. *Traumatic sites possess a special "magic of Antaeus."*[11] Beyond the valuable information imparted by non-location-specific monuments, museums, and documentation centers, we expect the actual historical sites where atrocities took place to generate a more powerful experience, by virtue of our direct sensory perception. As we saw earlier, this attitude of ours corresponds to the age-old spiritual readiness of pilgrims and educational tourists alike to strengthen their historical knowledge by means of subjective experience. Having concrete and sensory experience of a particular site—with all the affective coloring that implies—should deepen our understanding of that past event in terms of personal experience, engagement, and appropriation. Otherwise our understanding of what happened remains purely intellectual.

   About those who travel to Auschwitz, Ruth Klüger has written, "Whoever claims to find something there must actually have brought it with them in their baggage."[12] Of course, survivors returning to these places of horror also bring baggage with them, but it is of an entirely different sort than those whose knowledge about Auschwitz has come solely from books and images. The baggage of those not directly affected by what took place there is inevitably going to be easier to carry than the baggage of those who have personal memories and connections to the place. Perhaps one could even say that the lighter the baggage of the visitor, the higher their expectation will be about the affective power of the place.

   Whatever one no longer brings oneself, since one is already too distant from the events, must be compensated for by a site-specific power of memory, or by the way in which the site itself makes a powerful appeal. The magic of Antaeas is grounded in whatever authenticity can be attributed to the historical site. But references to the category of authenticity are not easily made these days. The formerly clear distinction between the terms *authentic* and *construed* or *staged* has subsequently been replaced with talk of "performances of authenticity."[13] Which brings us to our second point:

2. *Traumatic sites are both authentic and staged.* They exist in the space between authenticity and performance, between retention and

reconstruction. For sites of memory that have been reconfigured into memorials and museums are governed by a paradox: the conservation of these sites in the interests of authenticity unavoidably entails a loss of authenticity. When a site is preserved, there is no way to avoid changing it and replacing it by something else. Only a small proportion of the material inventory of the concentration camp can be maintained as emblematic; even here dilapidated material always has to be restored or replaced. Over time, the authenticity of a site tends to go from being embodied in relics or remnants to being a sheer "This is where it happened"; that is, it gets reduced to a pure index of location.

Whoever places too much emphasis on a site's power of memory runs the risk of confusing the reconstructed commemorative site of the visitors for the historical site of the prisoner: "I once visited Dachau," writes Ruth Klüger, "with some Americans who had asked me to come along. It was a clean and proper place, and it would have taken more imagination than your average John or Jane Doe possesses to visualize the camp as it was forty years earlier. Today a fresh wind blows across the central square where the infamous roll calls took place, and simple barracks of stone and wood suggest a youth hostel more easily than a setting for tortured lives."[14]

From the perspective of the witness who has a living memory of "tortured lives," not only do these sites possess no power of memory but they actually work to conceal memory. According to Klüger, musealized sites of memory have turned into screen memories. In order to avoid their becoming pernicious tourist attractions, we must disabuse ourselves of the illusion that they offer the possibility of a window onto the past. The difference between the site for the victim and the site visited by the tourist, in whom sympathy and compassion can always be blanked out, must be made apparent if the affective potential mobilized at the site of memory is not to lead to a "fusing of horizons" and an illusory identification.

3. *Traumatic sites are palimpsests.* Time never stands still, and it certainly does not at these sites, either. Although singular histories were brought to a catastrophic end at these sites, history has carried on there too and has turned out to be a layered [*geschichtete*] one. Immediately after the war, as Koselleck experienced it, Russian POWs were interred in Auschwitz, and then later it became a prison for political dissidents and critics of the Communist regimes, as

was also the case with the Soviet special camps of Buchenwald and Sachsenhausen. The period during which governments tried to turn traumatic sites like Auschwitz or Buchenwald into politically motivated commemorative centers by emphasizing a particular aspect of what happened has now come to an end. Ever more diverse voices are now coming to light, including the different perspectives offered by survivors' memories and the heated issue of their incompatibility.

4. *Traumatic sites are overdetermined and multiperspectival.* In contrast to the ways in which meaning is symbolically constructed in museums and monuments, the memory of sites is disunified and irreducibly complex. The same site can be constituted by many different affective frames. For some groups of former prisoners, because the concentration camps and death factories are saturated with the experience of the suffering they endured, it validates their experience and serves as the concrete affirmation of a collective experience. For survivors and their children who mourn their murdered relatives there, it is primarily a cemetery. For those who have no personal connection to the millions of victims, it is primarily an educational tourist site, supported by the onsite museum and its presentation of the preserved scene of the crime through exhibits and tours. For heads of state, the historical location becomes the setting for acts of public recognition, for reminders, declarations, and claims. For historians, it continues to be the archeological setting for ongoing search and preservation. The site becomes what one is looking for, what one knows about it, what brings about a connection. The more objectively concrete it is, the more multifaceted it becomes in relation to these various perspectives.

With historical sites, one enters an in-between world: one can neither completely rely on the magic of an authentic site, nor can the site completely be captured by being given symbolic value. Different in this respect from monuments, commemorative sites, and rituals, the memory of traumatic sites is not even taken up in "constructions of a survivor identity."[15] As historical locations with exiguous material remnants, despite all of their symbolic interpretations and exploitations, they are still something other than a symbol; namely, they are the locations themselves. While cultural symbols are often established and then later dismantled, the persistence of these places suggests a long-term obligation to remember that exceeds the memory frameworks of survivors, of nations, and of Europe.

Analyses and Case Studies

Commemorating and Forgetting

We have just discussed how East German commemorative sites were brought under the aegis of a reunified Germany following the Unification Treaty of 1990. Just as with commemorative sites in the former West German federal states, professional memory workers are at work in those former East German sites too, carrying out the work of conservation, education, and memorialization. But such an arrangement is certainly not in place for each and every traumatic site. Therefore I would like to introduce a counter-example here, of which there are certainly many other instances. A young Austrian artist drew my attention to the concentration camp in Gusen situated next to Mauthausen, near the area where he grew up.[16] From 1940 to 1945, political prisoners, forced laborers, and deported Jews were interned there; 37 000 people died or were killed there (a third of whom were Jewish) as a consequence of hard labor, brutal prison conditions, and torture. According to the website of the Austrian Holocaust Memorial Service, the site can be classified as the largest humanitarian catastrophe of the twentieth century to have happened on present-day Austrian territory.[17]

But there are no professional memory workers here because in contrast to the Mauthausen camp, this one never became an official commemorative site.[18] Following decades of neglect, in 1962 survivors and families of those murdered took it upon themselves to purchase a piece of land and erect the only monument to mark the site. Aside from that one monument, this site was hardly the proverbial water under the bridge that Semprun had dreamed of. This site had been completely transformed, not through the work of nature, however, but through culture or, more precisely, through postwar development. Idyllic single-family dwellings on a quiet street, complete with flourishing gardens in front yards, took the place of the prisoners' barracks. The artist who grew up here in the 1980s had no idea about the site's history: it was simply never discussed as an aspect of the area's social memory. Only when a visitor's center was opened in 2004 did he find out about the concentration camp. "My music school was located in the kitchen barracks of the SS. And during a club party, I had a gun put in my hand for the first time ever in a building that had formerly been the SS shooting gallery."

More than sixty years after the liberation of this camp, it is not just survivors, their families, and the relatives of the murdered who are taking an active interest in the site's history. Members of citizens' initiatives and artists' groups are, too. They are now in a position to bring a certain degree of stability to the lived memory of those personally affected—a lived memory that is on the verge of completely disappearing—by translating it into a cultural memory for those born afterward. And the medium through which this will be accomplished, through which this site of forgetting will be transformed into a site of memory, is headphones. Visitors who come to the area of the former camp will experience something of the history of the place by means of an audio installation of interviews available on headphones. The project Audiowalk Gusen creates a temporal corridor between the everyday present, in which all traces of history have been ineradicably altered, and the traumatic past, which is brought back into memory. The spoken words of survivors, complemented by a sound installation, transport the visitors to the former setting. A site of memory emerges, as it were, from acoustic signals. At this site, where authenticity has literally been reduced to the pure index of "It happened here," where the eye would have to pass through the layers of history to see anything, the ear opens up a more direct route back into the past. Hence the motto of the installation: "You will hear what you can no longer see."

Traumatic Anniversaries

April 26, 2003, marked an anniversary that only very few people remembered. A large memorial service took place in the square of the Erfurt Cathedral, and a minute of silence was observed. At 10:45 the bells began to ring, the very moment at which a year earlier the heavily armed student Robert Steinhäuser had forced his way into Gutenberg secondary school and shot sixteen people. The steps of the school and the cathedral were covered with flowers. The media reports of the service brought the Erfurt incident back into German national memory; whoever followed the service on television or in the papers were not commemorating but rather remembering. By contrast, those who were directly affected were neither commemorating nor remembering; rather they were living through the event again. The televised images showed how the bodies of those in mourning convulsed as if the shots had been fired just yesterday.

The memorial service in Erfurt echoed the tradition of the institutional remembrance of the dead. In many cultures, the first anniversary following a death is given special observance—through the placing of a gravestone or other similar rites. For instance, a son must recite Kaddish, the Jewish prayer for the dead, for his deceased father every day for a year. Such rites help to shape the experience of grief, which can otherwise be so overwhelming: they give a more stable form to these amorphous and volatile emotions. In this respect, we could speak here of the emotional magic of dates: wounds break open again, feelings that, without fail, recede into the distance with time, and its intervening problems suddenly regain all of their undiminished strength with the yearly return of the date of death. Still, the Erfurt anniversary was more than an institutional commemoration of the dead. The memorial service was marked by a trauma that was both individual and social and that not only affected teachers, students, and parents but cast a shadow over the entire city. In this context, the memorial service performed another socio-psychological function: it was supposed to give a ritualized form to the feelings associated with this incident—feelings that were as overwhelming as they were diffuse, of terror, anger, and agonizing affliction—and at the same time to articulate those feelings in a social field and to give them boundaries. It is not expected that this traumatic incident will be repeated in subsequent years with a similarly intense public ceremony. For that to happen, other conditions would have to be met. An incident can only turn into a regularly observed date if the identity of a group is inextricably bound to the memory.

A comparison with another traumatic incident might be instructive here, one also associated with April 26: the nuclear accident of Chernobyl in 1986. The year 2003 was the seventeenth anniversary of the disaster. Since seventeen is not an especially significant "round-numbered" anniversary, the anniversary was only minimally observed. Nonetheless, the television network *Arte* did air a one-hour documentary on the course of events leading up to the nuclear disaster and its aftermath, and *Der Spiegel* ran an article by Henryk M. Broder that draws attention to the high follow-up costs of these nuclear worst-case scenarios. It is not yet clear whether this traumatic event will ever be made into a regular social commemoration. What is at stake here is a still-latent social memory, one whose "coming-out" [English in orig.—Trans.] as an official day of commemoration still lies in the future (if indeed it ever comes to that). And for such a coming-out to happen, of course more is required than a significant round-number anniversary, such as the twentieth anniversary of 2006: an official day of commemoration can only be established when a community of memory is developed that not only combines this anniversary date with specific concerns and a clear message but that also succeeds in generalizing its message by having it anchored in relevant institutions. Unsurprisingly, those responsible for the Chernobyl reactor—whose preferred *modus operandi* has been nondisclosure—have shown little interest in any such strengthening of memory or increased public attention. So it remains to be seen where the initiative will come from to cultivate such a memory.

The trauma that befell the city of New York is a completely different matter. September 11, 2001, the day of the terrorist attacks on the World Trade Center and the Pentagon during which nearly 3,000 people died, had already been commemorated six months after the attacks, on March 11, 2002, before being commemorated on the first anniversary in an enormous public ceremony. Alongside the Fourth of July, this date could potentially become the second national day of commemoration in the United States. The cover of the *Economist* from September 11, 2002, had a single word on it: "Remember." There are already many indications that this imperative to remember (similar to the Hebrew word *Zakhor* in connection with the Holocaust) will continue to be recognized in the future and that it will take on the form of a regulated commemoration. Alongside the excessive, repetitive, and widespread dissemination of the events of September 11 in text, image, and film, the trauma also triggered a wave of artistic engagements and prolonged discussions about the meaning of the attacks, which have been identified as a watershed moment in American history. One often hears it said that the new millennium only really began on this date. So, as it has been anchored in time, it has also been anchored in space. The setting of the event, Ground Zero in South Manhattan, is on the verge of turning into a site of memory with a distinctively national symbolic value. The glass tower that, alongside other building complexes, is part of the design of architect Daniel Liebeskind is 1,776 feet high, which corresponds to the year of the American Declaration of Independence. With that, the site of the trauma became connected to a triumphalist message, and the threat to American democracy is answered with a signal of defiance and a gesture of national self-assertion. Along with the two wars that President Bush has led thus far, the global meaning of the date is being engraved ever deeper into history.

The examples of traumatic memorial days that we have cited here—Erfurt, Chernobyl, September 11—are recent in the sense that there are still witnesses for them. This means that the external temporal framework is still in a subtle relation to the internal rhythm of psychodynamics: for witnesses and survivors, the abstract logic of yearly dates still corresponds to the dynamics of their own inner shock. The example of Helena Janeczek shows how the fine line separating the past from the present in the memory of traumatized survivors can break down on such dates. In her memoir, Janeczek recounts an episode during a trip that she and her mother took to Auschwitz. Before arriving at their destination, her mother suddenly broke down in tears in a Warsaw hotel. It was August 25, 1993. Exactly fifty years ago to the day, the daughter now discovers, her mother had left her parents and her brother Jerzy behind in the ghetto. She had screamed at her parents on that day, saying that she knew exactly where she would be taken and that she "didn't want to be burned up in the ovens!" She left her family immediately afterward and never saw them again.[19]

In the aftermath of traumatic events, yearly dates have a complex function: insofar as they channel and direct mourning, they give shape to trauma. In addition to this function oriented toward the past, these yearly anniversaries also point to the future. In stabilizing memory by repeating it at regular intervals, they articulate the possibility that meaning and identity can be tied to remembrance or that remembrance can be tied to a forward-looking obligation to act for future generations. One condition of this future orientation is that a social, political, or cultural meaning can be developed in relation to the traumatic event. This meaning is developed by memory activists who become the spokespeople for memory communities, using appropriate forms of public discourse to ensure that a certain memory will be taken up in long-term memory. With generational shifts the dynamics of memory undergo fundamental changes once again, even more so when lived memory gives way to a memory that is wholly disseminated by the media. With the help of yearly anniversaries, a memory can be reactivated and renewed not just for decades but for centuries. That way, an event that has lost all connection to personal experience can be given over to an abstract collective of groups and be symbolically and mythically condensed. In this process, individual memory turns into collective commemoration. Anniversaries also offer the possibility of important interactions between individual and collective memory.

Remembering as Repeating—Memory between Myth and History

Generally speaking, there are two kinds of time, the linear time of history and the cyclical time of nature or myth. Whereas in linear time, things irreversibly disappear and are lost forever, in cyclical time, they always predictably return. The embodiments of cyclical time—in myth, the eternal return of the same, and in nature, the renewal that happens each spring—stand in sharp contrast to the historical past as the embodiment of linear time, as what is definitively no longer there. It is not just the cyclical time of nature and myth that exists alongside linear time, the time of history, but so too does the periodic time of memory. What in linear time recedes into the distance and eventually disappears is continually brought back and remembered at specific intervals in periodic time.

Commemoration is a kind of memory that, framed by regular anniversaries, can be conveyed to any number of people and extended for any length of time. The rites and symbols used in commemorative practices turn the inherently unreliable and spontaneous activity of remembering into something more durable. "All rites are repetitive," writes Paul Connerton, "and repetition automatically implies continuity with the past. But there is a distinctive class of rites which have an explicitly backward-looking and calendrical character."[20] Indeed, generally speaking, that is a good working definition of repeatability, but the "what" and the "how" of repetition must be understood in terms of its frameworks.

Commemoration that is framed by anniversaries and repetitions can tend more strongly in the direction of the pole of history or the pole of myth, depending on whether the recollection of a past event takes on the form of a historical memory or a mythic renewal. Whether we are dealing with memory or renewal depends on how the ritual commemoration is carried out—that is, whether or not it is geared toward eliminating the difference between the past and the present or between different past events. Such was the form in which Judaism transformed history back into myth right up until the advent of modernity. Historical experiences could not be recognized as one-time historical events so long as they were immediately subsumed under a few archetypal or perpetually repeated models of history; the binding of Isaac, the destruction of the temple, and the sanctification of the name (martyrdom) are examples of such archetypes. Liturgy, myth, and ritual: these patterns of repetition still play a role in stabilizing Holocaust memory. And there are many examples of yearly political commemorations in which history is transformed into myth. For instance, the names of fallen Serbian heroes in the 1389 Battle of Kosovo were written into the calendar of saints and are commemorated every year throughout the cycle of the seasons and church festivals. Just as the seasons constitute the matrix for religious festivals, so too do those religious festivals constitute a matrix for political anniversaries, which in turn benefit from the aura of sacred calendar time.

We can distinguish three important functions of anniversaries.[21] *First*, they are occasions for interaction and participation. This corresponds to the most basic meaning of anniversaries as a performative form of recollection, *Wieder-Holen* [lit. *bringing-back*—Trans.], and reactivation, which is connected to the possibility of generating a new collective experience. Remembering is about bringing something back through repetitions (*Wieder-Holen mittels Wiederholungen*), so that what is repeated is in the end the repetition itself. In other words, nothing concrete is brought back but what is created is a publicly accessible space and time for the organized return of the past. Repetition re-embodies, reactivates, reanimates. It weaves the past into the present and accomplishes this recollection through these performative acts of return. The most radical form of repetition and participation is the liturgical commemoration, the goal of which according to Gabrielle Spiegel is to "revivify the past and make it live in the present, to fuse past and present, chanter and hearer, priest and observer, into a single collective entity."[22]

A *second* function of anniversaries consists in their providing the opportunity for the staging of a particular group. Imagined communities such as nations; corporate identities such as universities, companies, and cities; interest groups such as opponents of nuclear war or expellees: all such groups require a stage upon which they can, from time to time, be perceived and represented in terms of what they claim to be: a collective identity with a clear image in the midst of an otherwise anonymous and individualistic democratic society. Anniversaries supply the necessary occasion for this. A specific example of such a staging of group identity is the 1951 decision made by the Israeli Knesset to focus Holocaust Remembrance Day on the heroes of the ghetto resistance on the one hand and, on the other, to hold it on the Twenty-seventh of Nisan (in April/May). This decision reflects a desire to bring the memory of the extermination of the Jews in the Second World War into close calendric proximity with other Jewish catastrophes and to frame these traumas in terms of Independence Day and the triumphant birth of the new state.

The *third* function of anniversaries is that they act as triggers for reflection. Through the regular return of a powerfully ritualized liturgical memory, history turns into myth; through the irregular return in intervals of decades or centuries and through controversial new interpretations of the underlying event, myth turns into history. The festivities that took place in 1989 on the occasion of the bicentennial of the French Revolution are a good example of this, as is the occasion of the five hundredth anniversary of the discovery of America by Columbus in 1992.

These three functions simply mark different dimensions and accents on the broad spectrum of commemoration. Only through their interaction are they able to ensure the transgenerational durability of memory and turn an anniversary into a living support for cultural memory.

TEN

The Future of Holocaust Memory

For survivors who experienced the catastrophe of the Holocaust firsthand, it is virtually impossible to accept that the living memory of the event is decreasing with every passing generation and that this gradual forgetting is part of a normal social process. For them, such a normalized forgetting is a scandal. They themselves feel internally pressured to record their experiences in books or on video so that these memories can be passed on to the next generation and safeguarded for posterity's sake. Jewish philosopher Emil Fackenheim added another commandment to the 613 listed in the Hebrew Bible, the 614th, which is the commandment to remember the Holocaust. And not only for the victims is there an imperative to remember this traumatic event—one that produced unimaginable forms of degradation, torture, and mass murder of human life from out of the technologically advanced civilization of the Nazi state. Regardless of how broad the imperative to remember may be, the emphasis on the injunction to remember the atrocities inevitably comes up against the problem of the inability to imagine, or indeed to represent, those atrocities.

Representation

The condition and basis for cultural memory is the ability to preserve memories and experiences in a material storage medium. Without the codification of signs and symbols, without the form that texts and images bring, there is no cultural memory.[1] Put in a more positive way, representations are the very foundation of cultural memory. In the case of the Holocaust, however, this claim touches on a fundamental problem, for the question of whether or not this historical trauma can even be represented has been an inseparable part of the history of this memory from the very beginning.

Over the course of that history, one tendency has always been to deny the ability to represent the Holocaust and, out of that denial, to construe a prohibition on representation. The famous line from Adorno has become a kind of adage: that after Auschwitz poetry can no longer be written.[2] The prohibition on representation that Adorno formulated for language was later extended to include visual presentations. In 1978 Elie Wiesel sharply criticized the American television series *Holocaust*, accusing its producers at NBC of turning an ontological event into a soap opera in which everything became just a phony illusion. He insisted that the Holocaust transcends history and that it can neither be explained nor visualized.[3] At the beginning of the 1990s, author and filmmaker Claude Lanzmann—who engaged the topic solely through the medium of documentary film—expressed much the same viewpoint in the context of Steven Spielberg's *Schindler's List*. Like Wiesel, Lanzmann also emphasizes that some things cannot and should not be represented: "The Holocaust is unique in that, with a circle of fire, it builds a border around itself that cannot be transgressed, because a certain absolute kind of horror cannot be conveyed. To pretend that one is nevertheless conveying it makes one guilty of an offence of the worst transgression. Fiction is such a transgression and I am deeply convinced that there is a ban on representation."[4]

Lanzmann is a purist not only in the sense that he subjects the Holocaust to a strict ban on images but also insofar as he speaks out against notoriously inaccurate and misleading individual memories. His strict conception of truth places him in the tradition of Proust, though he differs from Proust in that he does not locate the authenticity of past moments in involuntary memory but solely in the gestures that are made as the trauma is being acted out, and through which its (literally) overwhelming power is once again reproduced against the will (that is, bypassing memory altogether). So for Lanzmann, only the involuntary memory of the traumatic reflex is authentic. Whereas Lanzmann permits no illusion whatsoever and his audience becomes a would-be direct witness to the event itself, Spielberg can be considered a media virtuoso who performs cinematic operations with an eye to the desired effect (at times the historical setting is recreated; at other times filming takes place on-site; sometimes he films in black and white, sometimes he films in color or colors in the footage afterward).[5]

The idea that it is impossible to represent the trauma of the Holocaust is a leitmotif running through the memory discourse. There is no suitable narrative for Auschwitz, Dan Diner observes; rather, there are only statistics.[6] However, the problem of the representability of the Holocaust has fundamentally changed over time; over the years, it has gradually become less of a problem regarding the production of representations and more of a problem regarding their reception. Are mass murders even imaginable for those on the outside or for those who come after? How much of such histories can really be acquired and become a part of a cultural memory through processes of psychological identification or emotional and intellectual involvement?

These questions regarding the limits of representation, as well as the artistic and ethical decisions they generate, are posed differently by every generation. This is largely because the representation of the Holocaust is not guided by a central responsible body, but has developed in the context of a complex historical, social, and political process. As the twentieth century came to a close, it became possible to approach this process as the "social creation of a cultural fact."[7] As a consequence, a remarkable shift occurred with respect to the position of authors like Adorno and Lanzmann: whereas they were referring directly to the Holocaust as the belated presence of a historical event, we are already referring to a Holocaust that is mediated as a social construction and a cultural representation. Well *before* the time came when survivors and witnesses would no longer be able to contribute their lived memory, a media Holocaust memory has been developed that uses representations as support. It is a memory that we take to be a self-evident part of our social and cultural environment, and it is one into which future generations will grow. The future of memory has definitively begun.

The fact that the Holocaust has been entrenched in the media sixty years after the event does not mean that its representation is fixed or indeed closed. Writer, historian, and Holocaust survivor Ivan Ivanji emphasizes the impossibility of ever exhausting the Holocaust in representations. To express this idea, he takes up the formula spoken in English courts by which the witness commits him- or herself to "the truth, the whole truth, and nothing but the truth."

> The *whole truth* about the concentration camps and all the deaths, the mass executions, the interrogations and the acts of torture committed by people in German uniform would be much more than the sum of all the memories not only of those who were executed, tortured, exiled or endangered people, but obviously also of all of their guards, the administrators of the persecuted, the train personnel of the transports to the camps, the by-standers and everyone who looked away. In a word, the experience of an entire generation. Let's not kid ourselves: the *whole truth* is so unattainable for us, it is as if it didn't exist, and this will be the case in an even more extreme way in fifty or a hundred years.[8]

The "whole truth" of history is and always will remain inaccessible, and this is precisely why we are constantly being forced to find new ways of approaching it. The future of memory essentially depends on whether the impulse to do this remains alive. In this sense, Ivanji also emphasizes that the point of the task of remembering lies "more in the search than it does in the possibility of finding the definitive truth."

Institutionalization

If we do take a media-generated and representation-based memory of the Holocaust to be a self-evident part of our social and cultural environment, this is because of the many forms of institutionalization that work to strengthen and stabilize this memory. Institutions are social establishments in the form of buildings, organizations, hierarchies, bureaucracies, and salaried personnel that help to frame long-term cultural decisions. Institutions embody values, norms, and programs that are not redefined every day or even every generation but are oriented toward long-term validity. Forms of safeguarding longevity as well as forms of safeguarding repetition can be addressed in terms of institutions. Examples of institutions that are oriented toward longevity are monuments, museums, libraries, archives, commemorative centers, and commemorative sites; examples of institutions that focus on ritualized repetitions are vibrant customs, embodied traditions, rites, ceremonies that are occasioned by anniversaries and commemorative years. Cultural memory—along with its promise of the cross-generational longevity of its content—is based on such institutions that safeguard those contents and ensure their continued vitality. With a view to the Holocaust, one could say that this phase of institutionalization was entered into at the international level in the 1990s, or that it was given a new foundation. The memorial site of Yad Vashem in Jerusalem belongs to this history of institutionalization, as does the Holocaust museum in Washington or the new conception of German memorials and the Holocaust memorial in Berlin.

Forms of institutionalization play an important role in the kind of research that falls under catch-phrases like "the politics of the past" and "the politics of history." What Norbert Frei calls "the politics of the past"[9] can be understood in terms of the process of "coming to terms with the past" [*Vergangenheitsbewältigung*] along with its political, ethical, judicial, financial, and pedagogical dimensions and their institutional supports—those of the political system, of the administration of justice, of science, of the economy, and of the educational system. Whenever the issue is above all to come to terms with the past, institutions that focus on preservation and memory do not necessarily play an important role. Under the rubric of what Leggewie and Meyer call "the politics of history," processes of public discussion and political-administrative decision-making are undertaken: "Initiatives centering on the politics of history are not limited . . . to the staging of 'symbolic politics' and events focused on political education: they include tangible decisions (administrative procedures and legislation) as well as mobilizing campaigns at the levels of the state and of civil society, and they have a trickle-down effect on a nation's foreign policy and its security politics."[10] What needs to be added here is of course a consideration of the economic dimension, the question of financing, allocation of resources, the economic budget, and donations, since national and cultural memory not only involve decision-making but are also extremely expensive undertakings.

Institutions strengthen cultural memory not only by securing appropriate sites, collecting traces, recording memories, and exhibiting representations, but they also pool a great deal of unrelated information and make it available as knowledge to be acquired. They select information, condense it through a process of evaluative interpretation, and frame it as stored memory. Institutions bring information onto a higher level. Evolutionary anthropologists speak of a ratchet effect in this context,[11] which means that details can be integrated and tightly packed and so become retrievable and transmissible by others. It is on this basis that knowledge and experience can be carried over into other contexts, that they can be acquired by other individuals and become the basis for further knowledge and new experiences. Institutions embody and ensure important agendas for the future. The future of Holocaust memory will only be as enduring, we could say, as the institutional structures that house it are stable. Architect Peter Eisenman's enormous field of stelae in the middle of Berlin is not only impossible to ignore, but it also evokes a sense of permanence in that it could never be easily removed.

Of course, decisions must first be made regarding which memories are to be raised to the level of institutionalization, and those decisions are made in the context of processes of and struggles over interpretation. Instructive in this regard are instances of memories that have not (yet) reached this level of institutionalization. The 1915 Armenian genocide is one such event that has not yet found its way into the history books. That is because Turkey, as the legal successor to the Ottoman Empire, has not only not condemned the perpetrators, but actually honors them as national heroes and founding fathers. Monuments to them are established; streets and buildings are named after them. Under these kinds of conditions, the archives that would be required for a scholarly investigation of the traumatic events remain inaccessible. As a consequence of this nonrecognition, this memory has not been brought forth into tangible representations and has not been made an object of scholarly research. So the orally transmitted memories of survivors have had to be conveyed to the cultural memory of those who come after without the support of external structures and institutions. Under these conditions, the forms in which memories are preserved and transmitted must rely solely on ritualized repetition. In Armenian society, there is "no being together, no daily routine, no celebration at which the experiences of the parents, the grandparents and the great grandparents are not recounted. With the recounting, the experiences are made present and passed on."[12] It follows that Armenians constitute a community of memory, of narrative, and of experience of the kind that is typical of the family. The temporal limits of about eighty to one hundred years (up to the third generation) that generally define family memory are surpassed in this case through institutionalized forms of transmission and occasions for commemoration. In this exceptional case, an orally transmitted memory has turned into a cultural memory. Cultural modes of securing continuity and strengthening identification, as well as models for transmission (something like medieval dirges) also play important roles, all of which can be drawn on to shape the traumatic memory.

Another example of a memory that for the time being lacks an institutional basis but for which huge efforts are being made to raise it over the limit of a three-generation memory is the memory of the expellees. The Centre against Expulsion that Erika Steinbach has proposed could lend institutional support to what is still mostly an orally transmitted memory, thereby making it into a cultural memory.[13] In this context, questions regarding how appropriate or inappropriate the memory is, how functional or dysfunctional (but *not* regarding how correct or incorrect it is), still need to be addressed and decided upon in the fields of history and politics.

Mass Media

Together with processes of institutionalization, the mass-mediatization of Holocaust memory has also made huge advances. This development, which also involves the commercialization of memory, is looked upon critically by many, but nonetheless has become an unavoidable social fact.[14] Looking back, historian Saul Friedländer observes that before historians took it up, the mass media in the guise of the television series *Holocaust* had already placed Holocaust memory on the agenda. Elie Wiesel had vehemently polemicized against this same series at the end of the 1970s, and his insistence on the singularity and sacred character of the Holocaust would subsequently be taken up in Germany eight years later with the Historians' Debate.[15] After his work *Night* was chosen as an official selection for the book club of the popular American television host Oprah Winfrey in late 2006, he refused to acknowledge it or to appear on her show. The Holocaust as an ontological evil can no longer be spared the vicissitudes of mass culture today, as Adorno had still demanded. Even Henryk M. Broder's cynical catch-phrase of "Shoah business" does not go far enough, since business and memory are always bound up with each other in a world that is more and more mediatized.

One often hears it said that the mass media are the real media of cultural memory today.[16] To be sure, mass media generate the cultural environment for individual and social remembering. What reaches us through books and films, through television documentaries and talk shows, through videos and websites, confirms, supplements, corrects, and unavoidably colors our memory. But are they really the media of cultural memory? The catalogues of publishers accommodate occasions from the cultural memorial calendar. Films and television series increase public awareness about certain events and make the past present through effective processing. They achieve a resonance with the public that gets further developed in print media and prolonged by means of word-of-mouth. As Ivan Ivanji has observed, though, the notion of the public is a "somewhat confusing concept."[17] It is less an independent sphere for open dialogue and discussion than a costly and elaborate staging of topics that will be the center of attention for a while and then will cool down again after a certain amount of time. Whatever makes an appearance on the stages of the mass media must immediately exit again to make room for new things. The mass media are tethered to attention spans, which are short, and not to memory, which is ruminative and has a prolonged effect.

Mass media create important impulses and triggers for cultural memory, but they do not produce memory themselves. While they might be essential for the activation of memory, other bodies are required to shape it. Most of what is on offer in terms of mass media is irretrievably lost; a small portion of it ends up in storage memory, a tiny segment of which becomes an element of functional memory. What ends up being preserved in cultural memory, and what does not, is not solely determined by the number of Oscars, visitor numbers, and ratings, however, but depends more on whether debates succeed in tapping into something, whether elements of certain works are taken up by others, or whether certain books or films are repeatedly cited and are given new kinds of reception.

The significance of the market lies in how it mobilizes scarce resources of attention for the dynamics of cultural memory. However, the market itself is solely focused on the present; its task is to allow for the circulation of products and information in the here and now. It is responsible neither for the maintenance of inventory (storage memory) nor for the formulation of lasting values (functional memory). Its approach to cultural memory is determined by the commerce that can be made of it. Sixty years after 1945, books appear about the end of the war; there are books about Mozart during Mozart Year, and during the celebratory year of Heine's birth, books come out about Heine. The mass media take up the theme of memory and cause it to circulate throughout society. Within democratic societies, the market not only generates attention but also activates cultural memory and relates it to the memory of individuals. Disconnected from bodies of cultural memory, though, the market tends to be more destructive of memory insofar as it positions itself in relation to the ever-changing present day.

Nevertheless, the market and the public sphere are the media in which the levels of cultural and individual memory constantly become intertwined with one another in new ways. Memory becomes ossified when only the political framework of memory is involved, as is the case with some official commemorative speeches that do not correspond to anything at the levels of social discourse or personal memories. In turn, when memories are framed exclusively in terms of individuals and small groups, no dialogue or exchange results at the level of society as a whole, and no stable reference points regarding the past are made in the culture to which the collective as a whole might refer. Without the market and the public sphere, the disparate worlds of memory cannot come together.

The Internet as Medium of Memory?

For memories to go from personal communicative networks to the cultural memory, media are needed both to record the memories and to disseminate them. The dissemination of texts and images is the business of the book market and the publishing industry; the dissemination of animated images is the business of the film and television industry and of the growing market in videos and DVDs, which is now being organized in a similar way to the book market. Because of its hybrid nature, the Internet diverges from the structure of all these markets. It is hybrid not only in the sense that it seamlessly brings together all the forms of recording like writing, image, and sound, but also in that it combines the functions of recording, communicating, and dissemination in completely new ways. The Internet is an individualized mass medium that bypasses the usual institutions of publication and dissemination. On the Internet, the distinction between public and private collapses; anyone who has access to this medium can produce his or her own public sphere. The Internet is a medium of global interaction and communication, but is it also a medium of memory?

In his novella *Crabwalk*, Günter Grass draws attention to the significance of the Internet as a catchment for what is collectively repressed. He shows how this medium thrives on raising and remembering issues that contradict the official frameworks of social and political memory. "With the zeal fueled by his passion for thoroughness," writes the narrator, "my son had succeeded in using his Web site to draw the right-wing circles' muddled attention to the forgotten ship and its human cargo."[18] He depicts very precisely how memory happens in this medium:

Now there ensued the kind of no-holds-barred total communication possible on the Internet. Voices from home and abroad joined in. One contribution even came from Alaska. You could see how current the sinking of the long-forgotten ship had become. With the exclamation, seemingly emanating from the present, "The *Gustloff* is sinking!," my son's home page opened a window to the entire world, launching . . . "a much overdue discourse." Yes, of course! Now everyone could know and judge for himself what had happened on 30 January 1945 off the Stolpe Bank; the Webmaster had scanned in a map of the Baltic and marked with didactic precision all the sea-lanes leading to the site of the tragedy.[19]

The Internet is articulated by Grass as a theater for a battle of memories, for the return of the repressed and the revitalization of age-old prejudices: "The chat room promptly filled with hate. 'Jewish scum' and 'Auschwitz liar' were the mildest insults. As the sinking of the ship was dredged up for a new generation, the long-submerged hate slogan 'Death to all Jews' bubbled up to the digital surface of contemporary reality: foaming hate, a maelstrom of hate. Good God! How much of this has been dammed up all this time, is growing day by day, building pressure for action."[20] The Internet exists outside of social institutions, and by and large it also continues to lie beyond the authority of regulatory bodies. Everyone has to find out for him- or herself what is true and documented, what is false and invented, what is the product of individual fantasy and what is academic research, what is serious information and what is blasphemy or pornography. In complete contrast to newspapers and publishers, there is no process of selection or evaluation of the information floating around there. In this respect, Grass also speaks of "information roaming worldwide" and a "global playground."[21]

Political theorists Erik Meyer and Claus Leggewie have also investigated the Internet as a medium of memory.[22] They analyze how private memories of September 11, 2001, get transformed on the Internet into a collective or even cultural memory. Their results suggest that the Internet as an interactive medium with the potential for mass communication has developed into an important virtual site of memory that intertwines the private and the public, what is close and what is far, what is local and what is global. Novel in this development are primarily the forms within which history and memory are constituted "from below." Alongside many different individual activities, approaches are also being developed for the construction of frameworks and the integration of memorial activities. For instance, the September 11 Digital

Archive consists of a website that is being maintained by two universities. It begins with the following description of its aim: "The September 11 Digital Archive uses electronic media to collect, preserve and present the history of September 11, 2001 and its aftermath." To achieve that end, there is a virtual museum to which everyone can contribute. "Tell your story" is the prompt to submit written contributions; under the rubrics of "photo or other images" and "video," further material is collected. We are clearly being confronted here with the most radical instance of what Clemens Wischermann has called "history under the paradigm of individualism"[23]: thanks to the Internet, everyone can take part in writing the history of this event. By being framed in terms of this professionally initiated and maintained archive, testimonies that would otherwise be quite ephemeral or fleeting achieve a degree of stability and orderliness that is lacking in other such Internet submissions. For, as a storage medium the Internet does not have much to offer: what is written on a piece of paper has much better chances of surviving than an electronic data-set, whose staying power often lasts not much longer than forty days. We are often unsure whether or not what we find on the Internet today will still be there tomorrow. Secondary initiatives such as this one, which require advanced technical know-how and not inconsiderable maintenance costs, are the first to establish something along the lines of structure and stability in the fluid medium of the Internet. In the context of the structured online archive and its theme-specific Internet portal, Meyer and Leggewie speak of approaches that are being developed to "institutionalise individualized mass commemoration."[24]

What Keeps Memory Alive? Dangers and Opportunities

In stark contrast to the Armenian genocide, the Holocaust is currently the best documented among all cases of crimes against humanity. It has a presence in commemorative sites, museums, archives, exhibitions, documentation centers, memorials, and art installations, as well as in books, television series, films, and video testimonies. In view of the exponential growth in the amount of research material on the topic and the levels of engagement in the mass media, we can actually spare ourselves the question of whether Holocaust memory has a future. In fact, there is no memory whose course is more clearly set in terms of cultural memory. The question is thus not whether this memory will continue to exist once it is no longer sustained by survivors' testimonies, but rather, what will the quality of this memory be once it has completely passed over into cultural memory?

There is no danger that the Holocaust will be forgotten in the future, but there is a danger that it will be subject to a flattening out and a narrowing. So, a few concluding remarks shall be made here that pertain to this diminishing quality of memory as well as to ways of possibly enhancing it.

Ossification. One question would involve the forms that can best stabilize memory without at the same time causing it to become ossified. Development of such forms will depend in particular on processes that are able to draw memory away from the lure of stereotyping. Memory must reanimate stored knowledge in a lively engagement involving problems and issues in the present. Such a renewal resists the routinized and ossified use of clichés. The arts play an important role in this renewal to the extent that they make important cultural contributions to the preservation of truth through exhibitions, texts, and film. By developing insightful and provocative approaches to representing the past, artists can broaden the historical imagination.

Neutralization. A French maxim of memory that arose in the context of the defeat against the German-Prussian army in the War of 1870–71 (in reference to the loss of Alsace-Lorraine) goes as follows: "Never speak of it, always think of it!" The inversion of this maxim approximates the reality of an excessively mediatized memory: "Always speak of it, never think of it." This criticism is directed solely toward the tendency of the mass media to streamline their programming and the deflation in value that results from oversaturation. In no way is this meant to be a blanket argument against the exploration of memory on the part of the mass media. Maxim 40 of Adorno's *Minima Moralia* goes in that direction. There was still consensus between Heidegger and Adorno in the 1950s on this point, which, in the context of a traumatic past, talking was silver and silence gold. This silence can only be an option, however, when everyone is still aware of what is at stake. Once communicative memory has largely passed over into a cultural memory, the mass media in particular becomes indispensable as a support for this memory.

Delegating. As memory culture becomes more and more institutionalized and professionalized—and that includes substantial numbers of memory workers—the danger arises that memory is simply delegated to specialists. The task of remembering might be in good hands as a consequence, but by largely disregarding the general population, individuals could feel that they were relieved of the burden.

Trivialization. The problem of the flattening of memory necessarily arises when memory is taken out of its context. Standardization, commercialization, and sentimentality are the expressions of a memory that is both uncontroversial and cost-free. For instance, Jewish American historian Peter Novick disputes the idea that Holocaust memory in the United States is a memory of central and vital importance. In his opinion, it is much too "cost-free" for that to be the case.[25] In his opinion, a memory of slavery, of the decimated native population, of the civil war, or of Hiroshima would be controversial.

Narrowing. It will therefore be a matter of gradually dismantling the exclusive focus on the Holocaust that has resulted in all kinds of omissions and of introducing greater differentiations. In concrete terms, that means helping other victim groups gain recognition in the public eye, groups like the Sinti and the Roma, homosexuals, and those persecuted on religious or political grounds. When it is no longer a matter of a competition between claims and when practices of mutual exclusion in a broadened European memory have been overcome, public recognition could take the place of other forms of traumatization that alongside the Holocaust are also connected to the Second World War, such as the bombing of German cities and the experience of expulsion in Eastern Europe.

On the basis of these considerations of both the contents of memory and the forms in which those contents are being remembered, possible answers arise in response to the question of what, then, is keeping Holocaust memory alive, particularly in Germany.

Controversies. In a democratic culture of debate, memory is especially invigorated through conflicts and debates.[26] Thus, for instance, the title of the publication documenting the various debates about the Holocaust memorial (*Der Denkmalstreit—das Denkmal?* [The Dispute over the Memorial—The Real Memorial?])[27] suggests that the controversies surrounding the memorial might themselves be considered part of the memorial. Likewise, the exhibit about the crimes of the Wehrmacht achieved an even great resonance due to the controversy triggered by it, traveling to cities across Germany twice in quick succession.

Scandals. Nothing enlivens memory discourse as much as scandals do. Touching on taboos always brings about flare-ups. In Germany, memory is activated through periodic uproars on the spectrum between taboos on the one hand and norms of commemoration on the other. One only need think of the (very different) protagonists Jenninger, Walser, Möllemann, and Hohmann.

Regeneration. A decontextualized memory needs to make contact with individual life stories, develop points of reference to its own existence, make bridges to the present, and have a concrete, spatial, and temporal life world. Through modes of regeneration such as these, an otherwise abstract and depersonalized history can become a meaningful part of one's own memory. The "Stolpersteine" (Stumbling Stones) project by Gunter Demnig is an excellent example of this. The *Stolpersteine* are brass plaques onto which are stamped the name, date of birth, and the fate of individual victims of National Socialism who were deported and murdered. The Stolperstein is then laid flush into the sidewalk in front of the last residence of the victim. To date, the artist has installed over 45,000 stones in over 610 localities.[28]

Multimediality. The many languages of memory and their different media (academic history, memoirs, testimonies, films, exhibitions, documentaries) each develop their own perspectives, and each offers a different view of traumatic events. As a consequence these different treatments can supplement each other and find points of intersection, but competition and friction between them also arise that prevent a rigid and unified image of this past from ever developing. The multiplicity of the different memory media can help to refer us back—as Ruth Klüger puts it—to "the grainy resistance of what happened," instead of it being filtered out "until it's unrecognizable in the telling."[29]

We need historians to reconstruct this past for us, and we need artists to put it in concrete terms. Above all, there needs to be retrospective connections made to concrete life histories and authentic sites, in order to shield this memory from generalizations, from being delegated to specialists and from becoming gradually derealized. The future of memory will depend on its ability to renew itself. Confronted by the ongoing threat of being reduced to stereotyped images and formulations, we particularly need the arts to extend the historical imagination and to invent powerful forms of recollecting the past through the different forms and media of expression that are available to them. But in this respect as well, ritualized and symbolic forms of commemoration should not be automatically discredited, as so often happens these days; remembering requires not only the factual basis of sites and archives on the one hand and artistic expression on the other. It also needs to be supported through repeated occasions and repeatable gestures. Those who adamantly reject the task of giving cultural shape to memory must be prepared to be visited by the past in unexpected and uncontrollable ways. For a traumatic past that is not remembered will, at some point, begin to haunt.

ELEVEN

Europe as a Community of Memory

At the very height of the development of nationalism during the late nineteenth century, a prescient Ernst Renan succinctly claims that "nations are not eternal. . . . They were begun, they will end. A European confederation will probably replace them."[1] The nation as the basis for collective identity has in fact begun to wane as the dominant reference point for collective identities, and new forms of collective identity are being developed, both above and below the level of nationhood. In this process, the tendency toward the splintering of identities from *below* national identity seems to be quite a lot stronger than the tendency toward unification from *above*; the disintegrative trend is more pronounced than the trend toward integration. The most obvious example of this splintering is to be found in the United States, where national myths and visions have lost their color and persuasive force and have given way to ethnic identities. The national myth once demanded that every immigrant give up his or her origin and history in order to devote him- or herself fully to the collective national project. The nation was united not by a common heritage but by a promise, a common dream: "To be an American (unlike being English or French or whatever) is precisely to imagine a destiny rather than to inherit one."² It was thought that what people had in common would gradually replace whatever divided them. What counted was what bound people together, and this was the vision of a world in which people enjoyed equal rights and opportunities.

The metaphor for this concept of nationhood, "the melting pot," was subsequently replaced by "the salad bowl," in which multiple origins and different experiences are retained. In general, one could say that the future has lost much of its power to integrate while the past has become much more important in the formation of identity. This shift toward the past occurred when suppressed, silenced, and unrecognized stories of suffering began to return. How does Renan put this? "Shared suffering unites more than joy does. As far as national memories go, acts of mourning are more potent than those of triumph, since they impose duties and require common effort."³ The tremendous persuasive power and effective force of the national myth made ethnic, regional, and internal social differences *invisible*; class distinctions, power relations, and gender hierarchies could also be overlooked (and so untouched) in a society in which it was possible to imagine a symbolically integrated national unity. In our day, allegiances that are tied to group-specific experiences of victimhood are now taking the place of that national unity. This fragmentation of national identity has resulted in the so-called hyphenated identities that emerged in the aftermath of colonialism and the Holocaust, such as African-American, Native American, Caribbean-British or Jewish-Austrian.

European Identity Formation

While the United States is witnessing the formation of identities from below the level of the nation, Europe is engaging the opposite issue: the formation of supranational identities. In hindsight, the year 1989 has been dubbed "the year of Europe" since, despite manifest resistances to the constitutional treaty, the consolidation of the European Union could be described as a success story. However, it still remains to be seen whether the economic and administrative achievements will be matched in the cultural sphere. A nation, Renan wrote, is not only a voluntary collective but also has "a soul" and is based on a spiritual principle.⁴ A cultural idea of Europe or a European identity could "remedy the absence of European identification and solidarity." There is indeed widespread agreement that the project of European unity "suffers from a serious deficit of emotional ties."⁵ Can we conceive of something like a European identity?⁶ Is such a thing even desirable? How could Europe become an imagined community? And what would contribute to these collective ideas?

There are basically two possibilities of forming a European identity that I differentiate here as eclectic and relational. *Eclectic identity* arises from a collection of specific traits, characteristics, properties, and events that can be identified as genuinely European and so lend a certain European quality to those who identify with them. The list of attributes that are considered European is long and highly variable.⁷ They include inventions, achievements, and institutions that originated in Europe, such as democracy, universities, free cities, progress of the sciences, innovation in the arts, human rights, professional history writing, and the romantic idea of a self-determining nation as a collective subject of history. The problem of such lists is that they are always eclectic. Athenian democracy, Roman law, Montesquieu's division of powers, and human rights are all well and good but what about the Inquisition, slavery, iconoclasm, and pogroms, all of which are also European inventions? We boast about tolerating difference and multiplicity but, as we do so, we must not forget Europe's history of divisiveness and schisms, of its religious and national wars. We emphasize humanistic values, but we also need to think of Auschwitz and Bosnia as being a part of Europe.⁸

Relational identity is a process whereby European identity arises out of the specific arrangements it has with what it perceives to be its "other." For the Greeks of antiquity, Asia, represented by the Persians, was the "other" against whom they established their first great alliance; in late antiquity, the Western Roman Empire was defined as the "other" to the Eastern Roman Empire; in the eighteenth and nineteenth centuries, the Orient became Europe's "other"; in twentieth-century Germany, the Occidental West [*Abendland*] was defined as the third way between "West" (capitalist America) and "East" (Communist Russia). Of course, Europe was also the "other" against which nation-states outside of Europe defined themselves, as was done, for example, in the United States during the nineteenth century in a bid to develop its own cultural identity. After WWII, a close alliance was established between the United States and Western Europe in the face of tensions with the Communist East. The idea of "the West" that replaced the Christian "Occident" stood for a complex of values including democracy, secularization, modernity, technology, and capitalism. Following September 11, 2001, and America's "War on Islamic Terrorism," the American part of this West has been obliged once again to base its own identity more strongly on its Christian fundamentalist values. At the beginning of the Iraq war, this Western alliance further disintegrated into (in the estimation of Donald Rumsfeld) a reluctant Old Europe and a loyal New Europe. To summarize this brief overview, European identity is clearly still in flux and will be formed out of the development of new political arrangements. These shifting configurations reflect the embeddedness of Europe within larger structures of global problems and political conflicts.

For Renan, *collective identities* require both a common goal for the future and a shared past experience. So they consist of two separate components: past experiences and values. Is the same true of Europe? There is widespread agreement about values for the future: the basic rights of democratic civil society are compulsory for all member states. Political theorist Bassam Tibi, a German Muslim, a former student of Max Horkheimer and a professor of political science and Islamic studies at the University of Göttingen, developed the idea of European *Leitkultur*, or a European core culture, which is defined entirely on the basis of values and disregards experiences in the past. Tibi's idea of *Leitkultur* was quickly appropriated by politicians in such a way that has distorted its original meaning. By *Leitkultur* or core culture, Tibi means "a framework for integration."[9] Beginning with the premise that every community needs a "consensus of values and an identity," he formulates the standard of a "European identity for Germany":

> To sum up in a few words: Priority of reason over religious revelation, that is to say, over the authority of absolute religious truths; *individual* human rights (over communal rights); secular democracies based on the separation of church and state; *universally recognized* pluralism as well as a mutually effective secular tolerance. Alone the acceptance of these values forms the substance of a civil society.[10]

Tibi limits the problem of European identity to a consensus on values. From his German Muslim perspective, the emphasis on pluralism and rights to cultural and religious difference is entirely understandable. However, at the same time other people are raising questions about the possibility of developing a collective European heritage. In October 1999 a conference took place in the European Parliament in Brussels to prepare for the foundation of a museum of Europe that was to open in 2007 on the fiftieth anniversary of the European Community. It was mandated to strengthen the historical consciousness of a transnational European identity by giving it concrete and visible shape. The conference, led by Romano Prodi and attended by former German chancellors Helmut Schmidt and Helmut Kohl, encountered difficulties concerning the geographic and historical extent of Europe. Consensus was achieved on Charlemagne as the founder of Europe and on the definition of Europe as the "off-spring of Catholicism and northern barbarians," a formula that from the outset excludes the sources of Europe in ancient Israel, Greece, and Roman antiquity.[11]

Another initiative to determine the historical parameters of Europe began when an international group of historians met in March 2000 to decide on European sites of memory. The precedent for this initiative was Pierre Nora's project of *Les lieux de mémoire* (1984–92), for which Nora, in collaboration with over a hundred historians, succeeded in turning the question of national sites of memory into a huge research and publication project. Since its publication, the work had resonated well beyond the borders of France and had found adherents in many European countries such as Holland, Spain, Austria, and Germany. Therefore it made sense to apply this national model to the transnational case of Europe and ask whether Europe could also be considered a "continental community of memory."[12] In addition to this project, various other politicians, historians, and image makers are working on a collective European memory that is regulated by means of school textbooks, collective symbols, and commemorative days. Of course, this initiative will only be effective if it resists the abstract top-down method of implementation and draws on the local conditions of existing national and regional communities of memory.

The Holocaust as the Memory of Europe?

Alongside various initiatives for the development of historical museums and *lieux de mémoire*, another framework for a collective European memory is also being explored. In fact, historians like Dan Diner had long argued that there is only one answer to the question about a collective European point of reference in the past—namely, the Holocaust. This, he argues, is the paradigmatic European *lieu de mémoire*, and every cultural construction of a European identity must begin with it as its point of departure. And in fact, institutional steps have been taken to enshrine this collective memory as the core of European identity. On January 27, 2000, Sweden's Prime Minister Göran Persson invited representatives from sixteen nations (among which thirteen were current and future European Union member states) to a conference in Stockholm to discuss the forms that Holocaust commemoration and education should take. In the first year of the new millennium, fifty-five years after the liberation of Auschwitz, consensus was achieved on the point that the murder of six million European Jews should become a collective memory and that this memory should form the basis of a commitment to the values of civil society and serve as a reminder of the obligation to protect the rights of minorities. The inaugural declaration of the *Task Force for International Cooperation on Holocaust Education, Remembrance, and Research*—first established in 1998 and now including twenty-two nation-states—clearly sets the course for the commitment to perpetuate the memory of the Holocaust. The last article of the Stockholm declaration states:

> It is appropriate that this, the first major international conference of the new millennium, declares its commitment to plant the seeds of a better future amidst the soil of a bitter past. We empathize with the victims' suffering and draw inspiration from their struggle. Our commitment must be to remember the victims who perished, respect the survivors still with us, and reaffirm humanity's common aspiration for mutual understanding and justice.[13]

Five years later, on January 24, 2005, the United Nations held a special session for the first time in its history in commemoration of the Holocaust. In his address, Kofi Annan emphasized that "the evil that exterminated six million Jews and others in these camps still threatens all of us today"; the crimes of the Nazis are "not something that we can relegate to the distant past in order to forget about them."[14]

The project of universalizing the lessons of a specific memory requires the extension of the boundaries of collective memory. As to our question from earlier as to *Who is remembering?* the answer is, namely, an unlimited number of people. Those who take up the obligation to remember the Holocaust are far greater in number than the Jewish victims, their descendants, and the common destiny of the Jewish people; this collective also includes the descendants of the perpetrators, bystanders, and those who looked away, as well as all ethically minded future generations. So, as the memory of the Holocaust becomes universalized, it also becomes fundamentally open. However, this universalization will become a problem if it leads to a leveling down or a homogenization of different memories. In Germany for instance, taking on the obligation to remember the victims could result in the disappearance of its own perpetrator memory. That is why Volkhard Knigge objected to the universalization of victim memory and warned against "naïvely importing notions like 'Holocaust education'"[15] But our second question is also relevant—namely, *Who is being remembered?* With the phrase "six million Jews and others," Annan at least insinuated that even the boundaries of the group being remembered are porous. In the run-up to the establishment of the central Holocaust memorial in Berlin, this question played an important role; some of the most heated debates focused largely on the many victims' groups to be remembered (aside from the Jews, there are the Roma and Sinti, homosexuals, and Jehovah's witnesses) and their hierarchization. As Peter Novick reminds us, there was a similar controversy in the late 1970s, between Simon Wiesenthal and Elie Wiesel. Both are famous Jewish survivors of the Holocaust; the one devoted his life to the pursuit of perpetrators while the other has devoted his life to the memory of the victims. The number "six million," which has become a virtual synonym for the Holocaust, was modified by Simon Wiesenthal. He realized that, for many people today, the real number of Holocaust victims came to about eleven million: "Six million Jews and some five million other peoples." Elie Wiesel resisted redefining the terms of the Holocaust on the grounds that it could "falsify it in the name of a misguided universalism."[16]

Proper universalization for Wiesel involves extending the group who remembers but not the groups who are being remembered. In *The Holocaust and Memory in the Global Age*, Daniel Levy and Natan Sznaider also support a globalization of memory of the Holocaust that extends beyond the boundaries of Europe. Their argument is that in the globalized modern world, whose most important feature is deterritorialization and the transcendence of borders, the "cosmopolitization of Holocaust memory" provides the foundation for a global culture of memory whereby remembered barbarism can become the basis for a global politics of human rights.[17] Sociologist Jeffrey Alexander makes a similar point when he emphasizes how raising the memory of the Holocaust to the universal level of ethical memory for a global humanity requires the transcendence of localized constructions of collective memory. However, he sees things in a slightly more differentiated way and suggests that non-Western nations cannot remember the Holocaust in the same way as Western nations can. Nonetheless, in the context of cultural globalization, they certainly have become aware of its symbolic meaning and social significance. Therefore, Alexander imagines that "non-Western nations could develop trauma dramas that are functional equivalents to the Holocaust." Thanks to this kind of social process, the cultures of East and West could learn "to share the experiences of one another's traumas and to take vicarious responsibility for the other's afflictions."[18] So, while a collective memory is always going to be limited, images and symbols from one area can be extended beyond borders and, along with them, so too can solidarity and responsibility.[19]

We need to differentiate between the universalization of moral values and the particularity of historical memories. But what further complicates the issue is the fact that a global struggle for recognition within the veritable minefield of identity politics is taking place between these levels of universalization and particularity. Victims compete for recognition in the current post-traumatic age and are not yet assured that "the destruction of the foundation of their collective identity" will be "recognized as a crime."[20] The global struggle for recognition responds to experiences of extreme violence in the form of genocides, colonial exploitation, and repression, along with the systematic cultural destruction of minorities. "The oppressed people who are the majority of the people in the world expect recognition for what they suffered, at a time when we failed to hear their cries of suffering and distress. The echoes today are a call for justice. Recognition includes our responsibility toward the past. It is the precondition for any true dialogue in the future."[21] That the memory of the Holocaust has a well-entrenched position in this struggle no longer necessarily implies that the suppression of the claims of other victims' groups is supplanted; rather, it helps these claims to assert themselves. As such, references made by other victims' groups to the Holocaust are less and less about making competing or relativizing claims and can be increasingly understood in terms of a globally recognized paradigm in the struggle for recognition.

European Memories after 1945

Persson's initiative was undeniably effective and important, and it must remain a responsibility for the future. Of course, it is important to remember that a memory is a vibrant cultural force only when it is not solely determined from above but is supported at local levels as well. In the United States, the forms that have developed for the memory of the Holocaust are entirely divorced from local conditions. Indeed, this memory does not have the same quality and resonance everywhere. We therefore have to consider the difference between a global and a European memory of the Holocaust and, furthermore, between a European and a national Holocaust memory. If we overlook these different historical levels and identities or paint them with too broad a brush, we run the risk of ending up with a rather abstract memory construct.

In Europe, the historical site of the genocide of the Jews, Holocaust memory is anything but abstract or removed. The Holocaust has left memory traces in practically every country. These traces are embedded in the history of the Second World War, which all nations in Europe experienced but which each experienced differently. In other words, what Persson defines in terms of a transnational memory encounters a variety of national memory constellations and collisions in the different European countries.[22] This problem was emphatically pointed out by Swiss author Adolf Muschg when he wrote that "what binds Europe together and what divides it is essentially the same thing: the common memory."[23] More than sixty years after the events, we Europeans are still far from a unified memory; on the contrary, it has to be said that the Second World War and the Holocaust remain subjects of conflict, debate, and controversy. Apparently, national memories cannot be integrated within European memory as easily as the *Task Force for International Cooperation on Holocaust Education, Remembrance, and Research* might wish. To understand the national subtexts for European memory more clearly, we need to turn to the history of European memory prior to and after 1945.

Prior to the First World War, in the heyday of nationalism, memories were more strongly attached to the collective. There existed something like an absolute sovereignty of memory, with a strongly self-referential component. What was remembered in a neighboring country was not taken into account; along with its arsenal of weapons, every nation was also armed with precisely those memories that bolstered its positive self-image, its will to power, and its claim to superiority. This politics of memory was an aspect of national ideology that would lead directly to the Second World War.

One can hardly say that the age of memory dawned after the end of the Second World War. Memories were politically explosive and indeed useless during an era when Europe was both divided and bound together by a sharp ideological contest between the two superpowers of East and West, of communism and capitalism. During this period, the enemy had to be given a new image, making it inopportune to recall that the Soviet Union had recently been one of the Allies in the war against Hitler and the Axis powers. Once Hitler was gone, this alliance quickly collapsed and was replaced by the new frontline of the Iron Curtain. As a result, memories were frozen and the images of history were realigned to conform to the political status quo of the Cold War.

This situation changed dramatically in 1989, which brought about a radical political change. As has often been emphasized, the collapse of the polarized political framework triggered an eruption of suppressed memories and a reawakening of history. Following 1989, after a period of extremely stylized and standardized images of the past, many European nations were finally confronting conflicting, painful, and shameful memories. When the East-West conflict came to an end, the thaw after the deep freeze revived not only memories of the past but also the idea of Europe. However, the return of memories in Western and Eastern Europe had very different and even opposed consequences.

In the West, the nations' closing of the ranks led to a crumbling of national myths and the opening of archives following the collapse of the Soviet Union, all of which contributed to the breakthrough of memory. In light of new historical research, official interpretations of history and national myths were being questioned and new lines of conflict were opening up. In an essay entitled "Myth and Memory in Postwar Europe" (1992), New York political theorist Tony Judt showed that during the Cold War, the national memories of Europe were frozen in such a way as to support the political status quo. According to Judt, the official version of history, according to which "responsibility for the war, its suffering and its crimes, lay with the Germans," had the effect that many memories of what happened during and after the war "got conveniently lost."[24] For Judt, this did not entail minimizing German guilt; rather, he points to the exonerating effect it had on the memory of other European nations. The Hungarian writer Peter Esterházy expressed a similar idea when, in the speech he gave in St. Paul's Church in Frankfurt upon receiving the 2004 Peace Prize, he said, "Concealing one's own guilt by referring to Germany's crimes is a European habit. Hatred for the Germans is the foundation of the post-war period."[25]

During this period, there were two generally recognized and honorable roles that European nations could make use of: victim and resister. Austria is a good example of the first—the nation as victim, while France, especially as regards the significance attached to the Résistance, exemplifies the second—the nation as resister. In both countries, of course, there were people who were victims of Hitler's Germany and there were those who engaged in acts of resistance. Therefore, it is not a question of how memory was distorted, but alone a question of the ways in which such memories were generalized and politically instrumentalized after the war. In this regard, psychoanalysts speak of screen memories that serve to protect a positive self-image. In other words, one remembers something in order to be better able to forget something else. When applied to the realm of national memory, this means that one remembers one's own suffering in order to avoid being reminded of one's own guilt. Remembering oneself in the role of victim can also block out the memory of other victims, in particular Jewish victims. National myths arise when convenient partial memories supported by experience are claimed as the homogeneous and exclusive memory for the entire national collective. In that way, inconvenient memories are excluded from the national discourse and erased from the self-image. In the 1990s, these defensive strategies became more and more the subject of controversy, and over the last ten years, nations across Europe have shifted the coordinates for national images of history, making way for more complex representations.[26] In France, the acknowledgment of the collaboration of the Vichy regime shattered the national myth of the resistance; in post-Waldheim Austria, the official version of Austria as "the first victim of Hitler" became problematic; the Polish, who were particularly made to suffer persecution and extermination at the hands of the Germans, have also had to confront their own history of anti-Semitism; in Italy, the communist and Fascist memories remain as divided as ever; and even Switzerland, the neutral state and haven for so many refugees, has been confronted with its own sites of memory in the form of its banks and its borders.

Differences between East and West

While in Western Europe national myths were challenged and debunked, that was by no means equally the case in Eastern Europe. Here we may invoke another of Renan's claims from 1882: "Forgetting—I almost said historical error—plays an essential role for the creation of a nation, and so the progress of the historical sciences is often a danger for the nation."[27] While Western European nations increasingly brought their national constructions of the past into line with the standards of historical scholarship, such has not been the case with the nations that emerged from the Eastern bloc. If anything, new national myths possessing explosive political power are being established and finding fertile ground. Here, historical consciousness often stops at national borders, and the self-edifying function of national myths carries on from the period before the two world wars.

Poland is a good example of this, where the national myth continues to revolve around the role of victim. Unlike in Austria, the Polish sense of victimhood is backed by centuries of historical experience and cultural tradition. The Polish self-image as the "Christ of the nations" indicates the sacrosanct status of Polish martyrdom. In light of this deeply ingrained cultural model of experience, it is virtually impossible to acknowledge the status of other victims—such as the Jews—and to confront their own guilt, say, in the context of Catholic anti-Semitism. Once again, the generalizing of *one* model of experience covers up *other* uncomfortable memories. The national status as victim can lead to a self-immunization against guilt and responsibility.[28]

Hungarians also saw themselves, in the *longue durée* of European history, as the victims of repression and foreign domination by the Ottomans, the Habsburgs, the Nazis, and the Communists. After the fall of the Berlin Wall, in its new phase of national self-definition, Hungary could once again deploy these old models of experience and exploit their enduring appeal in the public eye. A similar situation arose in the Czech Republic, whose national historical myth revolves around the recurring experience of a legendary defeat (the Battle of White Mountain on November 8, 1620). With the abolition of the obligatory socialist image of history, these old national patterns of interpreting history resurfaced and structured the way in which the historical experience of the Second World War was processed.

Russia offers a further example of the reconstruction of a national historical myth that disregards the memories of others and also ignores, in a supposedly sovereign way, the achievements of increased historical awareness. As the victors in 1945, Russia claims the privilege of not having to submit its memories to scrutiny and will tolerate no opposition. The official history focuses on the heavy losses incurred in the efforts of the Great Patriotic War where Hitler was defeated and a collapsing Europe was ensured a future. The core of this historical interpretation of the liberation of 1945 is a self-validating image determined by historical greatness, one that prevents other conflicting features from entering into the picture, such as the victims of communist terror, of the Stalinist dictatorship or the Gulag.

At the level of national memory, the problems are differently situated than they are at the level of individual memory. Whereas at the individual level the problem lies in how notoriously inaccurate and easily falsified memories are, the problem on the national level lies in how selective nations can be in the search for expedient memories. That is how, in the case of Russian national memory, the historically accurate recollection of the difficult and costly victory over National Socialism can act as a broad defensive shield against recalling the victims of the communist terror. The victors who write history have the power to suppress counter-memory and to prevent the writing of different histories by keeping archives under lock and key. As the victors of 1945, Russia claims for itself the privilege of not having to submit its memories to close European scrutiny. Thus memory reveals itself to be inseparable from the question of power. In this context, sovereign is not only whoever decides on the state of exception but also whoever has the privilege of selecting which memories will go into the self-serving construction of national myths. In such states, it falls to civic initiatives to develop a counter-memory and to keep it alive. While in Russia, the nationalist group *Pamyat* was able to gain official acceptance of their memory, the nongovernmental organization *Memorial*, by contrast, is dedicated to the historical investigation of the crimes of the totalitarian Communist regime on behalf of the victims. Fully in the spirit of Renan, this group is counting on the power of historical research to destroy national myths.[29]

By contrast, if national myths are gradually being eroded in the western part of the European Union, this is because a perspective that transcends national borders is steadily becoming the European norm. This inward and outward perspective is making it increasingly difficult to sustain the self-validating function of national myths. As far as I can tell, that is an important reason for the fact that at the present time, national memories in the western part of Europe are becoming more inclusive and more complex. Not least, the global wave of ritual apologies whereby heads of state are assuming responsibility for historical crimes committed in the name of their countries shows just such an ethical turn taking place in the construction of memories.

Guidelines for Dealing Peaceably with National Memories

All of this shows that we have not yet arrived where Dan Diner and President Persson would like us to be: at the point where the Holocaust has become a clear point of common historical reference for the new Europe. We have become highly conscious of the fact that memories are not only a means of unification but also can stand in its way; they not only promote a more critical self-image, but they can also produce new conflicts by opening up old wounds and reanimating irreconcilable differences. They cannot therefore be viewed as solely beneficial for the project of Europe, especially considering how often they appear in populist media campaigns to enflame old stereotypes. Surprisingly enough, sixty years after the end of the Second World War certain prejudices and emotions are still lurking at the ready to be reignited. On October 30, 2004, the headline on the front page of the *Daily Express* read, "Queen refuses to say sorry for war!" This headline appeared shortly before her fourth visit to Germany and was written in reaction to the headline on the German *Bild-Zeitung* that, two days earlier, had asked, "Will the queen finally apologize?" To be sure, this is a trivial example from the daily media but it does show that the struggle for memories in Europe continues in a subterranean way, prolonging old fronts.[30] "In light of the conflict of national memories and the fragmentation of collective memories, is there a risk of forgetting in the name of the future? In other words, can European integration be achieved only at the price of mutual oblivion, because no one wants to re-open old wounds?" asks Ulrike Ackermann, pointing out some of Europe's memory blocks.[31] We are clearly still very far away from Esterházy's vision of a "common European self-knowledge."

This knowledge might not be a reality yet but it certainly is the great potential of the project of European integration. It includes the opportunity to "face history and ourselves," as the American phrase has it,[32] and also to see our national histories from a transnational perspective. Europe was the stage for an unimaginable unleashing of extreme violence. The network of death camps and labor camps that covered Europe during the Nazi dictatorship like a rash, the battlefields of both world wars, from Marne to Stalingrad and the bombed-out cities, from Guernica to Coventry and Dresden—all these have become Europe's *lieux de mémoire*. To remember them within a transnational framework is a European task. At the same time, it is equally important that the national external borders of EU nation states be transformed into European internal frontiers, whereby these border regions can become paradigmatic European zones of contact.[33]

This development can draw on the work of historians, who are now shifting their historical research from a national to a European perspective. The paradigm of comparative history, representing a dialogical and comparative project, amounts to the preservation of national heritage and the legitimation of national interests. However, the phenomenon of migration, the movement of millions of people in endless streams of refugees, is a key experience in the Europe of the twentieth century that can only be treated from within a transnational perspective. Converting national external borders into European internal borders and introducing a trans-European perspective into historical research have contributed to the fact that quite a number of proverbial minefields have been defused and made into zones of dialogue and communication.

But unfortunately these achievements can also be reversed. In 2002 the Polish professor of German Karol Sauerland pointed out that "there are no more problems surrounding the theme of the expulsion of Germans," to which he added, "the fact that this is no longer the subject of disagreements is seen by historians as one of the most important successes of the German–Polish relationship in the post–Cold War period."[34] But these hard-won successes were undone in a single blow when, a year later, Erika Steinbach, the president of the Federation of Expellees, put forward a proposal to establish a Centre against Expulsion in the symbolically charged central location of Berlin. Many Polish neighbors immediately began to worry that this German experience of suffering would be tied to political demands, be it for the redrawing of borders or for the restitution of lost property.

While there is a lot of discussion these days about the politics of history, or the politics of the past, one hears very little about guidelines that could be established to promote peaceable ways of dealing with collective memories. I should now like to make a few practical suggestions in this regard. Since the dynamics of collective memory take place in the domain between the political and the psychological, any universally recognized principles that we establish must move between strategic and therapeutic considerations.

DIFFERENTIATING MEMORY FROM ARGUMENT

There is a difference between a memory and the arguments that are built upon it. A good example is the commemorative ceremonies that marked the sixtieth anniversary of the bombing of Dresden. Some of the city's residents participated in the official commemoration, with the mayor and representatives of Britain, France, and the United States all in attendance. Some marched through the streets carrying banners that read "Bombing Holocaust," and others set up a series of large posters bearing the names of the cities Dresden, Nagasaki, New York, and Baghdad. In all of these commemorative acts, the same event, the bombing of Dresden, was associated with three completely different messages: one was aggressive and reactionary; one was diplomatic and conciliatory; and one was pacifist. Memories are often bound up with arguments, but these arguments are not an intrinsic part of the memories themselves. To neutralize the potential of memories to trigger feelings of revenge, hatred, and resentment, a clear line must be drawn between what was experienced and what follows from that experience in terms of interpretations, evaluations, demands, or consequences.

INJUNCTION AGAINST THE OFFSETTING OF GUILT

A widespread and completely untenable logic used in the battle of memories is the tactic of offsetting. In such cases, a historical situation is presented as a zero-sum game: proof of your opponent's guilt automatically reduces or effaces your own guilt. In this form of competition, memories become a kind of weapon with which to beat the opponent. The only important memory in this case is the guilt of the other, which is seen as the grounds upon which one's own guilt is dismissed. While the connection between a memory and an argument leads to the instrumentalization and politicization of memory, the offsetting of guilt leads one to relativize one's own guilt.

INJUNCTION AGAINST COMPETITION FOR VICTIMHOOD

Whereas offsetting guilt is a way to minimize one's own share of it or to nullify it completely, competition between victims is often a battle for the recognition of one's own suffering. This sort of memory contest takes the form of a hierarchy of suffering, in which victims' groups vie with each other for public recognition. We could recall here how the dedication to Toni Morrison's *Beloved*, "Sixty million and more," draws an unmistakable parallel between the Jewish victims of the Holocaust and the victims of slavery. In drawing this parallel, Morrison was not so much setting one set of victims off of another as she was drawing attention to a less recognized experience of victimhood. Privileging one trauma over another can serve to eclipse awareness of the other, in accordance with the idea that what is worse tends to cover up what is bad. That is, because what is worse (the Holocaust) has been experienced, what is bad (the aerial war, expulsion) is deemed unworthy of recognition. A strategy like this could easily end up fostering the sense that what is worse ought to be covered up by what is bad, called into question, and suppressed again. Placing victims in a hierarchy was certainly an important transitional phase in engaging with historical traumas and working for their recognition, but it must be confronted with the idea that every individual has a human right both to memory and also—in particular frameworks—to recognition for the suffering they have endured. This will never happen if the failure to empathize, one that is often scandalously upheld regarding Jewish victims, gets perpetuated in the context of other victim groups.

FROM EXCLUSIVITY TO INCLUSIVITY

Memories that support a collective identity not only are selective but also function as a protective shield against other memories. Such memories tend to expand and crowd out others; one memory is used to immunize against another. Therefore the crucial question is: how inclusive or exclusive is a collective memory? For many European states after the war, fixating on Germany's crimes helped to make their own crimes conveniently disappear. For the Germans, the negative privileging of the Holocaust minimized their own experience of victimhood, as Günter Grass has emphasized. But, as Christian Meier has pointed out, it also cast a shadow over other atrocities, shielding them from public awareness. He asks, "Have not atrocities like those we perpetrated against Poland and Russia . . . disappeared under the shadow of the Holocaust?"[35]

FROM A DIVISIVE TO A COMMON MEMORY

In his speech at St. Paul's Church in Frankfurt, Esterházy summed up a negative aspect of European memory: "What was supposed to be united has been torn apart in self-hatred and self-pity. . . . Alongside the untruth of the exclusive perpetrator, there is the untruth of the exclusive victim, and the unspoken 'we' of the national memory lies hidden beneath both. . . . A common European knowledge about ourselves as both perpetrators and victims is not yet in sight."[36] For Esterházy, the road to a common European community of memory passes through the memory of one's own guilt and the acknowledgment of the suffering of others. This failure to empathize is what made the war and the Holocaust possible; in our own day, memory is what can help improve the situation. A divisive memory leaves the memory of suffering to the affected victims' groups, while the descendants of the perpetrators forget those memories and so perpetuate the divisions of the original murderous constellation. This deadly polarity can be overcome and lead to a common memory only through empathic acknowledgment of the victim's memories.

CONTEXTUALIZATION

Another way to defuse the potentially destructive energy of memory is to place experience and memory into larger contexts. This is only possible in retrospect; it is an intellectual achievement of historical pedagogy. Experiencing and remembering never take place in such a context; those who lost everything in 1945 and took part in dangerous and uncertain journeys westward did not automatically view the experience as a just punishment for Hitler's criminal war of aggression. Yet nothing is gained by disregarding lived experiences merely because they do not conform to a broader historical perspective. Everyone has a human right to his or her memories, and those memories should not be muzzled by the retrospective insight of greater historical context. However, memories that have been articulated and recognized should also be understood in terms of a broader horizon. Only by being placed in such contexts do memories lose something of their irreconcilable solipsism and become compatible with other memories; this is entirely different from retrospective falsification.

FRAMING

The European project of unification depends upon a common framework that can accommodate multiple memories. Accommodation in this sense has two roles: on the one hand, it implies that memories are recognized and preserved, and on the other hand, it also means that whatever is psychologically or politically damaging or divisive can be neutralized. The common framework reflects a desire for mutual understanding on the basis of a canon of values and goals. Memories are not just systematized but are also framed within this horizon of values, which restricts or contains their tendency to proliferate or escalate in damaging ways. Here, the double aspect of identity, based on memories and values, comes into play again. Memories can retain their unmistakable variety and diversity without becoming divisive. Only through integration into a common framework of identity and values can they be made to coexist without reigniting old conflicts by adding new fuel. In this way, the task of preserving the past intersects with the task of coming to terms with it.

Writer Adolf Muschg once described Europe as "a community of destiny."[37] This community of destiny could become a community of memory in which, after the unthinkable atrocities and terrors of the twentieth century, all histories of suffering are remembered, including precisely those one would most like to forget. In such a community of memory, different levels of identity—

subnational, national, supranational—should not be excluded, but rather they should point to the irreducible diversity of perspectives, loyalties, and alliances. Of course, the ability to integrate smaller entities into larger contexts will be crucial to this enterprise. The dangers of a divisive particularism and a battlefield of memories can only be avoided if Europe can be successfully established as a transnational framework of memory based on a common historical consciousness. This common historical consciousness, stabilized and promoted by the schools, must be positioned alongside each episodic or autobiographical memory as a generalized fact-based memory (so-called semantic memory), in which the history of one's own biography, family, generation, and nation can be preserved. This would be a step in the direction of Peter Esterházy's vision of a common European knowledge of ourselves as both perpetrators and victims.

The common European knowledge of ourselves bridges different formations of storage memory. As an awareness of historical events *in terms of their interconnectedness*, this historical consciousness rises above the potential divisiveness of memories. Identifying with historical events produces a national memory; historicizing them nullifies that memory once again. Historical consciousness rises above this tense oscillation in that it does not *eliminate* national memories, but rather *integrates* them. Within such a framework, Europeans could learn to face up to their own memories and to listen to others' with empathy. Such a European memory would not provide a platform for political legitimation; rather, it would militate against grandiose self-images and antagonistic images of others. Unless history is taught to future generations of Europeans within a common European framework of memory, the idea of Europe will remain an empty fantasy.[38] As the European Union continues to expand due to the accession of new member states, a process of internal entrenchment is needed to sustain this expansion. In a lecture Peter Steinbach gave in 2002 during a celebration at the Goethe Institute in Weimar, he spoke of Europe as an educational project. "What we need right now," he said, "is not the extension of Europe, but its improvement." Sixteen years earlier, in the essay "The Idea of Europe (One more Elegy)," Susan Sontag had said something quite similar. She wrote, "The new idea of Europe is not of extension but of retrenchment: the Europeanization not of the rest of the world but of Europe. . . . Make Europe . . . European."[39]

CONCLUSION

Shadows of Trauma

Twenty years ago, following the 1985 commemorative ceremonies that marked the fortieth anniversary of the liberation of Auschwitz and the Historians' Debate in 1986, historian Christian Meier wrote an urgent and critical case study under the heading *Vierzig Jahre nach Auschwitz* [Forty Years after Auschwitz].[1] The commitment to memory expressed in that work has only gotten stronger in the intervening years, although the historical standpoint has certainly changed. Are we further distanced from Auschwitz today? How does the younger generation feel about it? Here is the opinion of someone born in 1962: "'We feel nothing'—that is the disturbing reality of German Holocaust emotionalism in 2005, but it simply must be acknowledged. The time of emotional 'commemoration' is irretrievably over."[2] Joachim Landkammer is referring here to the "unavoidable disappearance of the past," and he emphasizes that only an "abstract idealism" can fail to see the reality of a progressive erosion of memory by the ravages of time. He argues that the time factor, or what he describes as an "inevitable and gradual distancing," is the most effective way for Germany to come to terms with the past (55).

However, Landkammer's assessment is contradicted by the fact that, over the last two decades, a national and transnational memorial landscape has been established in which the Holocaust has become a crucially important common reference point, at least in the Western European nations. What was still a living memory twenty years ago and so depended on the willingness or unwillingness of individuals to remember has today been transferred into long-term cultural memory, and these once-living memories have been consolidated at many different sites in a variety of forms. The hard work of a citizens' initiative, begun at the end of the 1980s in the face of so much resistance, has resulted in the establishment of the national Holocaust memorial in the heart of Berlin. In the midst of all this hard work, what has fallen by the wayside? Has the emotionalism of this history been dissipated as it has been converted from a living and orally communicated memory into a cultural memory, as Landkammer suggests? Has the social culture of memory that was so closely connected to the engagement of the '68 generation turned into an abstract politics of history?

The idea that the history of National Socialism is becoming abstract or de-emotionalized has more to do with wishful thinking than it does with a description of what is actually the case. As we have seen, engaging with history has become powerfully emotional in the context of the memory boom currently taking place not just in Germany but all over the world. Now that this history no longer falls under the exclusive purview of professional historians and is increasingly being treated by the media and in exhibitions, autobiographies and family novels, video testimonies and installations, as well as in documentaries and feature films, this widespread engagement has brought about an unprecedented emotional investment in history. People might be increasingly confused as to how they should engage with this history, but that does not necessarily mean that the hot topic of memory has cooled down. For it is absurd to suggest that this memory be carried by a self-enclosed and homogeneous German nation; those who engage with memory only ever do so as individuals or groups dispersed throughout society, across generations and classes.

Judging from Meier's manifesto of twenty years ago, though we are *not* further distanced from Auschwitz, the memory of the Holocaust today has been mediatized to a much greater extent. We no longer confront the Holocaust in an immediate way as the pure content of consciousness; rather, we refer to the forms in which it is represented and recollected. In other words, we do not directly confront the incomprehensible, but rather are part of a world that is marked by this memory in fundamental ways. Memory is both presented and represented, and so it both imparts something and processes it at the same time. Experiences as such are never transmitted, but are always already processed through linguistic or visual forms; we do not react to bare historical facts, but we do to the representation of facts, to their interpretation and evaluation. One focus of this book has therefore been to consider the mediatization of memory as the basis for the broadened dissemination and further development of remembered history.

The two phrases in the original German subtitle to this book are useful for analyzing this level of mediatized memory—namely, "cultures of memory" and "politics of history."[3] The phrases overlap with one another, but they also capture a spectrum ranging from rather informal, variable, and heterogeneous forms of remembering to more stable and institutionalized forms. Political theorists Leggewie and Meyer introduced the idea of a politics of history so they could sharply distinguish their own research from studies in the humanities and cultural theory, grouped (as they are in the Collaborative Research Center at the University of Giessen) under the heading of "memory cultures."[4] With the idea of politics of history, Leggewie and Meyer focus on a dimension that is often neglected in the humanities: they are interested in questions of organization, financing, management, bureaucracies, and above all, the political decision-making process, all of which "co-determine structures of memory and the capacity to remember, particularly in modern pluralistic societies where commemoration and remembering can no longer be prescribed from the top down and have become critically self-reflective."[5]

The phrases *cultures of memory* and *politics of history* are often opposed to each other, and not infrequently with a strong bias. In this particular constellation, *cultures of memory* is cast in a positive light insofar as it represents an independent, cultural, and bottom-up approach, while *politics of history* is associated with a top-down, authoritarian, and homogenizing form of remembering. As Jutta Sherrer has shown, this oppositional structure is ideally suited to the case of Russia, where a state-centered politics of history dominates and the aim is to generate internal unity and a "meaningful representation of Russia as a super-power." The increasingly precarious *Memorial* is an independent historical and civil-rights organization in Russia that opposes these politics by taking on unwelcome memories through an engagement with the Stalinist terror.[6]

The idea of cultures of memory is often used in reference to the whole ensemble of forms and media of cultural mnemo-techniques that helps groups and cultures develop a collective identity and an orientation in time, while politics of history are defined in terms of an instrumentalized relation to the past. The term *instrumentalization* is more polemical than analytical and is often used to identify something from which one wishes to distance oneself. Peter Novick has criticized this use of language on the basis that, as he points out, there would be no collective memory whatsoever without instrumentalization. Since memories are always selected and represented in particular ways, there are always other goals being pursued in relation to them that are at the service of the present and the future.[7] Memories perform many functions: they create forms of legitimation, promote communalization, are the basis of an at-times critical self-image, and not least, they also at times serve to block other memories. It is therefore inadequate to criticize the social uses of memory on the basis of instrumentalization; rather, a specific abuse must be identified and set off from the more positive uses of memory.

Today, most would agree that one such abuse occurs when the dead are retrospectively made into the agents of particular goals and aims and are used to strengthen a political cause. We could also speak of the instrumentalization of history in the negative sense where one's own political goals are legitimated by means of ad-hoc arguments drawn from history. At the security conference held in Munich (!) in February 2006, for example, Angela Merkel warned about appeasement in the context of the threat posed by Iran's President Ahmadinejad. By using the term *appeasement*, she was implicitly recalling the British and French politics of concession in relation to Nazi Germany in 1938, the year that saw the annexation of the Sudenten-German areas of the former Czechoslovakia.[8] Both the Gulf War in 1990 and the Iraq War in 2002 were legitimated by American presidents George Bush Sr. and George W. Bush with the catchword *appeasement*. That one word made it possible to establish a parallel between the Iraqi or Iranian presidents and Hitler, a parallel that prevented further dialogue and negotiations from taking place and morally justified the war as the only appropriate means of engagement.

Merkel certainly meant well in using this catchword in the discussion. It reflects the position of German politics, which must in every respect distance and distinguish itself from the disastrous prehistory of the Federal Republic. The political imperative reads as follows: never again appeasement, never again foster or encourage an equivalent development through feigned innocence or opportunism. The imperative "never again" suggests that history can repeat itself and that one can work to prevent this repetition. "Never again" is of course also a moral imperative about Auschwitz. As clear as this directive may be, its use in particular situations is not so, for there are never crystal-clear lessons to be gleaned from history. In arguing for and against the deployment of German troops in Kosovo, German politicians appealed to Auschwitz. On the basis of the memory of German aggression during the Second World War, the imperative was never again to engage Germany in military operations; on the basis of the memory of Auschwitz, Germany could never again be indifferent to genocide. Michael Jeismann has made the sobering observation that the imperative of "never again" has not yet sufficed to prevent a new historical catastrophe.[9] In 1994, as the film *Schindler's List* was running in theaters, the world looked on in horror at the genocide of the Tutsis in Rwanda. In 1995, the exhibition "Crimes of the Wehrmacht" was being shown at the same time as a genocide was taking place in Srebrenica with Bosnian Serbs slaughtering Bosnian Muslims.

The catchword *appeasement* is only one typical case of the politics of history. Many nations remain captivated by key events in their histories: they perceive the challenges faced in the present through these events, which seem to generate normative standards for action. These formative and deeply engrained historical memories constitute the cultural lens through which reality is processed, and the degree to which this can be avoided varies a great deal. The term *instrumentalization* is somewhat confusing in this respect, since these historical associations often arise as a knee-jerk reaction, and, if no distancing historical education is in place to prevent it, they can easily determine the orientation of the present. Nations that always interpret the challenges of the future in light of a sensitive event in the past have not yet emerged from under the spell (not to mention the shadow) of their histories. To overcome this dynamic, it is not necessary that such events be forgotten, but they do have to be reshaped in such a way that the past loses the character of an appeal that overrides all other considerations and so also loses its power over the present. In other words, memories require active shaping, but we are also passively influenced by them. The notion of instrumentalization suggests that the present has the past firmly in its grip, but it is also the case that the past—especially a traumatic past—often has the present in its grip. In such cases, it is not we who possess it, but it that possesses us.

On both the individual level and the collective level, memories are not always beneficial, for they are also the stuff of which conflicts and aggressive mythologizing are made. They are both dangerous and essential; they are both a means of stirring up violence and they are a means of preventing violence.[10] Just as it is the work of psychotherapy to neutralize memories that inhibit development and to transform them into positive forces, it must also be the concern of cultural research—this is another focus of this book—to expose the dangerous dynamics of constructions of collective memory and to develop criteria according to which the destructive power of memory can be objectively measured. Here are a few questions in this regard regarding constructions of memory:

- Exclusivity or openness: can they cope with historical truth or are they closed off to it?
- One-sided or inclusive: how many contradictory elements can they integrate?
- Self-centered or tolerant: how well do they get along with those of their neighbors?
- Heroization and victimization: are they exclusively characterized in terms of honor, or do they focus solely on the role of victim?
- Externalization or internalization: is guilt avoided or accepted?

We have repeatedly talked about an ethical turn in memory, one that is at the same time a turn away from heroic memory to a post-heroic one. By *post-heroic*, I am referring to the increased significance of the notion of trauma in our day, which privileges the defenseless and passive victim for the first time after a long history of using memory for the purposes of self-glorification. With Holocaust memory, a new phase in the elevation of the victim was introduced, one that allowed new modes of approaching the question of violence in history to develop (one thinks of slaves forcibly taken from Africa or the colonized aboriginals of various continents) and that led, in the end, to a competition for the role of victim. It is quite possible that we have already moved beyond the peak of this phase. But the notion of post-heroic can also be understood in relation to a move away from a moralizing discourse of memory. The entirely pragmatic notion of contemporary memory management belongs to this context, which is a turn away from the style of memory of the '68 generation, characterized as it was by consternation and awareness of guilt, and toward a cool and ideology-free engagement with the memory constructions of younger generations: "Engaging with unpleasant aspects of a history must in any case be somehow 'managed'; this problem will not be solved by generating some kind of future-oriented collective consciousness but rather by addressing the concrete tasks of avoiding conflict and normalizing social relations for communication and trade."[11]

The fact that a trace of disconcertion remains in the memory of National Socialism is something that even this easy pragmatism cannot entirely brush aside. "It is unusual," writes Christian Meier, "for a past to hold the present under its spell for more than four decades."[12] This unusual situation—the anomaly that has upset the balance of remembering and forgetting—is related to the exceptionalism of the crimes represented by the name *Auschwitz*. One image that is often used to depict the hold of a past that will not pass is the image of the shadow. No other image is used as frequently in Germany's memory discourse, and a plethora of books have titles containing the word.[13] *Shadow* does not just mean *reverberating presence* in this context, but also obfuscation and darkening. Once again, Christian Meier: "As little as Auschwitz . . . could have been the goal of German history, so much does it retrospectively cast its dark shadow over it."[14]

When will we emerge out from under the shadow of the period of National Socialism and the Holocaust? Twenty years ago, Christian Meier countered those who ask such a question with the following response: "No, we will never achieve a naïve relation to our history. Even an awareness of its richness will always remain overshadowed" (73). If we understand *shadow* to mean the lasting effects of the traumatic past, we will just have to live with it. Because the Holocaust represents a quantum leap in the history of evil, we must live with this irreversible darkening of our idea of the human from now on. And as Germans, we must take historical responsibility for it. To know this history has nothing to do with what Martin Walser calls the "grim service of memory" and must be an educational imperative from now on. Someone who "is perennially surprised that depravity exists, who continues to feel disillusioned (even incredulous) when confronted with evidence of what humans are capable of inflicting in the way of gruesome, hands-on cruelties upon other humans, has not reached moral or psychological adulthood."[15]

However, we should not understand the term *shadow* here as an absence of a future, a dark melancholy or even a self-hatred. A negative memory is in no way the same as a negative self-image. Negative memory is emblazoned into the foundation of the German state. This stigma can, however, be converted into a positive value for the present and the future, for instance, in terms of the affirmation of human rights written into the preamble of the constitution. The most brutal form of a complete absence of human solidarity can be translated into the positive value of the recognition of others. It is these basic values (and not only those of industriousness, aptitude, and efficiency) that have allowed our country to enter once again into the community of civilized nations, and they are the standard by which it will be measured in the future.

"What was once rejoicing and sorrow shall now become insight," wrote Jacob Burckhardt in the middle of the nineteenth century, confident in the belief that rational historiography could prevail over the emotions of historical players.[16] At the beginning of the twenty-first century, we are experiencing rather the opposite: the growing interest in memory has reinvigorated an engagement with history accompanied by feelings, ones that have a lot more to do with sorrow than they do with rejoicing. Should we want to ask how long this shadow will last, we might find an answer in the work of another nineteenth-century thinker: "Only that which never ceases to *hurt* stays in the memory—this is a main clause of the oldest (unhappily also the most enduring) psychology on earth."[17] Nietzsche's claim here is particularly relevant to the victims, those who determine the extent of our memory. What the victims *cannot* forget is precisely what the descendants of the perpetrators *must not* forget. Therefore, a claim made by artist Horst Hoheisel in the interview cited at the very beginning of this book shall continue to resonate for a while longer: "As we pass under the Brandenburg Gate, as we lead official guests there from all over the world and use it to establish a new national identity, we must always keep that other gate in mind—the one we want to push aside, the one very far away in Poland—we must think about them together, see them together, experience them together."

NOTES

INTRODUCTION: TRIUMPH AND TRAUMA

1. "Gespräch mit Horst Hoheisel" [In Conversation with Horst Hoheisel], in *Nachträgliche Wirksamkeit: Vom Aufheben der Taten im Gedenken* [Delayed Effects: On Taking up Crimes in Memory], ed. Christian Staffa and Jochen Spielmann (Berlin: Institut für Vergleichende Geschichtswissenschaften, 1998), 254.

2. Gustav Seibt, "Das Brandenburger Tor" [The Brandenburg Gate], *Deutsche Erinnerungsorte* [German Places of Memory], ed. Étienne François and Hagen Schulze, vol. 2 (Munich: Beck, 2001).

3. Reinhart Koselleck, "Formen und Traditionen des negative Gedächnisses" [Forms and Traditions of Negative Memory], in *Verbrechen erinnern: Die Auseinandersetzung mit Holocaust und Völkermord* [Remembering Crimes: Engaging the Holocaust and Genocide] (Munich: Beck, 2002), 22.

4. Ibid., 23.

5. Italo Svevo, *Zeno's Conscience* (Reinbek: Rowohlt, 2000), 467.

6. Dirk Baecker and Alexander Kluge, *Vom Nutzen ungelöster Probleme* [On the Use of Unsolved Problems] (Berlin: Merve, 2003).

1. FROM INDIVIDUAL TO COLLECTIVE CONSTRUCTIONS OF THE PAST

1. Sir Thomas Browne, "Hydriotaphia or Urne Buriall," in *The Prose of Sir Thomas Browne*, ed. Norman J. Endicott (New York: Anchor, 1967), 283.

2. Daniel L. Schacter, ed., *Memory Distortion: How Minds, Brains, and Societies Reconstruct the Past* (Cambridge, Mass.: Harvard University Press, 1995); see also Schacter's "The Seven Sins of Memory: Insights from Psychology and Cognitive Neuroscience," *American Psychologist* 54, no. 3 (March 1999): 182–203.

3. See William Lowell Randall, *The Stories We Are: An Essay on Self-Creation* (Toronto: University of Toronto Press, 1995).

4. See Jan Assmann, *Das kulturelle Gedächtnis: Schrift, Erinnerung und politische Identität in frühen Hochkulturen* (Munich: Beck, 1992), 48–66; English translation: *Cultural Memory and Early Civilization: Writing, Remembrance, and Political Imagination* (Cambridge: Cambridge University Press, 2011); Harald Welzer, *Das kommunikative Gedächtnis: Eine Theorie der Erinnerung* [Communicative

Memory: A Theory of Remembering] (Munich: Beck, 2002); Maurice Halbwachs, *On Collective Memory*, trans. and ed. Lewis A. Coser (Chicago: University of Chicago Press, 1992); Halbwachs, *The Collective Memory*, introduction by Mary Douglas (New York: Harper and Row, 1980). On Halbwachs, see Gérard Namer, *Halbwachs et la mémoire sociale* [Halbwachs and Social Memory] (Paris: L'Harmattan, 2000); Gerald Echterhoff and Martin Saar, eds., *Kontexte und Kulturen des Erinnerns: Maurice Halbwachs und das Paradigma des kollektiven Gedächtnisses* [Contexts and Cultures of Remembrance: Maurice Halbwachs and the Paradigm of Collective Memory] (Constance: UVK Verlagsgesellschaft, 2002); and Annette Becker and Halbwachs, *Un intellectuel en guerres mondiales 1914–1945* [An Intellectual in the World Wars] (Paris: Agnès Viénot, 2003).

5. Howard Schuhmann and Jacqueline Scott, "Generations and Collective Memory," *American Sociological Review* 54 (June 1989): 359–81; Henk A. Becker, "Discontinuous Change and Generational Contracts," in *The Myth of Generational Conflict: The Family and State in Ageing Societies*, ed. Sara Arber and Claudine Attias-Donfurt (London: Routledge Press, 2000), 114–32.

6. Karl Mannheim, "The Problem of Generations," in *Essays on the Sociology of Knowledge by Karl Mannheim*, ed. P. Kecskemeti (New York: Routledge and Kegan Paul, 1952), 276–321.

7. Martin A. Conway, "The Inventory of Experience: Memory and Identity," in *Collective Memory of Political Events: Social Psychological Perspectives*, ed. James W. Pennebaker, Dario Paez, and Bernard Rime (Mahwah, N.J.: Lawrence Erlbaum Associates, 1997), 43.

8. Helmut Schelsky, "Die Generationen der Bundesrepublik" [The Generations of the Federal Republic], in *Die andere deutsche Frage* [The Other German Question], ed. Walter Scheel (Stuttgart: Klett-Cotta, 1981), 178.

9. Heinz Bude, "Generationen im sozialen Wandel [Generations in Social Transition]," in *Alt und Jung: Die Abenteuer der Generationen; A Publication of the German Hygiene Museum Dresden* (Frankfurt am Main: Basel, 1997), 65.

10. James W. Pennebaker and Becky L. Banasik, "On the Creation and Maintenance of Collective Memories: History as a Social Psychology," in *Collective Memory of Political Events: Social Psychological Perspectives*, ed. Pennebaker, Dario Paez, and Bernard Rim (Mahwah, N.J.: Lawrence Erlbaum Associates, 1997), 11–13.

11. Welzer, ed., *Das soziale Gedächtnis: Geschichte, Erinnerung, Tradierung* [Social Memory: History, Memory, Transmission] (Hamburg: Hamburger Edition, 2001), 16.

12. Ibid., 15–18.

13. Reinhart Koselleck: "There is no collective memory, but there are collective conditions for possible memories" ("Gibt es ein kollektives Gedächtnis?" *Divinatio* 19, no. 2 [Spring 2004]: 1–6, 6.) See also Koselleck, "Gebrochene Erinnerungen? Deutsche und polnische Vergangenheiten" [Broken Memories? German and Polish Pasts], in *Jahrbuch der Deutschen Akademie für Sprache und Dichtung* (2000): 19–32.

14. In a review of a book by Halbwachs for example, historian Marc Bloch suggests that the notion of "collective memory" is "admittedly handy, but a little fictitious" (Bloch, "Mémoire collective, tradition et coutume" [Collective Memory, Tradition and Custom], *Révue de Synthèse Historique* 40 (1925): 78–83. When set against the backdrop of the essentialist discourse of the early twentieth century, where souls and unified subjectivities were attributed to nations and cultures, this kind of suspicion regarding the notion of collective memory is certainly understandable. New branches in memory research have since opened up, with the development of psychoanalytic and constructivist concepts like the "social imaginary" (Lacan) and "imagined communities" (Anderson).

15. Susan Sontag, *Regarding the Pain of Others* (New York: Picador, 2004), 85–86.

16. We might describe this kind of fabricated political memory, to use Nietzsche's phrase, as a "memory of the will," insofar as it does not arise spontaneously but is intentionally constructed and strengthened by the use of symbols; Friedrich Nietzsche, *On the Genealogy of Morals and Ecce Homo*, trans. Walter Kaufmann and R. J. Hollingdale (New York: Vintage, 1967), 58. This theme of "willed memory" is powerfully illustrated in the exhibition curated by Étienne François and Monia Flacke on the German nation and its myths; see the exhibition catalogue *Ausstellungskatalog: Germania—Mythen der Nationen, 1945—Arena der Erinnerungen* [Exhibition Catalogue: Germania—National Myths 1945—Arena of Memories] (Berlin: Von Zabern, 2004).

17. Nietzsche, "On the Uses and Disadvantages of History for Life," in *Untimely Meditations*, trans. R. J. Hollingdale (Cambridge: Cambridge University Press, 1983).

18. Ernst Renan, *What Is a Nation?* trans. Wanda Romer Taylor (Toronto: Tapir Press, 1996).

19. Christian Meier, *Vierzig Jahre nach Auschwitz: Deutsche Geschichtserinnerungen heute* [Forty Years after Auschwitz: German Memory Today] (Munich: Beck, 1990), 75; 63.

20. Ian Buruma, *The Wages of Guilt: Memories of War in Germany and Japan* (New York: Farrar, Straus, and Giroux, 1994), 69. At another point, he writes, "I like the idea of 'constitutional patriotism.' Maybe it isn't enough. Perhaps more is needed to transform a once dangerous nation" (305).

21. Peter Novick. *The Holocaust in American Life* (Boston: Houghton Mifflin, 1999), 4.

22. John Borland, "Graffiti, Paraden und Alltagskultur in Nordirland" [Graffiti, Parades and Everyday Culture in Northern Ireland], in *Das Soziale Gedächtnis*, ed. Harald Welzer (Hamburg: Hamburger Edition, 2001), 278.

23. See Jan Assmann, *Moses the Egyptian: The Memory of Egypt in Western Monotheism* (Cambridge, Mass.: Harvard University Press, 1998), chap. 1.

24. On the concept of *Mythomotorik*, see Jan Assmann, "Frühe Formen politischer Mythomotorik: Fundierende, kontrapräsentische und revolutionäre Mythen" [Early Forms of Political Myth-Making: Foundations, Anachronisms,

Revolutions], in *Revolution und Mythos*, ed. Dietrich Harth and Jan Assmann (Frankfurt am Main: Fischer, 1992), 39–61.

25. Benedict R. Anderson, *Imagined Communities: Reflections on the Origin and Spread of Nationalism* (London: Verso, 2006).

26. Halbwachs, *The Collective Memory*, 84.

27. Pierre Nora, "Between Memory and History: *Les Lieux de Mémoire*," trans. Marc Roudebush, *Representations* 26, Special Issue, *Memory and Counter-Memory* (Spring 1989): 8–9.

28. See Frei, *Vergangenheitspolitik: Die Anfänge der Bundesrepublik und die NS-Vergangenheit* (Munich: Beck, 1996); English translation: *Adenauer's Germany and the Nazi Past: The Politics of Amnesty and Integration*, trans. Joel Golb (New York: Columbia University Press, 2002).

29. See John H. Plumb, *The Death of the Past* (London: MacMillan, 1978).

30. Herodotus, *The Histories of Herodotus*, trans. C. E. Godley, vol. 1, book 1 (Cambridge, Mass.: Harvard University Press, 2004).

31. In antiquity, therefore, Herodotus was chided for being "philo-barbaric"; see Plutarch, *De Malignatate Herodoti* 12 (857A); *Malice of Herodotus*, trans. Anthony Bowen (Warminster: Aris and Phillips, 1992).

32. Ibid.

33. Nora, "Between Memory and History," 9.

34. Halbwachs, *The Collective Memory*, 84.

35. Johann Gustav Droysen, cited in "Erinnern—Lernen—Geschichte: Sechzig Jahre nach 1945" [Remembering—Learning: History Sixty Years after 1945], by Jürgen Kocka, *Österreichische Zeitschrift für Geschichtswissenschaften* 16 (2005): 72.

36. Bernard Lewis, *History: Remembered, Recovered, Invented* (Princeton: Princeton University Press, 1975), 54. On the objectivity of the historian, see Novick, *That Noble Dream: The "Objectivity Question" and the American Historical Profession* (Cambridge, Mass.: Harvard University Press, 1988).

37. Oral history is a new paradigm in historical research that was developed in the 1960s and can, in certain ways, be understood as a precursor to the development we are considering here.

38. See Chapter 2 of this volume.

39. Saul Friedländer, *When Memory Comes* (New York: Farrar, 1979).

40. Friedländer, "Im Angesicht der 'Endlösung': Die Entwicklung des offentlichen Gedächtnisses und die Verantwortung des Historikers" [Confronting the "Final Solution": The Development of Public Memory and the Responsibility of the Historian], in *Das Judentum im Spiegel seiner kulturellen Umwelten: Symposium zu Ehren von Saul Friedländer* [Judaism in Cultural Context: Symposium in Honor of Saul Friedländer] ed. Dieter Borchmeyer and Helmut Kiesel (Neckargemund, Germany: Edition Mnemosyne, 2002), 207–23.

41. According to Vaget's "Saul Friedländer," what is involved here is a "new kind of interweaving of history and memory, to such an extent that the voices

of memory and the demands of history as an academic discipline interlock and reciprocally advance the concerns of the other"; Hans Rudolf Vaget, "Saul Friedländer und die Zukunft der Erinnerung" [Saul Friedländer and the Future of Memory], in *Judentum im Spiegel seiner kulturellen Umwelten*, 18.

42. Johan Huizinga, "A Definition of the Concept of History," in *Philosophy and History: Essays Presented to Ernst Cassirer*, ed. Raymond Klibansky and Herbert James Paton (New York: Harper and Row, 1963), 9. I am grateful to Jan Assmann for providing this reference.

43. Hayden White, *Metahistory: The Historical Imagination in Nineteenth-Century Europe* (Baltimore: Johns Hopkins University Press, 1975); Carlo Ginzburg, *The Judge and the Historian: Marginal Notes on a Late-Twentieth-Century Miscarriage of Justice*, trans. Antony Shugaar (Verso: London, 1999); Peter Burke, "History as Social Memory," in *Memory: History, Culture and the Mind*, ed. Thomas Butler (Oxford: Blackwell Press, 1989), 110.

44. Charles S. Maier, "A Surfeit of Memory? Reflections on History, Melancholy and Denial," *History and Memory* 5, no. 2 (1993): 143.

45. Browne, "Hydriotaphia," 281.

46. Harald Weinrich, *Lethe: The Art and Critique of Forgetting*, trans. Steven Rendell (Ithaca: Cornell University Press, 2004). On the idea of forgetting as a resource, see Chapter 2 of this volume.

47. Hubert Wolf, *Index: Der Vatikan und die verbotenen Bücher* [Index: The Vatican and the Banned Books]. Munich: Beck, 2007.

48. Inaugural lecture of the "Konstanz Master class" organized by Bernhard Giesen at the University of Konstanz in September 2002. In his study *Liquid Modernity* (Cambridge: Polity, 2000), Zygmunt Bauman defends the argument that enduring objects, ones symbolizing eternity, were characteristic of the long-term orientation of a "stable modernity" and that this temporal perspective has meanwhile given way to the short-term orientation of a "liquid modernity." If this were true, there would be no museums, libraries, archives, or monuments, and the imperative never to forget the Holocaust would certainly not exist.

49. Siegfried Kracauer, "Photography," in *The Mass Ornament: Weimar Essays*, trans. Thomas Y. Levin (Cambridge, Mass.: Harvard University Press, 1995), 48. Marianne Hirsch coined the term *postmemory* in *Family Frames: Photography, Narrative and Postmemory* (Cambridge, Mass.: Harvard University Press, 1997) to emphasize the significance of photography as a support for social memory in which the experiential memory of individuals expands to include the experience of other family members.

50. Susan Warner, *The Wide, Wide World*, afterword by Jane Tompkins (New York: Feminist Press, 1987), 583.

51. Philip Fisher, "Local Meanings and Portable Objects: National Collections, Literatures, Music and Architecture," in *The Formation of National Collections of Art and Archaeology*, ed. Gwendolyn Wright (Hanover, N.H.: University Press of New England, 1996).

52. Friedrich Georg Jünger speaks in his book *Gedächtnis und Erinnerung* [Memory and Recollection] (Frankfurt am Main: Klostermann, 1957), of "forgetting to store."

53. The question will be addressed again in Chapter 8, "Points of Intersection between Lived Memory and Cultural Memory."

54. Hans Georg Gadamer, *Truth and Method*, trans. W. Glen-Doepel (London: Continuum, 2004), 276–77.

55. Alasdair MacIntyre, *After Virtue: A Study in Moral Theory* (Notre Dame: University of Notre Dame, 2007), 221.

2. BASIC CONCEPTS AND THEMES OF INDIVIDUAL AND COLLECTIVE MEMORY

1. In *Opa war kein Nazi* (Frankfurt am Main: Fischer, 2002), Harald Welzer differentiates between the following types of transmission: victimhood, justification, distancing, fascination, and being overwhelmed; available in English translation as *Grandpa Wasn't a Nazi: The Holocaust in German Family Remembrance* at http://www.ajc.org/site/apps/nlnet/content3.aspx?c=7oJILSPwFfJSG&b=84498 63&ct=12485707, accessed 15 July 2014.

2. Astrid Erll's *Kollektives Gedächtnis und Erinnerungskulturen: Eine Einführung* [Collective Memory and Cultures of Remembering: An Introduction] (Stuttgart: Metzler, 2005) makes an impressive contribution to a new level of integration in research. On the problem of the integration of interdisciplinary traditions of research, see also Aleida Assmann, "Vier Formen von Erinnerung" [Four Forms of Memory], *Forum Ethik Streitkultur* 13 (2002): 183–90.

3. Reinhart Koselleck, "Formen und Traditionen des negativen Gedächtnisses" [Forms and Traditions of Negative Memory], in *Verbrechen erinnern: Die Auseinandersetzung mit Holocaust und Völkermord* [Remembering Crimes: Engaging the Holocaust and Genocide], ed. Volkhard Knigge and Norbert Frei (Munich: Beck, 2002), 26.

4. Ernst Renan, *What Is a Nation?* trans. Wanda Romer Taylor (Toronto: Tapir Press, 1996), 47.

5. Wolfgang Schivelbusch, *The Culture of Defeat: On National Trauma, Mourning, and Recovery*, trans. Jefferson Chase (New York: Henry Holt, 2003), 125.

6. See Bernard Lewis, *History: Remembered, Recovered, Invented* (Princeton: Princeton University Press, 1975).

7. "DHM übernimmt Langemarckhalle," in *Die Welt*, 29 March 2006.

8. Schivelbusch, *Culture of Defeat*, 29.

9. Vamik D. Volkan, "Großgruppenidentität und auserwähltes Trauma" [Large Group Identity and Selective Trauma], *Psyche* 9/10 (2000): 931–53. At times, Volken's argument sounds like a paraphrase of Renan: "The articulation of an ethnic or large group identity through the selective use of traumatic experiences is far more powerful than one articulated by means of victories or triumph, because the psychological processes involved go much deeper" (946).

10. Walter Benjamin, "Theses on the Philosophy of History," in *Illuminations*, trans. Harry Zohn, ed. Hannah Arendt (New York: Schocken, 1968), 256.

11. Koselleck, "Erfahrungswandel und Methodenwechsel: Eine historisch-anthropologische Skizze" [Changes in Experience and Transformations in Method: A Historical-Anthropological Sketch], in *Historische Methode* [Historical Method], ed. Christian Meier et al., Theorie der Geschichte 5 (Munich: dtv, 1988), 76.

12. Ibid., 76–77.

13. Peter Burke, "History as Social Memory," in *Memory: History, Culture and the Mind*, ed. Thomas Butler (Oxford: Blackwell Press, 1989), 97–113, 106.

14. In the American edition, the notion of archetypes is used in this context; Schivelbusch, *Culture of Defeat*, 10.

15. On what follows, see Wolfgang Stegemann, "Zur Metaphorik des Opfers" [On the Metaphor of the Victim], in *Opfer: Theologische und kulturelle Kontexte* [Victimhood: Theological and Cultural Contexts], ed. Bernd Janowski and Michael Welker (Frankfurt am Main: Suhrkamp, 2000).

16. Ian Buruma, *Wages of Guilt: Memories of War in Germany and Japan* (New York: Farrar, Straus, and Giroux, 1994), 77.

17. Ibid., 80.

18. Louis Begley, *Wartime Lies* (New York: Ivy, 1991), 122.

19. Geoffrey Hartman, ed., *Bitburg in a Moral and Political Perspective* (Bloomington: Indiana University Press, 1986).

20. Henry Rousso, "Das Dilemma eines europäischen Gedächtnisses" [The Dilemma of a European Memory], in *Zeithistorische Forschungen*, online edition, http://www.zeithistorische-forschungen.de/site/40208268/default.aspx, accessed 15 July 2014.

21. Axel Honneth, *The Struggle for Recognition*, trans. Joel Anderson (Cambridge, Mass.: MIT Press, 1996); Charles Taylor, *Multiculturalism and "The Politics of Recognition,"* ed. Amy Gutmann (Princeton: Princeton University Press, 1994). I am following Taylor's distinction here between dignity as the foundation of the Western concept of individuality and the concept of person on the one hand and honor as a (usually collective) characteristic of distinction in the construction of identity on the other.

22. Ulrich Baer understands "critical secondary witnessing" as a "dialogical appeal and call for responsibility"; Baer, ed., *Niemand zeugt für den Zeugen: Erinnerungskultur und historische Verantwortung nach der Shoah* [No One Bears Witness for the Witness: Memory Culture and Historical Responsibility after the Shoah] (Frankfurt am Main: Suhrkamp, 2000), 16.

23. On this point, see the examination of the Wilkomirski case in Chapter 4 of this volume.

24. Yehuda Elkana, "The Need to Forget," *Ha'aretz*, 2 March 1988. Similar arguments were later put forward by Jewish historians Peter Novick and Charles Maier in the context of American-Jewish identity as a historical community based exclusively on the Holocaust.

25. See Friedrich Nietzsche, *Beyond Good and Evil*, trans. Marion Faber (Oxford: Oxford University Press, 1998).

26. This idea of pride about guilt arises in the context of the extreme right and has polemical rather than descriptive power: after all, one can hardly attribute a pride about guilt to Germans who are obsessed with the idea of guilt to a narcissistic or neurotic degree.

27. Günther Anders, *Wir Eichmannsöhne: Offener Brief an Klaus Eichmann* [We Sons of Eichmann: Open Letter to Klaus Eichmann] (Munich: Beck, 1964), 79–80.

28. See Giorgio Agamben, *Homo Sacer: Sovereign Power and Bare Life*, trans. Daniel Heller-Roazen (Stanford: Stanford University Press, 1998).

29. C. K. Williams, "Das symbolische Volk der Täter" [A Symbolic People of Perpetrators], *Die Zeit*, 7 November 2002. Williams defines the status of symbolic identity in opposition to normality: "To be normal means that one doesn't feel oneself to be observed. One could add that normality means not being bound to a symbolic identity."

30. Ibid.

31. On the theme of collective guilt, see Aleida Assmann and Ute Frevert, *Geschichtsvergessenheit—Geschichtsversessenheit: Vom Umgang mit deutschen Vergangenheiten nach 1945* [Forgetting History—Obsessing over History: On the Engagement with Germany's Pasts after 1945] (Stuttgart: Deutsche Verlags-Anstalt, 1999), 112–39; Norbert Frei, "Von deutscher Erfindungkraft, oder Die Kollektivschuldthese in der Nachkriegszeit" [On German Inventiveness, or The Thesis of Collective Guilt in the Postwar Period], in *1945 und Wir: Das Dritte Reich im Bewusstsein der Deutschen* [1945 and Us: The Third Reich in the German Psyche] (Munich: Beck, 2005). Norbert Frei doubts that there were official documents of the victorious powers in which this notion was used and talks about "German powers of invention" in this context. That the notion is discredited in the literature does not prevent it from being taken up periodically or from surfacing every once in a while as a populist gaffe, as for instance in the more recent discussion regarding the "Beneš-Decree"; see Ulrike Ackermann, "Vergessen zugunsten der Zukunft?" [Forgetting for the Sake of the Future?] *Merkur* 643 (November 2002): 993.

32. Anders, *Wir Eichmannsöhne*, 81–82.

33. Ibid.

34. Hannah Arendt, "Organized Guilt and Universal Responsibility," in *Essays in Understanding, 1930–1954: Formation, Exile, and Totalitarianism* (New York: Schocken Books, 2005): 121–32, 122.

35. Primo Levi, *If This Is a Man*, trans. Stuart Woolf (New York: Orion, 1959), 11.

36. "The Figure of the Third" was the title of a Humanities Graduate Colloquium at the University of Konstanz.

37. Cited in Jacques Derrida, "'A Self-Unsealing Poetic Text': Poetics and Politics of Witnessing," in *Revenge of the Aesthetic*, ed. Michael Clark (Berkeley: University of California Press, 2000), 186.

38. On the witness- or "canon-formula," see Aleida Assmann, "Fiktion als Differenz" [Fiction as Difference], *Poetica* 21 (1989): 239–60.

39. Benveniste defines the word *superstes* as follows: "*Superstes* describes the 'witness' either as the one who 'subsists beyond,' witness at the same time as survivor, or as 'the one who holds himself to the thing,' who is present there"; cited in Derrida, "Self-Unsealing Poetic Text," 187.

40. Burke, *Eyewitnessing: The Uses of Images as Historical Evidence* (Ithaca: Cornell University Press, 2001). Carlo Ginzburg develops the analogy between judge and historian in *The Judge and the Historian: Marginal Notes on a Late-Twentieth-Century Miscarriage of Justice*, trans. Antony Shugaar (Verso: London, 1999).

41. Lutz Niethammer, ed., *Lebenserfahrung und kollektives Gedächtnis: Die Praxis der "Oral History"* [Life Experience and Collective Memory: The Practice of Oral History] (Frankfurt am Main: Syndikat, 1985).

42. Hans Quecke, "Ich habe nichts hinzugefügt und nichts weggenommen: Zur Wahrheitsbeteuerung koptischer Martyrien" [I have added nothing and taken nothing away: On the Truth Claims of Coptic Martyrdom], in *Fragen an die altägyptische Literatur: Studien zum Gedenken an Eberhard Otto* [Questions regarding Ancient Egyptian Literature: Studies in Memory of Eberhard Otto], ed. Eberhard Otto, Jan Assmann, Erika Feucht, and Reinhard Grieshammer (Wiesbaden: Reichert, 1977), 399–416.

43. See Shoshana Felman and Dori Laub, *Testimony: The Crisis of Witnessing in Literature, Psychoanalysis, and History* (New York: Routledge, 1992); Felman, *The Juridical Unconscious: Trials and Traumas in the Twentieth Century* (Cambridge, Mass.: Harvard University Press, 2002).

44. See Sigrid Weigel, "Zeugnis und Zeugenschaft, Klage und Anklage" [Evidence and Testimony, Grievance and Accusal], in *Zeugnis und Zeugenschaft*, ed. Rüdiger Zill (Berlin: Akademie Verlag, 2000), 116–20.

45. Paul Celan, *Breathturn*, trans. Pierre Joris (Los Angeles: Green Integer, 2006); compare Baer, *Niemand zeugt fuer den Zeugen*.

46. Bernhard Giesen, *Triumph and Trauma* (London: Paradigm, 2004), 46. See also Günter Grass's novel *Crabwalk*, trans. Krishna Winston (New York: Harcourt, 2002), in which the notion of witness is applied to Germans as well as to civilian victims of the Second World War (see Chapter 7 of this volume).

47. Giesen, *Triumph and Trauma*, 65.

48. Avishai Margalit, *The Ethics of Memory* (Cambridge, Mass.: Harvard University Press, 2002), 147–82.

49. I am citing Ulrich Baer here (a little contrary to his intention), *Niemand zeugt fuer den Zeugen*, 16.

50. Jay Winter, *Remembering War: The Great War between Memory and History in the Twentieth Century* (New Haven: Yale University Press, 2006), 271; Winter, *The Arts of Remembrance in the Century of Total War* (New Haven: Yale University, 2003), 13, 38 (unpublished manuscript).

51. Dirk Rupnow, *Vernichten und Erinnern: Spuren nationalsozialistischer Gedächtnispolitik* [Annihilate, Commemorate: Traces of a National Socialist Politics of Memory] (Göttingen: Wallstein, 2005).

52. Anders, *Wir Eichmannsöhne*, 79ff.

53. Winter, *Remembering War*, 263. A relevant example is the lawsuit *David Irving v. Deborah Lipstadt*, where the pursuit of truth was carried into the context of academic history.

54. The idea of dissociation can be traced back to Pierre Janet (a contemporary of Freud's) who developed an alternative theory of repression.

55. Ruth Leys, *Trauma: A Genealogy* (Chicago: University of Chicago Press, 2000).

56. Ilany Kogan, *The Cry of Mute Children: A Psychoanalytic Perspective of the Second Generation of the Holocaust*, trans. Janine Chassegut-Smirgel (London: Free Association Books, 1995).

57. Bernhard Giesen argues that the destruction of *subjectivity* and its reduction to the *status of an object* is an essential characteristic of the traumatized victim. Although this description is exactly right, it is too vague a formulation. When Giesen argues that "there is a deeply rooted elective affinity between the impersonal order of modern society and the construction of victims" (*Triumph and Trauma*, 53), he is applying the idea of the traumatized object to structural phenomena like alienation and anonymity, in the context of which we cannot speak either of perpetrators or of particular triggers for incidences of violence. "Fordism" or "Taylorism," industrial methods of production that reduce human beings to their specialized labor, must be distinguished from the sort of biopolitics in which the ruling powers have full power over the bodies and souls of the exploited, as happened in the concentration camps. That the crimes of National Socialism profited from such structures of modernization, however, as Hannah Arendt, Zygmunt Baumann, and Giorgio Agamben, among others, have forcefully emphasized, should not be denied.

58. See Werner Bohleber, "Die Entwicklung der Traumatheorie in der Psychoanalyse" [The Development of Trauma Theory in Psychoanalysis], *Psyche* 9/10 (2000): 797–839.

59. Cathy Caruth, *Unclaimed Experience: Trauma, Narrative, and History* (Baltimore: John Hopkins University Press, 1996).

60. Cited in Irmtrud Wojak, *Eichmanns Memoiren: Ein kritischer Essay* [Eichmann's Memoirs: A Critical Essay] (Frankfurt: Campus, 2001), 69ff.

61. Giesen and Christoph Schneider, eds., *Tätertrauma: Nationale Erinnerungen im öffentlichen Diskurs* [Trauma of the Perpetrator: National Remembrance in Public Discourse] (Constance: UVK Verlagsgesellschaft, 2004), 22. "For the perpetrators, that is, for all those who directly and willingly participated in the persecution and murder of the Jews, perpetrator trauma applies in the sense of a suddenly destroyed triumphalism and of a destroyed phantasy of all-powerfulness. From now on, they are murderers who must either remain hidden or be discovered."

62. On this point, see the chapter on shame and guilt in Aleida Assmann and Frevert, *Geschichtsvergessenehit—Geschichtsversessenheit*, 86–96; 112–39.

63. As an example of how the concepts of taboo and trauma can be brought together, see Antoon van den Braembussche, "The Silence of Belgium: Taboo and Trauma in Belgian Memory," ed. Catherine Labio, *Yale French Studies*, no. 102 (2002): 35–52.

64. Giesen, *Tätertrauma*, 23.

65. Dan Bar-On, *Legacy of Silence: Encounters with Children of the Third Reich* (Cambridge, Mass.: Harvard University Press, 1989).

66. Levi, *If This Is a Man*, 64.

67. Wieviorka writes about the rich production of survivor testimonies and the disinterest on the part of publishers in the 1940s; Annette Wieviorka, "On Testimony," in *Holocaust Remembrance: The Shapes of Memory*, ed. Geoffrey Hartman (Oxford: Blackwell, 1994), 26ff.

68. Rupnow, *Vernichten und Erinnern*, 62.

69. Helmut Dubiel, *Niemand ist frei von Geschichte: Die nationalsozialistische Herrschaft in den Debatten des Deutschen Bundestages* [No One Is Free of History: The Legacy of National Socialism in the Debates of the German National Parliament] (Munich: Hanser, 1999).

70. An exception to this is the (politically motivated) thematization of the fate of the expellees in the 1950s.

71. Hermann Lübbe, "Der Nationalsozialismus im politischen Bewusstsein der Gegenwart" [National-Socialism in Contemporary Political Consciousness], in *Deutschlands Weg in die Diktatur* [Germany's Path to Dictatorship], ed. Martin Broszat (Berlin: Siedler, 1983), 329.

72. Arendt, "Organized Guilt and Universal Responsibility," in *Essays in Understanding, 1930–1954: Formation, Exile, and Totalitarianism*, 121–32 (New York: Schocken Books, 2005), 122.

73. Jeffrey C. Alexander, "On the Social Construction of Moral Universals: The 'Holocaust' from War Crime to Trauma Drama," in *Cultural Trauma and Collective Identity*, ed. Jeffrey C. Alexander (Berkeley: University of California Press, 2004).

74. Ernst Renan, "What Is a Nation?," trans. Wanda Romer Taylor (Toronto: Tapir Press, 1996), 21.

75. Nietzsche, "On the Uses and Disadvantages of History for Life," in *Untimely Meditations*, trans. R. J. Hollingdale (Cambridge: Cambridge University Press, 1983), 63.

76. Ralph Waldo Emerson, "Circles," in *Emerson's Essays* (New York: Viking, 1983), 179.

77. On this point, see Nicole Loraux's seminal study on Ancient Athens, *The Divided City: On Memory and Forgetting in Ancient Athens* (Cambridge, Mass.: Zone), 2002. Her work was the focus of a conference at the Einstein Forum in Potsdam; see Gary Smith and Avishai Margalit, eds., *Amnestie, oder die Politik der Erinnerung in der Demokratie* [Amnesty, or the Politics of Memory in a Democracy] (Frankfurt am Main: Suhrkamp, 1997).

78. Rudolf Burger, *Kleine Geschichte der Vergangenheit: Eine pyrrhonische Skizze der historischen Vernunft* [A Short History of the Past: A Pyrrhonic Sketch of Historical Reason] (Vienna: Styria, 2004), 25.

79. Ibid., 22. Further dichotomies resonate in this phrase on forgetting and remembering: those between logos and mythos and between Athens and Jerusalem.

80. The principle of impunity has not been adopted by all truth and reconciliation initiatives, which have in the interim spread all over the world. Following a civil war lasting eleven years, peace activists in Sierra Leone plan on including compensation packages in their community-oriented psychosocial programs. At the same time, as they put the following in their website material, "After years of brutal conflict in Sierra Leone there existed a need to confront the past. . . . The Commission heard the voices of a large number of victims, perpetrators, other witnesses to conflict and various stakeholders. Victims . . . came forward to testify . . . in order to relate their stories to Sierra Leone and the world"; http://www.sierraleonetrc.org/.

81. Kurt Meyer, *Geweint wird, wenn der Kopf ab ist: Annäherungen an meinen Vater—"Panzermeyer," Generalmajor der Waffen-SS* [Approaching My Father—"Panzermeyer," Brigadier General of the Waffen SS] (Freiburg: Herder, 1998).

82. Johanna Haarer, *Die deutsche Mutter und ihr erstes Kind* [The German Mother and Her First Child] (Munich: J. F. Lehmann, 1934).

83. Grass, *The Tin Drum*, trans. Breon Mitchell (New York: Houghton Mifflin Harcourt, 2009), 525.

84. Buruma, *Wages of Guilt*, 303.

85. W. G. Sebald, "Air War and Literature: Zurich Lectures," in *On the Natural History of Destruction*, trans. Anthea Bell (New York: Modern Library, 2004).

86. Werner Bohleber, "Trauma, Trauer und Geschichte" [Trauma, Mourning and History], in *Trauer und Geschichte* [Mourning and History], ed. Burkhard Liebsch and Jörn Rüsen (Cologne: Böhlau, 2001), 142.

87. Buruma, *Wages of Guilt*, 304.

88. See Cora Stephan, *Der Betroffenheitskult: Eine politische Sittengeschichte* [The Cult of Shock: A Political History of Morals] (Reinbek: Rowohlt, 1994).

89. Karl Heinz Bohrer, "Historische Trauer und Poetische Trauer" [Historical Mourning and Poetic Mourning], *Merkur* 12 (1999): 1141.

90. Burkhard Liebsch, "Trauer als Gewissen der Geschichte?" [Mourning as the Conscience of History?], in *Trauer und Geschichte*, 52.

91. Ibid., 56; Paul Ricoeur, *Das Rätsel der Vergangenheit* [The Riddle of the Past] (Göttingen: Wallstein, 2004).

92. See Jörn Rüsen, "Historisch Trauern: Skizze einer Zumutung" [Historical Mourning], in *Trauer und Geschichte*.

93. Ibid., 79.

94. Ibid., 78.

95. Alexander Mitscherlich and Margarete Mitscherlich, *Die Unfähigkeit zu trauern: Grundlagen kollektiven Verhaltens* (Munich: Piper, 1997), 41ff. English translation: *The Inability to Mourn: Principles of Collective Behavior* (New York: Grove Press, 1975).

96. On this point, see the excellent and informative contribution by Heidemarie Uhl, "Vom Opfermythos sur Mitverantwortunsthese: NS-Herrschaft, Krieg und Holocaust im 'Österreichischen Gedächtnis'" [From the Myth of Victimhood to Mutual Responsibility: National Socialism, War and the Holocaust in "Austrian Memory"], in *Transformationen gesellschaftlicher Erinnerung: Studien zur Gedächtnisgeschichte der zweiten Republik* [*Transformations in Social Memory: Studies in the History of Memory in the Second Republic of Austria*], ed. Christian Gerbel (Vienna: Turia and Kant, 2005).

97. Aleida Assmann and Ute Frevert, *Geschichtsvergessenheit—Geschichtsversessenehit*; Jeffrey Herf, *Divided Memory: The Nazi Past in the Two Germanys* (Cambridge, Mass.: Harvard University Press, 1997).

98. Ute Heimrod, Günter Schlusche, and Horst Seferens, *Der Denkmalstreit —das Denkmal? Die Debatte um das "Denkmal für ermorderten Juden Europas": Eine Dokumentation* [The Dispute over the Memorial—The Real Memorial? Documenting the Debate about the "Memorial for the Murdered Jews of Europe"] (Berlin: Philo, 1999).

99. Lübbe, *Ich entschuldige mich: Das neue politische Bußritual* [I'm Sorry: The New Ritual of Repentance] (Berlin: Siedler, 2001).

100. Ibid.

101. Peter Sloterdijk, *Luftbeben: An den Wurzeln des Terrors* [Airquake: On the Roots of Terror] (Frankfurt: Suhrkamp, 2002).

102. It is disturbing, however, that this ethical practice is not more extensive; in particular, it has no effect on political powers that are not pressured from the outside. The United States has had no occasion to confront its own historical guilt—one could refer here to the canceled Smithsonian exhibition of the Enola Gay, the plane that dropped the atom bomb on Hiroshima; Susan Sontag and Peter Novick have explicitly pointed to the problem of the Holocaust as a "screen memory" in the United States. The other example here is Russia, where there is still no sign that the crimes of Stalin and his regime are being officially condemned or that the victims of the Gulag are being recognized. This memory is still being passed over in silence, whereas a remythologization and heroization of Stalin in the popular and official historical consciousness is in full force (see Chapter 11 of this volume).

3. HOW TRUE ARE MEMORIES?

1. Along with Günter Grass, Czesław Milosz, Wisława Szymborska, and the Lithuanian writer Tomas Venclova also participated; Grass et al., *Die Zukunft der Erinnerung* [The Future of Memory], ed. Martin Wälde (Göttingen: Steidl, 2001), 27–34.

2. Grass, "I Remember . . . ," in *The Günter Grass Reader*, ed. Helmut Frielinghaus (Wilmington: Mariner, 2004), 282.

3. William Lowell Randall, *The Stories We Are: An Essay on Self-Creation* (Toronto: University of Toronto Press, 1995), 210–23.

4. Henri Bergson, *Matter and Memory*, trans. Nancy Margaret Paul and W. Scott Palmer (New York: Zone, 1988), 153.

5. This sentence was the heading for an exhibition about Christa Wolf on the occasion of her seventy-fifth birthday in 2004 at the Academie der Künste in Berlin.

6. Primo Levi, "If This Is a Man," in *If This Is a Man*, trans. Stuart Woolf (New York: Orion, 1959), 179–206.

7. Ibid., 204.

8. *Frankfurter Allgemeine Zeitung*, 6 May 1995; reprinted as "Vielerlei Abschied vom Krieg" [Many-Sided Farewell to War], by Reinhart Koselleck, in *Vom Vergessen, vom Gedenken: Erinnerungen und Erwartungen in Europa zum 8. Mai 1945* [On Forgetting, on Remembrance: Memories and Expectations in Europe on 8 May, 1945], ed. Brigitte Sauzay, Heinz Ludwig Arnold, and Rudolf von Thadden (Göttingen: Wallstein Verlag, 1995).

9. J. Brown and R. Kulik, "Flashbulb Memories," *Cognition* 2 (1997): 629–54.

10. Martin A. Conway, "The Inventory of Experience: Memory and Identity," in *Collective Memory of Political Events: Social Psychological Perspectives*, ed. James W. Pennebaker, Dario Paez, and Bernard Rime (Mahwah, N.J.: Lawrence Erlbaum Associates, 1997), 36; Conway, *Flashbulb Memories* (Hillsdale: Lawrence Erbaum Associates, 1995).

11. Samuel Butler, *Life and Habit* (London: J. Cape, 1924), cited in *On Collective Memory*, by Maurice Halbwachs, trans., ed. Lewis A. Coser (Chicago: University of Chicago Press, 1992), 80.

12. Daniel Schacter, *Searching for Memory: The Brain, the Mind, and the Past* (New York: Basic Books, 1997), 46.

13. Christa Wolf, *No Place on Earth*, trans. Jan van Heurck (New York: Farrar, 1983), 81.

14. Christa Wolf, "Lesen und Schreiben," in *Die Dimension des Autors* (Darmstadt: Luchterhand, 19870, 479–80; English translation: "Reading and Writing," in *The Author's Dimension: Selected Essays*, ed. Alexander Stephan, trans. Jan van Heurck (Chicago: University of Chicago Press, 1995).

15. Italo Svevo, *Zeno Cosini* (Reinbek: Rowohlt, 2000). 467. Svevo possibly read Bergson as well as Maurice Halbwachs.

16. Marcel Proust, *In Search of Lost Time*, vol. 6, *Time Regained*, trans. Andreas Mayor and Terence Kilmartin (New York: Random House, 1993), 275.

17. Carl Gustav Carus, *Lebenserinnerungen und Denkwürdigkeiten* [Life's Thoughts and Recollections] (Leipzig: Brockhaus, 1865), 1:13. On this, see Anton Philipp Knittel, "Bilder-Bücher der Erinnerung, 'Jugenderinnerungen eines alten Mannes' im Kontext ihrer Zeit" [Picture-Books of Memory: "An Ag-

ing Man's Recollections of his Youth" in Historical Context], *Weimarer Beiträge: Zeitschrift für Literaturwissenschaft, Äesthetik und Kulturwissenschaften* 42, no. 4 (1996): 545–60.

18. The notion of *engram*, which goes back to the work of psychologist Richard Semon, had a powerful influence on thinkers as different from each other as Sigmund Freud and Aby Warburg. On Semon, see Schacter, *Searching for Memory*, 56–60.

19. Schacter, *Searching for Memory*, 58–59.

20. Alan Baddeley, *Your Memory: A User's Guide* (New York: Firefly, 2004), 62. I am grateful to Ali Wacker for this reference.

21. Schacter, *Searching for Memory*, 101.

22. Wolf Singer, "Wahrnehmen, Erinnern, Vergessen" [Perceiving, Remembering, Forgetting], *Frankfurter Allgemeine Zeitung*, 28 September 2000.

23. However, the question becomes how we engage with these new perspectives. An example is the position of the medieval historian Johannes Fried, who, in his book *Der Schleier der Erinnerung: Grundzüge einer historischen Memorik* [The Veil of Memory: Toward a Historical Memorics] (Munich: Beck, 2004), takes the new brain research at its word, which causes the foundations of historical research to collapse. When people cannot produce any reliable memories, there are also no reliable sources on which to base history writing, since the eyewitness is the point of departure for all historical experience. On this point, see Peter Burke, *Eyewitnessing: The Uses of Images as Historical Evidence* (Ithaca: Cornell, 2001).

24. Hans J. Markowitsch and Harald Welzer, *Das autogiographische Gedächtnis: Hirnorganische Grundlagen und biosoziale Entwicklung* (Stuttgart: Klett-Cotta, 1995) 33; English translation: *The Development of Autobiographical Memory* (East Sussex: Pyschology Press, 2009).

25. For examples of people who are sentenced on the basis of false memories, see Schacter, *Searching for Memory*, 107–10.

26. Ibid., 133.

4. FALSE MEMORIES: PATHOLOGIES OF IDENTITY AT THE END OF THE TWENTIETH CENTURY

1. See Erik Erikson, "'Identity Crisis' in Autobiographical Perspective," in *Life History and the Historical Moment* (New York: W. W. Norton, 1975).

2. See Lutz Niethammer, *Kollektive Identität: Heimliche Quellen einer unheimlichen Konjunktur* [Collective Identity: Secret Sources of an Uncanny Negotiation] (Reinbek: Rowohlt, 2000).

3. Dieter Teichert, *Personen und Identitäten* [Persons and Identities] (Berlin: Walter de Gruyter, 1999), 152.

4. Javier Marías, *All Souls*, trans. Margaret Jull Costas (New York: HarperCollins, 1992), 3.

5. John Locke, "Of Identity and Diversity," in *Essay Concerning Human Understanding*, ed. P. H. Nidditch (Oxford: Oxford University Press, 1975). Locke's *Essay* appeared in 1689; the chapter on identity was added in the second edition

from 1694. See the illuminating commentary on this text by Teichert, *Personen und Identitäten* [Persons and Identities], 130–52.

6. Paul Ricoeur, *Oneself as Another*, trans. Kathleen Blamey (Chicago: University of Chicago Press, 1992), 118ff.

7. See Valentin Groebner, *Schein der Person* [The Appearance of the Person] (Munich: Beck, 2004).

8. In a personal correspondence, Dieter Teichert made the claim to me that Locke "cleared the way for later conceptions of ipseity, without himself representing this model. His successors will substantially broaden the terms of self-relation and self-consciousness, in order to think an ipse-identity."

9. One of these sieves was on display at the history museum of Viadrina in Frankfurt (Oder), in a special exhibit entitled "Necessity is the Mother of Invention: Everyday Objects During Times of Crisis in the 20th Century," marking the sixtieth anniversary of liberation.

10. The self-disclosure came after it was clear that Schwerte's secret was about to be uncovered in Belgian circles. In Germany, there had been indications circulating at the level of rumor from time to time that intensified at the beginning of the 1990s. Since the most vocal accuser did not enter into the matter without a degree of self-interest (he himself had applied for a professorship in Aachen), this source lost something of its credibility. On the willingness to keep silent and on secrecy as a characteristic of the postwar climate in the Federal Republic, see Rusinek, "Schneider/Schwerte: Die Karriere eines Spagatakteurs 1936–1995" [Schneider/Schwerte: The Career of a Balancing Act, 1936–1995]," in *Der Fall Schwerte im Kontext* [The Schwerte Case in Context], ed. Helmut König (Opladen: Westdeutscher, 1998), 34–41, as well as the editor's Introduction, 6–11.

11. For the particulars of this case, see Norbert Frei, "Identitätswechsel in der Nachkriegszeit: Die 'Illegalen' in der Nachkriegszeit" [Identity Reversal after 1945: The 'Illegals' in the Postwar Period], in *Vertuschte Vergangenheit: Der Fall Schwerte und die NS-Vergangenheit der deutschen Hochschulen* [The Silenced Past: The Schwerte Case and the Legacy of National Socialism in the German University], ed. Helmut König, Wolfgang Kuhlmann, and Klaus Schwabe (Munich: Beck, 1997). On the five falsified papers that Schwerte used to establish his new identity, see Rusinek, "Schneider/Schwerte," 32.

12. Ludwig Jäger, "Germanistik—eine deutsche Wissenschaft: Das Kapitel Hans Ernst Schneider" [German Studies: The Chapter on Hans Ernst Schneider]," in König, *Vertuschte Vergangenheit*, 44. For a more detailed account, see Jäger's "Seitenwechsel: *Der Fall Schneider/Schwerte und die Diskretion der Germanistik*" [Changing Sides: The Schneider/Schwerte Case and the Discretion of German Studies] (Munich: Fink, 1998).

13. Claus Leggewie, *Von Schneider zu Schwerte: Das ungewöhnliche Leben eines Mannes, der aus der Geschichte Lernen wollte* [From Schneider to Schwerte: The Unusual Life of a Man Attempting to Learn from the Past] (Munich: Hanser, 1998), 226. Another way of describing it is "switching masks"; see Joachim

Lerchenmüller and Gerd Simon, eds., *Maskenwechsel* [Switching Masks] (Tübingen: Gesellschaft für interdisziplinäre Forschung, 1999).

14. Cited in Leggewie, *Von Schneider zu Schwerte*, 85.

15. Jäger, "Germanistik."

16. Elena Lappin, "The Man with Two Heads," *Granta* 66 (1999): 10.

17. Daniel Ganzfried, . . . *alias Wilkomirski: Die Holocaust Travestie; Enthüllung und Dokumentation eines literarischen Skandals* [Aka Wilkomirski: The Holocaust Travesty; Unearthing and Documenting a Literary Scandal] (Berlin: Jüdische Verlagsanstalt, 2002); Lappin, "Man with Two Heads"; Stefan Mächler, *The Wilkomirski Affair: A Study in Biographical Truth*, trans. John E. Woods (New York: Schocken Books, 2001).

18. Binjamin Wilkomirski, *Fragments: Memoirs of a Childhood, 1939–1948*, trans. Carol Brown Janeway (New York: Picador, 1996), 4. In an interview, he describes his memories in the following way: "It was a process that lasted for decades because most of the imagistic memories were actually replaying in me on an almost daily basis, like a kind of film, triggered by some detail, some small association. But for the longest time, I couldn't interpret most of these images. They were there, and made me anxious but I couldn't put them into words, I couldn't explain them, perhaps because the memories, these images, went so far back into a phase where I didn't even speak, into what today we'd call a non-verbal phase, and so it took a long time before I found the vocabulary to represent these images"; Stefan Mächler, *Wilkomirski als Opfer: Das Wilkomirski Syndrom—Eingebildete Erinnerung oder Von der Sehnsucht, Opfer zu Sein* [Wilkomirski as Victim: The Wilkomirski Syndrome—Constructed Memory or, On the Desire to Be a Victim], ed. Irene Diekmann and Julius H. Schoeps (Zurich: Pendo, 2002), 42–43.

19. Cited in Philip Gourevitch, "The Memory Thief," *The New Yorker*, 14 June 1999.

20. Henry Krystal, "Oral History and Echoes of Cataclysms Past," *Address to the Social Science History Association*, Chicago, 17 November 1998, 4–5.

21. Ibid., 5.

22. Wilkomirski, *Fragments*, 153. He also talks about how he had invested in a counter-memory ever since his youth, which he told as a litany in rosary-bead fashion to shield himself from his environment. In that, he is emphatically distancing his own case from the notion of recovered memory, which became a key term in the debate about sexual child abuse. "Recovered memory means to re-discover through therapy lost things of your unconscious memory. And that is in my case absolutely wrong. Never in my life have I forgotten what I wrote in my book. I had nothing to re-discover again! . . . When I was a youngster, I spent hours and hours on free afternoons, at a secret place in our garden, loudly speaking and repeating all I could remember"; cited in Gourevitch, "Memory Thief."

23. Anthony Trollope, "On English Prose Fiction as a Rational Amusement," in *Four Lectures* (London: Folcroft, 1976), 108.

24. On this, see also Dieter Teichert, "Erinnerte Einbildungen und Eingebildete Erinnerungen: Erinnerung und Imagination in epistemologischer Perspektive" [Remembered Imaginings and Imagined Memories in Epistemological Perspective], in *Erinnerungsarbeit: Zu Paul Ricoeurs Philosophie von Gedächtnis, Geschichte und Vergessen* [The Work of Memory: On Paul Ricoeur's Philosophy of Memory, History, and Forgetting], ed. Andris Beitling and Stefan Orth (Berlin: Berliner Wissenschafts-Verlag, 2004).

25. Daniel Schacter, "The Seven Sins of Memory: Insights from Psychology and Cognitive Neuroscience," *American Psychologist* 54, no. 3 (March 1999): 182–203. I am grateful to Rudolf Cohen for providing me with this reference.

26. Schacter, "Seven Sins of Memory," 191.

27. Maurice Halbwachs, *On Collective Memory*, trans., ed. Lewis A. Coser (Chicago: University of Chicago Press, 1992), 38.

28. See Jan Assmann, "Erinnern, um dazuzugehören: Kulturelles Gedächtnis, Zugehörigkeitsstruktur und normative Vergangenheit" [Remembering in Order to Belong: Cultural Memory, Structures of Belonging and Normative Pasts], in *Generation und Gedächtnis: Erinnerungen und kollektive Identitäten*, ed. Kristin Platt and Mihran Dabag (Opladen: Leske and Budrich, 1995), 51–75.

29. Sebastian Rödl, *Selbstbezug und Normativität* (Münster: mentis, 1998), 49; English translation: *Self-Consciousness*, trans. Sibylle Salewski (Cambridge, Mass.: Harvard University Press, 2007).

5. INCORRECT RECOLLECTIONS: ON THE NORMATIVE
POWER OF SOCIAL FRAMEWORKS OF MEMORY

1. I have adopted the image of "shards of a mirror" from Günter Grass's essay "I Remember. . . ." (in *The Günter Grass Reader*, ed. Helmut Frielinghaus [Wilmington: Mariner, 2004] and the notion of multiple refractions from Shelly Berlovitz, an invaluable participant in the University of Konstanz memory seminars.

2. Peter Novick, *The Holocaust in American Life* (Boston: Houghton Mifflin, 1999), 8.

3. I am referring here to an oral reference from Moshe Barasch, who found himself caught up in the Holocaust from his hometown of Cernowitz on 22 June 1940 and became involved with a Jewish resistance organization.

4. Ivan Illich, *Fortschrittsmythen* [Myths of Progress] (Reinbek: Rowohlt, 1980), 30.

5. Novick, *The Holocaust in American Life*. The German subtitle of the book, "der Umgang mit dem Massenmord," is incorrect; it undoubtedly should have read "The *American* Engagement with Mass Murder."

6. Jeffrey C. Alexander, "On the Social Construction of Moral Universals: The 'Holocaust' from War Crime to Trauma Drama," in *Cultural Trauma and Collective Identity*, ed. Jeffrey C. Alexander (Berkeley: University of California Press, 2004), 201.

7. Maurice Halbwachs, *On Collective Memory*, trans., ed. Lewis A. Coser (Chicago: University of Chicago Press, 1992), 51.

8. Ibid., 50.

9. Halbwachs suggests that the more firmly grounded people are in their particular social groups, the more clearly their memories will reflect the pre-given frameworks. Since these social groups have a weaker hold on children and older people, their memories are less dependent on those frames of reference. There are doubtless differentiations to be made in Halbwachs's brilliant and still influential concept of frameworks. For instance, he does not differentiate clearly enough between the social framework of the family and that of society as a whole, each of which can indeed come into conflict with the other: this differentiation between a private and a public framework is crucial for the context of German postwar society.

10. George Herbert Mead, *The Philosophy of the Present*, ed. Arthur E. Murphy (Chicago: University of Chicago Press, 1980), 28–29.

11. Jean-Paul Sartre, *Being and Nothingness*, trans. Hazel E. Barnes (New York: Washington Square Press, 1992), 640; Rudolf Burger, *Kleine Geschichte der Vergangenheit: Eine pyrrhonische Skizze der historischen Vernunft* [A Short History of the Past: A Pyrrhonic Sketch of Historical Reason] (Vienna: Styria, 2004), 31–32.

12. Michael Jeismann, "Voodoo Child: Die verhexten Kinder" [Voodoo Child: The Cursed Children], *Literaturen* (May 2005): 15: "If notions like fatherland, resistance or honour had the same meaning today that they did at the end of the war, these histories would also not be narratable today." The same goes for the conceptual trio of nation-guilt-identity, which relegate still other histories to the realm of the unspeakable.

13. "In short, the most painful aspects of yesterday's society are forgotten because constraints are felt only so long as they operate and because, by definition, a past constraint has ceased to be operative"; Halbwachs, *On Collective Memory*, 51.

14. My sense is that Bergson's powerful influence caused Halbwachs to side with the constructivists and to wholly reject theorists of memory who emphasized the more shadowy aspects of individual consciousness.

15. Martin Walser, *Ein springender Brunnen* [A Leaping Fountain] (Frankfurt am Main: Suhrkamp, 1998), 282.

16. Ibid., 283.

17. Walser, *Über Deutschland Reden* [Discussing Germany] (Frankfurt am Main: Suhrkamp, 1988), 76–78.

18. Max Frisch, *Wilhelm Tell: A School Text*, trans. Lore Segal and Paul Stern, in *Max Frisch: Novels Plays Essays* (New York: Continuum, 1989), 111.

19. On the importance of forgetting in this respect, see Halbwachs, *On Collective Memory*, 47.

20. Walser, *Ein springender Brunnen*, 282.

21. "'Niemand muß mir Glauben schenken' [Nobody Has to Believe Me], interview with Binjamin Wilkomirski," by Peter Teuwsen, *Tagesanzeiger*, 31 August 1998.

22. Sigrid Weigel, "Zeugnis und Zeugenschaft, Klage und Anklage" [Evidence and Testimony, Grievance and Accusal], in *Zeugnis und Zeugenschaft*, ed. Rüdiger Zill (Berlin: Akademie Verlag, 2000), 116.

23. http://www.teachsam.de/deutsch/d_rhetorik/rede/pol_rede/pol_rede/brd/Jenninger_1.1.htm, accessed 30 May 2015.

24. Christian Meier, *Vierzig Jahre nach Auschwitz: Deutsche Geschichtserinnerungen heute* [Forty Years after Auschwitz: German Memory Today] (Munich: Beck, 1990), 84.

25. http://www.teachsam.de/deutsch/d_rhetorik/rede/pol_rede/pol_rede/brd/Jenninger_I.htm.

26. Andreas Schreitmüller, *Alle Bilder lügen* [All Images Lie] (Constance: UVK Universitätsverlag, 2005), 14–16.

27. Interview with Ian Buruma, quoted in Buruma, *Wages of Guilt: Memories of War in Germany and Japan* (New York: Farrar, Straus, and Giroux, 1994), 242.

28. Philipp Jenninger's speech was also used as an educational tool in schools. Werner Hill made a searing film about the speech in 1989. In that film, he recreates the Bundestag "history lesson" using such high-profile stage actors as Ulrich Wildgruber (as Jenninger), Dietrich Mattausch, Gustav Peter Wöhler, Hermann Lause, Barbara Nüsse, Klaus Nägelen, Gisela Trowe, Heiko Deutschmann, and Heike Falkenberg (http://www.klick-nach-rechts.de/ticker/2003/II/Jenninger.htm).

29. Buruma, *Wages of Guilt*, 247.

30. Novick, *The Holocaust in American Life*, 5.

31. Ibid., 85.

32. Ibid., 85–86.

6. FIVE STRATEGIES OF REPRESSION

Cf. Chapter 2 of this volume.

2. Cited in Niklas Frank, *Der Vater: Eine Abrechnung* (Munich: Goldmann, 1987), 304; English translation: *In the Shadow of the Reich* (New York: Alfred A. Knopf, 1991).

3. Ibid., 312.

4. Rainer M. Lepsius, "Das Erbe des Nationalsozialismus und die politische Kultur der Nachfolgestaaten des 'Großdeutschen Reiches'" [The Legacy of National Socialism and the Political Culture of Successor States to the "Greater German Reich"], in *Kultur und Gesellschaft.*, ed. Max Heller et al. (Frankfurt: Campus, 1989), 247–64.

5. Hannes Heer, *Hitler war's: Die Befreiung der Deutschen von ihrer Vergangenheit* ["It Was Hitler!": The Liberation of the Germans From Their Past] (Berlin: Aufbau Verlag, 2005).

6. Saul K. Padover, *The Experiment in Germany: The Story of an American Intelligence Officer* (New York: Duell, Sloan, and Pearce, 1946); German translation: *Lügendetektor: Vernehmungen im besiegten Deutschland 1944/45* (Frankfurt: Eichborn, 1999).

7. Although the American officer Saul Padover carried out his interviews with militarily defeated Germans in his role as an occupier, his tone was in no way that of an interrogation. For him it was a question of learning something about the inner motives, dispositions, hopes, and attitudes of his informants; he wanted to get at the "German character" and the German mentality. So he quickly learned how to guide the discussions so as to draw his interlocutors out and to get them to talk.

8. Padover, *Lügendetektor*, 93–94.

9. Uwe Timm, *In My Brother's Shadow*, trans. Anthea Bell (New York: Farrar, Straus and Giroux, 2005), 67.

10. Heer, *Hitler war's*.

11. Christian Meier, *Vierzig Jahre nach Auschwitz: Deutsche Geschichtserinnerungen heute* [Forty Years after Auschwitz: German Memory Today] (Munich: Beck, 1990), 41.

12. The historian Robert Gellately pursues the question of how much the Germans knew or were aware of in *Backing Hitler: Consent and Coercion in Nazi Germany* (Oxford: Oxford University Press, 2002).

13. Sigmund Freud, "Remembering, Repeating, and Working Through," in *The Standard Edition of the Complete Psychological Works of Sigmund Freud*, ed. James Strachey (London: Hogarth Press, 1958), 12:149.

14. Daniel Schacter, "The Seven Sins of Memory: Insights from Psychology and Cognitive Neuroscience," *American Psychologist* 54, no. 3 (March 1999): 186.

15. Regarding the ambivalence of silence, see "Remaining Silent" in this chapter.

16. George Steiner, *After Babel: Aspects of Language and Translation* (Oxford: Oxford University Press, 1998).

17. Wolfgang Emmerlich, ed., *Der Bremer Literaturpreis 1954–1987: Reden der Preisträger und andere Texte* [Bremen Literature Prize 1954–1987: Speeches of the Award Winners and Other Texts] (Bremerhaven: Verlag für Neue Wissenschaft, 1988), 69–76; Paul Celan, *Selected Poems and Prose of Paul Celan*, trans. John Felstiner (New York: W. W. Norton, 2002), 395.

18. Celan, "Todtnauberg," in Celan, *Selected Poems and Prose*. On Heidegger's silence, see Rüdiger Safranski, *Ein Meister aus Deutschland: Heidegger und seine Zeit* (Frankfurt: Fischer, 1995), 483ff; English translation: *Martin Heidegger: Between Good and Evil*, trans. Ewald Osers (Cambridge, Mass.: Harvard University Press, 1998). Safranksi explores the demand confronting Heidegger to distance himself from the murder of millions of Jews. This, says Safranski, "Heidegger rightly experienced as an utter abomination" because he would have implicitly had to recognize his complicity with the murderers. By contrast, "when Heidegger speaks about the perversion of the modern will to power that makes nature

and the human into mere material of its machination, . . . Auschwitz is always explicitly or implicitly meant."

19. Hermann Lübbe, "Der Nationalsozialismus im politischen Bewusstsein der Gegenwart" [National Socialism in Contemporary Political Consciousness], in *Deutschlands Weg in die Diktatur* [Germany's Path to Dictatorship], ed. Martin Broszat (Berlin: Siedler), 1983, 329. Dirk van Laak also sees the pragmatic silence of the period as a mechanism geared toward integration, though one that had clear "operating noises" associated with it; see van Laak, *Gespräche in der Sicherheit des Schweigens: Carl Schmitt in der politischen Geistesgeschichte der frühen Bundesrepublik* [Conversations in the Safety of Silence: Positioning Carl Schmitt in the Political Intellectual History of the Young German Republic] (Berlin: Akademie Verlag, 2002), 130.

20. Lutz Niethammer, *Lebenserfahrung und kollektives Gedächtnis: Die Praxis der "Oral History"* [Lived Experience and Collective Memory: The Practice of Oral History] (Frankfurt am Main: Syndikat, 1985), 178.

21. Martin Heidegger, *Being and Time*, trans. Joan Stambaugh (Albany: SUNY Press, 2010), §164ff.

22. Ibid., §127.

23. Harald Welzer, "Der Holocaust im deutschen Familiengedächtnis" [The Holocaust in German Family Remembrance], in *Verbrechen erinnern* [Remembering Crimes], ed. Norbert Frei and Volkhard Knigge (Munich: Beck, 2002), 342–58.

24. Ibid.

25. Welzer, *Opa war kein Nazi* (Frankfurt am Main: Fischer, 2002), 11; English translation: *Grandpa Wasn't a Nazi: Nazism and the Holocaust in German Family Remembrance*, available at http://www.ajc.org/atf/cf/%7BF56F4495-CF69-45CB-A2D7-F8ECA17198EE%7D/Grandpa_wasnt_nazi.pdf, accessed 15 July 2014.

26. Welzer, *Opa War Kein Nazi*, 12.

27. On the concept of experiential memory, see Michael Theunissen, *Reichweite und Grenzen der Erinnerung* [The Scope and Limits of Memory] (Tübingen: Mohr Siebeck, 2001).

7. GERMAN NARRATIVES OF VICTIMHOOD

1. Klaus Naumann, *Der Krieg als Text: Das Jahr 1945 im kulturellen Gedächtnis der Presse* [The War as Text: 1945 in the Cultural Memory of the Media] (Hamburg: Hamburger Edition, 1998). On this point, see Herfried Münkler, "Opfer der Geschichte? Das Jahr 1945 im Gedenken und Erinnern der Deutschen" [Victims of History? 1945 in German Memory], in *Die Zeit*, 16 May 2000.

2. Helke Sanders's documentary film *BeFreier und BeFreite* [Liberator and Liberated] (Bremen: Bremer Institut Film/Fernsehen, 1992) is of great significance in this context, since it brought the theme back into memory at the beginning of the 1990s. But beyond group initiatives and intellectual circles, it didn't trigger any debates at a more general social level.

3. I myself first heard detailed accounts of the nights of bombing in the 1970s after having asked, and not from family members. Interestingly, it was always women who told these histories; they were perhaps supplementing the (male) soldier's experience of war with a (female) civilian side.

4. Sebald's lecture series was held in Zurich in 1997 and published in W. G. Sebald, "Air War and Literature: Zurich Lectures," in *On the Natural History of Destruction*, trans. Anthea Bell (New York: Modern Library, 2004).

5. Ibid., 10.

6. Reissued, Gert Ledig, *Vergeltung* (Frankfurt am Main: Suhrkamp, 2001); English translation: *Payback*, trans. Shaun Whiteside (London: Granta, 2009).

7. Klaus Rainer Röhl, *Verbotene Trauer: Ende der deutschen Tabus* [Forbidden Mourning: The End of a German Taboo] (Munich: Universitas, 2002). He prefaces his book with the following: "Fifty-seven years after the end of the Second World War, we mourn the victims of Hitler's regime almost every week and in almost every German city. The million-fold suffering of innocent victims should never be forgotten. That is the way it should be. But this public mourning is a divided mourning. For many millions of innocent Germans were also victims of the war against the totalitarian Hitler regime. They were murdered and deported, most of them through a no-less totalitarian regime, that of Stalin. No observances, no ceremonial acts and no commemorations take place for these millions of German victims, and no national memorial is even planned. That is not the way it should be. Should not, should not, should not" (9).

8. *The New Yorker*, 2 December 2002.

9. Sebald, "Air War and Literature," 70.

10. See Jörg Friedrich, *The Fire: The Bombing of Germany, 1940–1945*, trans. Allison Brown (New York: Columbia University Press, 2006); see also the Spiegel report in Nr. 49 (2002), 2 and 4 (2003) and Lothar Kettenacker, ed., *Ein Volk von Opfern? Die neue Debatte um den Bombenkrieg 1940–1945* [A People of Victims? Recent Perspectives on the Bombing 1940–1945] (Berlin: Rowohlt, 2003).

11. Hans-Ulrich Wehler, "Vergleichen—nicht moralisieren: Spiegel-Gespräch mit Hans-Ulrich Wehler" [Compare—Don't Moralize: A Conversation with Hans-Ulrich Wehler], *Der Spiegel* 2 (2003): 51.

12. Dieter Forte, *Schweigen oder Sprechen* [Remaining Silent or Speaking] (Frankfurt am Main: Fischer, 2002), 67.

13. Günter Grass, "I Remember . . . ," in *The Günter Grass Reader*, ed. Helmut Frielinghaus (Wilmington: Mariner, 2004), 286.

14. Ulrich Raulff, *Süddeutsche Zeitung*, 30 January 2003.

15. Uwe Timm, *In My Brother's Shadow*, trans. Anthea Bell (New York: Farrar, Straus, and Giroux, 2005), 29.

16. Ibid., 29–32.

17. Aleida Assmann, "Persönliche Erinnerung und kollektives Gedächtnis in Deutschland nach 1945" [Personal Recollection and Collective Memory in Germany after 1945], in *Erinnern und Verstehen: Der Völkermord an den Juden im politischen Gedächtnis der Deutschen* [Remembering and Understanding: The

Genocide of the Jews in German Political Memory] ed. Hans Erler (Frankfurt: Campus, 2003), 126–38.

18. See the contributions to the collection of Jürgen Danyel and Phillip Ther, eds., *Flucht und Vertreibung in Europäischer Perspektive* [Flight and Expulsion in European Perspective], Zeitschrift für Geschichtswissenschaft 51 (Berlin: Metropol, 2003).

19. Here I am referring to the so-called "Hohmann Affair" of 2003, wherein Defense Minister Peter Struck fired Brigadier General Reinhard Günzel, commander-in-chief of the German Special Forces (KSK), for apparently praising the conservative MP Martin Hohmann (CDU), who had been accused of anti-Semitism; http://news.bbc.co.uk/2/hi/europe/3240799.stm, accessed 6 June 2015.

20. East German author Reinhard Jirgl's 2002 novel *Die Unvollendeten* [The Incomplete] (Munich: Hanser, 2002) in no way belongs to this category. In this brilliant and widely acclaimed book, which is based partially on the facts of his own life, the narrator is written into a family history spanning four generations, all of which are represented exclusively by women. The novel begins in 1945 with the expulsion out of Komotau, a Südenten-German city, proceeds through GDR history, and then ends in present-day Berlin.

21. Examples of memory literature in which the diaries and letters of deceased family members are taken up, continued, and rewritten are Timm, *In My Brother's Shadow*, and Stephan Wackwitz, *Ein unsichtbares Land: Familienroman* [An Invisible Land: A Family Novel] (Frankfurt am Main: Fischer, 2003).

22. Grass, "I Remember . . . ," 286.

23. Ibid., 286.

24. From a psychoanalytic perspective, one might say that the suffering of Jewish victims "silenced" members of the children's generation, so that they "could not speak of their own traumatization"; Werner Bohleber, "Trauma, Trauer und Geschichte" [Trauma, Mourning and History], in *Trauer und Geschichte* [Mourning and History], ed. Burkhard Liebsch and Jörn Rüsen (Cologne: Böhlau, 2001), 143.

25. "No matter what plan we make for the future," Grass writes in his Vilnius speech, "the past has already marked the supposedly virgin territories with its scent and everywhere staked signposts pointing back to our history"; "I Remember . . . ," 286.

26. Grass, "I Remember . . . ," 287.

27. Heidemarie Uhl, in the *Süddeutsche Zeitung*, 29 November 2003.

28. Hannes Heer, *Vom Verschwinden der Täter: Der Vernichtungskrieg fand statt, aber keiner war dabei* [On the Disappearance of the Perpetrators: The War of Extermination Took Place, but No One Was Present], (Berlin: Aufbau, 2004).

29. The citations are compiled by Heer, *Vom Verschwinden der Täter*, 287.

30. Ibid., 294.

31. Ibid., 304.

32. Grass, "I Remember . . . ," 286.

33. Musil Bogdan, quoted in Heer, *Vom Verschwinden der Täter*, 272.

8. POINTS OF INTERSECTION BETWEEN LIVED MEMORY AND CULTURAL MEMORY

1. Reinhart Koselleck, "Afterword to Charlotte Beradt's The Third Reich of Dreams," in *Practice of Conceptual History: Timing History, Spacing Concepts*, trans. T. S. Presner, Kerstin Behnke, and Jobst Welge (Stanford: Stanford University Press, 2002), 327.

2. Hans J. Markowitsch and Harald Welzer, *Das Autobiographische Gedächtnis: Hirnorganische Grundlagen und biosoziale Entwicklung* (Stuttgart: Klett-Cotta, 1995), 33; English translation: *The Development of Autobiographical Memory* (East Sussex: Pyschology Press, 2009).

3. Ibid.

4. Peter Reichel, *Erfundene Erinnerung: Weltkrieg und Judenmord in Film und Theater* [Invented Memory: World War and the Holocaust in Film and Theatre] (Munich: Fischer, 2004), 46.

5. On that point, see Valentin Groebner, *Der Schein der Person* [The Appearance of the Person] (Munich: Beck, 2004).

6. John Borland, "Graffiti, Paraden und Alltagskultur in Nordirland" [Graffiti, Parades and Everyday Culture in North Ireland], in *Das Soziale Gedächtnis*, ed. Harald Welzer (Hamburg: Hamburger Edition, 2001), 278.

7. Peter Novick, *The Holocaust in American Life* (Boston: Houghton Mifflin, 1999), 8.

8. Ibid.

9. Jürgen Trabant, "Wissen als Handeln und die Vermittlung der Zeichen" [Knowledge as Action and the Transmission of Signs], *Rechtshistorisches Journal* 18 (1999): 265.

10. Ibid., 268.

11. Edward A. Shils, *Tradition* (Chicago: University of Chicago Press, 2006), 50–51.

12. Jeffrey C. Alexander, "On the Social Construction of Moral Universals: The 'Holocaust' from War Crime to Trauma Drama," in *Cultural Trauma and Collective Identity*, ed. Jeffrey C. Alexander (Berkeley: University of California Press, 2004), 199.

13. Martin Walser, "Ein springender Brunnen" [A Leaping Fountain] (Frankfurt am Main: Suhrkamp, 1998), 9f.

14. Jorge Semprun, *Literature or Life*, trans. Linda Coverdale (Toronto: Penguin, 1997), 198–200.

15. http://www.antisemitismus.net/antisemitismus/debatte/texte/nblatt-03.htm, accessed 3 June 2015.

16. Elena Lappin, "The Man with Two Heads," *Granta* 66 (1999): 5.

17. Ibid.

18. On the medium of video testimony, see Aleida Assmann, "History, Memory, and the Genre of Testimony," *Poetics Today* 27, no. 2 (2006): 261–73.

19. The difference between self-representation and the representation of/by others is instructive here. Whereas the victims speak of Germans and mean Nazis, Germans always speak of Nazis as their others.

20. Friedrich Nietzsche, "On the Uses and Disadvantages of History for Life," in *Untimely Meditations*, trans. R. J. Hollingdale (Cambridge: Cambridge University Press, 1983), 76.

21. Uwe Timm, *In My Brother's Shadow*, trans. Anthea Bell (New York: Farrar, Straus, and Giroux, 2005), 58–59.

22. Ibid., 59.

23. Timm, *In My Brother's Shadow*; Tanja Dückers, *Himmelskörper* [Heavenly Bodies] (Berlin: Aufbau-Verlag, 2003); Stephan Wackwitz, *Ein unsichtbares Land: Familienroman* [An Invisible Land: A Family Novel] (Frankfurt am Main: Fischer, 2003); Dagmar Leupold, *Nach den Kriegen: Roman eines Lebens* [After the Wars: Novel of a Life] (Munich: Beck, 2004); Malte Ludin, dir, *2 oder 3 Dinge, die ich von ihm weiß* [2 or 3 Things I Know about Him] (Berlin: Absolut Medien, 2005).

9. COMMEMORATIVE SITES IN SPACE AND TIME

1. Niklas Luhmann, "Gleichzeitigkeit und Synchronisation" [Simultaneity and Synchronization], *Soziologische Aufklärung 5: Konstruktivistische Perspektiven* (1990): 95–130.

2. Marcus Tullius Cicero, *De finibus*, in *On Moral Ends*, trans. Raphael Woolf, ed. Julia Annas (Cambridge: Cambridge University Press, 2001), 394–96. See also my treatment of places as media of memory in Aleida Assmann, *Cultural Memory and Western Civilization: Functions, Media, Archives* (Cambridge: Cambridge University Press, 2011).

3. Moritz Csáky and Peter Stachel, eds., *Die Verortung von Gedächtnis* [Placing Memory] (Vienna: Passagen, 2001); on the theme of monuments, see the useful collection edited by the Akademie der Künste Berlin: *Denkmale und kulturelles Gedächtnis nach dem Ende der Ost-West-Konfrontation* [Monuments and Cultural Memory after the End of the East-West Conflict] (Berlin: Jovis, 2000).

4. Volkhard Knigge, Afterword, in *Verbrechen erinnern: Die Auseinandersetzung mit Holocaust und Völkermord* [Remembering Crimes: Engaging the Holocaust and Genocide], ed. Knigge and Norbert Frei (Munich: Beck, 2002), 443.

5. Knigge, Jürgen Maria Pietsch, and Thomas A. Seidel, *Versteinertes Gedenken: Das Buchenwalder Mahnmal von 1958* [Petrified Remembrance: The Buchenwald Memorial of 1958] (Leipzig: Editions Akanthus, 1997), 1:81.

6. Jorge Semprun, "In den Wind gestreut" [Strewn in the Wind], in Knigge, Pietsch, and Seidel, *Versteinertes Gedenken*, vol. 2.

7. http://www.stiftung.hsh.de/document.php?cat_id=CAT_163&special=0.

8. http://www.braunschweig.de/kultur/museen/gedenkstaettenkonzept_vernetztes.html.

9. http://keom.de/denkmal/sigurdsson.html.

10. http://keom.de/denkmal/impressum.html.

11. The term "the magic of Antaeus" was used by the cultural theorist Aby Warburg in the context of historical relics that emanate "mnemic energy." According to Greek legend, Antaeus is a giant whose power comes from touching

the earth. Heracles succeeded in overcoming him by preventing him from having any physical contact with the earth.

12. Ruth Klüger, *Weiter leben: Eine Jugend* [Still Alive: A Youth] (Göttingen: Wallstein Verlag: 1992), 75.

13. This is the name of a cultural studies postgraduate program at the University of Hildesheim.

14. Klüger, *Still Alive* (New York: Feminist Press at the City University of New York, 2001), 67.

15. The quotation is taken from a title of a work by Reinhart Koselleck, "Kriegerdenkmale als Identitätsstiftungen der Überlebenden" [War Memorials as Sources of Identity for Survivors], *Poetik und Hermeneutik* 8 (1979): 255–76.

16. I am grateful to Christoph Mayer and his project group named "A So-called Peripheral Camp" for the information presented here.

17. http://www.gusen.org, accessed 3 June 2015.

18. Bertrand Perz, *Die KZ-Gedenkstätte Mauthausen 1945 bis zur Gegenwart* [The Mauthausen Memorial from 1945 to the Present] (Innsbruck: StudienVerlag, 2006), 195–208.

19. Helena Janeczek, "Excerpt from *Lessons of Darkness*," trans. Stephen Sartarelli, in *Nothing Makes You Free: Writings by Descendants of Jewish Holocaust Survivors*, ed. Melvin Jules Bukiet (New York: W. W. Norton, 2002), 259.

20. Paul Connerton, *How Societies Remember* (Cambridge: Cambridge University Press, 1989), 45.

21. I am gratefully incorporating elements of Beate Binder's entry "Jahrestag" [Anniversary] found in the *Lexikon Gedächtnis und Erinnerung*, ed. Jens Ruchatz and Nicholas Pethes (Reinbek: Rowohlt, 2001).

22. Gabrielle M. Spiegel, "Memory and History: Liturgical Time and Historical Time," *History and Theory* 41 (2002): 232.

10. THE FUTURE OF HOLOCAUST MEMORY

1. This is the case above all for cultures that use writing; in cultures with oral or gestural forms of transmission, cultural transmission is not stored in external media but in the body. On this point, see Jan Assmann, Aleida Assmann, and Christoph Hardmeier, eds., *Schrift und Gedächtnis: Beiträge zur Archäologie der literarischen Kommunikation* [Writing and Memory: Contributions to the Archaeology of Literary Communication] (Munich: Fink, 1983).

2. Theodor W. Adorno, *Prisms*, trans. Shierry Weber and Samuel Weber (Cambridge, Mass.: MIT Press, 1983), 34.

3. Elie Wiesel, "Trivializing the Holocaust," *New York Times*, 16 April 1978.

4. Claude Lanzmann, dir., *Shoah* (New York: New Yorker Films, 1985). On Lanzmann's argument, see the Cultural Office, City of Marburg, ed., *Formen von Erinnerung: Eine Diskussion mit Claude Lanzmann: Ein Anderer Blick auf Gedenken, Erinnern und Erleben* [Forms of Memory: A Discussion with Claude Lanzmann; Another Perspective on Commemorating, Remembering and Experiencing] (Marburg: Cultural Office, 1998); Lanzmann, "*Schindler's List* Is an Impossible

Story," http://www.phil.uu.nl/~rob/2007/hum291/lanzmannschindler.shtml, accessed 15 July 2014; first published in *Le Monde*, 3 March 1994; published in German as "Ihr sollt nicht weinen: Einspruch gegen 'Schlinders Liste,'" in *"Der gute Deutsche"* ["The Good German"], ed. Christoph Weiss (St. Ingbert: Röhrig Universitätsverlag, 1995), 175; see also Alan Mintz, *Popular Culture and the Shaping of Holocaust Memory in America* (Seattle: University of Washington Press, 2001), 146.

5. *Schindler's List*, directed by Steven Spielberg (U.S.: Universal Pictures, 1993), docudrama/war drama; 197 min. On the reception of the film in Germany, see Christoph Weiss, ed., *"Der gute Deutsche"* ["The Good German"].

6. Dan Diner, *Beyond the Conceivable: Studies on Germany, Nazism, and the Holocaust*. (Berkeley: University of California Press, 2000).

7. Jeffrey C. Alexander, "On the Social Construction of Moral Universals: The 'Holocaust' from War Crime to Trauma Drama," in *Cultural Trauma and Collective Identity*, ed. Jeffrey C. Alexander (Berkeley: University of California Press, 2004), 197.

8. Ivan Ivanji, "Die Macht der Erinnerung, die Ohnmacht der Worte" [The Power of Memory, the Powerlessness of the Word], in *Verbrechen erinnern* [Remembering Crimes], ed. Volkhard Knigge and Norbert Frei (Munich: Beck, 2002), 12f.

9. Norbert Frei, *Vergangenheitspolitik: Die Anfänge der Bundesrepublik und die NS-Vergangenheit* (Munich: Beck, 1996); English translation: *Adenauer's Germany and the Nazi Past: The Politics of Amnesty and Integration*, trans. Joel Golb (New York: Columbia University Press, 2002).

10. Claus Leggewie and Erik Meyer, *"Ein Ort an den man gerne geht": Das Holocaust-Mahnmal und die deutsche Geschichtspolitik nach 1989* ["A Place That One Likes to Go": The Holocaust Memorial and German Political History after 1989] (Munich: Hanser, 2005), 13.

11. Michael Tomasello, *The Cultural Origins of Human Cognition* (Cambridge, Mass.: Harvard University Press, 1999), 37ff.

12. Mihran Dabag, "Der Genozid an den Armeniern im Osmanischen Reich" [The Armenian Genocide in the Ottoman Empire], in Knigge and Frei, *Verbrechen Erinnern*, 49.

13. On this point, see Leggewie and Erik Meyer, "Ort," 322–32.

14. Geoffrey Hartman discusses this question with his own differentiations and ethical sensibilities in "Democracy's Museum," from his book *Scars of the Spirit: The Struggle against Inauthenticity* (New York: Palgrave Macmillan, 2002).

15. Wiesel, "Trivializing the Holocaust."

16. Herfried Münkler, "Opfer der Geschichte? Das Jahr 1945 im Gedenken und Erinnern der Deutschen" [Victims of History? 1945 in German Memory], in *Die Zeit*, 16 May 2000.

17. Ivanji, "Macht der Erinnerung," 12.

18. Günter Grass, *Crabwalk*, trans. Krishna Winston (New York: Harcourt, 2002), 142.

19. Ibid., 159.
20. Ibid., 160.
21. Ibid., 142.
22. Erik Meyer and Leggewie, "'Collecting Today for Tomorrow,'"—Medien des kollektiven Gedächtnisses am Beispiel des 'Elften September'" [Collecting Today for Tomorrow: 9/11 and the Media of Collective Memory], in *Medien des Kollektiven Gedächtnisses: Konstruktivität, Historizität, Kulturspezifizität* [The Media of Collective Memory: Constructivism, Historicity, Cultural Specificity], ed. Astrid Erll and Ansgar Nünning (Berlin: Walter de Gruyter, 2004), 277–91.
23. Clemens Wischermann, ed., *Vom kollektiven Gedächtnis zur Individualisierung der Erinnerung* (Stuffgart: Franz-Steiner, 2002).
24. Ibid., 287.
25. Peter Novick, *The Holocaust in American Life* (Boston: Houghton Mifflin, 1999), 15.
26. *Long Shadows: Truth, Lies and History* (Toronto: Knopf Canada, 2000), by Canadian Erna Paris, is an important book on the sacred cow of memory and the friction that exists between historical research and the stylizations of memory.
27. Ute Heimrod, Günter Schlusche, and Horst Seferens, *Der Denkmalstreit—das Denkmal? Die Debatte um das "Denkmal für ermorderten Juden Europas" Eine Dokumentation* [The Dispute over the Memorial—The Real Memorial? Documenting the Debate about the "Memorial for the Murdered Jews of Europe"] (Berlin: Philo, 1999).
28. Here is an excerpt from the homepage: "Gunter Demnig cites the Talmud saying that 'a person is only forgotten when his or her name is forgotten.' The Stolpersteine in front of the buildings bring back to memory the people who once lived here. Each 'stone' begins with HERE LIVED. . . . One 'stone.' One name. One person. For 120 euros, anybody can sponsor a stone, its manufacture and its installation. Please contact info@stolpersteine.eu for more information."
29. Ruth Klüger, *Still Alive* (New York: Feminist Press at the City University of New York, 2001), 38.

11. EUROPE AS A COMMUNITY OF MEMORY

1. Ernst Renan, "What Is a Nation?," trans. Wanda Romer Taylor (Toronto: Tapir Press, 1996), 49.
2. Leslie Fiedler, *Cross the Border, Close the Gap* (New York: Stein and Day, 1972), 73. The sentence continues, "since we have always been, insofar as we are Americans at all, inhabitants of myth rather than history."
3. Renan, "What Is a Nation?," 47.
4. Ibid., 47.
5. Ute Frevert, *Eurovisionen: Ansichten guter Europäer im 19. und 20. Jahrhundert* [Conceptions of the Good European in the 19th and 20th Centuries] (Göttingen: Fischer, 2003); Frevert, "Braucht Europa eine kulturelle Identität? Zehn

kritische Anmerkungen" [Does Europe Need a Cultural Identity? Ten Critical Remarks], *Europäische Revue* 28 (2005): 109–14.

6. The argument seems very plausible to me that Europe needs to adopt a pragmatic understanding of identity, one that does not push national identities into the background and that can be generated through the emergence of a European public sphere; cf. Bettina Thalmaier, *Die zukünftige Gestalt der Europäischen Union* [The Future Form of the European Union] (Baden-Baden: Nomos, 2005).

7. Rémi Brague calls this means of identity construction "spectral analysis"; Brague, *Europa—eine exzentrische Identität*, trans. Gennaro Ghiradelli (Frankfurt: Campus, 1993), 25–28; English translation: *Eccentric Culture: A Theory of Western Civilization*, trans. Samuel Lester (South Bend, Ind.: St. Augustine's Press, 2002).

8. Christian Meier, *From Athens to Auschwitz: The Uses of History*, trans. Deborah Lucas Schneider (Cambridge Mass.: Harvard University Press, 2005).

9. Bassam Tibi, *Europa ohne Identität Die Krise der multikulturellen Gesellschaft* [Europe without Identity? The Crisis of Multiculturalism], 3rd ed. (Munich: Siedler, 2002), xiv.

10. Ibid., 183. Tibi's distinction between multiculturalism and pluralism is undoubtedly important. Whereas the former is an unstructured product of migration and of market globalization that on the one hand reflects a postmodern arbitrariness and on the other hand has dangerous political potential (that is, potential for a cultural racism), the latter stands for a consensual framework of values within which both difference *and* integration are safeguarded.

11. The decision to name Charlemagne as Europe's founding father has direct territorial consequences—though the author of the article on Charlemagne contained in *Deutsche Erinnerungsorte* claims that Charlemagne is not relevant to a new Europe that is expanding eastward, beyond the boundaries that were once known as Latin in origin.

12. Heinz Duchhardt, Julia Schmidt, and Manfred Sicking, eds., *Schwerpunktthema: Europäische lieux de mémoire?* [Discussion Topic: European Sites of Memory?], *Jahrbuch für Europäische Geschichte*, vol. 3 (Munich: Oldenbourg, 2002). See also Alexandre Escudier, ed., *Gedenken im Zwiespalt: Konfliktlinien europäischen Erinnerns* [Divided Memories: Lines of Conflict in European Remembering] (Göttingen: Wallstein, 2001); Benedikt Stuchtey, "Bericht" zur Tagung 'European Lieux de Mémoire'" [Report on the Conference "European Sites of Memory"], German Historical Institute London, 5–7 July 2002, *GHIL Bulletin* 24 (2002): 121–25.

13. http://taskforce.ushmm.org/about/index.php?content=stockholm/.

14. *Süddeutsche Zeitung*, lead article, 25 January 2005; UN website: http://www.un.org/News/Press/docs/2005/sgsm9686.doc.htm.

15. Volkhard Knigge, "Afterword," in *Verbrechen erinnern: Die Auseinandersetzung mit Holocaust und Völkermord* [Remembering Crimes: Engaging the Holocaust and Genocide], ed. Knigge and Norbert Frei (Munich: Beck, 2002), 445.

Reinhart Koselleck expresses himself especially clearly in this respect: "We can never hide behind victims' groups like the Jews, as if through it we were to gain a Holocaust monument like other countries of the globe too"; Koselleck, "Formen und Traditionen des negative Gedächtnisses" [Forms and Traditions of Negative Memory], in Knigge and Frei, *Verbrechen erinnern*, 28.

16. Peter Novick, *The Holocaust in American Life* (Boston: Houghton Mifflin, 1999), 218.

17. Daniel Levy and Natan Sznaider, *The Holocaust and Memory in the Global Age*, trans. Assenka Oksiloff (Philadelphia: Temple University Press, 2006), 10ff. They also write, "Nothing was more 'cosmopolitan' than the concentration and extermination camps of the Nazis" (25).

18. Jeffrey C. Alexander, "On the Social Construction of Moral Universals: The 'Holocaust' from War Crime to Trauma Drama," in *Cultural Trauma and Collective Identity*, ed. Jeffrey C. Alexander (Berkeley: University of California Press, 2004), 262.

19. Levy and Sznaider, *Holocaust and Memory*, 9.

20. Jean-Michel Chaumont, *Die Konkurrenz der Opfer: Genozid, Identität und Anerkennung* [Competing Victims: Genocide, Identity and Recognition] (Lüneburg: Lüneburg Press, 2001), 294; originally published as *La Concurrence des Victimes: Génocide, identité, reconnaissance* (Paris: La Découverte, 1997).

21. Luc Ferry, cited in Chaumont, *Konkurrenz der Opfer*, 302.

22. This is the theme of a research project being undertaken by Sibylle Quack at Hannover University: "The European Process of Integration and the Memory of the Holocaust in Transatlantic Dialogue."

23. Adolf Muschg, "Kerneuropa": Gedanken zur europäischen Identität" [Thoughts on a European Identity], *Neue Zürcher Zeitung*, 31 April 2003; see also Muschg, *Was ist europäisch? Reden für einen gastlichen Erdteil* [What Is European? Discussions about a Convivial Continent] (Munich: Beck, 2005).

24. Tony Judt, "The Past Is Another Country: Myth and Memory in Postwar Europe," *Daedelus* 12 (1992): 87, 89. Ian Buruma presents this logic in the following manner: "It was comforting to know that a border divided us from a nation that personified evil. They were bad, so we must be good. To grow up after the war in a country that had suffered German occupation was to know that one was on the side of the angels"; Buruma, *Wages of Guilt: Memories of War in Germany and Japan* (New York: Farrar, Straus, and Giroux, 1994), 4–5. Regarding members of the Committee for Jewish Claims on Austria, the Austrian government stated that "all the suffering of the Jews during this time was inflicted by the Germans and not by the Austrians; Austria bears no guilt for all these awful things and where there is no guilt, there is no obligation to make restitution"; cited in Heidemarie Uhl, "Vom Opfermythos zur Mitverantwortungsthese": NS-Herrschaft, Krieg und Holocaust im 'Österreichischen Gedächtnis'" [From the Myth of Victimhood to Mutual Responsibility: National Socialism, War and the Holocaust in "Austrian Memory"],

in *Transformationen gesellschaftlicher Erinnerung: Studien zur Gedächtnisgeschichte der zweiten Republik* [*Transformations in Social Memory: Studies in the History of Memory in the Second Republic of Austria*], ed. Christian Gerbel (Vienna: Turia and Kant, 2005), 57.

25. Peter Esterházy, "Alle Hände sind unsere Hände" [All Hands Are Our Hands], *Süddeutsche Zeitung*, 11 October 2004.

26. Annette Leo, ed., *Die wiedergefundene Erinnerung: Verdrängte Geschichte in Osteuropa* [Recovered Memory: Repressed History in Eastern Europe] (Berlin: BasisDruck, 1992).

27. Renan, "What Is a Nation?," 45; see also Chapter 1 of this volume.

28. Rudolf Jaworski, "Geschichtsdenken im Umbruch" [Historical Thinking in a State of Upheaval], in *Umbruch im östlichen Europa: Die nationale Wende and das kollektive Gedächtnis* [Upheaval in Eastern Europe: The National Turn and Collective Remembrance], ed. Rudolf Jaworski, Andrei Corbea-Hoisie, and Monica Sommer (Vienna: StudienVerlage, 2004); Ewa Kobylinska and Andreas Lawaty, eds., *Erinnern, Vergessen, Verdrängen: Polnische und deutsche Erfahrungen* [Remembering, Forgetting, Repressing: Polish and German Experiences] (Wiesbaden: Otto Harrassowitz Verlag, 1998).

29. http://www.memorial.de/nachr.php?nid=50, accessed 6 June 2015.

30. John Theobald, *The Media and the Making of History* (Burlington: Ashgate, 2004), Chapter 10, "The Longevity of Wartime Discourses and Identities: The Case of Britain and Europe." Theobald cites the *Observer* from 26 March 2000: "Paradoxically, the more the Second World War retreats into the past the more its legacy seems to poison modern attitudes" (153).

31. Ulrike Ackermann, "Vergessen zugunsten der Zukunft?" [Forgetting for the Sake of the Future?] *Merkur* 643 (November 2002): 992–1001.

32. "Facing History and Ourselves" is the name of an organization that was founded in 1976 and concerns itself with the origins and effects of racism and collective violence. This educational history project is based on the premise that the citizens of a country should not only know about the high points of their national history but also that they should confront its burdens.

33. Pim de Boer does not exclude collective forgetting as a consequence of collective remembering either: "Europe needs sites of memory, not only as a mnemotechnical way of identifying the dead, but also to promote understanding, forgiveness, and forgetting"; Pim de Boer, "Lieux de mémoire et identité de l'Europe" [Places of Memory and European Identity], in *Lieux de mémoire et identitées nationales*, ed. Pim de Boer and Willem Frijhoff (Amsterdam: Amsterdam University Press, 1993), 29.

34. Karol Sauerland, "Minenfelder: Schwieriger Dialog—Deutsche und polnische Historiker" [Minefields: A Difficult Dialogue Between German and Polish Historians], *Frankfurter Allgemeine Zeitung*, 27 December 2002.

35. Christian Meier, *Vierzig Jahre nach Auschwitz: Deutsche Geschichtserinnerungen heute* [Forty Years after Auschwitz: German Memory Today] (Munich: Beck, 1990), 14.

36. Esterhazy, *Alle Hände sind unsere Hände*.

37. Muschg, "Kerneuropa."

38. At first, this idea was not developed in reference to the Holocaust, but more generally arose out of the sense of the "complete elimination of the economic and political causes of the two world wars." At an EU Summit in Milan in 1985, it was decided that 9 May would be celebrated as Europe Day, with reference back to the famous speech made by Robert Schuman in Paris on that day in 1950.

39. Susan Sontag, "The Idea of Europe (One more Elegy)," in *Where the Stress Falls* (New York: Picador, 2001), 288. For Brague, the project of Europe consists in its "de-barbarization"; *Europa—eine exzentrische Identität*, 40.

CONCLUSION: SHADOWS OF TRAUMA

1. Christian Meier, *Vierzig Jahre nach Auschwitz: Deutsche Geschichtserinnerungen heute* [Forty Years after Auschwitz: German Memory Today] (Munich: Beck, 1990).

2. Joachim Landkammer, 'Wir spüren nichts': Anstößige Thesen zum zukünftigen Umgang mit der NS-Vergangenheit ["We Feel Nothing": Objectionable Arguments about Engaging with the Nazi Past], in *Erinnerungsmanagement: Systemtransformation und Vergangenheitspolitik im internationalen Vergleich* [Managing Memory: International Perpectives on the Transformation of Systems and the Politics of the Past], ed. Joachim Landkammer, Thomas Noetzel, and Walther Zimmerli (Munich: Fink, 2006), 76.

3. [The original German title of the book is *Die Lange Schatten der Vergangenheit: Erinnerungskultur und Geschichtspolitik*, or *The Long Shadow of the Past: Cultures of Memory and Politics of History*—Trans.]

4. Günter Oesterle, ed., *Erinnerung, Gedächtnis, Wissen: Studien zur kulturwissenschaftlichen Gedächtnisforschung* [Memory, Recollection, Knowledge: Examinations of Cultural Studies Memory Research] (Göttingen: Vandenhoeck and Ruprecht, 2005).

5. Claus Leggewie and Erik Meyer, *"Ein Ort an den man gerne geht": Das Holocaust-Mahnmal und die deutsche Geschichtspolitik nach 1989* ["A Place That One Likes to Go": The Holocaust Memorial and German Political History after 1989] (Munich: Hanser, 2005), 12.

6. Jutta Scherrer, "Russlands neue-alte Erinnerungsorte" [Russia's New-Old Sites of Memory], *Aus Politik und Zeitgeschichte* 11 (2006): 5, Bundeszentrale für politische Bildung, http://www.bpb.de/publikationen/7VR557.html.

7. Peter Novick, *The Holocaust in American Life* (Boston: Houghton Mifflin, 1999), 6.

8. "Great Britain and France saw this decision as a necessary measure to prevent a war (politics of appeasement) and guaranteed for it the continued existence of the rest of the Czechoslovakian state. The representatives of Czechoslovakia, who weren't allowed to take part in the conference—with President Edvard Beneš leading the way—felt betrayed, which is why the Czech people call

the Munich Agreement the Munich dictate or, jokingly, as 'About us, Without us.' Even today, the Munich agreement remains a dark day in history for Czech consciousness"; http://de.wikipedia.org/wiki/Münchener_Abkommen. This example clarifies a problem in the subterranean network of European memory. For the Munich agreement is closely tied to the Beneš decrees, and this is a real problem in domestic European communications; see Barbara Coudenhove-Kalergi and Oliver Rathkolb, eds., *Die Beneš-Dekrete* [The Beneš Decrees] (Vienna: Czernin, 2002).

9. Michael Jeismann, "Die Holocaust-Erinnerung als Passepartout" [Holocaust Memory as *Passe-partout*], in *Erinnerungsmanagement: Systemtransformation und Vergangenheitspolitik im internationalen Vergleich* [Managing Memory: International Perspectives on the Transformation of Systems and the Politics of the Past], ed. Joachim Landkammer, Thomas Noetzel, and Walther Zimmerli (Munich: Fink, 2006), 258.

10. Edgar Wolfrum, *Geschichte als Waffe: Vom Kaiserreich bis zur Wiedervereinigung* [History as Weapon: From Kaiserreich to Reunification] (Göttingen: Vandenhoeck and Ruprecht, 2001); Wolfrum and Petra Bock, eds., *Umkämpfte Vergangenheit: Geschichtsbilder, Erinnerung und Vergangenheitspolitik im internationalen Vergleich* [Contested Past: An International Comparison of Views on History, Memory and the Politics of the Past] (Göttingen: Vandenhoeck and Ruprecht, 1999).

11. Landkammer, Noetzel, and Zimmli, eds, *Erinnerungsmanagement*, 279.

12. Ibid., 19.

13. Just a couple of examples here: Peter Graf Kielmannsegg, *Lange Schatten: Vom Umgang der Deutschen mit der nationalsozialistischen Vergangenheit* [Long Shadows: On the Struggle of Germany with the Legacy of National Socialism] (Berlin: Siedler, 1989); Uwe Backes, Eckhard Jesse, and Rainer Zitelmann, eds., *Die Schatten der Vergangenheit: Impulse zur Historisierung des Nationalsozialismus* [The Shadows of the Past: The Historicizing Tendency of National Socialism] (Berlin: Propyläen, 1990); Konrad Brendler and Günter Rexilius, eds, *Drei Generationen im Schatten der NS Vergangenheit: Beiträge zum Internationalen Forschungskolloquium "Lernen und Pseudolernen in der Aufarbeitung des Holocaust"* [Three Generations in the Shadow of the Nazi Past: Proceedings of the International Research Colloquium "Learning and Pseudo-Learning in the Engagement with Holocaust"] (Wuppertal: Bergische Universität Gesamthochschule Wuppertal, Fachbereich Gesellschaftswissenschaften und Fachbereich Erziehungswissenschaften, 1991); Josef Foschepoth, *Im Schatten der Vergangenheit: Die Anfänge der Gesellschaften für Christlich-Jüdische Zusammenarbeit* [In the Shadow of the Past: The First Societies for Christian-Jewish Cooperation] (Göttingen: Vandenhoeck and Ruprecht, 1993); Michael Daxner, *An der Schwelle zum Neuen—im Schatten der Vergangenheit: Jüdische Kultur in Deutschland Heute* [On the Threshold of the New—In the Shadow of the Past: Jewish Culture in Contemporary Germany] (Oldenburg: Isensee, 1997); Geoffrey Hartman, *The Longest Shadow: In the Aftermath of the Holocaust* (Bloomington: Indiana University

Press, 1996); Erna Paris, *Long Shadows: Truth, Lies and History* (Toronto: Knopf Canada, 2000); Stefan Aust, *Die Gegenwart der Vergangenheit: Der lange Schatten des Dritten Reichs* [The Presence of the Past: The Long Shadow of the Third Reich] (Munich: Deutsche Verlags-Anstalt, 2004); Hartmut Radebold, *Die dunklen Schatten unserer Vergangenheit: Ältere Menschen in Beratung, Psychotherapie, Seelsorge und Pflege* [The Dark Shadows of Our Past: The Elderly in Counseling, Psychotherapy, Spiritual Welfare and Care] (Stuttgart: Klett-Cotta, 2005).

14. Meier, *Vierzig Jahre nach Auschwitz*, 10.

15. Susan Sontag, *Regarding the Pain of Others* (New York: Picador, 2004), 114.

16. Jacob Christoph Burckhardt, *Weltgeschichtlichen Betrachtungen*, 51.

17. Friedrich Nietzsche, *On the Genealogy of Morals and Ecce Homo*, trans. Walter Kaufmann and R. J. Hollingdale (New York: Vintage, 1967), 61.

BIBLIOGRAPHY

Ackermann, Ulrike. "Vergessen zugunsten der Zukunft?" [Forgetting for the Sake of the Future?]. *Merkur* 643 (November 2002): 992–1001.
Adorno, Theodor W. *Negative Dialectics*. Trans. E. B. Ashton. London: Routledge, 1973.
———. *Prisms*. Trans. Shierry Weber and Samuel Weber. Cambridge, Mass.: MIT Press, 1983.
Agamben, Giorgio. *Homo Sacer: Sovereign Power and Bare Life*. Trans. Daniel Heller-Roazen. Stanford: Stanford University Press, 1998.
Akademie der Künste Berlin, ed. *Denkmale und kulturelles Gedächtnis nach dem Ende der Ost-West-Konfrontation* [Monuments and Cultural Memory after the End of the East-West Conflict]. Berlin: Jovis, 2000.
Alexander, Jeffrey C. "On the Social Construction of Moral Universals: The 'Holocaust' from War Crime to Trauma Drama." In *Cultural Trauma and Collective Identity*, ed. Jeffrey C. Alexander. Berkeley: University of California Press, 2004.
Anders, Günther. *Wir Eichmannsöhne: Offener Brief an Klaus Eichmann*. [We Sons of Eichmann: Open Letter to Klaus Eichmann]. Munich: Beck, 1964.
Anderson, Benedict R. *Imagined Communities: Reflections on the Origin and Spread of Nationalism*. London: Verso, 2006.
Arendt, Hannah. "Organized Guilt and Universal Responsibility." In *Essays in Understanding, 1930–1954: Formation, Exile, and Totalitarianism*, 121–32. New York: Schocken Books, 2005.
Assmann, Aleida. *Cultural Memory and Western Civilization: Functions, Media, Archives*. Cambridge: Cambridge University Press, 2011.
———. "Fiktion als Differenz" [Fiction as Difference]. *Poetica* 21 (1989): 239–60.
———. "History, Memory, and the Genre of Testimony." *Poetics Today* 27, no. 2 (2006): 261–73.
———. "Persönliche Erinnerung und kollektives Gedächtnis in Deutschland nach 1945" [Personal Recollection and Collective Memory in Germany after 1945]. In *Erinnern und Verstehen: Der Völkermord an den Juden im politischen*

Gedächtnis der Deutschen [Remembering and Understanding: The Genocide of the Jews in German Political Memory], ed. Hans Erler, 126–38. Frankfurt: Campus, 2003.

———. "Vier Formen von Erinnerung" [Four Forms of Memory]. *Forum Ethik Streitkultur* 13 (2002): 183–90.

Assmann, Aleida, and Ute Frevert. *Geschichtsvergessenheit—Geschichtsversessenheit: Vom Umgang mit deutschen Vergangenheiten nach 1945* [Forgetting History—Obsessing over History: On the Engagement with Germany's Pasts after 1945]. Stuttgart: Deutsche Verlags-Anstalt, 1999.

Assmann, Jan. "Erinnern, um dazuzugehören: Kulturelles Gedächtnis, Zugehörigkeitsstruktur und normative Vergangenheit" [Remembering to Belong: Cultural Memory, Structures of Belonging and Normative Pasts]. In *Generation und Gedächtnis: Erinnerungen und kollektive Identitäten*, ed. Kristin Platt and Mihran Dabag, 51–75. Opladen: Leske and Budrich, 1995.

———. "Frühe Formen politischer Mythomotorik: Fundierende, kontrapräsentische und revolutionäre Mythen" [Early Forms of Political Myth-Making: Foundations, Anachronisms, Revolutions]. In *Revolution und Mythos*, ed. Dietrich Harth and Jan Assmann, 39–61. Frankfurt am Main: Fischer, 1992.

———. *Das kulturelle Gedächtnis: Schrift, Erinnerung und politische Identität in frühen Hochkulturen*. Munich: Beck, 1992. English translation: *Cultural Memory and Early Civilization: Writing, Remembrance, and Political Imagination*. Cambridge: Cambridge University Press, 2011.

———. *Moses the Egyptian: The Memory of Egypt in Western Monotheism*. Cambridge, Mass.: Harvard University Press, 1998.

Assmann, Jan, Aleida Assmann, and Christoph Hardmeier, eds. *Schrift und Gedächtnis: Beiträge zur Archäologie der literarischen Kommunikation* [Writing and Memory: Contributions to the Archaeology of Literary Communication]. Munich: Fink, 1983.

Aust, Stefan, ed. *Die Gegenwart der Vergangenheit: Der lange Schatten des Dritten Reichs* [The Presence of the Past: The Shadow of the Third Reich]. Munich: Deutsche Verlags-Anstalt, 2004.

Backes, Uwe, Eckhard Jesse, and Rainer Zitelmann, eds. *Die Schatten der Vergangenheit: Impulse zur Historisierung des Nationalsozialismus*. [The Shadows of the Past: The Historicizing Tendency of National Socialism]. Berlin: Propyläen, 1990.

Baddeley, Alan. *Your Memory: A User's Guide*. New York: Firefly, 2004.

Baecker, Dirk, and Alexander Kluge. *Vom Nutzen ungelöster Probleme* [On the Use of Unsolved Problems]. Berlin: Merve, 2003.

Baer, Ulrich, ed. *Niemand zeugt für den Zeugen: Erinnerungskultur und historische Verantwortung nach der Shoah* [No One Bears Witness for the Witness: Memory Culture and Historical Responsibility after the Shoah]. Frankfurt am Main: Suhrkamp, 2000.

Bar-on, Dan. *Legacy of Silence: Encounters with Children of the Third Reich*. Cambridge, Mass.: Harvard University Press, 1989.

Bauman, Zygmunt. *Liquid Modernity*. Cambridge: Polity, 2000.
Becker, Annette, and Maurice Halbwachs. *Un intellectuel en guerres mondiales 1914–1945* [An Intellectual in the World Wars]. Paris: Agnès Viénot, 2003.
Becker, Henk A. "Discontinuous Change and Generational Contracts." In *The Myth of Generational Conflict: The Family and State in Ageing Societies*, ed. Sara Arber and Claudine Attias-Donfurt, 114–32. London: Routledge Press, 2000.
Begley, Louis. *Wartime Lies*. New York: Ivy, 1991.
Benjamin, Walter. "Theses on the Philosophy of History." In *Illuminations*, trans. Harry Zohn, ed. Hannah Arendt, 253–64. New York: Schocken, 1968.
Beradt, Charlotte. *The Third Reich of Dreams: The Nightmares of a Nation, 1933–1939*. Trans. Adriane Gottwald. Northamptonshire: Aquarian, 1985.
Bergson, Henri. *Matter and Memory*. Trans. Nancy Margaret Paul and W. Scott Palmer. New York: Zone, 1988.
Bhabha, Homi. *Nation and Narration*. London: Routledge, 1990.
Binder, Beate. "Jahrestag" [Anniversary]. In *Lexikon Gedächtnis und Erinnerung*, ed. Jens Ruchatz and Nicholas Pethes. Reinbek: Rowohlt, 2001.
Bloch, Marc. "Mémoire collective, tradition et coutume" [Collective Memory, Tradition and Custom]. *Révue de Synthèse Historique* 40 (1925): 78–83.
Bohleber, Werner. "Die Entwicklung der Traumatheorie in der Psychoanalyse" [The Development of Trauma Theory in Psychoanalysis]. *Psyche* 9/10 (2000): 797–839.
———. "Trauma, Trauer und Geschichte" [Trauma, Mourning and History]. In *Trauer und Geschichte* [Mourning and History], ed. Burkhard Liebsch and Jörn Rüsen. Cologne: Böhlau, 2001.
Bohrer, Karl Heinz. "Historische Trauer und Poetische Trauer" [Historical Mourning and Poetic Mourning]. *Merkur* 12 (1999): 1127–41.
Borland, John. "Graffiti, Paraden und Alltagskultur in Nordirland" [Graffiti, Parades and Everyday Culture in Northern Ireland]. In *Das Soziale Gedächtnis*, ed. Harald Welzer, 276–95. Hamburg: Hamburger Edition, 2001.
Brague, Rémi. *Europa—eine exzentrische Identität*. Trans. Gennaro Ghiradelli. Frankfurt: Campus, 1993. English translation: *Eccentric Culture: A Theory of Western Civilization*. Trans. Samuel Lester. South Bend, Ind.: St. Augustine's Press, 2002.
Brendler, Konrad, and Günter Rexilius, eds. *Drei Generationen im Schatten der NS-Vergangenheit: Beiträge zum Internationalen Forschungskolloquium Lernen und Pseudolernen in der Aufarbeitung des Holocaust* [Three Generations in the Shadow of the Nazi Past: Proceedings of the International Research Colloquium Learning and Pseudo-Learning in the Engagement with Holocaust]. Wuppertal: Bergische Universität Gesamthochschule Wuppertal, Fachbereich Gesellschaftswissenschaften und Fachbereich Erziehungswissenschaften, 1991.
Brown, R., and J. Kulik. "Flashbulb Memories." *Cognition* 2 (1997): 629–54.

Browne, Thomas. "Hydriotaphia or Urne Buriall." In *The Prose of Sir Thomas Browne*, ed. Norman J. Endicott, 241–86. New York: Anchor, 1967.

Bude, Heinz. "Generationen im soziale Wandel" [Generations in Social Transition]. In *Alt und Jung: Die Abenteuer der Generationen; A Publication of the German Hygiene Museum Dresden*. Frankfurt am Main: Basel, 1997.

Burckhardt, Jacob Christoph. *Force and Freedom: Reflections on History*. Ed. James Hastings Nichols. New York: Pantheon, 1943.

Burger, Rudolf. *Kleine Geschichte der Vergangenheit: Eine pyrrhonische Skizze der historischen Vernunft* [A Short History of the Past: A Pyrrhonic Sketch of Historical Reason]. Vienna: Styria, 2004.

Burke, Peter. *Eyewitnessing: The Uses of Images as Historical Evidence*. Ithaca: Cornell University Press, 2001.

———. "History as Social Memory." In *Memory: History, Culture and the Mind*, ed. Thomas Butler. Oxford: Blackwell Press, 1989.

Buruma, Ian. *Wages of Guilt: Memories of War in Germany and Japan*. New York: Farrar, Straus, and Giroux, 1994.

Butler, Samuel. *Life and Habit*. London: J. Cape, 1924.

Carus, Carl Gustav. *Lebenserinnerungen und Denkwürdigkeiten* [Life's Thoughts and Recollections]. Leipzig: Brockhaus, 1865.

Caruth, Cathy. *Unclaimed Experience: Trauma, Narrative, and History*. Baltimore: Johns Hopkins University Press, 1996.

Celan, Paul. *Breathturn*. Trans. Pierre Joris. Los Angeles: Green Integer, 2006.

———. *Gedichte in Zwei Bände*. Frankfurt: Suhrkamp, 1975.

———. *Selected Poems and Prose of Paul Celan*. Trans. John Felstiner. New York: W. W. Norton, 2002.

Chaumont, Jean-Michel. *Die Konkurrenz der Opfer: Genozid, Identität und Anerkennung* [Competing Victims: Genocide, Identity and Recognition]. Lüneburg: Lüneburg Press, 2001. Originally published as *La Concurrence des Victimes: Génocide, identité, reconnaissance*. Paris: La Découverte, 1997.

Cicero, Marcus Tullius. *De finibus*. In *On Moral Ends*. Trans. Raphael Woolf. Ed. Julia Annas. Cambridge: Cambridge University Press, 2001.

Connerton, Paul. *How Societies Remember*. Cambridge: Cambridge University Press, 1989.

Conway, Martin A. *Flashbulb Memories*. Hillsdale: Lawrence Erlbaum Associates, 1995.

———. "The Inventory of Experience: Memory and Identity." In *Collective Memory of Political Events: Social Psychological Perspectives*, ed. James W. Pennebaker, Dario Paez, and Bernard Rime, 21–43. Mahwah, N.J.: Lawrence Erlbaum Associates, 1997.

Coudenhove-Kalergi, Barbara, and Oliver Rathkolb, eds. *Die Beneš–Dekrete* [The Beneš Decrees]. Vienna: Czernin, 2002.

Csáky, Moritz, and Peter Stachel, eds. *Die Verortung von Gedächtnis* [Placing Memory]. Vienna: Passagen, 2001.

Cultural Office, City of Marburg, ed. *Formen von Erinnerung: Eine Diskussion mit Claude Lanzmann; Ein Anderer Blick auf Gedenken, Erinnern und Erleben* [Forms of Memory: A Discussion with Claude Lanzmann; Another Perspective on Commemorating, Remembering, and Experiencing]. Marburg: Cultural Office, 1998.

Dabag, Mihran. "Der Genozid an den Armeniern im Osmanischen Reich" [The Armenian Genocide in the Ottoman Empire]. In Knigge and Frei, *Verbrechen Erinnern*, 33–55.

Danyel, Jürgen, and Phillip Ther, eds. *Flucht und Vertreibung in Europäischer Perspektive* [Flight and Expulsion in European Perspective]. Zeitschrift für Geschichtswissenschaft 51. Berlin: Metropol, 2003.

Daxner, Michael. *An der Schwelle zum Neuen—im Schatten der Vergangenheit: Jüdische Kultur in Deutschland Heute* [On the Threshold of the New—In the Shadow of the Past: Jewish Culture in Contemporary Germany]. Oldenburg: Isensee, 1997.

De Boer, Pim. "Lieux de mémoire et identité de l'Europe" [Places of Memory and European Identity]. In *Lieux de mémoire et identitées nationales*, ed. Pim de Boer and Willem Frijhoff. Amsterdam: Amsterdam University Press, 1993.

Derrida, Jacques. "'A Self-Unsealing Poetic Text': Poetics and Politics of Witnessing." In *Revenge of the Aesthetic*, ed. Michael Clark, 180–207. Berkeley: University of California Press, 2000.

Diner, Dan. *Beyond the Conceivable: Studies on Germany, Nazism, and the Holocaust*. Berkeley: University of California Press, 2000.

Dubiel, Helmut. *Niemand is frei von Geschichte: Die nationalsozialistische Herrschaft in den Debatten des Deutschen Bundestages* [No One Is Free of History: The Legacy of National Socialism in the Debates of the German National Parliament]. Munich: Hanser, 1999.

Duchardt, Heinz, Julia Schmidt, and Manfred Sicking, eds. *Schwerpunktthema: Europäische lieux de mémoire?* [Discussion Topic: European Sites of Memory?]. *Jahrbuch für Europäische Geschichte*. Vol. 3. Munich: Oldenbourg, 2002.

Dückers, Tanja. *Himmelskörper* [Heavenly Bodies]. Berlin: Aufbau-Verlag, 2003.

Echterhoff, Gerald, and Martin Saar, eds. *Kontexte und Kulturen des Erinnerns: Maurice Halbwachs und das Paradigma des kollektiven Gedächtnisses* [Contexts and Cultures of Remembering: Maurice Halbwachs and the Paradigm of Collective Memory]. Constance: UVK Verlagsgesellschaft, 2002.

Elkana, Yehuda. "The Need to Forget." *Ha'aretz*, 2 March 1988.

Emerson, Ralph Waldo. "Circles." In *Emerson's Essays*. New York: Viking, 1983.

Emmerich, Wolfgang, ed. *Der Bremer Literaturpreis 1954–1987: Reden der Preisträger und andere Texte* [Bremen Literature Prize 1954–1987: Speeches of the Award Winners and Other Texts]. Bremerhaven: Verlag für Neue Wissenschaft, 1988.

Erikson, Erik. "'Identity Crisis' in Autobiographical Perspective." In *Life History and the Historical Moment*. New York: W. W. Norton, 1975.

Erll, Astrid. *Kollektives Gedächtnis und Erinnerungskulturen: Eine Einfuhrung* [Collective Memory and Cultures of Remembering: An Introduction]. Stuttgart: Metzler, 2005.

Escudier, Alexandre, ed. *Gedenken im Zwiespalt: Konfliktlinien europäischen Erinnerns* [Divided Memories: Lines of Conflict in European Remembering]. Göttingen: Wallstein, 2001.

Esterházy, Peter. "Alle Hände sind unsere Hände" [All Hands Are Our Hands]. *Süddeutsche Zeitung*, 11 October 2004.

Felman, Shoshana. *The Juridical Unconscious: Trials and Traumas in the Twentieth Century*. Cambridge, Mass.: Harvard University Press, 2002.

Felman, Shoshana, and Dori Laub. *Testimony: The Crisis of Witnessing in Literature, Psychoanalysis, and History*. New York: Routledge, 1992.

Fiedler, Leslie. *Cross the Border, Close the Gap*. New York: Stein and Day, 1972.

Fisher, Philip. "Local Meanings and Portable Objects: National Collections, Literatures, Music and Architecture." In *The Formation of National Collections of Art and Archaeology*, ed. Gwendolyn Wright. Hanover, N.H.: University Press of New England, 1996.

Forte, Dieter. *Schweigen oder Sprechen* [Remaining Silent or Speaking]. Frankfurt am Main: Fischer, 2002.

Foschepoth, Josef. *Im Schatten der Vergangenheit: Die Anfänge der Gesellschaften für Christlich-Jüdische Zusammenarbeit* [In the Shadow of the Past: The First Societies for Christian-Jewish Cooperation]. Göttingen: Vandenhoeck and Ruprecht, 1993.

François, Étienne, and Monika Flacke. *Ausstellungskatalog: Germania—Mythen der Nationen 1945—Arena der Erinnerungen* [Exhibition Catalogue: Germania—National Myths 1945—Arena of Memories]. Berlin: Von Zabern. 2004.

François, Étienne, and Hagen Schulze, eds. *Deutsche Erinnerungsorte* [German Sites of Memory]. Munich: Beck, 2001.

Frank, Niklas. *Der Vater: Eine Abrechnung*. Munich: Goldmann, 1987. English translation: *In the Shadow of the Reich*. New York: Alfred A. Knopf, 1991.

Frei, Norbert. "Identitätswechsel in der Nachkriegszeit: Die 'Illegalen' in der Nachkriegszeit" [Identity Reversal after 1945: The 'Illegals' in the Postwar Period]. In *Vertuschte Vergangenheit: Der Fall Schwerte und die NS-Vergangenheit der deutschen Hochschulen* [The Silenced Past: The Schwerte Case and the Legacy of National Socialism in the German University], ed. Helmut König, Wolfgang Kuhlmann, and Klaus Schwabe, 207–22. Munich: Beck, 1997.

———. *Vergangenheitspolitik: Die Anfänge der Bundesrepublik und die NS-Vergangenheit*. Munich: Beck, 1996. English translation: *Adenauer's Germany and the Nazi Past: The Politics of Amnesty and Integration*. Trans. Joel Golb. New York: Columbia University Press, 2002.

———. "Von deutscher Erfindungskraft, oder Die Kollektivschuldthese in der Nachkriegszeit" [On German Inventiveness, or The Thesis of Collective Guilt in the Postwar Period]. In *1945 und Wir: Das Dritte Reich im Bewusst-*

sein der Deutschen [1945 and Us: The Third Reich in the German Psyche]. Munich: Beck, 2005.

Freud, Sigmund. "Remembering, Repeating, and Working Through." In *The Standard Edition of the Complete Psychological Works of Sigmund Freud*, ed. James Strachey, 12:145–56. London: Hogarth Press, 1958.

Frevert, Ute. "Braucht Europa eine kulturelle Identität? Zehn kritische Anmerkungen" [Does Europe Need a Cultural Identity? Ten Critical Remarks]. *Europäische Revue* 28 (2005): 109–14.

———. *Eurovisionen: Ansichten guter Europäer im 19. und 20. Jahrhundert* [Conceptions of the Good European in the 19th and 20th Centuries]. Göttingen: Fischer, 2003.

Fried, Johannes. *Der Schleier der Erinnerung: Grundzüge einer historischen Memorik* [The Veil of Memory: Toward a Historical Memorics]. Munich: Beck, 2004.

Friedländer, Saul. "History, Memory, and the Historian: Dilemmas and Responsibilities." *New German Critique*, no. 80, Special Issue on the Holocaust (Spring–Summer 2000): 3–15.

———. "Im Angesicht der 'Endlosung': Die Entwicklung des offentlichen Gedächtnisses und die Verantwortung des Historikers" [Confronting the "Final Solution": The Development of Public Memory and the Responsibility of the Historian]. In *Das Judentum im Spiegel seiner kulturellen Umwelten: Symposium zu Ehren von Saul Friedländer* [Judaism in Cultural Context: Symposium in Honor of Saul Friedländer], ed. Dieter Borchmeyer and Helmut Kiesel, 207–23. Neckargemund, Germany: Edition Mnemosyne, 2002.

———. *When Memory Comes*. New York: Farrar, 1979.

Friedrich, Jörg. *The Fire: The Bombing of Germany, 1940–1945*. Trans. Allison Brown. New York: Columbia University Press, 2006.

Frisch, Max. *Wilhelm Tell: A School Text*. Trans. Lore Segal and Paul Stern. In *Max Frisch: Novels Plays Essays*. New York: Continuum, 1989.

Gadamer, Hans Georg. *Truth and Method*. Trans. W. Glen-Doepel. London: Continuum, 2004.

Ganzfried, Daniel. . . . *alias Wilkomirski: Die Holocaust Travestie; Enthüllung und Dokumentation eines literarischen Skandals* [Aka Wilkomirski: The Holocaust Travesty; Unearthing and Documenting a Literary Scandal]. Berlin: Jüdische Verlagsanstalt, 2002.

Gellately, Robert. *Backing Hitler: Consent and Coercion in Nazi Germany*. Oxford: Oxford University Press, 2002.

Giesen, Bernhard. *Triumph and Trauma*. London: Paradigm, 2004.

Giesen, Bernhard, and Christoph Schneider, eds. *Tätertrauma: Nationale Erinnerungen im öffentlichen Diskurs* [Trauma of the Perpetrator: National Remembrance in Public Discourse]. Constance: UVK Verlagsgesellschaft, 2004.

Ginzburg, Carlo. *The Judge and the Historian: Marginal Notes on a Late-Twentieth-Century Miscarriage of Justice*. Trans. Antony Shugaar. Verso: London, 1999.

Gourevitch, Philip. "The Memory Thief." *The New Yorker*, 14 June 1999.
Grass, Günter. *Crabwalk*. Trans. Krishna Winston. New York: Harcourt, 2002.
———. "I Remember. . . ." In *The Günter Grass Reader*, ed. Helmut Frielinghaus. Wilmington: Mariner, 2004.
———. *The Tin Drum*. Trans. Breon Mitchell. New York: Houghton Mifflin Harcourt, 2009.
Grass, Günter, Czesław Milosz, Wisława Szymborska, and Tomas Venclova. *Die Zukunft der Erinnerung* [The Future of Memory]. Ed. Martin Wälde. Göttingen: Steidl, 2001.
Groebner, Valentin. *Der Schein der Person* [The Appearance of the Person]. Munich: Beck, 2004.
Haarer, Johanna. *Die deutsche Mutter und ihr erstes Kind* [The German Mother and Her First Child]. Munich: J. F. Lehmann, 1934.
Halbwachs, Maurice. *On Collective Memory*. Trans. and ed. Lewis A. Coser. Chicago: University of Chicago Press, 1992.
———. *The Collective Memory*. Introduction by Mary Douglas. New York: Harper and Row, 1980.
Hartman, Geoffrey, ed. *Bitburg in a Moral and Political Perspective*. Bloomington: Indiana University Press, 1986.
———. *The Longest Shadow: In the Aftermath of the Holocaust*. Bloomington: Indiana University Press, 1996.
———. *Scars of the Spirit: The Struggle against Inauthenticity*. New York: Palgrave Macmillan, 2002.
Heer, Hannes. *Hitler war's: Die Befreiung der Deutschen von ihrer Vergangenheit* ["It Was Hitler!": The Liberation of the Germans From Their Past]. Berlin: Aufbau Verlag, 2005.
———. *Vom Verschwinden der Täter: Der Vernichtungskrieg fand statt, aber keiner war dabei* [On the Disappearance of the Perpetrators: The War of Extermination Took Place, but No One Was Present]. Berlin: Aufbau, 2004.
Heidegger, Martin. *Being and Time*. Trans. Joan Stambaugh. Albany: SUNY Press, 2010.
Heimrod, Ute, Günter Schlusche, and Horst Seferens. *Der Denkmalstreit—das Denkmal? Die Debatte um das "Denkmal für ermorderten Juden Europas" Eine Dokumentation* [The Dispute over the Memorial—The Real Memorial? Documenting the Debate about the "Memorial for the Murdered Jews of Europe"]. Berlin: Philo, 1999.
Herf, Jeffrey. *Divided Memory: The Nazi Past in the Two Germanys*. Cambridge, Mass.: Harvard University Press, 1997.
Herodotus. *The Histories of Herodotus*. Trans. C. E. Godley. Vol. 1, book 1. Cambridge, Mass.: Harvard University Press, 2004.
Hirsch, Marianne. *Family Frames: Photography, Narrative and Postmemory*. Cambridge, Mass.: Harvard University Press, 1997.
Honneth, Axel. *The Struggle for Recognition*. Trans. Joel Anderson. Cambridge, Mass.: MIT Press, 1996.

Huizinga, Johan. "A Definition of the Concept of History." In *Philosophy and History: Essays Presented to Ernst Cassirer*, ed. Raymond Klibansky and Herbert James Paton, 1–10. New York: Harper and Row, 1963.
Illich, Ivan. *Fortschrittsmythen* [Myths of Progress]. Reinbek: Rowohlt, 1980.
Ivanji, Ivan. "Die Macht der Erinnerung, die Ohnmacht der Worte" [The Power of Memory, the Powerlessness of the Word]. In Knigge and Frei, *Verbrechen erinnern* [Remembering Crimes], 1–20.
Jäger, Ludwig. "Germanistik—eine deutsche Wissenschaft: Das Kapitel Hans Ernst Schneider" [German Studies: The Chapter on Hans Ernst Schneider]. In König et al., *Vertuschte Vergangenheit* [Silenced Past], 5–47.
———. *Seitenwechsel: Der Fall Schneider/Schwerte und die Diskretion der Germanistik* [Changing Sides: The Schneider/Schwerte Case and the Discretion of German Studies]. Munich: Fink, 1998.
Janeczek, Helena. "Excerpt from *Lessons of Darkness*." Trans. Stephen Sartarelli. In *Nothing Makes You Free: Writings by Descendants of Jewish Holocaust Survivors*, ed. Melvin Jules Bukiet, 255–61. New York: W. W. Norton, 2002.
Jaworski, Rudolf. "Geschichtsdenken im Umbruch" [Historical Thinking in a State of Upheaval]. In *Umbruch im östlichen Europa: Die nationale Wende and das kollektive Gedächtnis* [Upheaval in Eastern Europe: The National Turn and Collective Remembrance], ed. Rudolf Jaworski, Andrei Corbea-Hoisie, and Monica Sommer. Vienna: StudienVerlage, 2004.
Jeismann, Michael. "Die Holocaust-Erinnerung als Passepartout" [Memory of the Holocaust as *Passe-partout*]. In *Erinnerungsmanagement: Systemtransformation und Vergangenheitspolitik im internationalen Vergleich* [Managing Memory: International Perspectives on the Transformation of Systems and the Politics of the Past], ed. Joachim Landkammer, Thomas Noetzel, and Walther Zimmerli. Munich: Fink, 2006.
———. "Voodoo Child: Die verhexten Kinder" [Voodoo Child: The Cursed Children]. *Literaturen* (May 2005): 15.
Jirgl, Reinhard. *Die Unvollendeten* [The Incomplete]. Munich: Hanser, 2002.
Judt, Tony. "The Past Is Another Country: Myth and Memory in Postwar Europe." *Daedelus* 12 (1992): 83–119.
Jünger, Friedrich Georg. *Gedächtnis und Erinnerung* [Memory and Recollection]. Frankfurt am Main: Klostermann, 1957.
Kerby, Anthony Paul. "The Language of the Self." *Philosophy Today* (Fall 1986): 210–23.
Kettenacker, Lothar, ed. *Ein Volk von Opfern? Die neue Debatte um den Bombenkrieg 1940–1945* [A People of Victims? Recent Perspectives on the Bombing 1940–1945]. Berlin: Rowohlt, 2003.
Kielsmannsegg, Peter Graf. *Lange Schatten: Vom Umgang der Deutschen mit der nationalsozialistischen Vergangenheit* [Long Shadows: On the Struggle of Germany with the Legacy of National Socialism]. Berlin: Siedler, 1989.
Klüger, Ruth. *Still Alive*. New York: Feminist Press at the City University of New York, 2001.

———. *Weiter leben: Eine Jugend* [Still Alive: A Youth]. Göttingen: Wallstein Verlag: 1992.
Knigge, Volkhard. "Afterword." In Knigge and Frei, *Verbrechen erinnern*, 445.
Knigge, Volkhard, and Norbert Frei, eds. *Verbrechen erinnern: Die Auseinandersetzung mit Holocaust und Völkermord* [Remembering Crimes: Engaging the Holocaust and Genocide]. Munich: Beck, 2002.
Knigge, Volkhard, Jürgen Maria Pietsch, Thomas A. Seidel. *Versteinertes Gedenken: Das Buchenwalder Mahnmal von 1958* [Petrified Remembrance: The Buchenwald Memorial of 1958]. 2 Vols. Leipzig: Editions Akanthus, 1997.
Knittel, Anton Philipp. "Bilder-Bücher der Erinnerung, 'Jugenderinnerungen eines alten Mannes' im Kontext ihrer Zeit" [Picture-Books of Memory: "An Aging Man's Recollections of his Youth" in Historical Context]. *Weimarer Beiträge: Zeitschrift für Literaturwissenschaft, Äesthetik und Kulturwissenschaften* 42, no. 4 (1996): 545–60.
Knopp, Guido, ed. *Geschichte im Fernsehen: Ein Handbuch* [History on Television: A Handbook]. Darmstadt: Wissenschaftliche Buchgesellschaft, 1988.
Kobylinska, Ewa, and Andreas Lawaty, eds. *Erinnern, Vergessen, Verdrängen: Polnische und deutsche Erfahrungen* [Remembering, Forgetting, Repressing: Polish and German Experiences]. Wiesbaden: Otto Harrassowitz Verlag, 1998.
Kocka, Jürgen. "Erinnern—Lernen: Geschichte Sechzig Jahre nach 1945" [Remembering—Learning: History Sixty Years after 1945]. *Österreichische Zeitschrift für Geschichtswissenschaften* 16 (2005): 64–78.
Kogan, Ilany. *The Cry of Mute Children: A Psychoanalytic Perspective of the Second Generation of the Holocaust*. Trans. Janine Chassegut-Smirgel. London: Free Association Books, 1995.
König, Helmut, ed. *Der Fall Schwerte im Kontext* [The Schwerte Affair in Context]. Opladen: Westdeutscher, 1998.
König, Helmut, Wolfgang Kuhlmann, and Klaus Schwabe, eds. *Vertuschte Vergangenheit: Der Fall Schwerte und die NS-Vergangenheit der deutschen Hochschulen* [The Silenced Past: The Schwerte Case and the Legacy of National Socialism in the German University]. Munich: Beck, 1997.
Koselleck, Reinhart. "Afterword to Charlotte Beradt's *The Third Reich of Dreams*." In *Practice of Conceptual History: Timing History, Spacing Concepts*, trans. T. S. Presner, Kerstin Behnke, and Jobst Welge. Stanford: Stanford University Press, 2002.
———. "Erfahrungswandel und Methodenwechsel: Eine historisch-anthropologische Skizze" [Changes in Experience and Transformations in Method: A Historical-Anthropological Sketch]. In *Historische Methode* [Historical Method], ed. Christian Meier et al. Theorie der Geschichte 5 Munich: dtv, 1988.
———. "Formen und Traditionen des negativen Gedächtnisses" [Forms and Traditions of Negative Memory]. In *Verbrechen erinnern: Die Auseinandersetzung mit Holocaust und Völkermord* [Remembering Crimes: Engaging the

Holocaust and Genocide], ed. Volkhard Knigge and Norbert Frei. Munich: Beck, 2002.

———. "Gebrochene Erinnerungen? Deutsche und polnische Vergangenheiten" [Broken Memories? German and Polish Pasts"]. *Jahrbuch der Deutschen Akademie für Sprache und Dichtung* (2000): 19–32.

———. "Gibt es ein kollektives Gedächtnis?" *Divinatio* 19, no. 2 (Spring 2004): 1–6.

———. "Kriegerdenkmale als Identitätsstiftungen der Überlebenden" [War Memorials as Sources of Identity for Survivors]. *Poetik und Hermeneutik* 8 (1979): 255–76.

———. "Vielerlei Abschied vom Krieg" [Many-Sided Farewell to War]. In *Vom Vergessen, vom Gedenken: Erinnerungen und Erwartungen in Europa zum 8. Mai 1945* [On Forgetting, of Remembrance: Memories and Expectations in Europe on 8 May, 1945], ed. Brigitte Sauzay, Heinz Ludwig Arnold, and Rudolf von Thadden. Göttingen: Wallstein Verlag, 1995.

Kracauer, Siegfried. *Mass Ornament: Weimar Essays*. Trans. Thomas Y. Levin. Cambridge, Mass.: Harvard University Press, 1995.

Krystal, Henry. "Oral History and Echoes of Cataclysms Past." *Address to the Social Science History Association*. Chicago, 17 November 1998.

Landkammer, Joachim. "'Wir spüren nichts': Anstößige Thesen zum zukünftigen Umgang mit der NS-Vergangenheit" ["We Feel Nothing": Objectionable Arguments about Engaging with the Nazi Past]. In *Erinnerungsmanagement: Systemtransformation und Vergangenheitspolitik im internationalen Vergleich* [Managing Memory: International Perpectives on Politics and the Transformation of Systems], ed. Joachim Landkammer, Thomas Noetzel, and Walther Zimmerli. Munich: Fink, 2006, 51–82.

Lanzmann, Claude. "*Schindler's List* Is an Impossible Story." http://www.phil.uu.nl/~rob/2007/hum291/lanzmannschindler.shtml. Accessed 15 July 2014. First published in *Le Monde*, 3 March 1994. Published in German as "Ihr sollt nicht weinen: Einspruch gegen 'Schlinders Liste,'" in *"Der gute Deutsche"* ["The Good German"], ed. Christoph Weiss. St. Ingbert: Röhrig Universitätsverlag, 1995.

———, dir. *Shoah*. New York: New York: New Yorker Films, 1985.

Lappin, Elena. "The Man with Two Heads." *Granta* 66 (1999): 7–65.

Ledig, Gert. *Vergeltung*. Frankfurt am Main: Suhrkamp, 2001. English translation: *Payback*. Trans. Shaun Whiteside. London: Granta, 2009

Leggewie, Claus. *Von Schneider zu Schwerte: Das ungewöhnliche Leben eines Mannes, der aus der Geschichte Lernen wollte* [From Schneider to Schwerte: The Unusual Life of a Man Attempting to Learn from the Past]. Munich: Hanser, 1998.

Leggewie, Claus, and Erik Meyer. *"Ein Ort an den man gerne geht": Das Holocaust-Mahnmal und die deutsche Geschichtspolitik nach 1989* ["A Place That One Likes to Go": The Holocaust Memorial and German Political History after 1989]. Munich: Hanser, 2005.

Leo, Annette, ed. *Die wiedergefundene Erinnerung: Verdrängte Geschichte in Osteuropa* [Recovered Memory: Repressed History in Eastern Europe]. Berlin: BasisDruck, 1992.

Lepsius, Rainer M. "Das Erbe des Nationalsozialismus und die politische Kultur der Nachfolgestaaten des 'Großdeutschen Reiches'" [The Legacy of National Socialism and the Political Culture of Successor States to the "Greater German Reich"]. In *Kultur und Gesellschaft.*, ed. Max Heller et al. Frankfurt: Campus, 1989.

Lerchenmüller, Joachim, and Gerd Simon, eds. *Maskenwechsel* [Switching Masks]. Tübingen: Gesellschaft für interdisziplinäre Forschung, 1999.

Leupold, Dagmar. *Nach den Kriegen: Roman eines Lebens* [After the War: Novel of a Life]. Munich: Beck, 2004.

Levi, Primo. *If This Is a Man*. Trans. Stuart Woolf. New York: Orion, 1959.

Levy, Daniel, and Natan Sznaider. *The Holocaust and Memory in the Global Age*. Trans. Assenka Oksiloff. Philadelphia: Temple University Press, 2006.

Lewis, Bernard. *History: Remembered, Recovered, Invented*. Princeton: Princeton University Press, 1975.

Leys, Ruth. *Trauma: A Genealogy*. Chicago: University of Chicago Press, 2000.

Liebsch, Burkhard. "Trauer als Gewissen der Geschichte?" [Mourning as the Conscience of History?]. In *Trauer und Geschichte* [*Mourning and History*], ed. Burkhard Liebsch and Jörn Rüsen, 15–62. Cologne: Böhlau, 2001.

Locke, John. "Of Identity and Diversity." In *Essay Concerning Human Understanding*, ed. P. H. Nidditch. Oxford: Oxford University Press, 1975.

Cambridge, Mass.: Zone, 2002.

Lübbe, Hermann. *Ich entschuldige mich: Das neue politische Bußritual* [I'm Sorry: The New Ritual of Repentance]. Berlin: Siedler, 2001.

———. "Der Nationalsozialismus im politischen Bewusstsein der Gegenwart" [National-Socialism in Contemporary Political Consciousness]. In *Deutschlands Weg in die Diktatur* [Germany's Path to Dictatorship], ed. Martin Broszat, 329–49. Berlin: Siedler, 1983.

Ludin, Malte, dir. *2 oder 3 Dinge, die ich von ihm weiß* [2 or 3 Things I Know about Him]. Berlin: Absolut Medien, 2005.

Luhmann, Niklas. "Gleichzeitigkeit und Synchronisation" [Simultaneity and Synchronization]. *Soziologische Aufklärung 5: Konstruktivistische Perspektiven* (1990): 95–130.

Mächler, Stefan. *The Wilkomirski Affair: A Study in Biographical Truth*. Trans. John E. Woods. New York: Schocken Books, 2001.

———. *Wilkomirski als Opfer: Das Wilkomirski Syndrom—Eingebildete Erinnerung oder Von der Sehnsucht, Opfer zu Sein* [Wilkomirski as Victim: The Wilkomirski Syndrome—Constructed Memory, or On the Desire to Be a Victim], ed. Irene Diekmann and Julius H. Schoeps. Zurich: Pendo, 2002, 42–43.

MacIntyre, Alasdair. *After Virtue: A Study in Moral Theory*. Notre Dame: University of Notre Dame Press, 2007.

Maier, Charles S. "A Surfeit of Memory? Reflections on History, Melancholy and Denial." *History and Memory* 5, no. 2 (1993): 136–51.
Mannheim, Karl. "The Problem of Generations." In *Essays on the Sociology of Knowledge by Karl Mannheim*, ed. P. Kecskemeti. New York: Routledge and Kegan Paul, 1952.
Margalit, Avishai. *The Ethics of Memory*. Cambridge, Mass.: Harvard University Press, 2002.
Marías, Javier. *All Souls*. Trans. Margaret Jull Costas. New York: HarperCollins, 1992.
Markowitsch, Hans J., and Harald Welzer. *Das autogiographische Gedächtnis: Hirnorganische Grundlagen und biosoziale Entwicklung*. Stuttgart: Klett-Cotta, 1995. English translation: *The Development of Autobiographical Memory*. East Sussex: Pyschology Press, 2009.
Mead, George Herbert. *The Philosophy of the Present*. Ed. Arthur E. Murphy. Chicago: University of Chicago Press, 1980.
Meier, Christian. *From Athens to Auschwitz: The Uses of History*. Trans. Deborah Lucas Schneider. Cambridge Mass.: Harvard University Press, 2005.
———. *Vierzig Jahre nach Auschwitz: Deutsche Geschichtserinnerungen heute* [Forty Years after Auschwitz: German Memory Today]. Munich: Beck, 1990.
Meyer, Erik, and Claus Leggewie. "'Collecting Today for Tomorrow'—Medien des kollektiven Gedächtnisses am Beispiel des 'Elften September'" [Collecting Today for Tomorrow: 9/11 and the Media of Collective Memory]. In *Medien des Kollektiven Gedächtnisses: Konstruktivität, Historizität, Kulturspezifizität* [The Media of Collective Memory: Constructivism, Historicity, Cultural Specificity], ed. Astrid Erll and Ansgar Nünning, 277–91. Berlin: Walter de Gruyter, 2004.
Meyer, Kurt. *Geweint wird, wenn der Kopf ab ist: Annäherungen an meinen Vater—"Panzermeyer," Generalmajor der Waffen-SS* [Approaching My Father—"Panzermeyer," Brigadier General of the Waffen SS]. Freiburg: Herder, 1998.
Mintz, Alan. *Popular Culture and the Shaping of Holocaust Memory in America*. Seattle: University of Washington Press, 2001.
Mitscherlich, Alexander, and Margarete Mitscherlich. *Die Unfähigkeit zu trauern: Grundlagen kollektiven Verhaltens*. Munich: Piper, 1997. English translation: *The Inability to Mourn: Principles of Collective Behavior*. New York: Grove Press, 1975.
Münkler, Herfried. "Opfer der Geschichte? Das Jahr 1945 im Gedenken und Erinnern der Deutschen" [A Victim of History? 1945 in German Memory]. In *Die Zeit*, 16 May 2000.
Muschg, Adolf. "Kerneuropa: Gedanken zur europäischen Identität" [Thoughts on a European Identity]. *Neue Zürcher Zeitung*, 31 April 2003.
———. *Was ist europäisch? Reden für einen gastlichen Erdteil* [What Is European? Discussions about a Convivial Continent]. Munich: Beck, 2005.

Namer, Gérard. *Halbwachs et la mémoire sociale* [Halbwachs and Social Memory]. Paris: L'Harmattan, 2000.

Naumann, Klaus. *Der Krieg als Text: Das Jahr 1945 im kulturellen Gedächtnis der Presse* [The War As Text: 1945 in the Cultural Memory of the Media]. Hamburg: Hamburger Edition, 1998.

Naumann, Michael, ed. *Erzählte Identitäten: Ein interdisziplinäres Symposion*. [Recounted Identities: An Interdisciplinary Symposium]. Munich: Fink, 2000.

Niethammer, Lutz. *Kollektive Identität: Heimliche Quellen einer unheimlichen Konjunktur* [Collective Identity: Secrets Sources of an Uncanny Negotiation]. Reinbek: Rowohlt, 2000.

Niethammer, Lutz, ed. *Lebenserfahrung und kollektives Gedächtnis: Die Praxis der "Oral History"* [Life Experience and Collective Memory: The Practice of Oral History]. Frankfurt am Main: Syndikat, 1985.

Nietzsche, Friedrich. *Beyond Good and Evil*. Trans. Marion Faber. Oxford: Oxford University Press, 1998.

———. *On the Genealogy of Morals and Ecce Homo*. Trans. Walter Kaufmann and R. J. Hollingdale. New York: Vintage, 1967.

———. "On the Uses and Disadvantages of History for Life." In *Untimely Meditations*, trans. R. J. Hollingdale, 57–123. Cambridge: Cambridge University Press, 1983.

Nora, Pierre. "Between Memory and History: *Les Lieux de Mémoire*." Trans. Marc Roudebush. *Representations* 26. Special Issue: *Memory and Counter-Memory* (Spring 1989): 7–24.

Novick, Peter. *The Holocaust in American Life*. Boston: Houghton Mifflin, 1999.

———. *That Noble Dream: The "Objectivity Question" and the American Historical Profession*. Cambridge, Mass.: Harvard University Press, 1988.

Oesterle, Günter, ed. *Erinnerung, Gedächtnis, Wissen: Studien zur kulturwissenschaftlichen Gedächtnisforschung* [Memory, Recollection, Knowledge: Examinations of Cultural Studies Memory Research]. Göttingen: Vandenhoeck and Ruprecht, 2005.

Padover, Saul K. *The Experiment in Germany: The Story of an American Intelligence Officer*. New York: Duell, Sloan, and Pearce, 1946. German translation: *Lügendetektor: Vernehmungen im besiegten Deutschland 1944/45*. Frankfurt: Eichborn, 1999.

Paris, Erna. *Long Shadows: Truth, Lies and History*. Toronto: Knopf Canada, 2000.

Pennebaker, James W., and Becky L. Banasik. "On the Creation and Maintenance of Collective Memories: History as a Social Psychology." In *Collective Memory of Political Events: Social Psychological Perspectives*, ed. James W. Pennebaker, Dario Paez, and Bernard Rim. Mahwah, N.J.: Lawrence Erlbaum Associates, 1997.

Perz, Bertrand. *Die KZ-Gedenkstätte Mauthausen 1945 bis zur Gegenwart* [The Mauthausen Memorial from 1945 to the Present]. Innsbruck: StudienVerlag, 2006.

Plumb, John H. *The Death of the Past.* London: MacMillan, 1978.
Plutarch. *Malice of Herodotus.* Trans. Anthony Bowen. Warminster: Aris and Phillips, 1992.
Proust, Marcel. *In Search of Lost Time.* Vol 6, *Time Regained.* Trans. Andreas Mayor and Terence Kilmartin. New York: Random House, 1993.
Quecke, Hans. "Ich habe nichts hinzugefügt und nichts weggenommen: Zur Wahrheitsbeteuerung koptischer Martyrien" [I have added nothing and taken nothing away: On the Truth Claims of Coptic Martyrdom]. In *Fragen an die altägyptische Literatur: Studien zum Gedenken an Eberhard Otto* [Questions regarding Ancient Egyptian Literature: Studies in Memory of Eberhard Otto], ed. Eberhard Otto, Jan Assmann, Erika Feucht, and Reinhard Grieshammer, 399–416. Wiesbaden: Reichert, 1977.
Radebold, Hartmut. *Die dunklen Schatten unserer Vergangenheit: Ältere Menschen in Beratung, Psychotherapie, Seelsorge und Pflege* [The Dark Shadows of Our Past: The Elderly in Counseling, Psychotherapy, Spiritual Welfare and Care]. Stuttgart: Klett-Cotta, 2005.
Randall, William Lowell. *The Stories We Are: An Essay on Self-Creation.* Toronto: University of Toronto Press, 1995.
Reichel, Peter. *Erfundene Erinnerung: Weltkrieg und Judenmord in Film und Theater* [Invented Memory: World War and the Holocaust in Film and Theatre]. Munich: Fischer, 2004.
Renan, Ernst. *What Is a Nation?* Trans. Wanda Romer Taylor. Toronto: Tapir Press, 1996.
Ricoeur, Paul. *Oneself as Another.* Trans. Kathleen Blamey. Chicago: University of Chicago Press, 1992.
———. *Das Rätsel der Vergangenheit* [The Riddle of the Past]. Göttingen: Wallstein, 2004.
Rödl, Sebastian. *Selbstbezug und Normativität.* Münster: mentis, 1998. English translation: *Self-Consciousness.* Trans. Sibylle Salewski. Cambridge, Mass.: Harvard University Press, 2007.
Röhl, Klaus Rainer. *Verbotene Trauer: Ende der deutschen Tabus* [Forbidden Mourning: The End of a German Taboo]. Munich: Universitas, 2002.
Rousso, Henry. "Das Dilemma eines europäischen Gedächtnisses" [The Dilemma of a European Memory]. In *Zeithistorische Forschungen,* online edition, http://www.zeithistorische-forschungen.de/site/40208268/default.aspx. Accessed 15 July 2014.
Ruchatz, Jens, and Nicolas Pethes, eds. *Lexikon Gedächtnis und Erinnerung.* Reinbek: Rowohlt, 2001.
Rupnow, Dirk. *Vernichten und Erinnern: Spuren nationalsozialistischer Gedächtnispolitik* [Annihilate, Commemorate: Traces of a National Socialist Politics of Memory]. Göttingen: Wallstein, 2005.
Rüsen, Jörn. "Historisch Trauern—Skizze einer Zumutung" [Historical Mourning]. In *Trauer und Geschichte* [Mourning and History], ed. Burkhard Liebsch and Jörn Rüsen, 63–84. Cologne: Böhlau, 2001.

Rusinek, Bernd-A. "Schneider/Schwerte: Die Karriere eines Spagatakteurs 1936–1995" [Schneider/Schwerte: The Career of a Balancing Act, 1936–1995]. In *Der Fall Schwerte im Kontext* [The Schwerte Case in Context], ed. Helmut König. Opladen: Westdeutscher, 1998.

Safranski, Rüdiger. *Ein Meister aus Deutschland: Heidegger und seine Zeit.* Frankfurt: Fischer, 1995. English translation: *Martin Heidegger: Between Good and Evil.* Trans. Ewald Osers. Cambridge, Mass.: Harvard University Press, 1998.

Sanders, Helke, dir. *BeFreier und BeFreite* [Liberator and Liberated]. Bremen: Bremer Institut Film/Fernsehen, 1992.

Sartre, Jean-Paul. *Being and Nothingness.* Trans. Hazel E. Barnes. New York: Washington Square Press, 1992.

Sauerland, Karol. "Minenfelder: Schwieriger Dialog—Deutsche und polnische Historiker" [Minefields: A Difficult Dialogue between German and Polish Historians]. *Frankfurter Allgemeine Zeitung*, 27 December 2002.

Schacter, Daniel, ed. *Memory Distortion: How Minds, Brains, and Societies Reconstruct the Past.* Cambridge, Mass.: Harvard University Press, 1995.

———. *Searching for Memory: The Brain, the Mind, and the Past.* New York: Basic Books, 1997.

———. "The Seven Sins of Memory: Insights from Psychology and Cognitive Neuroscience." *American Psychologist* 54, no. 3 (March 1999): 182–203.

Schelsky, Helmut. "Die Generationen der Bundesrepublik" [The Generations of the Federal Republic]. In *Die andere deutsche Frage* [The Other German Question], ed. Walter Scheel, 178–98. Stuttgart: Klett-Cotta, 1981.

Scherrer, Jutta. "Russlands neue-alte Erinnerungsorte" [Russia's New-Old Sites of Memory]. *Aus Politik und Zeitgeschichte* 11 (2006). Bundeszentrale für politische Bildung, http://www.bpb.de/publikationen/7VR557.html.

Schivelbusch, Wolfgang. *The Culture of Defeat: On National Trauma, Mourning, and Recovery.* Trans. Jefferson Chase. New York: Henry Holt, 2003.

Schreitmüller, Andreas. *Alle Bilder lügen* [All Images Lie]. Constance: UVK Universitätsverlag, 2005.

Schuhmann, Howard, and Jacqueline Scott. "Generations and Collective Memory." *American Sociological Review* 54 (June 1989): 359–81.

Sebald, W. G. "Air War and Literature: Zurich Lectures." In *On the Natural History of Destruction*, trans. Anthea Bell, 1–104. New York: Modern Library, 2004.

Seibt, Gustav. "Das Brandenburger Tor" [The Brandenburg Gate]. *Deutsche Erinnerungsorte* [German Places of Memory]. Vol. 2. Ed. Étienne François and Hagen Schulze. Munich: Beck, 2001.

Semprun, Jorge. "In den Wind gestreut" [Strewn in the Wind]. In Knigge, Pietsch, and Seidel, *Versteinertes Gedenken*. Vol. 2.

———. *Literature or Life.* Trans. Linda Coverdale. Toronto: Penguin, 1997.

Shils, Edward A. *Tradition.* Chicago: University of Chicago Press, 2006.

Singer, Wolf. "Wahrnehmen, Erinnern, Vergessen" [Perceiving, Remembering, Forgetting]. *Frankfurter Allgemeine Zeitung*, 28 September 2000.
Sloterdijk, Peter. *Luftbeben: An den Wurzeln des Terrors* [Airquake: On the Roots of Terror]. Shurkamps: Frankfurt, 2002.
Smith, Gary, and Avishai Margalit, eds. *Amnestie oder die Politik der Erinnerung in der Demokratie* [Amnesty, or the Politics of Memory in a Democracy]. Frankfurt am Main: Suhrkamp, 1997.
Sontag, Susan. "The Idea of Europe (One More Elegy)." In *Where the Stress Falls* (New York: Picador, 2001).
———. *Regarding the Pain of Others*. New York: Picador, 2004.
Spiegel, Gabrielle M. "Memory and History: Liturgical Time and Historical Time." *History and Theory* 41 (2002): 149–62.
Staffa, Christian, and Jochen Spielmann, eds. *Nachträgliche Wirksamkeit: Vom Aufheben der Taten im Gedenken* [Delayed Effects: On Taking up Crimes in Memory]. Berlin: Institut für Vergleichende Geschichtswissenschaften, 1998.
Stegemann, Wolfgang. "Zur Metaphorik des Opfers" [On the Metaphor of the Victim]. In *Opfer: Theologische und kulturelle Kontexte* [Victimhood: Theological and Cultural Contexts], ed. Bernd Janowski and Michael Welker, 191–216. Frankfurt am Main: Suhrkamp, 2000.
Steiner, George. *After Babel: Aspects of Language and Translation*. Oxford: Oxford University Press, 1998.
Stephan, Cora. *Der Betroffenheitskult: Eine politische Sittengeschichte* [The Cult of Shock: A Political History of Morals]. Reinbek: Rowohlt, 1994.
Stuchtey, Benedikt. "Bericht zur Tagung 'European Lieux de Mémoire'" [Report on the Conference "European Sites of Memory"]. German Historical Institute London, 5–7 July 2002. *GHIL Bulletin* 24 (2002): 121–25.
Svevo, Italo. *Zeno Cosini*. Reinbek: Rowohlt, 2000.
Taylor, Charles. *Multiculturalism and "The Politics of Recognition."* Ed. Amy Gutmann. Princeton: Princeton University Press, 1994.
Teichert, Dieter. "Erinnerte Einbildungen und Eingebildete Erinnerungen: Erinnerung und Imagination in epistemologischer Perspektive" [Remembered Imaginings and Imagined Memories in Epistemological Perspective]. In *Erinnerungsarbeit: Zu Paul Ricoeurs Philosophie von Gedächtnis, Geschichte und Vergessen* [The Work of Memory: On Paul Ricoeur's Philosophy of Memory, History, and Forgetting], ed. Andris Beitling and Stefan Orth, 89–100. Berlin: Berliner Wissenschafts-Verlag, 2004.
———. *Personen und Identitäten* [Persons and Identities]. Berlin: Walter de Gruyter, 1999.
Thalmaier, Bettina. *Die zukünftige Gestalt der Europäischen Union* [The Future Form of the European Union]. Baden-Baden: Nomos, 2005.
Theobald, John. *The Media and the Making of History*. Burlington: Ashgate, 2004.
Theunissen, Michael. *Reichweite und Grenzen der Erinnerung* [The Scope and Limits of Memory]. Tübingen: Mohr Siebeck, 2001.

Tibi, Bassam. *Europa ohne Identität? Die Krise der multikulturellen Gesellschaft* [Europe without Identity? The Crisis of Multiculturalism]. 3rd ed. Munich: Siedler, 2002.
Timm, Uwe. *In My Brother's Shadow*. Trans. Anthea Bell. New York: Farrar, Straus, and Giroux, 2005.
Tomasello, Michael. *The Cultural Origins of Human Cognition*. Cambridge, Mass.: Harvard University Press, 1999.
Trabant, Jürgen. "Wissen als Handeln und die Vermittlung der Zeichen" [Knowledge as Action and the Transmission of Signs]. *Rechtshistorisches Journal* 18 (1999): 260–69.
Trollope, Anthony. "On English Prose Fiction as a Rational Amusement." In *Four Lectures*. London: Folcroft, 1976.
Uhl, Heidemarie. "Vom Opfermythos zur Mitverantwortungsthese: NS-Herrschaft, Krieg und Holocaust im 'Österreichischen Gedächtnis'" [From the Myth of Victimhood to Mutual Responsibility: National Socialism, War and the Holocaust in "Austrian Memory"]. In *Transformationen gesellschaftlicher Erinnerung: Studien zur Gedächtnisgeschichte der zweiten Republik* [Transformations in Social Memory: Studies in the History of Memory in the Second Republic of Austria], ed. Christian Gerbel, 50–85. Vienna: Turia and Kant, 2005.
Vaget, Hans Rudolf. "Saul Friedländer und die Zukunft der Erinnerung" [Saul Friedländer and the Future of Memory]. In *Das Judentum im Spiegel seiner kulturellen Umwelten: Symposium zu Ehren von Saul Friedländer* [Judaism in Cultural Context: Symposium in Honor of Saul Friedländer], ed. Dieter Borchmeyer and Helmut Kiesel, 11–32. Neckargemünd: Editions Mnemosyne, 2002.
Van den Braembussche, Antoon. "The Silence of Belgium: Taboo and Trauma in Belgian Memory." Ed Catherine Labio. *Yale French Studies*, no. 102 (2002): 35–52.
Van Laak, Dirk. *Gespräche in der Sicherheit des Schweigens: Carl Schmitt in der politischen Geistesgeschichte der frühen Bundesrepublik* [Conversations in the Safety of Silence: Positioning Carl Schmitt in the Political Intellectual History of the Young German Republic]. Berlin: Akademie Verlag, 2002.
Volkan, Vamik D. "Großgruppenidentität und auserwähltes Trauma" [Large Group Identity and Selective Trauma]. *Psyche* 9/10 (2000): 931–53.
Wackwitz, Stephan. *Ein unsichtbares Land: Familienroman* [An Invisible Land: A Family Novel]. Frankfurt am Main: Fischer, 2003.
Walser, Martin. *Ein springender Brunnen* [A Leaping Fountain]. Frankfurt am Main: Suhrkamp, 1998.
———. *Über Deutschland reden* [Discussing Germany]. Frankfurt am Main: Suhrkamp, 1988.
Warner, Susan. *The Wide, Wide World*. Afterword by Jane Tompkins. New York: Feminist Press, 1987.

Wehler, Hans-Ulrich. "Vergleichen—nicht moralisieren: Spiegel-Gespräch mit Hans-Ulrich Wehler" [Compare—Don't Moralize: A Conversation with Hans-Ulrich Wehler]. *Der Spiegel* 2 (2003): 51.
Weigel, Sigrid. "Zeugnis und Zeugenschaft, Klage und Anklage" [Evidence and Testimony, Grievance and Accusal]. In *Zeugnis und Zeugenschaft*, ed. Rüdiger Zill, 116–20. Berlin: Akademie Verlag, 2000.
Weinrich, Harald. *Lethe: The Art and Critique of Forgetting*. Trans. Steven Rendell. Ithaca: Cornell University Press, 2004.
Weiss, Christoph, ed. *"Der gute Deutsche": Dokumente zur Diskussion um Steven Spielbergs "Schindlers Liste" in Deutschland* ["The Good German": Discussing Stephen Spielberg's "Schindler's List" in Germany]. St. Ingbert: Röhrig Universitätsverlag, 1995.
Welzer, Harald. "Der Holocaust im deutschen Familiengedächtnis" [The Holocaust in German Family Remembrance]. In *Verbrechen erinnern* [Remembering Crimes], ed. Norbert Frei and Volkhard Knigge, 342–58. Munich: Beck, 2002.
———. *Das kommunikative Gedächtnis: Eine Theorie der Erinnerung* [Communicative Memory: A Theory of Remembering]. Munich: Beck, 2002.
———. *Opa war kein Nazi*. Frankfurt am Main: Fischer, 2002. English translation: *Grandpa Wasn't a Nazi: The Holocaust in German Family Remembrance*. Available at http://www.ajc.org/site/apps/nlnet/content3.aspx?c=7oJILSPwFfJSG&b=8449863&ct=12485707. Accessed 15 July 2014.
Welzer, Harald, ed. *Das soziale Gedächtnis: Geschichte, Erinnerung, Tradierung* [Social Memory: History, Memory, Transmission]. Hamburg: Hamburger Edition, 2001.
White, Hayden. *Metahistory: The Historical Imagination in Nineteenth-Century Europe*. Baltimore: Johns Hopkins University Press, 1975.
Wiesel, Elie. "Trivializing the Holocaust." *New York Times*, 16 April 1978.
Wieviorka, Annette. "On Testimony." In *Holocaust Remembrance: The Shapes of Memory*, ed. Geoffrey Hartman, 23–32. Oxford: Blackwell, 1994.
Wilkomirski, Binjamin. *Fragments: Memoirs of a Childhood, 1939–1948*. Trans. Carol Brown Janeway. New York: Picador, 1996.
Williams, C. K. "Das symbolische Volk der Täter" [A Symbolic People of Perpetrators]. *Die Zeit*, 7 November 2002.
Winter, Jay. *The Arts of Remembrance in the Century of Total War*. New Haven: Yale University, 2003. Unpublished manuscript.
———. *Remembering War: The Great War between Memory and History in the Twentieth Century*. New Haven: Yale University Press, 2006.
Wischermann, Clemens, ed. *Vom kollektiven Gedächtnis zur Individualisierung der Erinnerung*. Stuffgart: Franz-Steiner, 2002.
Wojak, Irmtrud. *Eichmanns Memoiren: Ein kritischer Essay* [Eichmann's Memoirs: A Critical Essay]. Frankfurt: Campus, 2001.
Wolf, Christa. "Lesen und Schreiben." In *Die Dimension des Autors*. Darmstadt: Luchterhand, 1987, 479–80. English translation: "Reading and Writing." In

The Author's Dimension: Selected Essays, ed. Alexander Stephan, trans. Jan van Heurck. Chicago: University of Chicago Press, 1995.

———. *No Place on Earth*. Trans. Jan van Heurck. New York: Farrar, 1983.

Wolf, Hubert. *Index: Der Vatikan und die verbotenen Bücher* [Index: The Vatican and the Banned Books]. Munich: Beck, 2007.

Wolfrum, Edgar. *Geschichte als Waffe: Vom Kaiserreich bis zur Wiedervereinigung* [History as Weapon: From Kaiserreich to Reunification]. Göttingen: Vandenhoeck and Ruprecht, 2001.

Wolfrum, Edgar, and Petra Bock, eds. *Umkämpfte Vergangenheit: Geschichtsbilder, Erinnerung und Vergangenheitspolitik im internationalen Vergleich* [Contested Past: An International Comparison of Views on History, Memory and the Politics of the Past]. Göttingen: Vandenhoeck and Ruprecht, 1999.

INDEX

Ackermann, Ulrike 229, 250, 274
Adorno, Theodor W. 84, 203f., 208, 213, 269
Agamben, Giorgio 77, 250, 252
Ahmadinejad, Mahmoud 238
Alexander, Jeffrey C. 253, 260, 267, 270, 273, 279
Anders, Günther 64f., 72, 250
Andersch, Alfred 156
Anderson, Benedict R. 17, 27
Arendt, Hannah 66, 81, 249f., 252, 281
Aristotle 135
Assmann, Aleida 248, 250f., 253, 255, 266f., 268f.
Assmann, Jan 243, 245f., 247, 251, 260, 269
Aust, Stefan 277
Awerbuch, Marianne 190

Bach, Johann Sebastian 36
Backes, Uwe 276
Baddeley, Alan 109, 257
Baecker, Dirk 6, 243
Baer, Ulrich 249, 251
Bar-on, Dan 79, 82, 253, 280
Barasch, Moshe 260
Bauman, Zygmunt 36, 247, 252, 281
Becker, Annette 244,
Becker, Henk A. 244, 262, 281
Begley, Louis 57, 249
Benes, Edvard 275
Benjamin, Walter 39, 51, 89, 249
Benveniste, Emile 67
Beradt, Charlotte 267, 281
Bergson, Henri 24, 101, 256, 261
Berlovitz, Shelly 260
Bhabha, Homi 281
Binder, Beate 269
Bloch, Marc 245
Boer, Pim de 274, 283
Bogdan, Musil 266
Bohleber, Werner 87, 252, 254, 266, 281
Bohrer, Karl Heinz 88f., 254, 281
Böll, Heinrich 156
Borchert, Wolfgang 176

Borges, Jorge Luis 84
Borland, John 245, 267, 281
Bourdieu, Pierre 24
Braembussche, Antoon van de 253, 296
Brague, Rémi 272, 275, 281
Brendler, Konrad 276, 281
Britten, Benjamin 109
Broder, Henryk M. 196, 208
Brown, J. 256
Browne, Sir Thomas 12, 35f., 243, 247
Bubis, Ignatz 138
Bude, Heinz 14, 244, 282
Burckhardt, Jacob 242, 277, 282
Burger, Rudolf 16f., 84f., 254, 261, 282
Burke, Peter 34, 52, 247, 249, 257
Buruma, Ian 25f., 87f., 245, 249, 254, 262, 273, 282
Bush, George W. 197, 238
Butler, Samuel 105, 256

Carus, Carl Gustav 108, 256, 282
Caruth, Cathy 76, 252, 282
Castoriadis, Cornelius 17
Celan, Paul 70, 117, 137, 138, 148–50, 251, 263, 282
Chaumont, Jean-Michel 273, 282
Cicero 30, 186, 268, 282
Clinton, Bill 92
Columbus, Christopher 201
Connerton, Paul 199, 269, 282
Conway, Martin A. 244, 256, 282
Conze, Werner 162
Coudenhove-Kalergi, Barbara 276, 282
Cremer, Fritz 188
Csáky, Moritz 268, 282

Danyel, Jürgen 266, 283
Daxner, Michael 276, 283
Demnig, Gunter 215, 271
Derrida, Jacques 250f., 283
Deutschmann, Heiko 262
Diner, Dan 204, 220, 228, 270, 283
Dössecker, Bruno 120, 125

299

300 Index

Droysen, Johann Gustav 246
Dubiel, Helmut 253, 283
Duchardt, Heinz 283
Dückers, Tanja 184, 268, 283

Echterhoff, Gerald 244, 283
Ehre, Ida 137f.
Eichmann, Adolf 77, 79
Elizabeth II 228f.
Elkana, Yehuda 63, 249, 283
Emerson, Waldo Ralph 83, 253, 283
Emmerich, Wolfgang 283
Erikson, Erik 114
Erll, Astrid 248, 271, 284, 291
Escudier, Alexandre 272, 284
Esterhazy, Peter 225, 229, 232, 234, 274f., 284

Fackenheim, Emil 202
Felman, Shoshana 251, 284
Ferry, Luc 273
Fiedler, Leslie 271, 284
Finkelstein, Norman 130f.
Fisher, Philip 247, 284
Forte, Dieter 156, 159f., 265, 284
Foschepoth, Josef 276, 284
Franco, Francisco 53,
François, Etienne 245, 284, 294
Frank, Anne 120
Frank, Hans 142
Frank, Niklas 262
Frei, Norbert 206, 248, 250, 258, 264, 268, 270, 272, 288f., 297
Freud, Sigmund 75f., 105, 107, 126, 147, 252, 257, 263, 285
Frevert, Ute 250, 253, 255, 271, 280, 285
Fried, Johannes 257
Friedländer, Saul 32–34, 208, 246f., 285, 296
Friedrich, Jörg 155, 158f., 169–71, 245, 248, 250, 265, 285
Frisch, Max 134, 261, 285

Gadamer, Hans Georg 44, 248, 285
Galinski, Heinz 138
Ganzfried, Daniel 120, 259, 285
Gellately, Robert 263, 285
Giesen, Bernhard 3, 49, 70f., 77f., 247, 251–53, 285
Ginzburg, Carlo 34, 247, 251, 385
Ginzburg, Natalia 79
Girard, René 143
Goldhagen, Daniel 91, 145, 170
Gourevitch, Philip 259, 286
Grass, Günter 87, 97–101, 157f., 160, 162, 165–69, 171, 184f., 210f., 232, 251, 254–56, 260, 265f., 270, 286,
Graupner, Christoph 36
Groebner, Valentin 258, 267, 286
Günzel, Reinhard 162, 266

Haarer, Johanna 254, 286
Halbwachs, Maurice 13f., 16, 20, 29, 31, 105f., 124–26, 131–34, 139, 175, 244–46, 256, 260f., 281, 283, 286, 292
Hartman, Geoffrey 249, 253, 270, 276, 286, 297
Heer, Hannes 143, 169f., 262, 266
Heidegger, Martin 149–151, 213, 263f., 286, 294
Heimrod, Ute 255, 271, 286
Heine, Heinrich 209
Herder, Johann Gottfried 24, 254, 291
Herf, Jeffrey 255, 286
Herodotus 24, 30f., 246, 286, 293
Herzog, Roman 1, 187
Hilberg, Raul 182
Hill, Werner 262
Himmler, Heinrich 80, 118
Hirsch, Marianne 247, 286
Hitler, Adolf 2, 49, 72, 76, 81, 91, 105, 134, 137, 143–45, 152, 170, 176, 224–27, 233, 238, 262f., 265, 285f.
Hofmannthal, Hugo von 5, 148
Hoheisel, Horst 1–3, 242f.
Hohmann, Martin 162, 214, 266
Hölderlin, Friedrich 149
Holzbauer, Ignaz 36
Honneth, Axel 249, 286
Horkheimer, Max 219
Huizinga, Johan 34, 247, 287

Illich, Ivan 129, 260, 287
Irving, David 252
Ivanji, Ivan 204f., 209, 270, 287

Jäger, Ludwig 119, 258f., 287
Janeczek, Helena 198, 269, 287
Jaworski, Rudolf 274, 287
Jeismann, Michael 239, 261, 276, 287
Jirgl, Reinhard 266, 287
Joyce, James 101
Judt, Tony 225, 273, 287
Jünger, Friedrich Georg 248, 287

Kafka, Franz 117
Karl der Große 272
Kennedy, John F. 15, 105
Kerby, Anthony Paul 287
Kielmannsegg, Peter Graf 287
King, Martin Luther 15
Klemperer, Victor 170
Kluge, Alexander 243, 280
Klüger, Ruth 79, 191, 192, 215, 269, 271, 287
Knigge, Volkhard 187, 221, 248, 264, 268, 270, 272f., 283, 287–89, 294, 297
Knittel, Anton Philipp 256, 288
Knopp, Guido 288
Kobylinska, Ewa 274, 288
Kocka, Jürgen 246, 288

Index

Kogan, Ilany 252, 288
Kohl, Helmut 58, 88, 183, 219
König, Helmut 258, 284, 287f., 294
Koschorke, Albrecht 27
Koselleck, Reinhart 3-5, 16f., 28f., 46, 52, 102-7, 174f., 192, 243f., 248f., 256, 267, 269, 273, 288
Kracauer, Siegfried 37, 247, 289
Krystal, Henry 121, 259, 289
Kulik, J. 256, 281

Laak, Dirk van 264, 296
Lacan, Jacques 17, 245
Landkammer, Joachim 235f., 275f., 287, 289
Lanzmann, Claude 203f., 269f., 283, 289
Lappin, Elena 259, 267, 289
Laub, Dori 251, 284
Lause, Hermann 262
Lawaty, Andreas 274, 288
Ledig, Gert 156, 159, 265
Leggewie, Claus 119, 206, 211f., 237, 258f., 270f., 275, 289, 291
Lenin, Wladimir Iljitsch Uljanow 139
Leo, Annette 274
Lepsius, Rainer M. 143, 262, 290
Lerchenmüller, Joachim 259, 290
Leupold, Dagmar 184, 268, 290
Levi, Primo 66, 79, 102f., 250, 256
Levy, Daniel 222, 273
Lewis, Bernard 32, 246, 248, 290
Leys, Ruth 252
Liebeskind, Daniel 197
Liebsch, Burkhard 89, 254, 266, 281, 290, 293
Lipstadt, Deborah 252
Locke, John 114-17, 119f., 123-26, 163, 166, 184, 257f., 290
Lübbe, Hermann 81, 150, 253, 264
Ludin, Malte 184, 268
Luhmann, Niklas 268, 290

Mächler, Stefan 259, 290
MacIntyre, Alasdair 44, 248, 290
Maier, Charles S. 247, 249, 291
Maier, Christian 35
Manea, Norman 121
Mannheim, Karl 14, 244, 291
Margalit, Avishai 71f., 156, 251, 253, 291, 295
Marias, Javier 115, 257
Marinesko, Alexander 166
Markowitsch, Hans J. 257, 267, 291
Mattausch, Dietrich 262
Mauriac, François 79
Mayer, Christoph 269
Mead, George Herbert 132, 261, 291
Meier, Christian 25, 136, 145, 232, 235f., 241, 245, 249, 262f., 272, 274f., 277, 288, 291
Mendelssohn, Peter de 156
Merkel, Angela 238

Meyer, Erik 206, 211f., 237, 270f., 275, 289, 291
Meyer, Kurt 254
Milosevic, Slobodan 51
Milosz, Czeslaw 255, 286
Mintz, Alan 270, 291
Mitscherlich, Alexander und Margarete 86, 90f., 93, 255, 291
Möllemann, Jürgen 214
Montaigne, Michel de 40
Montcalm, Louis-Joseph 48
Morrison, Toni 158, 231
Mozart, Wolfgang Amadeus 36, 209
Münkler, Herfried 264, 270, 291
Muschg, Adolf 224, 233, 273, 275, 291

Nägelen, Klaus 262
Namer, Gérard 244, 292
Napoleon Bonaparte 2, 47
Naumann, Klaus 155, 264, 292
Naumann, Michael 292
Niethammer, Lutz 150, 251, 257, 264, 292
Nietzsche, Friedrich 22f., 31, 40, 63, 83, 101, 126, 183, 242, 245, 250, 253, 268, 277, 292
Nora, Pierre 29, 31, 33, 35, 100, 220, 246, 292
Novick, Peter 26, 128-131, 139f., 177, 214, 222, 238, 245f., 249, 255, 260, 262, 267, 271, 273, 275, 292
Nüsse, Barbara 262

Obuchi, Keizo 92
Oesterle, Günter 275, 292

Padover, Saul K. 143f., 146, 263, 292
Paris, Erna 271, 276
Pausanias 186
Pennebaker, James W. 244, 256, 282, 292
Persson, Göran 220, 223f., 228
Perz, Bertrand 269, 292
Pietsch, Jürgen Maria 268, 288, 294
Plumb, John H. 246, 293
Plutarch 246, 293
Prodi, Romano 219
Proust, Marcel 12, 39, 99, 101, 107f., 131, 133, 203, 256, 293

Quack, Sibylle 273
Quecke, Hans 251, 293

Radebold, Hartmut 277, 293
Randall, William Lowell 243, 256, 293
Rathkolb, Oliver 276, 282
Raulff, Uwe 161, 265
Reagan, Ronald 58
Reichel, Peter 267, 293
Renan, Ernst 23-25, 27f., 47-49, 83, 88, 168, 216f., 219, 226, 228, 245, 248, 253, 271, 274, 293

302 Index

Ricoeur, Paul 34, 89, 115, 254, 258, 260, 293, 295
Rivers, William H. 75
Rödl, Sebastian 125, 260, 293
Röhl, Klaus Rainer 157, 265, 293
Rothfels, Hans 162
Rousso, Henry 59, 249, 293
Ruchatz, Jens 269, 281, 293
Rupnow, Dirk 80, 252f., 293
Rumsfeld, Donald 219
Rüsen, Jörn 89f., 254, 266, 281, 290, 293
Rusinek, Bernd-A. 258, 294

Saar, Martin 244, 283
Safranksi, Rüdiger 263, 294
Sanders, Heike 264, 294
Sartre, Jean-Paul 132, 261, 294
Sauerland, Karol 229, 274, 294
Schacter, Daniel 110, 112, 123, 147, 243, 256f., 260, 263, 294
Schadow, Johann-Gottfried 2
Schelsky, Helmut 244, 294
Scherrer, Jutta 275, 294
Schieder, Theodor 162
Schinkel, Karl-Friedrich von 2
Schivelbusch, Wolfgang 50, 52, 248f., 294
Schlusche, G. 255, 271, 286
Schreitmüller, Andreas 262, 294
Schuhmann, Howard 244, 294
Schulze, Hagen 243, 284, 294
Schwerte, Hans 117f.
Sebald, W. G. 87, 155–58, 160, 162, 254, 265, 294
Seferens, Horst 255, 271, 286
Seibt, Gustav 163, 243, 294
Seidel, Thomas A. 268, 288, 294
Semon, Richard 257
Semprun, Jorge 180f., 188, 194, 267f., 294
Shils, Edward A. 178, 267, 294
Sigurdsson, Sigrid 190, 268
Simon, Gerd 259, 290
Singer, Wolf 110, 257, 295
Sloterdijk, Peter 93, 255, 295
Smith, Gary 253
Sontag, Susan 17, 234, 245, 255, 275, 277, 295
Spiegel, Gabrielle, M. 200
Spielberg, Steven 181f., 203f., 270, 297
Stachel, Peter 268, 282
Staffa, Christian 243, 295
Stalin, Josef 255, 265
Stegemann, Wolfgang 249, 295
Steinbach, Erika 172, 208, 230, 234
Steiner, George 148f., 263, 268, 271, 288, 294f., 297
Steinhäuser, Robert 195
Stephan, Cora 254, 295
Sternberger, Dolf 90
Stuchtey, Benedikt 272, 295

Svevo, Italo 5, 107, 243, 256, 295
Sznaider, Natan 222, 273, 290
Szymborska, Wislawa 255, 286

Tasso, Torquato 76
Taylor, Charles 249
Teichert, Dieter 124, 257f., 260, 295
Thalmaier, Bettina 272, 295
Theobald, John 274, 295
Theunissen, Michael 264, 295
Tibi, Bassam 219, 272, 296
Timm, Uwe 144, 161f., 183f., 263, 265f., 268, 296
Tocqueville, Alexis de 52
Tomasello, Michael 270, 296
Trabant, Jürgen 178, 296
Trilling, Lionel 148
Trollope, Anthony 123, 259, 296

Uhl, Heidemarie 169, 255, 266, 273, 296

Vaget, Hans Rudolf 246f., 296
Venclova, Tomas 255, 286
Volkan, Vamik D. 50f., 248, 296

Wackwitz, Stephan 184, 266, 268, 296
Waldheim, Bruno 91, 226
Walser, Martin 89, 133–36, 139, 179, 214, 241, 261, 267, 296
Warburg, Aby 257, 268
Warner, Susan 247, 296
Wehler, Hans-Ulrich 265, 297
Weigel, Sigrid 136, 251, 262, 297
Weinrich, Harald 247, 297
Weiss, Christoph 270, 289, 297
Weizsäcker, Richard von 138, 154
Wellington, Arthur Wellesley 47
Welzer, Harald 16, 151f., 176, 243–45, 248, 257, 264, 267, 281, 291, 297
White, Hayden 34, 247
Wicki, Bernhard 176
Wiesel, Elie 79, 128, 203, 208, 222, 269
Wiesenthal, Simon 222
Wieviorka, Annette 253, 297
Wilde, Oscar 101
Wildgruber, Ulrich 262
Wilkomirski, Binjamin 120–24, 126–28, 135, 249, 259, 262, 285, 290, 297
Williams, C. K. 65, 250, 297
Winfrey, Oprah 208
Winter, Jay 71, 73, 251
Wischermann, Clemens 212, 271, 297
Wöhler, Gustav Peter 262
Wojak, Irmtrud 252, 297
Wolf, Christa 102, 106, 256
Wolf, Hubert 247
Wolfrum, Edgar 276, 298
Woolf, Virginia 101

www.ingramcontent.com/pod-product-compliance
Lightning Source LLC
Chambersburg PA
CBHW030435300426
44112CB00009B/1006